"A refreshing new glimpse of how American Jews [...] and socio/cultural institutions to confront the deepening chasm between secularized folk Jewishness and synagogal Judaism. A thoughtful account of the 20th century development of American Judaism."

—Henry Feingold,
Baruch College and Graduate Center, CUNY

"David Kaufman's study presents wonderful new insights for a somewhat different view of American Jewish institutional history. Kaufman fuses a variety of disciplines to dissect the synagogue-center movement in a way that brings to life significant, but often lost, aspects of our immediate past."

—Tom L. Freudenheim,
Executive Director, YIVO Institute for Jewish Research, New York

"David Kaufman's *Shul with a Pool* is an important contribution to the history of the central institution of American Jewry—the synagogue—and a welcome addition to the unfolding account of the role of religion in American life. The reader will be grateful for a most readable, always interesting account of the endeavors of a singularly creative immigrant group striving to retain its spiritual and cultural identity in America's free and open society. A young scholar, gifted with mature skills and imagination, makes an auspicious debut."

—Rabbi Abraham Karp,
Professor Emeritus, University of Rochester

SHUL WITH A POOL

David Kaufman

SHUL WITH A POOL

The "Synagogue-Center" in
American Jewish History

BRANDEIS UNIVERSITY PRESS
Published by
University Press of New England
Hanover and London

Brandeis University Press
Published by University Press of New England, Hanover, NH 03755
© 1999 by the Trustees of Brandeis University
Printed in the United States of America   5 4 3 2 1
CIP data appear at the end of the book

BRANDEIS SERIES IN AMERICAN JEWISH HISTORY, CULTURE, AND LIFE

Jonathan D. Sarna, Editor

Sylvia Barack Fishman, Associate Editor

TO MY FAMILY, WITH LOVE

CONTENTS

FIGURES

ABBREVIATIONS

AHA	American Hebrew Association
AJA	American Jewish Archives
AJHS	American Jewish Historical Society
AJYB	*American Jewish Year Book*
BJC	Brooklyn Jewish Center
CCAR	Central Conference of American Rabbis
CEA	Council Educational Alliance
CHI	Chicago Hebrew Institute
CJI	Central Jewish Institute
CJW	Council of Jewish Women
CYMHKA	Council of Young Men's Hebrew and Kindred Associations
HES	Hebrew Educational Society
HFSA	Hebrew Free School Association
HUC	Hebrew Union College
IS	Institutional Synagogue
JCC	Jewish Community Center
JEA	Jewish Educational Alliance
JES	Jewish Endeavor Society
JPS	Jewish Publication Society
JTS	Jewish Theological Seminary
JWB	Jewish Welfare Board
NAJCW	National Association of Jewish Center Workers
NCJW	National Council of Jewish Women
PAJHS	*Publications of the American Jewish Historical Society*
PSA	People's Synagogue Association
UAHC	Union of American Hebrew Congregations
UHC	United Hebrew Charities
UOJC	Union of Orthodox Jewish Congregations
UTT	Uptown Talmud Torah
UYA	United YMHA of America
YI	Young Israel
YMHLA	Young Men's Hebrew Literary Association
YPHOL	Young People's Hebrew Orthodox League
YTT	Yorkville Talmud Torah
YWU	Young Women's Union

CHRONOLOGY

1875 Both the founding of Hebrew Union College in Cincinnati (a "religious" movement); and new YMHAs in New York and Philadelphia (a "social" movement).

1879 "Grand Revival" of Hanukah at the New York YMHA.

1883 The first graduation of Hebrew Union College, ordaining the first American-trained rabbis: Israel Aaron, Henry Berkowitz, Joseph Krauskopf, and David Philipson.

1885 The Pittsburgh Platform, to which Rabbi Emil G. Hirsch adds the new "social gospel."

1888 Rabbi Henry Berkowitz proposes a new congregational association, the L.A.C.E. Society.

1889 The YMHA, Hebrew Free School Association, and Aguilar Free Public Library merge to form the Hebrew Institute (later, Educational Alliance), the pioneer Jewish settlement.

1891 New buildings for the Hebrew Institute in New York and Touro Hall in Philadelphia, the latter including the first swimming pool in a Jewish center.

1893 Shaare Zion school founded in Brooklyn, first "National Hebrew School" in America.

1894 Rabbi Moses Gries turns his Cleveland congregation into an "open temple."

1896 Publication of *Jewish Life in the Middle Ages,* by Israel Abrahams, in which he describes the synagogue as "The Centre of Social Life."

1897 Sabbath and holiday services first instituted at the Educational Alliance.

1899 The "People's Synagogue" incorporated into the Educational Alliance by new director David Blaustein.

1900 New building erected for the New York YMHA; first high holiday services are held.

1901 At the annual meeting of the CCAR, Rabbi Moses Gries heralds: "a new spirit . . . widening the walls and purposes of narrow synagogues and temples . . ."

1902 Publication of "The School as Social Center," by John Dewey.

1903 The Chicago Hebrew Institute, the first major center founded by the immigrant community.

1904 First Community Passover Seder held at the New York YMHA.

1906 Albert Lucas establishes the Jewish Centres Association on the Lower East Side.

1908 The *Boston Advocate* announces the advent of a movement for "REJUDAISING"; at a conference of Jewish charities, Louis Marshall declares "the need of a distinctly Jewish tendency" in communal life.

1909 Jewish journalist and Zionist leader Jacob de Haas notes that the synagogue "was a house of learning, house of worship, meeting house, all rolled in one . . ."

1910 Ahad Ha'am writes to Judah Magnes to recommend that "the synagogue must be the center . . ."; a few months later, Magnes proposes to turn his synagogue into "a Jewish Center—a *bet ha'am,* a 'house of the Jewish people'."

1911 Rabbis Judah Magnes and Mordecai Kaplan help create the YMHA Congregation.

1912 Judah Magnes notes "the trend of the times that the old idea of having a single Jewish Centre, in which should be gathered all kinds of Jewish activities is again becoming fashionable.

1913 Merger of YMHA and Settlement movements to form the Council of Young Men's Hebrew and Kindred Associations, the birth of the "Jewish center" movement.

Professor Mordecai Kaplan urges his students to make "the synagogue a social centre."

1914 New building constructed for the YWHA on 110th Street, including a "shul and a pool."

1915 Mordecai Kaplan writes, "I find myself at the beginning of a new spiritual enterprise which holds out great promise. . . . I refer to the new movement that has been started by some of my friends on the West Side to establish a Jewish communal centre."

1916 Central Jewish Institute opens, the seminal "Jewish school center."

1917 Official founding of both the Jewish Center and the Institutional Synagogue.

1918 The Jewish Center opens for services, under Rabbi Mordecai Kaplan.

1919 Founding of the Brooklyn Jewish Center, under Rabbi Israel Levinthal.

1920s Hundreds of new synagogue-center institutions are built throughout the country.

1926 Deliberations of the New York Board of Jewish Ministers reveals some misgivings.

1927 Rabbi Israel Mattuck observes a "new" phenomenon: "The Community Centre with its synagogue, or the synagogue with a community house, is now the centre of Jewish life in America."

PREFACE AND ACKNOWLEDGMENTS

First, a word about the title. Many people have assumed that "shul with a pool" is my invention—it is not. The irreverent phrase was coined during the 1920s to refer to a new phenomenon in the American Jewish community, a combination synagogue (*shul* in Yiddish) and Jewish community center (whose swimming pool was often its chief attraction). This "synagogue-center" would come under sharp criticism, as when Rabbi Joel Blau derogatorily called it a "shul mit a pool." At other times, the phrase was used with pride, as when one contemporary rabbi assured me that it had originally applied to his Chicago congregation. In all likelihood, it gained popularity as a colloquialism expressing both fond affection and mild sarcasm. The humorous expression served the cultural purpose of deflating the pretensions of an upper-middle-class (hence elitist) institution, rendering it more accessible to the entire Jewish community, and bringing it "down to earth." It is in that populist spirit that I have chosen *Shul with a Pool* as the title of this book.

Shul with a Pool: The "Synagogue-Center" in American Jewish History is the revised and updated version of my doctoral dissertation at Brandeis University. The product of several years of research, and shaped by the exigencies of a graduate program, the book is a scholarly work in the field of American Jewish history. It examines the development of Jewish communal life in this country during the half century from 1875 to 1925 and is principally concerned with the story of the American synagogue and its close relation, the Jewish center. "Jewish center" is a broad (and often confusing) term that may apply to synagogues—whether Reform, Orthodox, or Conservative—as well as to social and educational institutions such as the YMHA, the Jewish settlement, and the Talmud Torah. The book has chapters devoted to each of them. Sources include the Jewish periodical press of the era, published and unpublished writings of some of the leading figures of the period, institutional records, and secondary historiography.

As is often the case in first books, my own life experience has gone into the writing as well. I grew up in many of the "Jewish centers" I write about; moreover, the complexities and contradictions of being an American Jew of the third generation inform my argument throughout. More than an academic exercise, therefore, the book is intended to be a commentary on the nature of Jewish identity in contemporary life. Its central thesis—the existence of a "social-religious dialectic" in American Judaism and Jewish community—is the cumulative observation of half a lifetime spent in Jewish environments as diverse as a Hebraist day school, a modern Orthodox high school, a Labor Zionist youth movement, several Judaic studies departments in academia—and of course, synagogues and other Jewish centers.

My first debt of gratitude, therefore, is to my parents, who thankfully did not join the exodus to suburbia in the late sixties and raised me in their hometown: Brooklyn, New York, the American "Jewish center" *par excellence.* My father, in fact, first learned to swim in the pool of the Brooklyn Jewish Center—whose interior adorns the cover of this book. One of my earliest childhood memories is of being taken by my dad, at the age of eight or nine, to the Center's pool and steam bath. I also remember running up the stairs to visit my grandmother who always insisted on sitting in the balcony for high holiday services—also at the Brooklyn Jewish Center, whose sanctuary is depicted on the cover as well (a view from the balcony, no less!). For school I attended the Bialik Hebrew Day School, housed at the Flatbush Jewish Center; and later the Yeshivah of Flatbush high school, also related to an early synagogue-center in Brooklyn, Young Israel of Flatbush. My parents gave me the very best Jewish education, and though they surely didn't intend it, the best possible background for this study of Jewish centers.

I also want to take this opportunity to thank my teachers in American Jewish Studies at Brandeis University: Leon Jick, Jonathan Sarna, and Marshall Sklare (z"l). Professor Sklare, who passed away in 1992, was both a mentor (in American Jewish sociology, a field he founded) and a friend. I remain eternally grateful to Marshall and his wife, Rose, for their emotional sustenance during some trying times. My other two academic advisors and mentors in American Jewish history were Professors Jick and Sarna, upon whom I continue to rely for their good counsel and unflagging support. I count myself extremely fortunate to have had three such exceptional teachers, and I humbly aspire to follow in their footsteps.

This book is a first step on that path, for all three have produced significant scholarly works which in some way prefigure *Shul with a Pool.* Leon Jick's *The Americanization of the Synagogue, 1820–1870* is a landmark study of the nineteenth-century synagogue, in which he argued for a social-historical reading of American Jewish religion. Marshall Sklare, too, interpreted American Judaism from a sociological perspective in his classic study, *Conservative Judaism—An American Religious Movement.* Both works clearly demonstrated how "religious" categories such as synagogues and movements may be interpreted as "social" phenomena. Jonathan Sarna, a leading member of the newer generation of American Jewish scholars, takes such duality for granted. In his 1988 publication *American Synagogue History: A Bibliography and State-of-the-Field Survey,* he wrote: "Much remains to be learned about the history of the American synagogue. We need more research, more syntheses, more conceptualizations. . . . We need more broadly framed studies that pay full attention to the larger contexts—secular and Jewish—

within which synagogues operate. . . . Finally, we need synagogue histories written with an eye toward the fundamental issues of American Jewish history." In *Shul with a Pool,* I have tried to respond to the challenge. Again, I must thank my teachers for showing the way.

I also give special thanks to those who actively assisted in the completion of this book: first, the many archivists who aided in the research, especially Julie Miller of the Ratner Center for the Study of Conservative Judaism, Kevin Proffitt of the American Jewish Archives, Jerry Schwarzbard of the Library of the Jewish Theological Seminary of America, and Steve Siegel of the 92d Street "Y." Steve was especially helpful in gathering the illustrations for Chapter 2 on the YMHA. Eric Robbins of the Educational Alliance and Amy Waterman of the Eldridge Street Synagogue also extended their professional courtesy and kind friendship. Several other illustrations were provided through the good graces of Peter Schweitzer, a private collector of Judaica Americana (and a man who should someday see a museum bearing his name). My good friend Rebecca Holtzman designed the cover, and I will be showing my gratitude for a long time to come. Phyllis Deutsch, my editor at UPNE, far surpassed the call of duty in cajoling, coaxing, and otherwise coercing me to finish the book. As the academic editor of this series (the Brandeis Series in American Jewish History, Culture, and Life), Jonathan Sarna deserves another note of thanks here. My gratitude extends also to Jack Wertheimer, Riv-Ellen Prell, Henry Feingold, and several other colleagues who served as readers of the manuscript. My greatest debt is to Karla Goldman, close friend (and tennis partner) throughout our school days in Cambridge, and now professor of American Jewish history at Hebrew Union College in Cincinnati. Karla has "been there" for me in at least two ways: she is the person who best knows the work, having aided in its conception through close readings and crucial leads, and is therefore the person I turn to for advice concerning the text; even more important, she has always believed in me, thereby providing the constant encouragement and emotional support so essential to the scholarly enterprise—and so lacking for those of us without families of our own. Karla, thank you.

A few concluding remarks: the book is divided into chapters devoted to discrete sources of the synagogue-center phenomenon. Since their individual chronologies overlap, I have provided a time-line that collapses the sequence of events and should help to encapsulate a complex set of developments. Following most contemporary usage, my transliterations of Hebrew or Yiddish words beginning with the guttural letter *[c]het* employ the letter "h" rather than "ch" (e.g., Hanukah, not Chanukah). A listing of abbreviations used in the text (mostly referring to the alphabet soup of American Jewish organizations) is provided as well.

Shul with a Pool is a work of American Jewish history whose main thesis concerns the critical tension in American Jewish life between the "religious" and the "social." Throughout the text, I have emphasized the word "social" rather than the more commonly employed "ethnic" and "secular." Though distinct terms, they are used here to refer to the same set of cultural meanings and behaviors that stands to the so-called "religious." Hence, social/ethnic/secular "Jewishness" (a loose translation of *Yiddishkeit,* as employed by Nathan Glazer) is Jewish by virtue of a relationship to other Jews—whether members of one's family, community, or nation. Religious Judaism, on the other hand, is Jewish by virtue of a relationship to God, as expressed through study of Jewish text and performance of Jewish ritual. This social-religious dichotomy makes perfect sense in the Jewish context. The Jewish commandments, for example, are traditionally divided into two categories: those "between Man and God" and those "between Man and his Fellow." The same dichotomy also applies to American Jewish life, which, as I argue throughout this book, tends to divide into separate social and religious expressions which then seek their missing half. If there is a message in all this, it is simply that Judaism encompasses both religion and peoplehood. Moving toward either extreme is inauthentic at best, self-destructive at worst. My sincere hope, therefore, is that this book will find an audience not only among academic students of American Jewish history, but also in the greater community. History may yet offer some useful answers to the questions of our day.

New York City   D.E.K.
February 1998

INTRODUCTION

Judaism cannot exist, for any length of time, without Jews, nor Jews without Judaism. Besides this inherent correlation which obtains between every creed and its believers, every culture and its bearers, there is a certain specific, and even more significant connection between Judaism as a creed and a culture. To Judaism the existence of the Jewish people is essential and indispensable, not only for its realization in life, but for its very idea; not only for its actuality, but for its potentiality. . . . The unity of Jews and Judaism thus has a deep meaning, and the interrelation between the two, the interplay of the social and the religious forces throughout the entire course of Jewish history, appears to be of controlling significance.

—S A L O   B A R O N, 1952[1]

THIS IS A book about Jews and Judaism. More precisely, it is about the tension between them—the tension between the social and religious spheres of Jewish life. As observed by the Jewish historian Salo Baron and others, the Jewish experience has always been characterized by an interlocked duality of people and faith. From a theological perspective, the core concerns of the Jewish religion are not only God and Torah, but also "Israel"—the Jewish people. From the historian's point of view, the essential element unifying the Jewish people through time and space was the religious tradition of Judaism. In the modern period, however, the duality has broken apart, its twin aspects cast into opposition. Following the civil emancipation of European Jewry, the modern world has witnessed the emergence of two distinct forms of Jewish identification: (1) Jews who see themselves primarily as members of a religious faith, forming one more "church" in Western society; and (2) Jews who identify in sociopolitical terms alone, whether as a nationality, an ethnic group, or as a "people." The split is most apparent in the contemporary State of Israel, where secular nationalists divide sharply from religious fundamentalists, but the division pervades the Jewish world. Thus has an ancient unity become a modern dichotomy.

The modern Jewish dialectic has special implications for Jewish life in the United States. At times the schism has been diametrically distinct, as when the American movement of Zionism was vehemently opposed by the American Council for Judaism. Yet far more often, the social-religious split of American Jewry falls across a continuum, each pole tending toward the center. We thus observe parallel tendencies in which the religious sphere shifts toward modern secularism and social activity, and the secular sphere moves "back" toward traditional Judaism. Here the social and religious spheres are forever in tension, continually energizing the dynamics of American Jewish life.

The phenomenon is most apparent in the interrelation of two institutions pivotal to the American Jewish experience, the synagogue and the community center. The social-religious dialectic underlying their relationship would ultimately produce a synthesis unique in Jewish history—the "synagogue-center"—whose essence it was to heal the rift between Jews and Judaism. On the most basic level, this book is a study of that distinctive American Jewish creation. It is the first full-length inquiry into the origins of the synagogue-center idea and the history of the synagogue-center movement.[2]

What is a synagogue-center? The term usually applies to the complex institution built by a Jewish congregation to serve the needs of its members. The physical structure tends to include a main sanctuary for worship, a smaller prayer chapel, a hall for social functions, classrooms, a library, offices, and so forth. But this merely describes the typical American synagogue (and, for that matter, the typical American church). The originality of the synagogue-center idea will emerge more clearly from an examination of the historical development of the institution. In 1875, the starting point for this study, the American synagogue was little more than a worship hall with a few dark and dingy schoolrooms in its basement. By 1925, the complex synagogue-center had become the leading trend in modern Jewish life, and a national "Jewish Center" movement was in full swing. The movement was expressed at the elite level by the ideological formulations of rabbis and Jewish social workers, and at the folk level by the sheer number of multimillion dollar structures erected in middle-class Jewish neighborhoods across the country.

By now, the concept of a synagogue-center has become so widely accepted that we no longer see the novelty. Marshall Sklare, the leading sociologist of American Jews, implied as much when he wrote, "the prototype of the contemporary American synagogue is the 'synagogue-center.'" Sklare explained that the synagogue had expanded its role for two purposes: to engage Jews who were thoroughly acculturated into America, and to provide for their (or their children's) reculturation to Judaism. Beyond religious services, therefore, extensive social and educational services were added to the synagogue program. The synagogue-center is most familiarly understood as a multipurpose synagogue that encompasses the three functions of religious worship, social activity, and education. The idea is echoed by the common description of the American synagogue as a threefold "house": a house of prayer, a house of assembly, and a house of study.[3]

Despite this seemingly traditional formula, the synagogue-center is the first synagogue type without precedent in the European past. It is originally and quintessentially American. The historical innovation lies in the development of a new institutional concept: the "Jewish center." Since the term was subsequently applied to various types of institutions, including both congregational synagogues and community centers, some confusion is apt to accompany its use today. Most famously, the term was applied to a key synagogue-center experiment: the Jewish Center, founded by Mordecai Kaplan in 1917. Thereafter, a "Jewish Center" movement arose that replicated the congregational self-definition of Kaplan's model. But the noncongregational sense of the term referred to another type of institution that had been in existence, in various forms, for half a century or more. This generic "Jewish center" (small c) may be traced back to the B'nai B'rith fraternal lodges of the mid-nineteenth century, and includes in its provenance the YMHA, the Jewish settlement, and the modern Talmud Torah. Its descendant today is the suburban Jewish Community Center (JCC).

All of the above share certain characteristics and so the generic institution may be defined as follows. A "Jewish center" is (1) a service agency, offering a variety of activities and social benefits to its mainly Jewish constituents; (2) a communal gathering place, housed in a centrally located building, and forming an integral part of the local Jewish neighborhood; (3) a unifying factor, open to all Jews of the community regardless of their religious affiliation or class status; and (4) a sectarian institution fostering Jewish culture and Jewish education, hence a primary locus of Jewish identification.[4]

The last point is crucial. By joining a center one affiliates with the voluntaristic American Jewish community, and feels that one has fulfilled the obligation to be "a good Jew." Through its educational and cultural programming the center then seeks to make him an even better Jew. In this sense, the Jewish center is not merely a center for Jews but also a center for Jewishness. The "Jewish" in its title signifies not only its constituency but also its content. The Jewish center thus presents itself *as an alternative to the synagogue,* the traditional and dominant form of public Jewish identification. As such, the creation of the center was a historic departure in the construction of Jewish community, and remains one of the most significant innovations of American Judaism.[5]

The institution was not entirely original, of course. As in the prototypical case of B'nai B'rith, the YMHA and all subsequent Jewish centers were created by some combination of American imitation and Jewish innovation. In the late nineteenth century, Jewish centers came to be more directly influenced by religious trends in American life; it was in that period that American Christianity underwent a significant revitalization. Three American-Christian institutions in particular were influential: the institutional church, the settlement house, and the Young Men's Christian Association (YMCA). As related trends within the greater ideological movement of "Protestant Social Service" or "Social Christianity," each of these institutions was born of the religious impulse to solve social problems, collectively foreshadowing the later Social Gospel movement. In their essence they were all syntheses of the religious and secular spheres, combining Christian mission and Progressive social service.[6]

In like manner, the religious synagogue and the secular Jewish center would come together to form a new institutional synthesis in Jewish life: the "synagogue-center." Though the term is most often associated with the congregational version, it may be applied as well to nonsynagogual Jewish centers that offer religious services. It may therefore be defined succinctly as follows: a synagogue-center is any combination of a synagogue and a center. This applies to any Jewish institution that combines the "religious" activities of the synagogue (worship, study, and public assembly) with the "social" services of the community center (recreation, special interest clubs, and informal education). The term *synagogue-center* is thereby broadened to denote any institution whose program merges the religious, the educational, and the social within one unified "center."

Locating the synagogue-center in its proper historical context is somewhat more complex. Imagine if you will an academic symposium on the origins of the synagogue-center. The panel consists of an American historian, a Jewish historian, a rabbi, and a sociologist. Opening the discussion, the first scholar describes the synagogue-center as the Jewish version of the institutional church, as the minority adaptation of a majority construct. The second historian, accustomed to surveying the entire sweep of Jewish history, insists that the synagogue was always the communal center; and since it had been a multipurpose institution from its inception in antiquity, any modern Christian influence only reinforced what had always been the case. Though sharing the notion of a multiple-use synagogue, the rabbi knows something of the development of American Judaism and offers the name of Mordecai M. Kaplan as the creator of the synagogue-center and the ideological father of the synagogue-center movement. The final participant takes exception to this elitist version of history and points to sociological factors such as generation, residential location, and economic status. In this view, the origins of the synagogue-center must be related to social forces acting upon the second generation of American Jews.

These four points of view are indeed the most commonly cited sources of the synagogue-center phenomenon: the church model, the historical synagogue, Mordecai M. Kaplan, and the sociological process of acculturation. Which of our theoreticians is right? They all are, to a degree; hence their theories may be offered in combination, as in the following instance: "The synagogue has been the focus and center of Jewish religious life throughout the 2,500 years of its history. It has been a center not only for prayer and instruction, but a communal center as well. . . . [Mordecai Kaplan's] synagogue center idea was, in fact, a reformulation and expansion in 20th century terms of what had always been the synagogue's role."[7] But essentially they are four very different arguments, each with its own merits and flaws. Let us consider each in turn.

(1) The *institutional church* is the model most like the synagogue-center in form, and an obvious direct influence. The institutional church movement was an important expression of "Social Christianity," the broader social-religious

trend characteristic of late nineteenth-century American Protestantism. As Aaron Abell explains, "the adjective 'institutional' was commonly employed to describe the numerous churches and missions which were expanding their functions to cover the entire life of man." Like the synagogue-center, the institutional church offered a wide variety of activities—religious, educational, and social. The "socialized" church was developed during the late 1880s and 1890s to provide social services to the populace of the rapidly changing American city. Some of its major representatives were the Broome Street Tabernacle of New York, Berkeley Temple of Boston, and Grace Church of Philadelphia, all created by established churches to minister to the urban lower classes, and all prominent institutions in their respective cities. Some of these may very well have inspired the founding of a neighboring synagogue-center. Quite understandably, the synagogue-center has been described as the Jewish version of the institutional church.[8]

Nevertheless, the church-synagogue connection applies mainly to the early synagogue-center of the Reform movement, as explored in Chapter 2. Even then there was sufficient distinction between the Christian and Jewish institutions to suggest parallel developments with only an indirect causal relationship. One such difference concerns the intended constituency. The synagogue-center was established by a Jewish community for its own benefit whereas the institutional church was most often conceived as a philanthropic project for others. A more critical distinction lies in the fact that the synagogue-center was the product of a dialectic between two competing ideologies: the religious Judaism of the synagogue and the ethnic Jewish secularism of the community center. By contrast, the institutional church was founded upon a single ideology and served one overarching purpose: to bring the gospel to the unchurched masses. The mission of the urban church may have included the relief of social ills, but its recreational/educational function was essentially a (social) means to a (religious) end, having no legitimating philosophy of its own. For this reason, the institutional church ought not to be considered the sole prototype for the synagogue-center, which also has its origins in the internal dynamics of Jewish life.

At the same time, many Reform congregations and their socially conscious rabbis were deeply affected by the general milieu of Social Christianity. Models provided by the Protestant environment included sewing circles, mission schools, settlement houses, and young people's societies. As immigrant Jews Americanized, they often borrowed the forms of such agencies, and even copied the names of such contemporary movements as the YMCA, the Christian Endeavor Society, Chautauqua retreats, People's Churches, and the Sunday School. In 1917—long after the first synagogue-center experiments—a modern Orthodox congregation was formed under the name of the Institutional Synagogue. Though the Jewish versions mimicked their Christian models by name, the process of adaptation would entail significant change. The final synthesis would be some combination of Christian influence and Jewish innovation.

(2) The *traditional synagogue* model, simultaneously a house of prayer, house

of study, and a house of assembly, is often cited as if its basis in historical Judaism were self-evident. Rabbi Marius Ranson, for example, stated in 1922: "Jewish tradition has ever maintained that the Synagog must serve three functions; viz., prayer, study and social gathering."⁹ Frequently advanced as proof are the original Hebrew terms for the three "houses." Since the synagogue has been denoted by *bet-tfila* (house of prayer), *bet-midrash* (house of study), and *bet-knesset* (house of assembly), then it must follow that those are its three traditional uses. A related etymological argument adds that the Greek word "synagogue" refers to a place of assembly; and similarly, the vernacular Yiddish term for synagogue is "shul," or school. A somewhat more sophisticated approach looks to the actual functioning of the synagogue throughout Jewish history to demonstrate its multipurpose nature. At various times, the synagogue has served as a hostel, a court, a charitable agency, a social hall, a town hall, a fort, and even a prison.

Above all, however, the synagogue has served as a house of worship. Though its exact origins remain unclear, it is certain that the synagogue blossomed as an institution following the destruction of the Second Temple in 70 c.e. Thereafter, the *tannaim* (rabbinic sages) of Yavneh accelerated the process of replacing the Temple ritual of priestly sacrifice with a synagogue-based ritual of communal prayer. It was this transposition of prayer for sacrifice that determined the chief function of the new institution. As a leading historian of the synagogue notes, "despite the plethora of activities that occurred in the ancient synagogue, the institution served first and foremost as a place for religious worship."¹⁰ No matter its secondary uses, the synagogue's primary role always remained communal worship. Hence it is misleading to call the synagogue a threefold house, implying the equal status within it of prayer, study, and assembly. The former was its main purpose whereas the latter two were secondary functions, each requiring a separate institution of its own.

Other facilities specifically intended to serve the needs of study and assembly included Jewish schools of varying sizes and scholarly levels, and communal "centers" such as the *bet din* (law court), the *Judaikei*, and the *kehillah* (centers in Hellenistic and medieval diaspora communities). In Jewish historical experience, therefore, the synagogue, school, and communal agency were most often three separate institutions. Even when offering multiple services in practice, the multifunctionality of the historical synagogue was never a matter of ideological intent. Nowhere in rabinic literature do we find a statement advocating the idea of the synagogue as an all-purpose institution; nowhere are all three terms found in unison. Yet in the contemporary era, they appear together with regularity.¹¹

The notion that the synagogue is rightfully a combination of all three is thus modern in origin, a twentieth-century invention of the synagogue-center movement. The unsubstantiated statement gained in frequency as attempts were made to reinstate the synagogue as the central institution of Jewish life and to legitimate the synagogue-center innovation. The statement thus became a sort of "mantra" for the movement (nowadays, it is merely cliché). That it is found throughout the literature of the American synagogue demonstrates the influence of the synagogue-center idea. The conscious evocation of that idea—emerging from the need to reestablish the center of Jewish life—belongs to the modern period and is especially relevant to the American Jewish community and its history.

(3) For similar legitimating motives, *Mordecai M. Kaplan* is frequently cited as the originator of the synagogue-center idea and the father of the movement. Kaplan was the outstanding American rabbi of this century, responsible for many significant developments in contemporary Judaism, both intellectual and practical. Kaplan's great intellectual achievement was his 1934 masterwork, *Judaism as a Civilization: Toward a Reconstruction of American-Jewish Life,* which ultimately served as the basis for the founding of Reconstructionism, the fourth branch of American Judaism. On the practical level he is perhaps best known for his central role in the formation of the Jewish Center, the influential synagogue-center founded in New York City in 1917.[12]

During the several-year process of planning and constructing the Jewish Center, Kaplan began to formulate an ideological rationale for the new institution. In no small part, his mature philosophy emerged from this early endeavor. Long before the emergence of Reconstructionism, therefore, Kaplan gained some prominence as the most articulate spokesman of the synagogue-center idea and hence the acknowledged leader of the synagogue-center movement. His reputation was enhanced by his pivotal teaching positions: professor of homiletics at the Jewish Theological Seminary and the principal of its Teachers Institute. His student-rabbis and student-teachers became enthusiastic proponents of the synagogue-center in pulpits and schools around the country.

Notwithstanding popular perception, however, Kaplan's responsibility for the creation of the synagogue-center was minimal. Here we must distinguish between the self-conscious movement, in which Kaplan's role was pivotal, and the full course of events leading to the advent of the synagogue-center, to which he was peripheral. Far from being the creation of one individual, the synagogue-center was the outcome of diverse trends. Once a movement coalesced, Kaplan was simply the right man at the right time, giving audible voice to less immediately observable—but far more pervasive—historical processes. Social historians have made this observation before, and yet the name of Mordecai Kaplan continues to be invoked as the sole progenitor of the synagogue-center.

(4) The *sociological perspective* has several variations. The prevailing model, first outlined by Marshall Sklare, relates the new synagogue type to changes in residential patterns and levels of acculturation. Here the evolution of the synagogue is traced through successive areas of settlement to demonstrate the emergence of a new type. The synagogue-center innovation is described as the response of the former immigrants to the challenges they confronted in their third areas of settlement, neighborhoods earlier inhabited by upper-middle-class Protestants and Reform Jews. The new environment was conducive to rapid acculturation, comprising both the trend toward secularism and the threat of assimilation. In

compromise with secularism and in defense against assimilation, the synagogue became a "multi-functional agency."[13]

More recent versions emphasize variables such as generation or economic class over residential location.[14] The generational emphasis attributes the rise of the synagogue-center to the immigrants' children, the second generation of American Jews. This view stresses the interwar years as the period in which the second generation came of age and began to create a community suited to its particular needs. One pressing need was to reconcile the Judaism of their parents with the American lifestyle they had adopted themselves. That lifestyle was solidly middle-class, and so the socioeconomic explanation focuses upon class status and economic prerogative. In either case, the synagogue-center provided the desired synthesis of provincial and cosmopolitan values. Without detracting from the legitimacy of any of these theories, we may suggest that all three factors—neighborhood, generation, and class—are inextricably linked. The question of which is the primary cause is less important than the integration of all three. This study will be careful to examine each relevant trend in Jewish life—a methodological decision that represents something of a departure in American Jewish studies.

In fact, this may be seen as a revisionist interpretation in several respects. Each of the forementioned theories of synagogue-center origins represents a distinct methodological perspective, each one valid in its own right. Thus, the perspective of American history has much to add to our understanding of the synagogue-center. Issues such as Social Christianity, Progressivism, immigrant adjustment, urban development, and the rise of leisure activity all played vital roles in the development of American Jewish life. But viewing the American context alone tends to eclipse those elements of Judaism and Jewish history that bear upon the formation of Jewish community. Lacking the perspective of the Jewish historian, we may overlook the historical models that have influenced the development of modern Jewish life. We might, for instance, be tempted to see the "Hebrew Free School" of the nineteenth century merely as an American-style mission school, rather than as the American version of the traditional Jewish public school, the *Talmud Torah*—itself an expression of the cherished Jewish values of communal philanthropy and universal education. For good reason, the more "parochial" perspective of Judaic studies will be employed to counter the tendency to dwell only in the realm of American studies.

Similarly, the opposing perspectives of the rabbi and the sociologist may be used to balance one another. If the error of the former is to focus upon the contribution of leading individuals (the intellectual "elite") then the latter tends to overemphasize the role of impersonal social forces (the "folk" impulse). In general, I have sought to combine or otherwise balance the two in delineating historical trends. Consequently, this is not a study of any one movement or institution, but of several. Far too often in the past, Jewish social and religious phenomena have been studied independently, as if they grew and developed in isolation. Yet precisely the opposite is the case, as movements and institutions evolve in response to one another and as constituent parts of a broader culture. In the evolution of the synagogue-center, religious movements conformed to social needs and social institutions resonated to religious imperatives, further demonstrating the need for a comparative and comprehensive approach.

This encompassing approach notwithstanding, the book is organized so as to treat each institutional movement within a separate chapter. On one level, each chapter may be considered a contribution to a specific topic in American Jewish history. But there is a larger point to be made. The chapters on the Reform temple, the YMHA, the Jewish settlement, the Talmud Torah, and the Orthodox shul will each present its subject as a singular source of the synagogue-center phenomenon. Two subsequent chapters on the rise of the synagogue-center movement will delve, respectively, into the role of leading rabbis and the impact of the second-generation neighborhood. Again, each will be shown to have individually engendered the synagogue-center synthesis; when taken together, they will be seen as the resolution of the rift between rabbinate and laity. Yet when all the chapters are added together, some larger theory will have to be advanced to explain the coincidence of synagogue-centers in every sector. It may then become apparent that the rift between rabbinate and laity is essentially the same as that between the older and younger generations, and as that between Germans and Russians: it is the modern divide between Judaism and the Jews that has given rise to the social-religious dialectic of American Jewish life.

The creation of the synagogue-center thus exemplified the synthesis of Jewish social and religious tendencies that has been maintained throughout Jewish history, always in tension yet rarely in equilibrium. The synagogue-center aspired to be that rare balancing act. It would be "house of worship, house of study, and house of assembly" all in one; or, in the colloquial phrase of the day, a "shul with a pool." The combination of those disparate activities may seem mundane to us today. But when placed within the context of the social-religious duality of Judaism, the rise of the synagogue-center proves to be of major significance to the history of American Jewish life.

1

TEMPLE
The Synagogue-Center of Classical Reform Judaism

The most interesting development in American Reform Judaism is the establishment of a new kind of Synagogue—one that stands not only for worship, but for all forms of social activity, from lessons in golf to lectures on art. The Community Centre with its synagogue, or the synagogue with a community house, is now the centre of Jewish life in America.

—RABBI ISRAEL MATTUCK, 1927[1]

AFTER SIXTEEN YEARS in England, the American Reform rabbi Israel Mattuck returned home for a visit. Writing for the American Hebrew, he reported his observations of the latest "developments in [the] Liberal Movement in America." One innovation in particular seems to have captured his attention, as he enthusiastically described "a new kind of Synagogue." It was a remarkable statement, as Mattuck first noted the emergence of a new Jewish institutional form: a combination synagogue and community center. Going further, however, he described the new type of synagogue as *the* central institution of American Jewish life, giving new meaning to the "center" in "synagogue-center." The effusive quality of the description is not entirely surprising, as 1927 was the height of the synagogue-center movement. Yet there is a seeming anomaly here. Mattuck was a leader of the Reform movement and a proponent of classical Reform Judaism. From our current perspective it may seem odd that such a figure would approve of a synagogue encompassing "all forms of social activity." While he reserved judgment as to "their effect on the religious life of American Jewry," Mattuck certainly did not disapprove. Rather, he seemed impressed by "this new adaptation of the ancient idea of the Synagogue [which] may be counted among America's contributions to Jewish life."[2]

Beyond mere approval, however, Mattuck added the following: "Most of these synagogues adhere to Reform Judaism, though I believe that some Conservative congregations have copied this development." He thus attributed the synagogue-center idea to the Reform movement! Our surprise is due first of all to the present historical understanding of American Reform Judaism, which tends to equate "classical" with "radical" Reform and therefore perpetuates the stereotypical notion that classical Reform regarded Judaism purely as a religion. Had not the definitive Reform platform declared: "We consider ourselves no longer a nation, but a religious community"? Many have since inferred that classical Reform Judaism had little interest in Jewish social life. As we shall see, it is a false assumption.[3]

Mattuck's comment also conflicts with the reigning image of the synagogue-center as Kaplan-inspired and Conservative-sponsored. Yet the current view overlooks the historical reality to which Mattuck alluded. An early version of the synagogue-center—in both theory and practice—had surfaced in the Reform movement before Mordecai Kaplan ever conceived the idea. Kaplan himself admitted this, pointing to the late nineteenth-century trend within Reform Judaism "toward enlarging the scope of the congregational activities beyond those of worship and elementary religious schooling," and the subsequent creation of so-called open temples by classical Reform rabbis.[4]

Whether Conservative rabbis and their congregations "copied this development" directly from the Reform movement remains open to question; what cannot be disputed is that the Reform version of the synagogue-center predated the advent of the Kaplanian synagogue-center. In fact, its earliest manifestation in Reform Judaism (in 1888) preceded the establishment of Kaplan's Jewish Center (in 1917) by nearly three decades. Mattuck has thus alerted us to a little-known aspect of the synagogue-center movement: its provenance in Reform Judaism. The observation is well worth exploring, especially insofar as the origin of the synagogue-center has so often been attributed to Kaplan and Conservativism alone.[5]

The Classical Reform Rabbi and the Problem of the Temple

When Mattuck arrived in 1927, the Reform movement in America was in transition. The era of "classical" Reform Judaism, that turn-of-the-century synthesis of Isaac Mayer Wise's pragmatism with the radicalism of David Einhorn, was in sharp decline. The new synagogue of which Mattuck wrote was the product of this era and the creation of its rabbis. Mattuck alluded to such a rabbi-synagogue nexus when he described the rise of the synagogue-center as having "coincided with—though it is not associated with—the establishment of an American Jewish ministry." His comment alludes to the close relationship of the synagogue and rabbinate throughout American Jewish history. The transformations of synagogual type—from colonial "synagogue-community" to Ashkenazic "rite-congregation" to Reform "temple"—paralleled the changing roles of the rabbinic leadership, from Sephardic *hazan* to German-Jewish "minister" to the fully Americanized "reverend-doctor." The synagogue and rabbinate have thus developed in tandem and are best studied within a dual framework.[6]

Indeed, the synagogue-rabbi relationship of classical Reform might even be described as symbiotic. The characteristic synagogue of this period was created largely by the rabbis, both as individuals and as an organized body (primarily, though not exclusively, the CCAR [Central Conference of American Rabbis]). In the reverse sense, those same rabbis were "made" by the synagogue, as the congregation now served as the platform from which the rabbi might attain fame and influence. Before the era of classical Reform, American rabbis derived their influence from the Jewish press, theological writings, rabbinic conferences, and organization on the national level (e.g., Isaac Leeser, David Einhorn, and Isaac Mayer Wise). In this period, the individual congregation would become the powerbase for an aspiring rabbi. A prominent congregation could enhance a rabbi's reputation immeasurably—which helps explain the competitive scramble for plum positions among the rabbis of the time. Accordingly, the subject of the classical Reform synagogue is here treated within the context of the classical Reform rabbinate.

Whereas the formative period of American Reform was effected as much by the laity as by the rabbis—together responding to changes in the social and economic status of the American Jew—classical Reform Judaism was largely the creation of the rabbinate. It was, in sum, the response of the late nineteenth-century leadership to the perceived inadequacies of the earlier phase of American Reform Judaism. Calling for religious revitalization, the Reform movement introduced a new type of rabbi in the 1880s and 1890s; subsequently, by the turn of the century, the new rabbis proposed the creation of a new type of synagogue: the classical Reform synagogue-center.[7]

The era of classical Reform was inaugurated by three related events of the 1880s: the first graduation of Hebrew Union College in 1883, the Pittsburgh Conference in 1885, and the establishment of the Central Conference of American Rabbis in 1889. All of these were epochal events in the formation of the American Reform rabbinate and consequently of classical Reform Judaism; yet all three events provide evidence of the decline, not the rise, of the synagogue.

The first, the 1883 graduation, was of the greatest import to the contemporary synagogue. Since Hebrew Union College had been established in response to the countrywide need for rabbis, the graduation of its first class was greeted with eager anticipation; the need was not simply for bodies to fill empty pulpits but for a new kind of rabbi altogether. In order to reach a generation that was native-born, English-speaking, and forward-thinking, and that seemed to have little interest in the synagogue, the new type of rabbi was required to "speak their language," which meant, above all, to speak English, beautifully enunciated and eloquently phrased. Also, as the institution that represented the Jews to the Gentile world, the synagogue now demanded a rabbi who would be as modern, as erudite, and as American as the minister of the church next door. Third, the new rabbi was asked to be an activist, combining the practical skills of a school principal, social worker, and charity organizer. The call for a new kind of rabbi came in response, therefore, to the changing needs of the American Jewish congregation. The call had become urgent due to the sorry state of congregational life at the time.[8]

By the 1880s the American synagogue had been thoroughly transformed into a "temple." The new designation for a synagogue stemmed from both Protestant example and from Reform's ideological rejection of Zion; more essentially, the term reflected the new understanding of the institution as a sacred hall of worship, a house of God, a Jewish church. Expressing the change both inside and out, the ritual pattern of the temple was Protestantized and its architecture became grandly impressive, or "cathedralized." Following the Civil War, Jewish congregations across the country built new structures of monumental proportion and fantastic architectural style. That they were willing and able to do so testifies to both a sound financial condition and to a secure sense of their Americanness. Americanization of synagogue ritual meant the introduction of English, mixed seating, organ and choir music, and a shorter and more decorous service with a sermon as its central feature—all calculated to appeal to a rapidly assimilating Jewish public.[9]

Yet despite such interior and exterior improvements, the new Reform temple was not a successful institution. From expressions of concern to the harshest of criticism, observations of religious impoverishment were commonplace. For example, the 1879 president's report of Chicago's Sinai Congregation reads in part:

> this congregation has during the past year not undertaken or accomplished any one thing or act, which could entitle it to any special credit or praise at this present meeting. . . . We claim to be the principal congregation in the Western country and we are thus classed, but we deserve it not. We own a temple erected by your liberality in days gone by, to-day we would not build it; we would be unwilling to bring a sacrifice. Service is held as stated but we do not attend. . . . We have a minister of whom we are justly proud [Kaufmann Kohler], but he preaches before empty benches. No doubt we lack inspiration; we are indifferent. And our children? Will they follow our examples, and if possible improve upon our evil ways, and still we remain indifferent. . . . In this manner we have brought religious matters to a standstill and have transformed our grand Temple in[to] a grand vacuum.[10]

Is it any wonder that Rabbi Kohler left soon thereafter?

By thus chastising the congregation for their "great indifference" and "lethargy," the president and board members hoped to reverse the trend and even believed that "a revival in our midst [would] cause a general revival among the Israelites of this city." Both the complaint and the hoped-for reversal were echoed time and again. During the winter of 1887–88, the pseudonymous "Auntie Apathy" (in reality Flora Brunn Berkowitz, the wife of Rabbi Henry Berkowitz) wrote several letters to the *American Israelite* sharply critical of the Jewish community of Mobile, Alabama. She employed somewhat macabre imagery, calling the town "dead as a doornail," and decrying the "fatal apathy" of her congregants.[11]

In the same vein, the *American Hebrew* editorialized: "our Jewish congregations have gradually loosened their hold upon the lives of the people, and . . . surrendered their influence to the social clubs. . . . There are no colors gloomy enough to paint too morbidly the conditions that are at present sustained. The real majority of our people come into actual contact with the organized religious forces but once a year—on the high holidays. When once a child has learned the alphabet of religion at Sunday-School and has been confirmed, its religious education is considered finished." Similar complaints are heard to this day.[12]

In the late nineteenth century, such admonishment was most often and most forcefully expressed by the rabbinic leadership. Their critique was neatly summed up by Rabbi Aaron Hahn at the first annual convention of the Central Conference of American Rabbis in 1890: "The general complaints in American Reformed Judaism are that the temple services are not so well attended as they should be; that there are, even among those who are very zealous for the preservation of Judaism, a great many who except on the great holidays are very seldom seen in the temple. . . . What is the cause of this evil? Why are the Reform temples not better attended?" To laypeople and rabbis alike, the problem appeared to be the widespread lack of attendance at services. Because congregational life was largely confined to public worship, this translated to lack of participation overall. While Rabbi Hahn's paper represented a new analytical approach to the role of the rabbi and his problems in the field, he offered no solutions. Others of his colleagues would.[13]

Kaufmann Kohler (1843–1926), the dominant intellectual of classical Reform, invited his fellow rabbis to convene and confer on the matter in 1885. The Pittsburgh conference, it has been observed, was called by Kohler in response to two ideological challenges: from Ethical Culture on the left, and from Conservatism on the right. Thus the most noted outcome of the conference was its famous platform of principles, which attempted to establish Reform Judaism as the theological middle ground between universalism and Jewish particularism. At the same time, the Pittsburgh conference was intended to respond concretely to the congregational malaise. In the preconference paper circulated to all the participants, Kohler stressed the pervasive religious decline, and claimed "it is high time to rally our forces to consolidate, to build."[14]

In addition to enunciating the principles that formed the basis for the platform, Kohler added the following practical recommendations:

After having drawn a large circle around the Jewish system of thought . . . we ought, I think, on this broad basis, proceed and organize a Jewish mission to work with the entire Jewish camp. . . . It ought to face the great social problems of today . . . [and furthermore] our congregations, owing to the large expenses with which they are maintained, are conducted on too narrow a basis. . . . We require a thorough reform of our congregational life.[15]

He continued by suggesting the increased participation of women, a Jewish publication society, a uniform system of religious instruction, further worship reform, a new translation of the Bible, improved Jewish-Gentile relations, and greater attention paid to the Jewish home; in short, anything that might help improve the quality of Jewish life (and all recommendations that were eventually enacted). Yet the conference that followed Kohler's initiative focused on the theoretical rather than the practical and such issues were left for the future. Kohler and his generation of European-born and -trained Reform rabbis had confronted the problem of Jewish religious life in America, offered some vague notions of how to proceed, but seemed unable or unwilling to take any effective course of action.

That was to be the contribution of the Americans, who in the next fifteen years (1885–1900) would transform the contours and functions of the American synagogue. The transformation would follow two concurrent but distinct paths. On the one hand, the Americanizing tendency so powerful in both the Reform rabbinate and the laity would bring about a greater openness in the temple. Rather than being a closed system of religious fellowship, a congregational *Gemeinschaft,* the new synagogue would be open to all people and to all ideas, truly an "open temple" on the American model.

The second tendency, often coexisting with the first, was also an "opening" of sorts; though here the expansion was not of form but of function. Rather than responding to the American invitation to open its doors to the outside world, the second transformation responded to certain imperatives of Jewish life by, metaphorically, adding more rooms within the temple itself. The scope of congregational life was widened by incrementally adding functions drawn from the culture of American Jewish communal life. Eventually, a comprehensive program was put forth, and a proto–synagogue-center was born. One trend, therefore, would model the synagogue after the freedoms and openness of American society, and the other would model the synagogue after the Jewish community, in all its secular and social variety. Both trends were the initiatives of the new generation of rabbis, post–Pittsburgh Platform reformers who understood that platforms are meant to be built upon.

Emil G. Hirsch, Americanizer of the Reform Temple

The impetus toward the creation of an "open temple" was provided by Emil G. Hirsch (1852–1923), the rabbi who personified the Americanization of classical Reform Judaism. Son of the radical reformer Samuel Hirsch, he was born in Luxembourg where his father served as chief rabbi. In 1866, Rabbi Hirsch was called to succeed David Einhorn in the pulpit of Keneseth Israel in Philadelphia. Emil thus emigrated to the United States at the impressionable age of fifteen, eager to begin his education in American ways. He continued his secular education first at the Episcopal Academy of Philadelphia and then at the University of Pennsylvania—where he played for the football team! But his true calling would be the rabbinate. As a university student, Emil most likely attended the rabbinical conference of 1869 held in his father's home. He returned to Europe to complete his doctoral and rabbinical degrees, and in 1876 was called to the pulpit of Har Sinai in Baltimore where he remained for one year until called to Adath Israel Congregation in Louisville, Kentucky. From there he moved to Chicago in 1880

Fig. 1. Rabbi Emil G. Hirsch, circa 1890. Courtesy
of the American Jewish Archives, Cincinnati, Ohio.

to replace Kaufman Kohler at Sinai Congregation, and served there for over four
decades. Like Kohler, he too married an Einhorn daughter.[16]

Yet unlike his more European brother-in-law, Hirsch was the consummate
American rabbi. Whereas Leeser and Wise had been the creative Americanizers,
and Einhorn and Kohler the radical Reformers of American Judaism, Hirsch was
the first of a new generation of rabbis who would be both completely Americanized and confidently Reformed. Rabbis before him had been active in both the
social and religious spheres, but he was the first activist for radical change in both
those arenas. As an early proponent of the Social Gospel movement in America
and a leading light of the classical Reform movement in Judaism, Emil G. Hirsch
set the standard for such dualism of purpose. In this sense, he would become the
prototype for the next generation of American rabbis.

That Hirsch was the principal Jewish advocate of the Social Gospel was due in
no small part to his collegial relations with his liberal Protestant contemporaries.
He most closely identified with Jenkin Lloyd Jones, the pastor of the Unitarian
All-Souls Church in Chicago. In the first issue of his newspaper, the *Reform Advocate,* Hirsch printed a sermon of Jones's entitled, "The Creedless Position"; in
the next issue, the rabbi responded in kind with his own article, "Creed Not the
Test of Religious Fellowship." Hirsch thus served as both a conduit and inter-
preter of contemporary Protestant thought to the world of Jewish discourse.[17]

Sinai Temple and Center, Grand Blvd. & 46th St., Chicago.

Fig. 2. Sinai Temple and Center, Chicago, Ill., built 1911–12. Collection of Peter Schweitzer.

As he wrote in the *Advocate* in 1892: "In a lecture published a few years ago, we emphasized the idea that congregations should stand for all those things that make for the higher life. We dwelt upon the many varied enterprises, which under the auspices of Christian churches and Unitarian societies, flourish, and do combine to make of the church the *center* of both the intellectual and social life of its members." Influenced by the trends of Social Christianity, therefore, Hirsch supported the inclusion of "social features" in Jewish "congregational life"; for example, in that same year, he also sponsored a renovation of his temple building in which space was added (in the basement) for a new kindergarten—a precursor of today's day-care services. As an early Social Gospeler, however, he was more interested in political activism than in congregational expansion.[18]

It was Hirsch who formulated and added the final plank of the Pittsburgh Platform regarding social justice. Such concern for the underprivileged also found expression in his call for an "open temple," a temple open to the entire Jewish community, rich and poor alike (that is, both German and East European Jews), with affordable pews for the middle class and free seating for the poor. Moreover, the "open temple" would be open to "all souls," both Jew and gentile; and, in fact, oftentimes more non-Jews than Jews were to be found listening to the pyrotechnic sermons of Hirsch and his fellow rabbis. These two separate intentions of the "open temple" were both derived from the "open church," which also strove to break down the barriers between people. (A specifically Jewish contribution was perhaps the biblical inscription above the doorway, "My house shall be called a house of prayer for all people.") However, there was an important difference between the open church and temple. For the temple, the "opening" of its doors had the unintended effect of expanding its schedule.

The expansion was due to the introduction of Sunday services, the most controversial ritual innovation of classical Reform and an idea most often associated with Hirsch. The proposed change was above all a practical response to the problem of inattendance. The problem was at first blamed on the situation of the Jewish workingman, who, forced by circumstance to work on the Sabbath, could not attend the traditional service. To a degree, this was a rationalization that obscured the fact that American Jews in general were becoming less interested in religion. Even so, the innovation was strictly a practical measure. The traditional Jewish Sabbath remained valid in theory, claimed the reformers; if it *could* have been preserved in practice, it *would* have been. The expedient of moving weekly services to the day of the Christian Sabbath was justified as being "the only remedy for the preservation and dissemination of prophetic Judaism." The adoption of Sunday services by many Reform congregations was thus a case of American pragmatism: the necessary means to an essential end—or so it was reasoned in the 1880s.[19]

It is significant that the more extreme view—that Sunday be adopted as the new Jewish Sabbath—is associated with Samuel Hirsch rather than with his son. While Emil G. Hirsch emulated his father's radicalism, most classical Reformers remained committed to the inviolable Jewishness of Saturday. At the same time, their willingness to switch days in practice is a peculiarly American habit. Being a new nation, America from the start created its own holidays—a practice that gives rise to the attitude that holidays are man-made and subject to change. An analogy is easily drawn to modern Judaism, which, having rejected *Torah m'Sinai* (the divine revelation at Mount Sinai) as literal fact, easily justifies its reforms of tradition. The Sunday service is analogous to the contemporary practice of moving holidays, such as presidents' birthdays, to the weekend for the sake of convenience. Neither actual birthdates nor the ancient tradition of the Sabbath-day seems to be very "sacred" in the free and secular society in which we live.

While the historic controversy has been covered elsewhere, the implications of the Sunday Sabbath for congregational life have been overlooked. Since the overwhelming majority of congregations who introduced the Sunday service kept their Saturday services as well, one effect was to extend the activity of the synagogue from one day a week to two. In such congregations, the Saturday service was often geared to the older folk by maintaining its traditional tone and delivering the sermon in German; while the Sunday service was more secular in character, employing English and current topics to appeal to the younger generation. Even those who abandoned the traditional Sabbath, such as Hirsch's Sinai Congregation, eventually found their scope broadened. With the growing importance of its Sunday service, Sinai in 1900 moved the day of its religious school from Sunday to Saturday, becoming a two-day-a-week temple as well. In either case, the precedent was set that the synagogue was no longer a one-day-a-week

institution. Of course, the premodern synagogue had been an everyday institution as prayer is a daily requirement in traditional Judaism. Alluding to this, the
rabbi of Temple Emanu-El in New York would write: "If it were feasible I would
have this Temple open every day of the week and an hour's service on each day,
but since the doors of the temple are ajar three days every week (on Friday, Saturday, and Sunday), there is little or no justification for the total absence of any one
from our services."[20]

Furthermore, the Sunday service represented the elevation of the secular
within the Reform temple, as the service now revolved around a sermon that had
taken on the character of a university lecture. Hirsch, for example, emphasized
the modern character of the sermon: "The new radical reformer . . . wishes his
congregation to learn this when they visit the 'teaching hall,' for that is what a
Temple is. . . . Not the cloister, but the university auditorium is the type of the
modern Jewish synagogue, the meeting place for teaching purposes." Yet, as
other reformers rationalized, this was nothing new to the Jewish experience.
Rabbi Henry Berkowitz explained: "With us the school and synagogue have
been and remain identical. 'Lernen,' study, is a form of worship, the pulpit itself
the legitimate place for the enunciation of all the ennobling lessons of truth. . . .
The 'Beth Hakeneses' and the 'Beth Hamidrash,' the 'house of worship' and the
'house of investigation,' have been one and the same place." In the classical Reform temple, however, the rabbi's sermon had displaced participatory prayer and
the reading of the Torah as the main feature of Jewish worship. The weekly service had become, in effect, Sunday school for adults.[21]

With the growing emphasis upon education, the temple had begun a process
of transformation: from a monolithic, worship-centered shrine into an institution with multiple priorities and departments (hence led by a rabbi with multiple
talents). The Sunday service may therefore be regarded as the first important step
toward widening the scope of the Reform temple. It furthermore set the stage for
the emergence of a Jewish "open temple," the phrase thereby gaining yet another
meaning: the temple would be "open" several days a week, not just one. It is no
coincidence that many of the same rabbis who were the strongest supporters of
the Sunday service—Hirsch, Moses Gries, Joseph Krauskopf, J. Leonard Levy,
Hyman G. Enelow, and Leo M. Franklin—would later become the foremost
proponents of an "open temple," that is, the classical Reform synagogue-center.

The agenda of the Reform congregation was thus liberalized and secularized,
that is, *Americanized*. Indeed, the "*open*" temple" mirrored the "*open*" society" of
America. This tendency, the absorption by the synagogue of American ideals and
imagery, continued through the coming decades. In 1898, William Rosenau
called for the creation of a "*People's* Reform Synagogue" to bring Reform's liberal
message to the denizens of the immigrant ghetto. Such Jewish "missions" were
established for short periods in several of the larger cities, beginning with
Philadelphia in 1904. Somewhat more successful was the "*Free* Synagogue"
movement founded by Stephen S. Wise in 1907. Wise's synagogue experiment

merged the Jewish ideal of community with the American ideal of democracy in unprecedented fashion. In 1913, Solomon Schechter founded a new synagogue movement and called it the "*United* Synagogue *of America*," perhaps the ultimate in such patriotic phrasing. The synthesis of Americanism and Judaism in the synagogue continued throughout the interwar era when rabbis' sermons were broadcast over the airwaves on Sunday mornings, temple architecture reflected the Neoclassicism of the United States capitol, and the American flag became a standard furnishing in the sanctuary. Therefore, the first trend in the creation of the classical Reform temple was Americanization—as epitomized by the American ministry of Emil G. Hirsch.

"Wise's Men" and the "Opening" of the Reform Synagogue

The second trend that transformed the American synagogue of the late 1880s and 1890s was the concurrent "opening" of the temple to greater Jewish possibilites. This entailed a broadening definition of the synagogue's purpose and the simultaneous increase of congregational functions. As early as 1883, a prominent lay officer of Temple Emanu-El in New York had called for such redirection of purpose. "The ideal church, temple, or synagogue of to-day," he declared, "is a place where men and women are to meet together, not merely for the culture of their religious sentiments (using that expression in its narrowest signification), but also for the furtherance of all measures of a philanthropic character." Two new ideas are in evidence here: one, that specifically religious sentiments "are but a means to an end," and second, that "public assemblage" for "good purposes" is fit and proper activity for the synagogue. If religion per se was too narrow, then some broadening of the program must occur. The related social functions of assembly and philanthropy stood ready to be incorporated as integral functions of the congregation; before such novelties could be accepted, however, they first required the imprimatur of the rabbis, a classical Reform "hechsher" (kosher authentification), so to speak.[22]

Also in 1883 was the first graduation of the first rabbinical seminary in America, hence, the advent of a new rabbinic type. Balancing their American and Jewish identities in Hirsch-like harmony, the new rabbis would serve as communal role models and provide an example of the ideal American Jew. At the turn of the century, when American Jewry seemed polarized between too-assimilated "Yahudim" and too-Jewish immigrants, such successful integration of commitments aroused great admiration. Thus, a 1902 newspaper account glowingly described one of the new breed, Moses Gries, as both "thoroughly American and thoroughly Jewish"; the same might have been said of any of his youthful colleagues.[23]

They were "thoroughly American" in dress, speech, and manner, as most were born here and had been educated in the public schools of America. Moreover, they were imbued with the optimism of post–Civil War America and were inspired by its ideals of religious universalism and social progressivism. They were individualists, pragmatists, and rationalists. Above all, however, the young rabbinic idealists evinced an unshakable faith in American democracy: the notion that since "all men are created equal" (a religious statement, of course) social hierarchies are un-American, and distinctions between rich and poor, Jew and Gentile, native and immigrant, men and women, ought to be eliminated as far as possible. Most studies of the Americanism of classical Reform focus upon the communal expression of these tendencies; that is, the Jewish correlate of the Social Gospel movement. Yet, as we shall see, their American ideals were expressed as much by their congregational activities as by their social activism.[24]

That they were "thoroughly Jewish" was somewhat less apparent. They spoke a perfect English, but could they and would they enunciate a full-bodied, resonant Judaism? Since most had never experienced the all-encompassing Jewish life of either the European ghetto or traditional Jewish practice, one might surmise that their Jewishness was less than consuming. Certainly the later critics of classical Reform would point to such a deficit. But, in truth, they had experienced eight arduous years of intensive Jewish education at Hebrew Union College, the first successful American rabbinical academy, established by Isaac Mayer Wise in 1875. As described by historian Michael Meyer, the curriculum offered by the new seminary was extraordinary for its depth and breadth. "The quantity of material . . . they managed to absorb is astounding," as it included ancient, classical, and modern languages, biblical and Talmudic texts, medieval Jewish philosophy and literature, Jewish history, Jewish theology, and homiletics. The curriculum itself thus infused the student rabbis with an overpowering sense of the vast scope of Jewish civilization. In addition, the comprehensive, systematized "university" method of instruction at the college would serve the students well as a model for their future educational roles as superintendents of the religious schools of their congregations.[25]

As important a molding influence as the academic curriculum was the community. Comprising students, faculty, and even members of the governing board, it was an intimate group setting that Meyer calls "a family in a very real sense." College life was furthermore characterized by a student literary society, a student journal, and later, sports teams. The literary society, instituted by Wise, met weekly for lectures, debates, music, and drama. The rabbinical students of Hebrew Union College learned in no uncertain terms that a Jewish institutional setting could relate to every aspect of life. This pervasive quality—Mordecai Kaplan would later call it "organic Jewish community"—would naturally be reflected in the congregational life that the young rabbis would seek to create, or really, re-create. Thus, their Jewish experience as well as their Americanism would shape the classical Reform conception of an American synagogue.[26]

One more word must be said about the influence of Wise. Upon their graduation, the young rabbis of Hebrew Union College were dubbed "Atzilei Bene Israel" (literally, the noblest of the sons of Israel) by their president and mentor; but really they might just as well have been called, "Atzilei Bene *Isaac*," for in their ardent Americanness and unyielding Jewishness, their capacity for innovation and pragmatism, and their penchant for organization and education, the young rabbis were without question the disciples of Isaac Mayer Wise. It is significant that all of the rabbis associated with the temple center were pre-1900 graduates of the college, all students of Wise. Yet as self-confident Americans (Wise, it must be recalled, was an immigrant) the younger men surpassed their mentor in their religious radicalism. One of the foremost members of this group once defended Sunday services—which Wise opposed—by declaring: "I am . . . a Sunday service man, first of all, because I am a Jew; secondly, because I love Judaism, and I love both with all my heart; thirdly, because on the 11th day of July, 1883, Rev. Dr. Wise placed his hand on my head and said: 'Go forth, preach Judaism.'"[27]

The speaker of those impressive words was Joseph Krauskopf, who, together with his Hebrew Union College roommate Henry Berkowitz, was to pioneer the expansion of the temple bounds. Like Kohler and Hirsch before them, Krauskopf and Berkowitz were brothers-in-law (Krauskopf married Berkowitz's sister); but, perhaps signified by their double wedding ceremony performed by Wise, they had much more in common; namely, the passionate commitment to Judaism inspired by their mentor. Krauskopf and Berkowitz also shared similar attitudes to the purpose of the synagogue. In September 1885, they were both present at the dedication of the new temple in Kansas City, and in their addresses expressed their images of the ideal temple. Whereas Wise, in his manifold dedicatory addresses, always stressed the sanctity of the temple as a "house of God," his students would introduce a broader conception.[28]

Krauskopf spoke first:

This house shall aim to show religion to be the greatest gift of God to Man, and if it realizes its aim, then it will be the soul's paradise. From it, as from the paradise of old, four life- and blessing-dispensing streams shall wind their course, one to the heart and one to the mind, one to the home and one to mankind, becoming to the heart a "Beth Elohim"—a house of God— and to the mind a "Beth Hamidrash"—a house of learning; to the home a "Beth Hakneseth"—that dearest spot on earth from which emanate those virtues that form the foundation of peaceful, progressive society, and to mankind a "Beth Hamikdash"—the house consecrated to be the shrine of the religion of humanity, within that holiest of all sanctuaries in which all good men worship alike.[29]

This is an early example of the use of the various Hebrew names of the synagogue to justify its multiple purposes. Furthermore, Krauskopf's prooftext for the fourfold function of the temple is the Midrashic description of the Garden of Eden, a traditional Jewish source. Of the four "Batim" (houses) he enumerates, the first two correspond to the already established functions of the Reform temple, worship and study, that are also of course two of the three functions of the synagogue-center. The fourth, "Beth Hamikdash," is defined as the "sanctuary in which all good men worship alike"; in other words, the open temple that we have previously discussed. However, his third suggestion is more novel and worth pausing over.

Krauskopf defines "Beth Hakneseth" not as the "house of" something exter-
nal but rather, as the home itself. Thus, the fourfold temple would cultivate both
worship and study, be directed outward toward "humanity," and inward to "that
dearest spot on earth," the private social realm of family and home. The home
was, in traditional Jewish life, the primary setting for religious education and
practice. According to one Reform rabbi of the older generation, "The Jewish
House [is] a Sanctuary of the Lord." The following generation would turn his
formulation around to read, "the sanctuary of the Lord [that is, the synagogue] is
the Jewish house [that is, the home of the community]." By expanding the educational and practical functions of the congregation, the intimate Judaism of the
home would be transferred to the public context of the synagogue. Hence Rabbi
Joseph Stolz, at another temple dedication, would proclaim: "[We] have therefore erected this *house,* not that it should be [God's] only resting place, but that it
should be unto [the congregation] a *home* where like members of one family they
might help each other, inspire each other, to lift up to thee their highest sentiments." Temple thus replaces the home as the wellspring of Jewish life—and the
imagery of the synagogue as center has begun.[30]

Wise foreshadowed the transference of home to synagogue through his advocacy of the Friday night service, thus bringing a formerly home-bound and family-
oriented custom—the Friday night "Oneg Shabbat"—into the congregational
realm. Yet his students would go a step further by redefining the synagogue as the
"home" of the entire Jewish community, and therefore began to introduce formerly communal functions into congregational life. The first of these was the literary society. Social and cultural clubs for young Jewish men and women had
been formed since the beginning of the German-Jewish settlement in America.
Societies were popular for their homelike atmosphere and informal camaraderie,
but their popularity derived mainly from the opportunity to raise one's social
standing through the acquisition of a higher culture; the major activities were
therefore lectures, debates, and reading. The same intellectual goals would later
be used to justify the inclusion of such social activity within the religious sphere
of the temple.[31]

At first providing a social alternative to the synagogue, the literary society
began intruding into Jewish religious life in various ways. The German Literary
Society of Albany was founded by the young Isaac Mayer Wise, and met in his
synagogue from its inception in 1849. It was an early development that foreshadowed later trends. As mentioned above, Wise would later incorporate a society
into the college's curriculum as part of its program of Americanization. In 1879,
Wise's colleague in Cincinnati, Max Lilienthal, initiated the short-lived Rabbinical Literary Association. The content was Jewish literature but the form was a literary society for rabbis. At the same time, the proliferating independent groups
had begun to request use of the temple facilities; thus turning the temple into an
ad-hoc "center" long before such an institution was conceptualized. Before the
official introduction of auxiliary groups into the congregation, therefore, such
groups came under the influence of the rabbis. For example, "The Sinai Literary

Association, a group of young men whom Kohler had hoped to influence religiously," was formed in the late 1870s. It was but a short step from literary societies for rabbis and literary societies meeting in the temple, to literary societies formed by the rabbi and with congregational sanction.[32]

In October 1887, Joseph Krauskopf came to the pulpit of Keneseth Israel, the leading Reform temple of Philadelphia. He soon organized the Society of Knowledge Seekers for "the purpose of mutual assistance in the acquirement of the knowledge contained in the articles published in the best current magazines." It was a young person's group organized by the young rabbi as an integral part of his expanding congregation. Not surprisingly, the development had been presaged by Emil G. Hirsch and his Sinai Congregation. As early as 1881, the Mendelsohn Literary Association was using the temple vestry for its meetings; in the same year, Hirsch recommended in his school committee report that his "post-graduate class" ought to be reorganized "on a social basis."[33]

Five years later, and a few months after the Pittsburgh conference, Hirsch proposed the following in his end-of-the-year report of March 1886: "I propose next winter to organize a young people's Union in our congregation for the purposes of both culture and entertainment. Under the auspices of this Union, I plan a number of lectures to be given by the young lawyers, physicians, and businessmen we are fortunate to have among our number. It is too early yet to speak of details. But let me even now bespeak your kind interest in the new movement."[34]

It was not only too early to talk details, it must also have been too early to act; the proposal only came to fruition in 1901 with the founding of the Sinai Young People's Association. But others took up the challenge at the time. Recent graduates of Hebrew Union College, such as Louis Grossmann (class of 1884) and Tobias Schanfarber (class of 1886), began to incorporate young people's societies into their congregations. In 1885, the Toledo correspondent to the *American Israelite* reported on the progress of its student rabbi:

The results which the Union College has shown since its existence—the education of ministers, whose activity is already beginning to work as a powerful religious motive in their respective congregations and communities—speaks volumes. . . . Mr. Schanfarber has begun to organize among the young ladies and gentlemen here a [literary and debating] society to obtain these results, and much has been accomplished so far in that direction. May success attend them.[35]

Likewise, Louis Grossmann "organized a society for the promotion of culture, named the Emerson Circle," in 1885, and one year later, "Dr. Grossmann organized the Beth El Alumnal Association (now the Young People's Society)" in his Detroit congregation. Also in 1886, the Reform congregation of Saint Joseph, Missouri, "organized a Young Israelite's Society for the purpose of furthering intellectual and ethical culture [!] among the rising generation."[36]

When Krauskopf introduced his youth group in 1887, therefore, it was not a true innovation. Yet the prominence of his congregation and the apparent appeal of the idea inspired wide imitation. For instance, Keneseth Israel's sister congregation in Philadelphia, Rodeph Shalom, established its Jewish Culture Society in 1888, under the guidance of Rabbi Jastrow. While not the first to attempt the experiment, Krauskopf may still be regarded as the first important sponsor of the congregational literary group. His Knowledge Seekers group provided the inspiration and organizational base for the creation of the Jewish Publication Society of America in 1888, which was, after all, a literary society for the entire American Jewish community.[37]

Henry Berkowitz, Inventor of the Reform Synagogue-Center

A quasi-literary society was partly responsible for inspiring the first synagogue-center experiment. Henry Berkowitz (1857–1924) was exposed to the Young Folks Reading Union of the Christian Chautauqua movement during his first pulpit assignment in Mobile, Alabama, between the years 1883 and 1888. In order to solve the problems of American Jewish life, he had begun to "cast about to see what others were doing," and in particular, "studied the methods of other religious bodies." As he later recalled:

I found that a distinctively American method was that evolved by Bishop John H. Vincent of the Methodist Episcopal Church which, from the center of its activities on the banks of Lake Chautauqua in western New York, was popularly known as the "Chautauqua Movement" (founded 1874). . . . My imagination was stirred and my ambition stimulated by what I learned from a young Baptist minister, Dr. Eager, who was conducting a Chautauqua Circle in Mobile, Alabama. I contrasted the enthusiasm its meetings engendered, with the lethargy and indifference of my own young people. . . . The Young Folks Reading Union of the Chautauqua gave me suggestions for assembling the boys and girls of post-Confirmation age to study and discuss topics of Jewish interest. It was gratifying to note the[ir]. . . enthusiasm.[38]

Berkowitz drew upon the example of the church-sponsored reading group to solve the problems he encountered as a young rabbi and would-be Jewish educator. Already familiar with the concept of a literary society under religious auspices, he did not glean the idea of a temple literary society per se from the Chautauqua model. He did learn from it the benefit of presenting religious education within informal settings and through pleasurable activities. Of Chautauqua, Berkowitz would later write: "It has revolutionized the Summer outings of thousands of people by teaching them to make of pleasure a wise pursuit, and of study a delightful pastime." He also learned that education is a broader concept than the traditional version constrained by the narrow confines of the classroom; that education, like religion, ought to apply to all of life. Since education was central to the role of the rabbi as Berkowitz understood it, such a progressive educational orientation might readily be applied to the synagogue itself.[39]

Thus, inspired by the example of the extra-congregational Chautauqua groups, Berkowitz began to evolve a radically new concept of the Jewish congregation. His 1888 innovation, an embryonic synagogue-center, was too radical

Fig. 3. Rabbi Henry Berkowitz, circa 1890. Courtesy of the American Jewish Archives, Cincinnati, Ohio.

perhaps for its time and inspired little contemporaneous imitation, but would find numerous supporters just a decade or so later. He was therefore less immediately influential than his friend Krauskopf but is more significant historically as the progenitor of an entirely new congregational constellation. The invention of the form is also significant for what it reveals of the rabbinic motivations for congregational expansion. Leaving the Chautauqua model aside, how and why did Berkowitz develop the revolutionary concept?

From the start, the young minister's sermons were on secular topics. While still at Hebrew Union College, the twenty-four-year-old student rabbi took a high holiday pulpit in La Crosse, Wisconsin. There, he wrote, "my sermons have met with the most flattering success. I preached on Rosh H. reviewing the important political and social events of the past year, dwelling particularly on the Jewish persecutions and on the lessons of Garfield's assassination." On the following weekday, Rabbi Berkowitz represented the Jewish community of La Crosse in a public parade and ecumenical service. As he described it, "the Jewish lodges also turned out and the whole community took great pride in having me represent them before their fellow citizens." The scope of the rabbi's leadership had widened to include the secular world of parades and memorial exercises. He represented the entire Jewish community, the "Jewish lodges" as well as his own congregation. Thus, the rabbi's role was both secularized and broadened in interdependent developments.[40]

Berkowitz's role would continue to expand in his first full-time pulpit in Mobile, Alabama. There he would spent most of the week preparing his "lecture" for Friday night and his "sermon" for Sabbath morning; but at the same time he would also be occupied in training teachers and serving as president of the local B'nai B'rith chapter. In addition, he wrote, "there are numerous societies of a charitable, literary or social kind which demand my attention—a society of S. School graduates, a Y.M.H.A., then the School Saturdays & Sundays." Accompanying the broadening of rabbinic responsibilities, therefore, would be the problem of time constraint. The young rabbi complained that "my time is pretty well taken up. . . the interruptions are countless. . . . The door bell is everlastingly ringing daily & the interruptions are of all imaginable kinds." Clearly, the division of his duties was a source of frustration for the rabbi, and we might expect a future attempt to alleviate the difficulty and to make his functioning more efficient.[41]

Toward the end of his tenure in Mobile he would suggest such a solution. In a sermon he described as "the greatest triumph I have ever achieved," he inspired the young men of the congregation to mount a membership drive. As a result, "Mobile can now boast of what is probably a unique record, viz. that every "man" in the city is now an interested & contributing member of the synagogue."[42] He thus acknowledged the desirability of congregational comprehensiveness: a synagogue whose membership was the entire community, in essence a throwback to the synagogue-community of early American Jewry. There was, however, a critical distinction in Berkowitz's vision of the synagogue-community. While the colonial archetype was a Jewish community recast in the form of a synagogue, the classical Reform version would be a synagogue reconstrued as community. The model for the first was the integrated Jewish community of Europe, whereas the inspiration for the second would be the fragmented Jewish community of America. Since the Reform rabbi had attained communal leadership in addition to his congregational responsibilities, the overlap of communal and congregational functions was inevitable.

Thus, in his second pulpit, Congregation B'nai Jehudah of Kansas City, Berkowitz would make a bold attempt to redefine both the congregation and his own role as rabbi. Upon arrival in Missouri, he began a series of lectures on the "New Education," which included the topics "Children, how they educate their parents," "The Voice of Nature in Education," and "Woman's part in the Drama of Life." According to the Kansas City correspondent of the *American Israelite,* "Rabbi Berkowitz made it clear in the course of his lectures that the work of Judaism, practically, in its various spheres, the synagogue, the school, and the home is primarily and essentially the work of education." As above, we again see the link between synagogue and home, but here the home is elevated to the level of the synagogue as a sphere of Judaism. Berkowitz would take the connection literally as he made it his practice to visit his new congregants in their homes. The rabbi

Fig. 4. B'nai Jehudah, Kansas City, Mo., built 1885. Collection of Peter Schweitzer.

thus extended his influence beyond the pulpit and into the parlor. The next logical step was to bring the people into the synagogue.[43]

Henry Berkowitz attempted just that when he proposed, in October 1888, the
creation of a congregational auxiliary organization. The idea of an auxiliary association was nothing new, of course, as the congregational *hevra* (literally, society)
was an age-old institution in Judaism, having arisen in the American synagogue
in various forms: first, as the burial society, then subsequently as the benevolent
society, the ladies' aid society, and as above, the literary society. Berkowitz's idea
was novel, however, in its use of the auxiliary "for the extension of the sphere of
congregational usefulness." The new society was not simply an appendage to the
main body of the congregation, but was consciously intended as the means to expand and improve congregational life overall.[44]

In his proposal to the congregation, publicized for a national audience in the
pages of the *American Israelite,* Berkowitz announced his "far-reaching purpose,"
and further declared: "The manner in which I propose that it should be met
may, therefore, seem very bold and ambitious, but it is a project not for a day nor
for a year. I would give my life's efforts towards its achievement." He begins by
noting the narrow scope of the contemporary synagogue and the consequent
lack of participation in the "hundreds of good purposes for which a congregation
should exist." Furthermore, he laments, there exists no opportunity for the rabbi
to lead "his people in the various departments of communal work." Thus, he
states the problem explicitly: as currently configured, neither the congregation

nor the rabbi encompasses the broader functions of community. His solution was to reconstruct the congregation to include communal functions, and to reconfigure the rabbi's role in order to widen his sphere of influence. Berkowitz's proposal—the formation of an auxiliary association—was therefore the culmination of his experience as a rabbi; it was a rational solution to the problems he had encountered in American Jewish life. He offered the following specifics:

Without in the slightest degree interfering with the workings of the congregation as at present managed, I would organize the adults of this Jewish community into an auxiliary association, for the purpose indicated. Such an association could co-operate with our educational enterprises. It should conduct a literary society, course of lectures, classes for advanced instruction, become auxiliary to the Sabbath School Union of America, found a library of Jewish science, history, and literature, and to this end affiliate with the Jewish Publication Society of America, just beginning its work.

Such a society could co-operate with our charities in subdividing and systematizing the care of the sick and needy, so as to bring the same into the plane of modern scientific charity; in rooting out pauperism by bringing the workman to the man who wants work done, through the agency of an employment bureau; and generally to look after the physical needs and advantages of the community furnishing a gymnasium and all means of healthful recreation.

Such a society could co-operate in the special work of the congregation in conserving the moral and spiritual health of the city. By affording all these benefits it would demonstrate in a utilitarian way the "good" of the congregation and thus attracting new accessions widen its scope of usefulness; it could help to sustain and enhance the interest in public worship by lay sermons, by a choral society, by undertaking all celebrations, anniversaries and festivities that every congregation should observe.[45]

Berkowitz concluded the proposal with an invitation to "one and all, and every Jewish adult of this community, to meet with me in this building on Sun. eve. next at 8:00, to confer upon the advisability and feasibility of forming such an organization." The community responded with enthusiasm and voted unanimously to form such an association. At the following meeting, the auxiliary was permanently organized and presented a constitutional preamble that repeated verbatim much of the original proposal.

At the auxiliary's second meeting, its functions were assigned to various committees: (1) the Intellectual Culture committee, (2) Lecture Course and Library, (3) Physical Culture and Employment Bureau, (4) Charity and Aid committee, and (5) Public Entertainments. Numbers 1 and 2 are obviously derived from the example of the literary society, being split here perhaps to create separate groups for the men and women (no. 1 was chaired by a Mr. Stern, whereas no. 2 was chaired by Miss Freddie Haas). Number 3 seems an odd coupling of functions until one remembers that these were the two classic functions of the young men's association, which therefore serves as the second model for the auxiliary (which employed the name "association" as well). Third, the Jewish charity is brought into the purview of the congregation: explicitly in the case of no. 4; and implicitly with the final addition of the "public entertainment," derived from the charity ball that had become popular in many communities, and that adumbrated the fund-raising campaign of the latter-day federation. The auxiliary proposed by Henry Berkowitz was simply a microcosmic version of the Jewish community, scaled down to the more efficient scope of the congregation.[46]

Kansas City Jews were pleased with their new organization for several reasons. For one, it attracted new members to the congregation: "Both members and non-members are taking active part in the meetings." It also united the generations in common cause: "Both young and old are lending their co-operation and support, and the enthusiasm and wide-awake interest manifested give assurance of its success." Not least of all, it provided the Kansas City Jewish community with an opportunity for national recognition and leadership. As the *American Israelite* editorialized: "This new movement has attracted attention in other cities, and, in a lengthy editorial in the *American Hebrew*, a leading Jewish publication in New York City, the plan and scope of the work is commented upon in terms of the highest praise. It was urged that the same be adopted and carried out in connection with all other congregations in the land." Rabbi Berkowitz was singled out for special praise, "not only for pointing out the difficulties that exist in the communal life of the Jewish community, but in offering a simple and practical remedy to overcome the same. The Kansas City community is thus made the pioneer and pattern in all kindred movements that may hereafter be inaugurated."[47]

Indeed, the Conservative editors of the *American Hebrew* heartily endorsed the new conception. Their editorial also pointed to a significant impetus for Berkowitz's action: "In a series of lectures . . . he demonstrated how our Jewish congregations have gradually loosened their hold upon the lives of the people, and how they have surrendered their influence to the social clubs." Apparently, the auxiliary society was formed in direct response to the threat of the secular Jewish lodges and clubs. If the synagogue had lost its hold on the people to such clubs, how better to win them back than to offer the identical social inducements (minus cardplaying of course)—"if you can't beat 'em, join 'em." The new idea would be attractive to any rabbi who felt threatened by competing social institutions and hoped to extend his influence within the community. The auxiliary would also recommend itself to the rabbi who sought greater sway within the congregation. Rabbi Berkowitz had long felt the frustration of being left out of the "power loop" of the synagogue's governing board. By creating his own organization within the congregation, he could win back much of the leverage and influence he felt denied. Indeed, the creation of the auxiliary, with the rabbi himself as president, lent him ever greater prestige and power.[48]

Over all other considerations, however, the introduction of the new auxiliary was intended to rationalize Jewish life, to combine all the functions of Judaism under one roof—the definition of a synagogue-center. Once again, what is new here is not the specific function of the proposed auxiliary, but the combination of all into an integrated whole: community as synagogue. This integration was indicated by the name finally chosen: the L.A.C.E. Society. The acronym may have suggested the lace curtains of the Victorian home, yet its main import was the combination of communal functions it represented: "The initial letters of Literary, Aid, Culture, and Employment, the aims and purposes for which the society exists, have thus been combined to form its title." In the following year, the committee assignments were changed again, to "L. Literary, Lecture, and Library Committee; A. Aid Committee; C. Congregational Cooperation Committee; E. Educational Committee." Subject to such continued experimentation, the L.A.C.E. Society proved to be a success.[49]

Two years later, Rabbi Berkowitz instituted yet another addition to congregational life drawn from communal example. Emulating Jewish periodicals such as the *American Israelite* and *American Hebrew,* Berkowitz introduced a congregational newsletter whose first issue was entitled, "Autumn Leaflet of Cong. B'nai Jehudah—Announcements for 5652, 1891–92." Its dedication page bore the biblical quotation, "And thy gates shall stand open continually" (Isaiah 60:11); in keeping with that sentiment, the rabbi's statement of purpose read as follows:

To make the congregational life a part of the people's life is to be our aim. The temple should stand open continually, i.e. some useful, uplifting influence should come from it day after day. We should strive to create opportunities for each individual in our community to participate actively in some one department at least, of the congregation's purpose. Each one must feel that he is serving Judaism by helping, however humbly, to conserve the religious, moral, educational or charitable life of the community.[50]

Berkowitz's statement is nothing less than a manifesto for an open temple. Yet here congregational life no longer centers upon the rabbi and his sermons, but rather involves the entire congregation through the instrumentality of the L.A.C.E. Society. As its founding rabbi continued: "The scope of the society is being enlarged from year to year as it gains in strength of membership and support." Unfortunately for B'nai Jehudah, Rabbi Berkowitz left for a new pulpit the following year, and his crowning achievement faded in his absence. Without the inspiration and vision of its founder, the L.A.C.E. Society lapsed into a merely auxiliary role. Hence, the rabbi was indispensable to both the creation and maintenance of the prototypical Reform synagogue-center.[51]

One might expect that rabbis in other cities would have been influenced by the example of Kansas City. In fact, the New York City–based Jewish Ministers of America, a combined group of Reform and Historical School rabbis, debated the idea in their winter conference of 1888. Undoubtedly, many of them had read of Berkowitz's experiment in the *American Hebrew* of the preceding month. The Reverend Henry Jacobs of Congregation B'nai Jeshurun offered a resolution to the conference that stated: "That it is believed that the establishment of semi-congregational Associations, which would draw together in close fellowship and communion those engaged in subordinate business capacities would make itself distinctly felt and would be productive of an incalculable amount of good, socially, morally and spiritually." Significantly, Jacobs's proposal was meant to provide "for the spiritual needs of the Jewish working classes," and to "minimize the evils which so largely prevail, in their irremediable and enforced absence from the House of God." It was the very same problem that had elsewhere prompted

the introduction of the Sunday Sabbath, a solution that could not be countenanced by the Conservative majority of the New York conference. The recommended alternative was an auxiliary association on the Kansas City model.[52]

Yet the specific scheme envisioned in Kansas City was not to be imitated just
yet; its comprehensiveness of purpose was too radical for the majority of rabbis
and their congregants in the 1890s. In its stead, a general trend arose of broadening the scope of the congregation by the addition of individual auxiliary societies. In New York especially, congregational women's groups came into vogue.
Formerly called the "Frauen Verein" or ladies' society, the distaff auxiliary matured into an integral element of congregational life during the 1880s, culminating in Rabbi Gustav Gottheil's founding of the Emanu-El Sisterhood in 1889.
Unlike its precedents, the synagogue sisterhood was founded to serve as a philanthropic agency, enabling the women of the community to exercise their activist
impulse, and concurrently, offering the rabbi an effective way to expand the
reach of his congregation.[53]

Commenting on the innovation, Emil G. Hirsch described the charitable
urge as "a long latent force" that had been earlier removed from the congregational sphere. Strangely, he remained somewhat ambivalent about its reintroduc-
tion. On the one hand, he approved of the erstwhile split between religion and
social service as "a wise thing," but then added, "at the same time we allowed to
lie fallow a mighty promise of moral power." More definitely, he credited Rabbi
Gottheil for taking the initiative: "To have seen the opportunity awaiting the
skilled organizer and to have practically inaugurated the movement is a merit of
no mean degree, for which the Rabbi of Temple Emanuel is entitled to thankful
recognition." Not only was the sisterhood the brainchild of the rabbi, Hirsch
concluded, it came straight out of Jewish tradition: "The work is a revival of the
old Jewish Chebrah adapted to the new surroundings and with this difference,
that the women are those who are enrolled in the service."[54]

Its Jewish authenticity aside, the prevalence of parallel church groups and the
prominence of Temple Emanu-El inspired other rabbis to organize such women's
societies: Frederick de Sola Mendes founded the Shaaray Tefila Sisterhood of Personal Service in 1890 (the same year in which he instituted the monthly Shaaray
Tefila Journal). In 1891, Aaron Wise encouraged the formation of The Rodeph
Shalom Sisterhood, Israel Aaron "urged the organization of the Sisterhood of
Zion" in Buffalo, and Louis Grossmann organized the Woman's Club of Temple
Beth El in Detroit. Concurrent with the rise of the sisterhood, the young peoples' associations grew more popular throughout the 1890s. Such congregational
youth groups began to sprout around the country, such as the Young Folks Association" founded in New York's Shaaray Tefila (the "West End Synagogue") in
1889, and the aforementioned Sinai Young People's Association in Chicago.[55]

Their popularity was such that even Henry Berkowitz was reduced to organizing youth groups. After joining Krauskopf in Philadelphia, Berkowitz attempted
to re-create the bold experiment of his former congregation. But the Quaker

City was not, as Kansas City had been, a blank slate on which to design from scratch. Philadelphia, called by Berkowitz "the Mecca of American Judaism," boasted a full range of Jewish social and philanthropic institutions. Within his new congregation there already existed a successful auxiliary group, the Jewish Culture Association, organized by his predecessor, Rabbi Marcus M. Jastrow. Thus, when Berkowitz introduced a new "Auxiliary Association" in January 1894, it appealed mainly to the younger generation (for whose sake he had been hired in the first place); though he made an attempt to explain its expanded functions, it was understood and utilized as a young people's society, subsidiary to the whole. While the innovation was said to have "superseded" the earlier group, Berkowitz's ambitions were frustrated by the presence of the earlier group, as they were by the continued participation of "Rabbi-Emeritus" Jastrow in congregational affairs.[56]

Berkowitz's original conception of 1888—a comprehensive synagogue-center program—was never fully realized by him and did not reappear until others took up the call after the turn of the century. During the 1890s, he followed the example of both his mentor Wise and his brother-in-law Krauskopf in expanding his congregational project into a nationwide movement. Like the blossoming of Krauskopf's Knowledge Seekers into the Jewish Publication Society, the L.A.C.E. Society inspired the later creation of the Jewish Chautauqua movement. Berkowitz's promotion of the idea began soon after his arrival in Philadelphia in 1892. He found an enthusiastic group of supporters in the Jewish Culture Society, and at a public meeting of the group in April 1893, the Jewish Chautauqua Society was born. Four years later, he expanded the local society into a national movement that gained wide attention in Jewish circles and became Berkowitz's main claim to fame. The connection of Chautauqua with the synagogue-center idea was not entirely forgotten, however, as a later observer of the American Jewish scene commented: "Thus the synagog of modern America comes to resemble . . . a 'busy place'; 'Activity' is its slogan; and 'something doing all the time' is the motto engraven in largest letters over its portals, like a Chautauqua center during camp meeting season."[57]

After launching his national project in 1897, Berkowitz continued to innovate on the congregational level. In the *Annual* of 1899, he referred to his ongoing efforts: "Year upon year I have emphasized to you the necessity of combating prevalent indifference and ignorance by making our congregational life a vital influence in the life of each individual, in the homes, in the Jewish community, and in the municipality." He concluded with a kind of summation of his own career: "Our efforts towards this end have, in this formative period of American Jewish life, necessarily been largely tentative and creative. We have been obliged to pioneer some new paths." He would end his career two decades later as one of the grand old men of the American rabbinate, revered as a surviving member of the first class of Hebrew Union College, the creator of the popular Jewish Chautauqua movement, and a universally beloved figure—the archetypal "beloved rabbi." He was also a kind of "rabbi's rabbi," seen by his peers as the foremost expert on the congregational function of the Reform rabbinate.[58]

He had gained the reputation after a long and productive career of synagogue administration and experimentation. Moved to action by the lethargy and inefficiency that characterized Jewish community life of the 1880s, and partly inspired by Christian examples of informal religious activity, Berkowitz began to try new congregational formulas. His L.A.C.E. Society of 1888 attempted to meet the diverse religious, educational, and social needs of the community within the single domain of the synagogue, and under the unified leadership of the rabbi. It was the first example in American Jewish history of the conscious attempt to create social-religious synthesis in the synagogue. It thereby foreshadowed and ultimately influenced the creation of the Reform synagogue-center. Berkowitz himself went on to related experiments, but others took up the cause he had begun. A new generation of classical Reform rabbis would now champion the open/institutional temple, and would thus create an independent synagogue-center movement under the aegis of classical Reform Judaism.

New Developments at the Turn of the Century

Before 1900, the synagogue-center existed as a vague concept in the mind of a few individuals and as a nascent institutional form; after the turn of the century, the new generation of classical Reform rabbis evolved a common ideology and the program was formally institutionalized in many leading Reform congregations around the country. The synagogue-center idea garnered support from both the rabbinate and laity and became a bona fide movement. The main circumstances giving rise to a movement at the turn of the century were the demographic growth of the Jewish community, a consequent boom in new synagogue construction, and a simultaneous generational shift within the Reform rabbinate. The confluence of such changes around 1900 sparked the emergence of a Reform synagogue-center movement in the early years of this century.

In the decades following the Pittsburgh Platform, second- and third-generation "German" Jews reached a peak of affluence and acculturation. They moved "uptown," bringing their established congregations with them; and, as the visible symbol of their newfound status, they would inevitably build a monumental temple edifice in the new neighborhood. Enlarged and improved facilities were also deemed necessary due to the rapid growth of membership and sudden expansion of activities. During this period therefore, new temples were built by classical Reform congregations in Jewish communities around the country. During the quarter-century from 1885 to 1910, more than thirty new temple structures were dedicated in locations as diverse as Boston (1885), Portland (1889), Salt Lake City (1891), Cleveland (1894), New Haven (1897), Denver (1899), Atlanta

(1902), Louisville (1906), and Brooklyn (1909). Similarly, renovations, new school buildings, social annexes, and even gymnasiums were added to the original temple plant in cities such as Philadelphia (1887), Chicago and New York (1892), Cincinnati (1903), and Detroit (1905).

More often than not, the new buildings followed soon upon the heels of a new rabbi—invariably an American-born, Hebrew Union College–trained activist of the classical Reform stamp. For example, just two years after Joseph Krauskopf's arrival in Kansas City (1883), the congregation dedicated a new temple (1885). When he moved to Philadelphia, the same pattern held (arrived, 1887/new temple, 1892). Similarly: Israel Aaron in Buffalo (1887/1890), William S. Friedman in Denver (1889/1899), William Rosenau in Baltimore (1892/1893), Moses Gries in Cleveland (1892/1894), David Levy in New Haven (1893/1897), Joseph Stolz in Chicago (1895/1899), David Marx in Atlanta (1895/1902), Leo Franklin in Detroit (1899/1903), Hyman G. Enelow in Louisville (1901/1906), and J. Leonard Levy in Pittsburgh (1901/1907).

These were no coincidences, of course. The same motives that prompted the acquisition of a modern, English-speaking rabbi—the desire for respectability in the eyes of the outside world and the need to draw the younger generation into the congregational sphere—motivated the construction of new facilities. The *American Israelite* reported on one such occasion: "the Pres. offered in this report some suggestions as to the enlarging of the Temple so as to accommodate the increased membership with pews, and also to be able to supply the new demands which the securing of members through the instrumentality of the Rabbi-elect will undoubtedly bring about."[59]

As described above, this was a time of renewed emphasis on education and the related rise of congregational agencies intended to promote Jewish life. Such priorities were often introduced by the new rabbi, making a new temple facility desirable. Either the rabbi himself militated for a building to house the new activities, or alternatively, the success of the new program itself made construction a necessity. In the former case, Emil G. Hirsch twice accomplished new construction through his intercession. In 1890, he recommended a new building for Sinai Congregation in order to "enlarge the sphere of our usefulness," resulting in the renovation of 1892; in 1900 he again advocated a new building, which culminated in the new temple of 1911 and its accompanying social center in 1912, later renamed the "E. G. Hirsch Center" (see fig. 2). The new buildings provided for an already expanded program and were thus synagogue-centers in the making.

In addition to the prompting of the rabbi, purely economic considerations played a role. Once a new structure was decided upon and a mortgage undertaken, the congregation began an urgent search for the means to pay for its construction and maintenance. When the resources of the standing membership were exhausted, attracting new members became a priority; thus strategies for outreach —such as the offering of manifold services and activities—were enthusiastically adopted. Often, therefore, rather than the new rabbi and his programmatic ambitions preceding the new facility, the temple structure itself and the financial burden it imposed served as impetus for the expansion of the program.

This expansion in turn required the acquisition of a new, often a second, rabbi. Thus, when J. Leonard Levy was hired to join Joseph Krauskopf in Philadelphia in 1893, it was not a matter of an English-speaking junior rabbi brought in to complement and assist an older German-speaking senior rabbi. Rather, the new Keneseth Israel temple complex of 1892 provided more services than one rabbi could handle, and so another was required. Levy was therefore asked to become "associate minister" to Krauskopf and to take over the administration of the newly enlarged school. This too was an early example of a synagogue-center in function if not in name.

Another example was Temple Isaiah of Chicago. "An offshoot of Zion Congregation, Isaiah was formed October 24, 1895, to provide a convenient house of worship." While the convenience spoken of was proximity to congregants' homes, the new congregation would provide other amenities as well. The founding rabbi was Joseph Stolz, graduate of the second class of Hebrew Union College and representative of the new generation of Reform rabbis. At the inauguration service, Stolz was joined in the pulpit by both Emil G. Hirsch and the Reverend Jenkin Lloyd Jones of All-Souls Church. Temple Isaiah would be an open temple, no doubt about it. In 1898, the congregation purchased a lot for a new temple and commissioned the architect Dankmar Adler, son of the revered Chicago rabbi, Liebmann Adler. With his partner Louis Sullivan, Adler had already designed three synagogues, including that of his father's congregation, K.A.M. But under the guidance of the new-age rabbi (and independent of the more aesthetically inclined Sullivan), Adler would now set a design precedent. His design was said to be "unique in its time for its separate—but connected— "annex" (that is, with a separate entrance) for the religious school and community center, a feature that would become commonplace in the early twentieth century."[60]

By its architectural innovation alone, therefore, Temple Isaiah of 1899 met the definition of a synagogue-center; its religious, educational, and social functions were all in place, "separate—but connected." Significantly, its building was designed by a Jewish architect, and its program was determined by an American rabbi; both of whom could "speak the language" of their clientele and provide for their changing needs. Such new temple buildings were the result of the economic rise and demographic shifts of American Jewish communities of the 1890s and early 1900s. The new temples were often accompanied by new rabbis, both of which played a role in the increase of social and educational activities. Congregational growth, new rabbis, and temple construction thereby combined to transform the life of the synagogue; and thus laid the groundwork for the rise of a conscious movement to create a temple center in every congregation and in every community.

"And Moses Shall Lead Them"

The leading figure of the temple-center movement would be a young American-born rabbi from Newark, New Jersey, named Moses J. Gries (1868–1918). Following the example of his mentor Emil G. Hirsch, Gries became a leading spokesman for the Open Temple (as well as for the Sunday Sabbath). Like Krauskopf and Berkowitz before him, he initiated the congregational groups and activities that made "The Temple [Tifereth Israel] among the leading houses of worship in Cleveland." The "full round of activity at The Temple" would lead the historian of Cleveland Jewry to call it "the first institutional synagogue in the United States." Whether or not this is accurate (an argument could be made for either Berkowitz's B'nai Jehudah in Kansas City [1888] or Krauskopf's Keneseth Israel in Philadelphia [1892]), the case of Moses Gries and The Temple provides a model of synagogue-center development at the turn of the century.[61]

Following his graduation from Hebrew Union College in 1889 he took his first pulpit in Chattanooga, Tennessee. Three years later, he was called to Cleveland's Tifereth Israel to replace Aaron Hahn, a Bohemian-born, yeshiva-trained, and radical Reform rabbi of the old school. By the 1890s the congregation was primed for a more modern, practical, and "thoroughly American" rabbi. Gries began innovating upon arrival: "soon after his coming he took up the untried task of establishing institutional work in the synagogue." First he would need a new building. At the cornerstone-laying ceremony in 1893, he declared that "at last we are able to erect a temple worthy to be called a house of God and fit for the works and needs of men." It would be nothing less than "an ideal temple, consecrated to ideal worship and ideal work." By contrast, Isaac M. Wise's speech on the same occasion described the temple as "an altar of the Lord, and it is sanctified as the place where God permits and causes his name to be invoked, to be praised and gloried." Certainly the imposing building—designed by the firm of Isadore (Israel) J. Lehman and Theodore Schmidt in the Romanesque style of Richardson's Trinity Church in Boston—earned its new title, The Temple.[62]

Yet the program instituted by the new rabbi would make of it an "open" temple. In November 1894, Rabbi Gries founded the Temple Society, whose scope and purpose were somewhat different from the congregational society of the Berkowitz model. As he explained:

With such thought in mind, we inaugurate a temple society instituted by and within a temple. I wish to declare it free; its temple open to all. We invite and welcome and hope to have as active workers MEMBERS OF OTHER CONGREGATIONS and members of no congregations at all. I assure them freedom. We have no thought of proselytizing. This is not a conversion agency or a membership formation scheme. . . . This work must be done within a church because it belongs to a church. The building of costly structures for mere ornament is bad economy. I hope to live to see the time when not a day shall dawn and set without some good work done within and from this temple. Every association for the betterment of ourselves and our fellows is welcome within these walls. Let the day come, and soon, when we shall be an association of toilers

Fig. 5. Rabbi Moses Gries, circa 1910. Courtesy of the American
Jewish Archives, Cincinnati, Ohio.

in blessed work, and this temple a shining center . . . for culture, education, helpfulness, and human upliftment of self and others.[63]

Later, the Temple Society was said "to bring culture and knowledge near to the people. It unites education with entertainment." A Junior Temple Society was founded at the same time. Two years later, Gries instituted the Educational League, which "conducted classes on a modified 'university extension' plan"; and established the Temple Course, a popular lecture series that brought to Cleveland the leading liberal theologians of the day, men such as Lyman Abbot, Washington Gladden, Jenkin Lloyd Jones, Josiah Strong, and even Felix Adler. Perhaps more surprising still, the Universalist convention of 1895 was held in The Temple. Gries thus combined the educational openness of Berkowitz with the Social Gospel proclivities of Hirsch.[64]

Gries continued to organize societies for his growing congregation. The Woman's Temple Association was founded in 1896, and the "Sunshine Club" of the Temple Sabbath School in the following year. In 1898, a Junior Temple Debating Club was formed, a Temple Library opened, and the first Temple *Annual*

The Temple, East Fifty Fifth and Central Avenue, Cleveland *Sixth City*

Fig. 6. Tifereth Israel, Cleveland, Ohio, built 1894. Collection of Peter Schweitzer.

published. Finally, in 1901 the Temple became the first congregation to build its own gymnasium—in response to popular demand. The development of the institutional synagogue thus exemplified the modern architectural dictum, "form follows function." As with the new facilities for the library and gymnasium, added functions led to an enlargement of form.

In some cases, the growth of the congregation itself necessitated added facilities. To illustrate, between 1892 and 1902 the Sabbath School grew from 80 students to 764, making it "the third largest Sabbath School among the Churches in the U.S., and the largest Jewish congregational school in the world." Under Rabbi Gries, therefore, the congregation had grown so rapidly (by 500 percent) that it is hard to determine whether added activities increased membership or vice versa. In either case, the incremental growth of a synagogue-center program is manifest. When Gries went public with the idea in 1901, his own congregation had been its testing ground during the first decade of his ministry.[65]

The forum he chose for the announcement was the Central Conference of American Rabbis. The CCAR was founded in 1889 as a regional conference, but soon became the representative body of the American rabbinate. With the passing of Isaac Mayer Wise in March 1900, the CCAR emerged as the powerbase of the Reform rabbinate. After Wise, no one rabbi ever again dominated the Reform movement as he had; rather, all gained in strength and in self-confidence. Their arrival as a group may be witnessed in the pages of the proceedings of the CCAR. The CCAR also provided the foundation for the movement to convert the Reform temple into the center of American Jewish life. Of the names that stand out as the champions of the synagogue-center, Moses Gries was most prominent among them. But he did not act alone.[66]

William Rosenau, Gries's classmate at Hebrew Union College (class of 1889), delivered a paper to the 1898 CCAR conference entitled "The Attitude of the Congregation to the Non-Member." In response, the "Committee on Unafiliated [sic] with Congregations" was formed, consisting at first of Joseph Krauskopf, Tobias Schanfarber, and William Rosenau. While in his first pulpit in Omaha, Nebraska, Rosenau had befriended Henry Berkowitz (then in Kansas City) and later helped him to found the Jewish Chautauqua Society. Both men moved east in 1892, when Berkowitz succeeded Jastrow in Philadelphia and Rosenau succeeded Szold in Baltimore. In the following year, Oheb Shalom Congregation of Baltimore erected a new temple edifice on Eutaw Place that would evolve into a complex of synagogue-center proportions during the forty-seven-year tenure of William Rosenau.

Prior to 1900, however, Rosenau could only express the idea in nonspecific terms. In his 1898 address, he asked what "is the real and only reason for the non-affiliation of many of the unsynagogued?" His answer was very definite: "It consists of nothing else but the gross materialism into which the present generation has plunged." Yet his solution was somewhat vague: "In the face of conditions such as these we dare not be inactive. We must be up and doing. Inactivity now means congregational decline."[67]

Similarly, in the following year, Joseph Krauskopf presented the committee's paper "How Can We Enlist Our Young Men in the Service of the Congregation?" Rather than recommend practical solutions to the problem, Krauskopf offered only a vitriolic attack on those avoiding the temple pews and, as if to further alienate them, more fiery pulpit rhetoric. Apparently, his own initiatives of the 1890s had not been fruitful and he was left unencouraged. Interestingly, he did cite the example of the "institutional churches," but only as an unacceptable usage of the religious sanctuary. Another rabbi then countered with a more forward-looking vision. In his response to Krauskopf's paper, Leo Franklin rejected the pessimism of his colleague and instead approached the problem directly and constructively. He also clearly articulated the theme of the synagogue as home:

Now since the home stands, and has ever stood, for so much in the life of the Jew, I would have the idea of home carried to a larger number of people, to a broader circle than those born under the same roof, dear to each other only by the ties of blood and kindred. I would have the influences of family life extended to an ever-widening circle. Yes, I would have the idea, and with the idea the influence of home, brought into our congregations, and I would have our synagogues stand in the life of the community for just the same things as the home does in the life of the individual. And if we achieve that we are safe, and we shall have the young men with us and the ready and the willing assistance and sympathy of the young men will be ours in our congregational activities.[68]

Franklin also repeated earlier themes by noting the detrimental effect of the social clubs, and by recommending to "so establish our synagogues that they shall exert an influence which shall counteract and overmeasure the influence of the club." He furthermore suggested "that we should so arrange our affairs that whatever social, educational, or charitable endeavor is distinctively Jewish should be part and parcel of the congregation." His ideas therefore echoed the earlier experiments of Henry Berkowitz, and similarly correspond to what we have referred to as the "synagogue-center idea." His 1899 statement was thus a summation of what had come before. Franklin would progress beyond precedent only in 1902, when he unabashedly recommended the transformation of the Reform temple into a new type of institution, the so-called open synagogue.[69]

What, we might ask, had changed between 1899 and 1902? Besides the generational shift signaled by the death of Wise, one other significant change must be noted. This was the intellectual influence of the new social science of the turn of the century. Contemporary American social philosophers such as William James and John Dewey were about to become widely influential, even upon the birth of a synagogue-center movement. In the Jewish world, secular ideologues such as Ahad Ha'am and Simon Dubnow would have equally far-reaching effect. Yet the idea that the Reform synagogue should stand at the center of Jewish communal life was not the contribution of Dubnow; nor should it be attributed to Ahad Ha'am, Dubnow's contemporary and fellow exponent of a "social" Judaism.[70]

Rather, the synagogue-center connection in Reform Judaism may be traced directly to the work of another Jewish historian of the day, the English scholar Israel Abrahams. Long before it became fashionable, Abrahams was a social historian, interested in the daily lives of ordinary people. His most famous work, *Jewish Life in the Middle Ages* (1896), was an anthropological compendium of medieval Jewish life ranging from "communal organization" to "home life," and from "trades and occupations" to "personal relations." The first chapter is entitled "The Centre of Social Life," which, asserted Abrahams, was the synagogue. His classic monograph began:

The medieval life of the Jews had for its centre the synagogue. The concentration of the Jewish populations into separate quarters of Christian and Moslem towns was initially an accident of Jewish communal life. The Jewish quarter seems to have grown up round the synagogue, which was thus the centre of Jewish life, locally as well as religiously.

This concentration round the synagogue may be noted in the social as well as in the material life of the middle ages. The synagogue, tended, with ever-increasing rapidity, to absorb and to develop the social life of the community, . . . throughout the middle ages proper the synagogue held undisputed sway in all the concerns of Jews. Nor was this absorption a new phenomenon. Already in Judea the Temple had assumed some social functions. The tendency first reveals itself amid the enthusiasm of the Maccabean revival, when the Jews felt drawn to the house of prayer for social as well as for religious communion. . . . The life within the synagogue reflected the social life of the Jews in all its essential features.[71]

In his second chapter "Life in the Synagogue," Abrahams continues:

The attitude of the medieval Jew toward his House of God was characteristic of his attitude towards life. Though the Jew and the Greek gave very different expressions to the conception, the Jew shared with the Greek a belief in the essential unity of life amidst its detailed obligations. It is not enough to say that the Jew's religion absorbed his life, for in quite as real a sense his life absorbed his religion. Hence the synagogue was not a mere place in which he prayed, it was a place in which he lived; and just as life has its earnest and its frivolous moments, so the Jew in the synagogue was at times rigorously reverent and at others quite at his ease.[72]

Thus, Abrahams located the center of Jewish life in the synagogue. In so doing, he demonstrated the inextricable nature of the social and religious spheres in Judaism. This compelling idea, as embodied by Abrahams's colorful description of Jewish life in the Middle Ages, naturally recommended itself for adaptation to Jewish life in modern-day America. Abrahams's understanding of the synagogue as "the centre of social life" could be and would be applied to the American synagogue by its proponents.

Jewish Life in the Middle Ages was published by the Jewish Publication Society in 1896 and became an instant classic. While it is unclear whether the book was included in the curriculum of Hebrew Union College, it was certainly considered required reading for the educated Jew, and would often have been read by the rabbinic aspirant even before his formal studies began. Thus, at the CCAR convention of 1902, Leo M. Franklin noted: "Israel Abrahams, whose work, as you note, we have followed quite closely, [and who] calls attention to . . . the intimate relation between the synagogue and the social life of the Jew." Throughout his address, Franklin cited the ideas of Abrahams as justification for the synagogue-center experiment. Apparently, he had read Abrahams sometime between 1899 and 1902.[73]

Another immediate influence on Franklin may have been the earlier initiative of his colleague from Cleveland, Moses J. Gries. After joining Krauskopf's Committee on Unaffiliated in 1900, Gries was chosen to deliver the keynote lecture of the next year's conference in Philadelphia. The address he gave was a rousing call for revival at the "dawn of the Twentieth Century." After invoking the memory of Isaac Mayer Wise, he bemoaned both the rise of antisemitism in Europe and the state of apathy in American Judaism, echoing Rosenau's complaint regarding "the commercialism of our synagogues and temples, selling the privilege to worship and retailing religious instruction." Moving beyond the vagueness of Rosenau, however, he heralded a new trend and issued the first public manifesto in support of the synagogue-center. In no uncertain terms, he declared for the "Open Temple" idea:

Thank God! a new spirit is widening the walls and purposes of narrow synagogue and temples. . . . Every effort and activity of life, all work and pleasure, are within the province of religion. Life is many-sided and life's interest[s] are varied. Temple and Judaism should meet the needs of life. . . . The temple shall be the larger home for the congregation—not a substitute for but a supplement to the home. It is the natural centre of all congregational and communal life. It should be the "social centre" for the well-to-do. The life of the community should grow and develop naturally about the temple. . . . Judaism should inspire, organize and direct Jewish life and activities. The congregation, rather than a social organization or a fraternal association of a charitable society, is and should be the centre. There is power in such centralization. One heart and one soul will unify the life of the community. The present never-ending conflict between rival interests may cease. . . . The temple, instead of forever begging for support, becomes the supporting influence. It is the power, the soul, the life-centre of the community. . . . All the interests of life are the interests of religion. Therefore, the activities of the temple should be larger than worship and religious school as life is larger than Sabbath and Sunday. I believe in the open temple—serving seven days in the week—"Thy gates shall stand open continually day and night, they shall not be closed."[74]

Gries's declaration encompassed all of the themes discussed earlier: Judaism is holistic, relating to all areas of life; competition between institutions is detrimental to the Jewish community; the natural center of Jewish life is the synagogue, which thus ought to provide services other than the religious and the educational. It seems this last point aroused the greatest opposition: at the conference of the following year, Leo Franklin delivered a paper entitled "Congregational Activities Outside the Pulpit and Sabbath School," which amounted to a defense of his friend Gries. In the 1902 address, Franklin stressed that such secular activities should remain subsidiary to the essential elements of prayer and study, but then went on to state "that it is the province of the synagogue to sanctify the secular, to make holy the affairs of the daily routine, to make every part of human activity an instrument to body forth the message of religion." He dwelt at length on the historical role of the synagogue in the Jewish community to bolster his argument that it ought to be re-created to solve the problem of the unaffiliated: "the idea of bringing people to the synagogue by persuasive measures is nothing new, but rather a return to the condition which made the synagogue the centre of the Jewish life of a community."[75]

Franklin also cited statistics on the unaffiliated. Based on a questionnaire he had circulated among his colleagues, he estimated "that the number of Jews in this country not identified with any congregation . . . outnumber those who are so identified [by] almost three to one, ranging from thirty per cent in the smaller cities to seventy or eighty per cent of the total Jewish population in the largest cities." He blamed their lack of interest on competing institutions that offered the "at home" feeling that the synagogue did not: "It is the curse of our day that the club and not the synagogue has become the centre of our life." Since the problem of the "unsynagogued" had reached such dire proportions, the immediate implementation of some practical solution was required. He ended his argument by specifying the activities that an open temple ought to include: "a library and reading room," "lecturers on Jewish and humanitarian themes," "musical entertainments," "literary meetings," "mothers' meetings," "philanthropic work," a "[congregational] bulletin, or newspaper, or year book," "Bible Classes, and Young People's Temple Societies, and Woman's Auxiliary Associations, and Junior Choirs, and Alumni Associations."[76]

Despite the past acceptability of most of these items, some rabbis remained unconvinced. Franklin himself indicated the opposition that might arise when he wrote, "the so-called open temple—I was about to say the institutional temple, but the name affrights too many." Some rabbis apparently balked at the seeming imitation of the Protestant institutional church. Similarly, Franklin mentions in closing "one other subject there is that properly should have been touched on as a part of the open synagogue, but which I have delayed to mention from sheer fright at the confusion the word may create. I mean the gymnasium, which has latterly been introduced in a few temples." He defended its introduction in Detroit as "a self-defensive measure, since the gymnasium of the Young Men's Christian Association—the only one available to our boys and young men—has become a menace." The objection to Christian influence was thus exacerbated by the "pagan" nature of the activity. In the closing discussion, veteran rabbis Lippman Mayer, Adolph Moses, and Henry Cohen objected to the proposal, provoking Franklin's exasperated response: "When Dr. Moses identifies poker parties with the institutional synagogue, he shows that he does not understand the scope and nature of the institution. It is almost inexplicable that ordinarily sensible men, should be quite illogical when dealing with this subject." One can almost visualize the generational gap between them.[77]

Gries's initiatives aroused the greatest opposition. Already in 1897, he was subjected to public chastisement on the subject of the Sunday Sabbath by no less a personage than Isaac M. Wise. But following his 1901 pronouncement, he became the center of controversy concerning the synagogue-center idea. His "notoriety" was further enhanced by the 1902 souvenir booklet issued by the congregation on the occasion of his tenth anniversary at The Temple. The booklet, which trumpeted the rabbi's achievement in creating an open temple, was widely distributed and prompted responses such as this personal communication from Gotthard Deutsch, then the editor of *Die Deborah,* to Gries:

Being not sufficiently in contact with the requirements of congregational life, and especially not with young people, I do not know whether your course of providing them with amusement and spiritual entertainment which has no connection with religious life, is the proper one. I say it frankly, . . . and am ready to admit that it may be due to my years or my foreign education. Nevertheless I appreciate whatever is done in maintaining Jewish consciousness amongst our young American people, and I highly esteem the courage which would not close its eyes before existing conditions.[78]

Harsher criticism was aired in public in the *American Israelite* by Max Heller. In the issue of December 25, 1902, Heller published an editorial, "The Philosophy of Institutionalism," in which he claimed that "there is something radically wrong with Cleveland Judaism" and attacked Gries's experiment as a "breach of religious propriety." The controversy appeared as far away as the *London Jewish Chronicle* in an article by Heller's fellow classical Reform Zionist Richard Gottheil. That two Reformers of the Zionist persuasion should oppose the synagogue-center idea makes eminent sense, for they had assigned Jewish peoplehood to a "center" far away from the temples of America. Unlike the cultural pluralists of the next generation, they had yet to reconcile Jewish social life with American Judaism. As opposed to Heller and Gottheil, Reform supporters of the synagogue-center were, by and large, opponents of Zionism. Their "center" would be in America.[79]

Moses Gries, meanwhile, responded to the attacks. In the *Jewish American* of Detroit he published an article in defense of Cleveland Judaism and his own open temple, complaining:

I have not the time and surely not the desire for newspaper controversy. Often, in the past ten years, I have been misquoted and misrepresented and the principles and policies of The Temple in Cleveland falsely judged. Our Jewish papers unfortunately take little or no pains to verify the reports upon which they base their criticisms. . . . In the present circumstance, the Israelite is at fault. . . . I do not hesitate to declare that the interest in things religious in Cleveland to-day, is as strong—I believe stronger—than in Cincinnati. . . . Our men and women reveal a reverence as deep and as genuine as any other Jews whom it has been my fortune to know. I ask Dr. Heller ["My good friend"] to *name specifically* one large community which is possessed of the reverence and awe and element of spirituality which Cleveland is said to lack. . . . To Dr. Heller and others, we may seem unJewish. My conviction is firm, and the facts sustain it, that we are as Jewish in thought and feeling as any community known to me [quotes from the tenth anniversary souvenir booklet on the success of the open temple]. . . . Few rabbis seem to understand the spirit and principles and methods of the Institutional Church of the Open Temple. Judging by the sweeping condemnation which Dr. Heller has pronounced, I am confident that he has very little actual knowledge of any institutional or open churches and temples. . . . My own position, Jewish, I believe, even though Dr. Heller says dogmatically, "This is not Judaism,"—I have stated clearly and emphatically enough. [closes by reprinting his CCAR address].[80]

Jewish editorialists joined sides. One wrote: "The argument of Rabbi Gries appears to be composed of a rather confused understanding of the scope of the synagogue, . . . there must be, and there is, a distinct line drawn between the scope of the synagogue, that of the home, of the school, and of the hundred and one other phases of life which the synagogue, as a matter of course, cannot undertake to direct." Whereas another wrote: "Of course it cannot be expected that every rabbi should endorse the Open Temple, if for no other reason than that the majority do not understand it. . . . The success of the Open Temple is at least tangible, which perhaps is basis for the assumption that it lacks in the spiritual. . . . Rabbi Gries has made out a good case for the Open Temple, and we hope that the "spiritual" gentleman of the other side will be just enough to heed the arguments presented."[81]

Rabbi Heller did seem somewhat more balanced in his reply. While still maintaining that "institutionalism['s] tendency is of a positivist, secularist, subtly materialist order . . . [and] it is deficient—so it appears to me—in reverence, historic loyalty, Jewish consciousness"; he did concede that "it abounds in earnestness, sincerity, and vigor." He even continued: "All honor, I say, to the energy and resourcefulness which seeks to make of the synagog an "Open Temple," a beehive of humane and educational endeavor." He would not, however, overcome his fear that the open temple implied an abandonment of authentic Judaism. He thought that Gries "may represent much of the younger element in this feeling or rather a lack of sentiment."[82]

His fear was well founded. Most of the younger generation of rabbis found great appeal in the words and deeds of Moses Gries. In 1905, the CCAR conference was held in Cleveland and met in The Temple precincts. There, Joseph Stolz accepted the welcome of the older Cleveland rabbi Michael Machol by praising the work of Machol's younger colleague in rather exuberant terms: "We are indeed happy . . . to meet in this temple reared so successfully by the executive skill, the impatient zeal, and the single-hearted devotion of the rabbi who stands out in our country as the enthusiastic champion of the Open Temple, the zealous advocate of widening the tent and strengthening the stakes, enlarging the usefulness and broadening the activities of the synagogue."[83]

The Movement Consolidates and Expands

At that same conference, a newly organized committee made its appearance. As the newly elected president of the CCAR, Joseph Krauskopf had offered several recommendations in his inaugural message of 1904. One was the formation of "Social Religious Unions" on the Christian model of monthly meetings between minister and laymen to discuss church issues. The new committee consisted of none other than Henry Berkowitz, Moses J. Gries, and Leo M. Franklin. In their report to the Cleveland conference, these three champions of the synagogue-center idea expanded upon Krauskopf's original suggestion and urged not only "a spirit of closer friendliness and better understanding between the pulpit and the pew, but more especially a closer fellowship between the members of our congregations themselves." Using language familiar from Berkowitz's earlier initiatives, the report advocated "the working out of a plan by which the members of the congregation can be brought under congregational auspices into closer fellowship, and so be made to feel a keener interest in congregational affairs." Intriguingly, the report then continued:

It need not be pointed out to you, who have yourselves individually had to face the perplexing situation, that in most communities the Jewish life, or what is commonly called the Jewish life, is predominantly *social* rather than *religious*. It shall be the work of the Social Union to restore the synagog to its rightful place, enabling it to direct not only the religious life of the Jew, but also to guide and ennoble his social life.[84]

Similarly, in 1906, committee chairman Franklin restated the committee's intention "to suggest and plan ways and means whereby the synagog may become a social as well as a religious center," but at the same time qualified that goal, adding, "its prime object is not to emphasize the social side of congregational life except insofar as the social functions recommended by it may be used as a lever to intensify the religious life of the community." Here the new conception is stated explicitly. Contrary to the stereotypical view of classical Reform Judaism, these classical Reform rabbis endorsed Jewish social life as a primary element of the synagogue. Perhaps to forestall criticism, Franklin assured his fellow rabbis that social life in the synagogue was but a means to an religious end. Thus qualified, the report was adopted by the conference and the Committee on Social and Religious Union became a standing committee of the CCAR.[85]

The committee prepared and distributed a questionnaire to determine the extent of center activity in the Reform synagogues around the country. They appended to their report a list of the congregations who responded affirmatively (from the one-third who replied at all), "congregations that, having introduced work of this character, have found it effective in stimulating the religious life of the people." These congregations included Ahawath Achim of Lafayette, Indiana; Bnai Israel of Galveston, Texas; Anshai Emeth of Peoria, Illinois; Rodeph Shalom of Philadelphia; Temple Isaiah of Chicago; Beth El of Detroit; Sons of Israel and David of Providence, Rhode Island; the "Temple Emanuels" of Dallas, Texas, Grand Rapids, Michigan, and Kingston, New York; and the "Temple Israels" of Harlem, New York, Paducah, Kentucky, and Terre Haute, Indiana. The survey concluded that many more congregations might be added to the list.[86]

Based on the replies to their questionnaire, the committee concluded that enhancement of the social life of the synagogue has "actually succeeded most splendidly in arousing a keener religious interest. . . . So the very thing that was originally hoped for by the advocates of this work is being accomplished." Flushed with their apparent success, they further recommended "that the scope of this Committee be enlarged so as to give it authority to deal with all those phases of congregational activity, outside the pulpit and Sabbath school, which may tend to bring the members and the minister of the congregation into closer fellowship and that in a general way are prepared to make the synagog a center for social and educational work."[87]

The synagogue-center movement of the Reform rabbinate was thereby institutionalized in the form of a CCAR committee whose power and influence would grow with the years. In 1907, summarizing the findings of their latest questionnaire, the committee lauded "institutional work" for encouraging the "more general celebration of Purim, Hannukah, and Succoth and the re-institution of the home ceremonies of our religion seem to have been a feature of the past year's activities. In a number of cities a Congregational Seder was instituted." Thus, in accordance with Marshall Sklare's "criteria for ritual retention," we see here the beginnings of the orientation toward holidays in American Judaism. The Jewish holiday celebration, formerly belonging to the spheres of home and community, would become a central feature of the synagogue-center program.[88]

Based on the questionnaires of the next two years, a continuing discussion ensued of the contemporary Reform celebration of the Jewish holidays. In 1909, under its new chairman Louis Wolsey, the committee report noted that "a significant fact of modern Jewish religious life is the transference of the Seder celebration from the home to the synagog." Similarly, the Sukkah moved "adjacent to the Temple," and both Purim and Hanukah, formerly religious functions of the home, were now celebrated with congregational parties and plays. While one rabbi objected on the grounds that the transfer of "home life to synagog life" is a false substitution, the committee responded that "the synagog has risen in importance because the home was first de-religionized and de-Judaized. . . . The

synagog is the victim of circumstances. It is compelled to do what the home either refuses or neglects to do. But the retort was unnecessary, for by then, the
consensus of both rabbinate and laity was staunchly in favor of a "home life"
within temple bounds.[89]

In 1908, the committee had declared

> that there can be little doubt that the "institutional idea" is gaining ground in modern congre-
> gations and that it seems altogether likely that in the near future all congregations will have to
> undertake institutional work of one kind or another if they are to hope for any real influence
> in their respective communities. . . . Our committee is not, in this place, making a plea for the
> Institutional Synagogue, but it is obvious, and this point is worthy of note, that practically all
> of our Synagogues are such in a greater or less degree.[90]

Three important points are made here: first of all, the "institutional idea" was
spreading rapidly; second, aside from the merits of the idea itself, temples were
led to "undertake institutional work" in order to aquire communal "influence";
and third, that nearly all Reform congregations already were "Institutional Synagogues" in some form or another. The 1908 report continued by enumerating the
number of congregations with men's clubs, women's organizations, young people's societies, Bible classes, congregational charities, lecture courses, libraries,
and various other societies and organizations meeting in the temple. All of these
together constituted "activities reverently conceived that have for their purpose
the establishing of the congregation as the central organization of the Jewish
communal life."[91]

By the time Moses Gries was elected president of the CCAR in 1913, his
synagogue-center idea—a radical proposal at the turn of the century—had become quite acceptable, even passé. The Committee on Social and Religious
Union continued its reporting based on questionnaires; as its function grew in
importance, it grew in membership. In 1916, the committee numbered fifteen
rabbis under the chairmanship of J. Leonard Levy. In that same year, the conference invited architect Albert S. Gottlieb to speak on the topic "Synagog and Religious School Architecture."[92] Not an eyelash was batted as he recommended the
addition of an "assembly room . . . class rooms . . . a library, a teachers room, an
exhibition room, possibly also a ladies' meeting room and a kitchen . . . [as well
as] the addition of club rooms and gymnasium" to the architecture of the Reform
congregation. In fact, many temples already had such facilities; and those that
did not would consider them in short order. Thus, well before the advent of Herbert Goldstein's Institutional Synagogue and Mordecai Kaplan's Jewish Center in
1917, the idea was firmly established in the Reform movement.[93]

Conclusion

In the first decade of the new century, two new developments arose that had profound implications for classical Reform Judaism and its synagogue-center idea.

The first was a newfound concern for the East European immigrant community. The Reform movement responded with a series of philanthopic initiatives, most notably the notion of a "People's Synagogue," essentially a Reform Jewish mission to the immigrant ghetto. Though it had a direct impact on the concept of the Reform synagogue-center—as reflected by Moses Gries's comments regarding rich and poor Jews—the subject will be taken up in a later chapter on settlement house activity.

Second, in a related development, the Reform movement began to be influenced by rabbis with a distinctly more Zionist orientation. Two of the leading Reform Zionists, Stephen S. Wise and Judah Magnes, each sought to create a new style of synagogue—both in reaction to the cold classicism of the uptown Temple Emanu-El. Wise's Free Synagogue, founded in 1907, was similar in intent and program to the People's Synagogue, and Magnes's dream of a *bet am* was a Zionist interpretation of the same; both will be addressed below in other contexts.

The ascent of Zionism signaled the decline of classical Reform Judaism. In the years following World War I, Zionism and cultural pluralism overtook American Jewish life. In reaction, most of the Reform rabbinate moved in the opposite direction. They turned more stridently anti-Zionist and conceded their role in communal development to the culturalists. Reform rabbis became more divided among themselves, split between the Zionist camp (of Wise–Magnes–Silver) and the apparent representatives of "classical" Reform Judaism. Yet the true classical Reformers—men such as Krauskopf, Berkowitz, Rosenau, Gries, and Franklin—had represented a centrist position. It was they who had therefore developed and supported the synagogue-center idea in the prewar period. After 1917, the ideological movement shifted to non-Reform quarters; co-opted by the Kaplans and Goldsteins, and abandoned by most Reform rabbis.

Nevertheless, the synagogue-center movement of the later period was preceded by an earlier trend in American Reform Judaism. To some degree, the classical Reform synagogue-center was a reflection of the institutional church movement and hence a prime example of the Americanization of Jewish life. And yet, the Jewish version had grown out of its own process of diversification, as construed by the Reform rabbi, as much as by direct imitation of the institutional church. The Reform synagogue-center would have a history of its own, emerging from its own past development.

The synagogue-center movement of Reform Judaism had emerged as an answer to the classic dilemma of American Jewish history, the dual imperative to adapt to American life and simultaneously perpetuate Jewish life. Faced with this challenge, the Reform movement evolved a new type of rabbinic leader who would combine American abilities and Jewish commitments. The classical Reform rabbi in turn conceived a new type of synagogue, again combining American and Jewish influences. The American model was the "open church," as interpreted by the archetypal Social Gospel rabbi, Emil G. Hirsch. The Jewish model was the Jewish community itself, as redefined by the great Jewish educator and communal organizer, Henry Berkowitz. After the turn of the century, the two trends coalesced in the newly ascendant CCAR. The movement soon began to spread around the country, championed by leading congregational rabbis such as Moses Gries and Leo M. Franklin. All these men were both "thoroughly Jewish and thoroughly American," and their institutions reflected it. In its Reform version, therefore, the synagogue-center was the ultimate resolution of the tensions created through three generations of German-Jewish communal life in America—and, lest we forget, as the first major exemplar of the social-religious synthesis of American Jewish life.

2

YMHA
The Jewish Associations of Young Men and Young Women

The Young Men's Hebrew Associations. The YMHAs are a new feature in American Jewish society, and a demonstration that American born Hebrews also belong to the House of Israel, and have no desire to be absorbed in the generality, or lose their identity, because they are American by birth, feelings and education. . . . Our Young America is the heir of that religiousness, benevolence and sociability in the Americanized form. Young people join all those institutions, but they must have something of their own, because they have a character of their own. This something of their own is the YMHA, which has as little in common with the YMCA, as the Jew and Christian have religiously in common.

—ISAAC MAYER WISE, 1878[1]

WHAT'S IN A NAME? In the case of the Young Men's Hebrew Association (YMHA), much it seems, for twice in the early years of the century the unwieldy phrase was adopted by groups forming new Jewish organizations. On February 6, 1902, a meeting of Jewish women was held in the home of Bella Unterberg on the Upper West Side of Manhattan. Mrs. Unterberg had called the ladies together to discuss the formation of a neighborhood center to serve the social, educational, and religious needs of young Jewish women. For a while they debated what to call their new institution, and, "after considerable discussion . . . it was agreed that it be called and known as the Young Women's Hebrew Association" (YWHA). Despite wanting an identity separate from the established YMHA, the women felt the undeniable pull of the name. In the second instance, on November 2, 1913, a group of communal leaders met to form a national federation of Jewish institutions. They too debated the name, considering options such as "United Jewish Educational Alliance" (favored by Louis Marshall) and "General Council of Jewish Centers" (Judah Magnes). They settled on "Council of Young Men's Hebrew and Kindred Associations" (CYMHKA), again, clearly inspired by the precedent of the YMHA. In both cases, the cachet of the name proved too strong to resist. By the turn of the century, the YMHA had built a solid reputation as a successful Jewish organization. A principal form of the Jewish center, it was to become an essential building block in the creation of the synagogue-center synthesis.

Paralleling the evolution of the Reform temple, the Young Men's Hebrew Association served in many ways as the youth wing of Reform Judaism. When founded in the mid-nineteenth century, the YMHA was not a religious institution in any sense, but rather a social and recreational clubhouse for young Jews of Central European descent. As it developed through the turn of the century, the YMHA began to take on more elements of a Jewish educational, cultural, and ultimately, religious nature. By World War I, the YMHA was adapted for the younger set of the East European immigrant community, and "reconstructed" as a young people's synagogue and center. In some instances it would provide the setting for the introduction of "progressive" Jewish services into the immigrant community. A survey of the history of the YMHA will reveal both its evolution as a Jewish center and its influence upon the formation of the later synagogue-center movement.[2]

The YMCA-YMHA Connection

Though its early history is clearly distinct from its Jewish counterpart, much in the development of the Young Men's Christian Association prefigures and parallels the YMHA. The YMCA was an import, brought to this country in 1851 by a Boston ship's captain named Thomas Sullivan. Sullivan had encountered the idea in London where the first YMCA had been established seven years earlier. On both sides of the Atlantic, the new institution was intended to appeal to the masses of young men drawn to the cities to provide cheap labor. The YMCA offered such men a "home away from home" and the civilizing influence of a Christian setting. The prospectus of the Boston YMCA declared itself "a social organization of those in whom the love of Christ has produced love to men; who shall meet the young stranger as he enters our city, take him to the church and Sabbath school, bring him to the Rooms of the Association, and in every way throw around him good influences, so that he may feel that he is not a stranger, but that noble and Christian spirits care for his soul." Early YMCAs thus sponsored Bible classes and prayer meetings, resembling "something of a cross between a Christian Science reading room and an old-fashioned Methodist revival."[3]

In addition, the YMCA provided a setting for informal gathering, in what might be termed a "Christian clubhouse." Besides encouraging such wholesome camaraderie, some YMCAs alleviated the difficulties of urban life by offering cheap food and lodging as well as employment bureaus. Even in these activities, however, the evangelical orientation of the new institution remained paramount. The idea succeeded beyond expectation; a parallel institution for women was begun in 1855 and by 1860 the nation's 205 associations counted

25,000 members. It is instructive to note the rapid changes undergone by the institution. Initially a grassroots organization intended to serve the working class, the YMCA became progressively more hierarchal: social service was offered to the poor, while full membership was extended only to those who could afford the dues (the middle class) and only to those of a certain background (white Anglo-Saxon Protestants).[4]

Sponsored at first by religiously inspired laymen—as evidenced by the "businessman's revival" of 1857–59—the YMCA soon allied itself with the evangelical churches, becoming a philanthropic institution supported by wealthy church members. In both instances, the YMCA "functioned not simply as an ecumenical service agency, but virtually as a church and as a Protestant denomination for the many young men and women who owed their Christian commitment to its Bible classes and religious services." Retaining its independence and ecumenical image, in practice the YMCAs "were to become the chief agency of the churches in promoting communitywide revival campaigns." Hence, membership in the YMCA required affiliation with an approved evangelical church. Originally fulfilling an informal function that the formal church could not provide, the YMCA was eventually co-opted as an extension of the church establishment.[5]

As the YMCA became more established in the post–Civil War period, its program became more secular in nature and greatly expanded at the same time. For example, "in 1884–85 the Boston association offered instruction in seventeen subjects to 1,014 men and 153 women; around 1890 industrial education classes were added." The rationale for such diversification was the YMCA's desire to provide for all aspects of a young man's life. Thus, in 1869, Robert McBurney developed a "Four-Fold Plan" that would compartmentalize the YMCA into four separate departments: physical, educational, social, and religious. When physical education came to predominate in the YMCA around the turn of the century, critics of the new secularism were silenced by the insistence that "it doesn't matter how you get a man to God provided you get him there."[6]

Through such rationalization, the YMCA leadership retained religion as their institutional purpose. At the same time, the youthful membership was becoming more interested solely in its social and physical offerings. That such contradictory sentiments could coexist was due to the synthetic nature of the institution: those who wished to see religiosity in the YMCA could point to the Bible classes, while those who were more interested in its secularism did not have to look much further. This pragmatic attitude was typically American, and accounts for the lasting success and broad influence of the YMCA.

Though the YMCA's program had expanded, its constituency had not. Blacks, Catholics, and Jews were excluded throughout the nineteenth century, setting the stage for the emergence of Young Men's and Young Women's Associations for these groups. The common assumption has it that the minority versions of the YMCA were merely imitations and nothing more. As indicated above, the Young Men's Hebrew Associations were not simply duplicates of the original, though many historians and other commentators have described the YMHA in derivative terms.[7] No less an authority than Horace Kallen would state:

In its primary intention the Young Men's Hebrew Association was to be a Jewish parallel to the Young Men's Christian Association. The parallel is specific, and specific for every item of activity in the early history of the "Y's." In the beginning, the whole difference between the YMHA and the YMCA may have lain simply in what is implied by the term "Hebrew" and by the term "Christian." And in this connection most of what is implied is very close to nothing at all.[8]

Others have countered with the opposite view that the YMHA was an original institution and actually preceded the YMCA; an organization calling itself the "Young Men's Hebrew Literary Association of Philadelphia" (YMHLA) was founded one year prior to the importation of the YMCA. The notion that the Jewish institution influenced the Christian nomenclature is unfounded, however, for the YMCA had preceded the YMHLA by several years—in England. More likely, the words "young men's association" in both the English YMCA and the American YMHLA were derived from the German "Jugendverein." The close identification of Central European immigrant Jews with German culture makes this all the more plausible.[9]

Overall, the YMHA was heavily influenced by the YMCA, while at the same time staking out new ground as a Jewish center. Like the early YMCA, argues historian Naomi Cohen, "the YMHA served as a weapon for preserving religious community in the secular city." Both were youth-oriented institutions that offered lecture courses, literary and musical programs, classes, debates, library facilities, and social activities. Even setting the name similarity aside, one thus sees much in the YMHA that was directly borrowed from or influenced by the YMCA. Such influences included direct inspiration for the founding of new YMHAs, borrowed forms such as an employment bureau or a gymnasium, a mission transcending divisions within the greater community, and an orientation toward outreach and social service that the impersonal churches and synagogues ignored.[10]

The following excerpt from an 1888 editorial of the *Jewish Messenger* illuminates the process of imitation:

Young Men's Work. The Jewish ministers' theory of the best way to improve the Hebrew Association of New York, seems to be the early erection of a handsome building that shall rival, if not excel, the complete and well-endowed edifice that dignifies the work of the Christian Association. They complain that many young Hebrews have joined the latter society, attracted by its superior physical and literary advantages, and have abandoned the former. . . . If the sole means that will commend a young men's organization to our young men be a gymnasium, bowling alleys, athletic grounds, and a collection of fashionable bath-rooms, we suppose that, in the interest of future congregations, such means must be provided.[11]

As the quote indicates, the YMCA was not perceived as a dangerous missionizing agency so much as a neighboring institution to be emulated. Of course, implicit within such friendly competition between the YMCA and YMHA is the age-old rivalry between the Jewish and Christian faiths, which helps to explain the active participation of "Jewish ministers" in the endeavor. Note also that their concern is for "future congregations," implying that youthful participation in a YMHA will lead to adult involvement in religious life. Thus the YMHA was seen by the Jewish religious establishment as a sort of youth synagogue, analogous to the YMCA in providing a training ground for later activity in the church.

Another example of YMCA influence is to be found in Boston, where the original Jewish congregation built its first synagogue building in 1851 (coincidentally the same year as the founding of the first YMCA in America—also in Boston). The "Warren Street Shul" of Congregation Ohabei Shalom immediately became the central address of the Jewish community. Another communal center, the Boston YWCA, was later built across the street, next to the Universalist church building, which the Jewish synagogue purchased and moved into in 1863. Thus, when Ohabei Shalom and its rabbi sponsored the founding of Boston's first YMHA in 1875, the YWCA was right next door. Its contiguous position could not help exercising a direct influence on its neighbor. Like the Boston YMCA and YWCA, the YMHA functioned as an employment bureau and philanthropic agency: "In the short time of three months since the organization of the Society, over 150 persons have been aided in various ways; some with money, clothing, employment, lodging, etc." Yet the description continues: "One of the most important of all was the supplying of matzos and groceries to eighteen Jewish families during the Passover." Thus was Christian influence converted to Jewish purpose.[12]

YMHAs would continue to be influenced by their neighboring YMCAs. In a 1910 meeting of the committee on social work of the New York YMHA, "Mr. Younker brought up the question of holding mid-day meetings in large establishments where young Jewish men are principally employed, with the view of advertising the work of the YMHA in a manner similar to that of the YMCA." Another time, "on the matter of pool tables . . . Mr. Younker reported as to the method pursued by the YMCA." And again: "As the YMCA Real Estate class meets on Tues. night it was deemed advisable that we select some night other than Tuesday. . . . As speakers of such course[s] we should try to get at least six not on the present YMCA course." Apparently, ambitious young Jewish men would attend such a course at both the Christian and Jewish Ys. In any case, the direction of influence is clear.[13]

In the final analysis, the comparison between the YMCA and YMHA presents an interesting paradox. On the one hand, both institutions were products of the peculiar American tendency to combine social and religious functions. The history of both institutions is marked by the troublesome tension between "hymn" and "gym," between "shul" and "pool." The development of the YMHA is similar in many respects to the history of the YMCA outlined above, with one major difference. Whereas the YMCA began as an intensely religious institution and grew progressively more secular, the YMHA developed in precisely the opposite direction: it began as an institution in revolt against the traditional definition of Judaism and grew more intensively Jewish as the years passed, becoming a particularly Jewish institution.

Jewish Influences on the Early YMHA

The process of Judaization began with the earliest influences on the YMHA. While clearly parallel to the YMCA, the YMHA was also evolved from and influenced by institutions in American Jewish life. Following Rabinowitz, later historians stressed the Jewish literary society as a forerunner of the YMHA: "Even more fashionable and numerous during the 1850s [than the Jewish fraternal orders] were Jewish young men's literary societies and associations. Ignoring the secret ritual appeal of the fraternal orders, they concentrated on cultural programs." As agencies of social and cultural improvement—and hence, of upward mobility—they became a staple of German-Jewish immigrant culture and would grow in popularity with succeeding generations. By the 1870s, Jewish literary societies would often serve as the model and direct influence on the formation of YMHAs.[14]

As already noted, in the pivotal Jewish community of Philadelphia, a literary society called the Young Men's Hebrew Literary Association was organized in 1850. Its subsequent history is unclear, but it likely survived in some form, for in 1875 there existed a literary society by the name of the "Hebrew Association." This, in turn, is believed to have been the origin of the YMHA founded in that same year. Adopting the mode of the literary society, its program was one of social betterment, including musical performances, recitations, debates, and lectures. But the YMHA had at least one other source. One of its founders and leading members was an intensely religious young man named Nathan Weissenstein. Like Weissenstein, many of the original members of the YMHA were alumni of the Jewish Foster Home, the Jewish orphanage of Philadelphia. As in the orphanage, a Jewish educational institution, the YMHA's program would also have "a Jewish tinge." The new association would combine the cultural ambience of the literary society with the Jewish spirit of the orphanage.[15]

Thus the literary society grew into a Jewish center. Like the fraternal lodge (as well as the Christian association), the literary society also held the potential for an underlying "religious" intent: by allowing Jews to associate with other Jews in a homogeneous social context, it would help them to remain Jewish in the American environment. This survivalist characteristic, latent in the YMHLA, would be realized by the new YMHA, but the change was gradual. Many early YMHAs were still essentially literary societies in form and content, while others were more akin to the YMCA model. Still others combined the two. In Cleveland, "A Hebrew Literary Association in 1869 decided 'to function as the local organization corresponding to the Young Men's Christian Association.'"[16]

But soon enough the YMHA would develop its own personality and agenda, and, like B'nai B'rith before it, would become a center for "the ethnic dimension of Judaism."[17] By exploring the growth in religious content of the early YMHA, we may discover the sources (or at least the adumbrations) of a later, more explicit integration of the synagogue and center. While both the 1850 YMHLA of Philadelphia and the 1854 YMHA of Baltimore have been cited as origins of the YMHA movement, a self-conscious movement did not arise until the creation of the New York YMHA two decades later. A distinction must be drawn therefore between the early YMHAs of the Civil War era and the more clearly defined YMHA that came later. Yet the earlier period is still relevant to our study, as it coincides with the initial adjustment of the German-Jewish immigrants to American society. Jewish communal life in those years was characterized by innovation and experimentation, ranging from the haphazard organization of imitative societies to the more thoughtful construction of Jewish culture by individuals such as Isaac Leeser and Isaac Mayer Wise.[18]

At first, we might be tempted to classify the early YMHA in the category of grassroots organization. Yet from the very beginning, the rabbinic leadership of the American Jewish community took an active roll in the YMHA. When the Young Men's Hebrew Literary Association of Philadelphia was organized in 1850, one of its main progenitors was *Hazan* Isaac Leeser. In 1855, Rabbi James K. Gutheim delivered "a course of lectures on history, ancient and modern, beginning with Abraham and down to the present time . . . [and offered] a class for Hebrew and religious instruction" to the Hebrew Young Men's Literary Association of New Orleans. In 1865, the first YMHA in Cincinnati was formed through the efforts of Rabbi Max Lilienthal, "who was actively interested in the movement over a long period of time and endeavored to extend it throughout the country." When, two years later, the second YMHA in Cincinnati was founded, Lilienthal and his close colleague Isaac Mayer Wise became "ardent supporters."[19]

Their view of the purpose of the institution no doubt corresponded to this excerpt from the constitution of 1867:

The association was organized for the purpose of cultivating and fostering a better knowledge of the history, literature and doctrines of Judaism; to develop and elevate our mental and moral character; to entertain and edify ourselves with such intellectual agencies as we may deem fit, and finally and above all, it is our mission to promulgate the sublime and eternal principles of Judaism to the world, and when necessary to defend though honorably and peaceably, the faith of our ancestors.[20]

When the Baltimore *Sinai* of 1856 hailed the "Hebrew Young Men's Literary Associations . . . as important elements in the development of American Judaism," we may take the last phrase in its literal sense. Though the editorialist intended "Judaism" to convey the broader idea of Jewish life, we may read the word as it specifically refers to Jewish religious life. While early YMHAs were often no more than literary societies formed of Jews, they were at other times conceived of as agencies of Judaism and Jewish culture. From their inceptions in 1856, the Young Men's Hebrew Literary Associations of both Davenport, Iowa, and Rock Island, Illinois, conducted religious services.[21]

Even without such services, Jewish religion was to be served. In Buffalo, New York, the "Hebrew young men" of the city met in October 1858 to form the Buffalo Hebrew Young Men's Association. Their stated purpose was the typical program of the literary society, "mutual improvement" through literature, as well as "debates on various topics." Yet in addition to general literature, Jewish literature was to be studied, and, together with socializing, the young men's "religious character" was to be fostered. Thus, the YMHLA and early YMHA moved beyond the secular program of the literary society in their newfound attention to things Jewish. It is no wonder that the religious establishment saw the nascent institution as an opportunity to extend its own influence beyond the pulpit.[22]

The main catalyst for the transformation from a largely secular literary society into a more positively Jewish institution was the rabbi. Indeed, many of the progressive rabbis of the time became deeply involved with the new YMHAs, assisting in their organization and often serving as their head officer. Some rabbis who served as presidents of YMHAs did so as active participants; for example, the young Sabato Morais served as the president and delivered weekly lectures to the early (pre-1875) YMHA of Philadelphia. Other rabbis were probably mere figureheads, but as we shall see, many more would later become instrumental as directors and superintendents of their YMHAs. In either case, whether passive or active, the rabbi's affiliation with the YMHA legitimated and motivated its "positive interest toward Jewish affairs."[23]

At the same time, lay organizers of YMHAs maintained their allegiance to the synagogue. The founders of the New York YMHA of 1874 were nearly all members of Congregation Shaaray Tefila, then a "conservative synagogue" located on West 44th Street. It was Sol B. Solomon, a trustee and a president of the congregation, who conceived the Young Men's Hebrew Association, and the first meeting was held in the home of Dr. Simon Newton Leo, another member of the congregation. Sometime later, Percival S. Menken and Falk Younker, also members of Shaaray Tefila, would lay the foundations of the reconstituted "Y."[24]

Similarly, membership lists of YMHAs and Reform temples usually overlapped considerably. Temple board members and YMHA officers were often the same individuals. The best example perhaps is the case of New York's Temple Emanu-El, whose lay leaders Jacob Schiff, Lewis May, and Myer Stern all served on the board of directors of the New York YMHA. For several months in 1874, the board met in the trustees' room of Temple Emanu-El. Lewis May served as president of both groups, simultaneously. Many other similar examples might be cited. Simply by virtue of their overlapping membership, therefore, the YMHAs were identified with leading Jewish congregations.[25]

Nevertheless, the coexistence of the institutions was based on mutual exclusivity of purpose, which inevitably led to conflict. In Baltimore, for example, the

YMHA of 1870 was criticized by one of the local rabbis for conducting Friday evening services. In his view, the YMHA and the synagogue stood in direct competition. Yet the opposite tendency appeared as well when the young David Philipson wrote to one of the leaders of the YMHA to register his support. Philipson, of course, would later become one of the first four graduates of Hebrew Union College. In his letter, he wrote that the rabbi's preaching would "have very little effect on the young men, as they mostly never visit the temple on a Sabbath" in any case, and thus expressed amazement that any rabbi would be opposed to religious programming at the YMHA. He apparently saw no contradiction between the existence of the Reform temple on the one hand and the YMHA on the other. Like his lay counterparts he assigned different roles to each, neatly dividing the religious and social functions of Jewish life.[26]

Yet not all of Philipson's fellow rabbinical students at Hebrew Union College were of the same mind. Their shared enthusiasm for the religious potential of the YMHA would create institutional friction between the explicitly social YMHA and the explicitly religious synagogue and therefore require some form of resolution. One path of resolution entailed bringing the "YMHA" into the synagogue, as when a number of New York City synagogues formed their own "Young Men's Associations," for example, Temple Ahavath Chesed in 1873 and Temple Beth El in 1880. The other, opposite path, meant bringing the "synagogue" into the YMHA, as we have seen. Eventually the two forms of conflict resolution would coalesce into one process of institutional synthesis. The creation of the synagogue-center in the twentieth century would thus provide an answer to the problem of synagogue-YMHA tension.[27]

In the period at hand, Rabbis remained intimately involved in the development of YMHA culture. For instance, the *American Israelite* of December 7, 1877, described the first literary entertainment of the Chicago YMHA:

The crowning feature of the evening's entertainment was the lecture on "Liberality and Judaism," by the Rev. Dr. Henry Gersoni, who spoke for nearly an hour, extemporaneously, keeping the large audience spell-bound during its recital, and when he concluded, his brilliant effort was received with round upon round of merited applause. . . . The Rev. Dr. [Liebmann] Adler, of the Indiana Avenue Temple, then addressed the Association in German, congratulating them on the success they have achieved in the past, and anticipating for them a prosperous career in the future.[28]

Still other Reform rabbis continued to participate in YMHA life. For example, the opening lecture at the Louisville YMHA in 1878 was delivered by Emil G. Hirsch, who was described as the "father of the association." Similarly, the Newark YMHA of 1878 boasted of the participation of the Reverend Joseph Leucht, pastor of the Washington Street Synagogue, who was elected to the Executive Committee at the founding meeting; and of the Reverend Dr. Isador Kalisch, who delivered a talk on Jewish ethics at the first public entertainment of the newly organized association.[29]

Also in 1878, Isaac M. Wise editorialized on the YMHA in the *American Is-*

raelite. Wise defended the YMHA as an anti-assimilationist institution, one that answered the specific needs of the younger American-born generation. If Jewish youth were attracted to the new institution, then ought not the future-thinking Jewish minister exert his influence and seek to "Judaize" the otherwise secular setting? In his travels, therefore, Wise would visit the YMHAs of the country just as he did the temples. In early 1883, visiting Boston for the first time in nine years, Wise made sure to deliver a lecture (on Moses) to the newly reorganized YMHA.[30]

Whenever given the opportunity, therefore, liberal rabbis would attempt to color their YMHAs in Judaic hues. A telling example of this is the minor controversy played out in the *Cleveland Hebrew Observer* of 1889 over the "paternity" of the YMHA. The writer of an article entitled, "The YMHA—Its Aims and Objects, and the Causes which led to its Organization—Why every Israelite should become a Member," claimed that it had descended from the Cleveland Literary Union; whereupon Rabbi Michael Machol responded rather testily, claiming that its patrimony lay instead in the Hebrew Congregation of the Scovill Avenue Temple. The issue was not so much the true course of historical development (both accounts might have been accurate) as the current emphasis of the YMHA. The rabbi, of course, sought a "religious" source for the institution to ensure its ongoing commitment to Judaism. Such was the indirect influence of the early YMHA rabbi.[31]

It must be emphasized, however, that the rabbis' involvement was not merely a strategy to bring the younger generation back to the synagogue. In addition to that goal, the YMHA leadership conceived of their movement as a bona fide branch of American Judaism, not opposed to, but in league with, the synagogue. The YMHA, they thought, could perhaps reach those whom the synagogue could not. As Jacob Schiff declared in 1884, "the YMHA's are better missionaries than nine-tenths of the congregations." The synagogue and the YMHA therefore cooperated with each other at times, and as we shall find, once even entertained the possibility of merger.[32]

In the spring of 1882, an effort was made to arouse public interest in the YMHA through the medium of the synagogue. The Sabbath before Passover was designated as "Association Day," and the rabbis were asked to deliver sermons on the subject of the YMHA. On Saturday evening, the various YMHAs were to conduct mass meetings and celebrations. There are several innovations here. First, the YMHAs began to act in unison, as an organized movement; second, the aid of the rabbis was solicited by the YMHA organizers; third, the subject of the YMHA was deemed suitable for the rabbi's sermon; and most significant, the YMHA evening program was seen as an appropriate follow-up to the morning services in synagogue. While the YMHA meetings and celebrations are intended primarily as social mixers for young people, the influence of religion is ensured as well by integrating the YMHA into the life of the synagogue.[33]

And, as before, the synagogue came to the YMHA in the form of rabbis' lectures; though now, the lectures were more regular and better organized. In 1886

New York, for example, the following course was announced in the *American Hebrew*:

A course of lectures pertaining to Judaism, from a strictly religious standpoint, has been arranged for the current season by the YMHA. These lectures are specially arranged to arouse young men and women of our faith from the apathy and indifference to religious matters that now prevail among them. . . . The Association of Jewish Ministers of this city has agreed to co-operate with the association, and has prepared a course of lectures. . . . The first lecture, entitled, "Why am I a Jew?" will be delivered by Rev. Dr. G[ustav] Gottheil at the Temple Beth El . . . all will be welcomed.[34]

Parallel to this, and worth noting, the same issue contained the following announcement: "The opening of the series of entertainments by the Young Men's Association [of] congregation Ahawath Chesed took place last Thu. evening, Nov. 18th, in the lecture room of the Temple, . . . then introduced the Rev. Dr. A[lexander] Kohut. For the first time in public, he used the English language in introducing the lecturer of the evening, the Rev. Dr. Bettelheim of Baltimore." Again, the appeal to youth is evident.[35]

On at least one occasion, an out-of-town rabbi invited to speak to a New York congregation avoided the appearance of a trial sermon by addressing the YMHA instead. In 1886, Rabbi Joseph Krauskopf of Kansas City (he moved to Philadelphia the next year) appeared before members of Temple Emanu-El in the neutral setting of the YMHA, which functioned, therefore, as a surrogate synagogue.[36] If the synagogue was the principal platform for the American rabbi, then the YMHA had become a kind of auxiliary pulpit.

The "Classical" YMHA (1875–1900)

The last quarter of the nineteenth century saw the rise of a more self-confident YMHA, in a phase that might be termed the "classical" period of the YMHA. The period was inaugurated in 1874–75 when two new YMHAs burst on the scene and together offered leadership and direction to the newborn movement. The first was founded in 1874 in New York, and the second the following year in Philadelphia. Both cities were poised to experience a "religious revival" and would become centers of nascent "Conservative" Judaism—which was itself, at the time of its origin, a youth movement. The two YMHAs would be hubs of the new revivalist activity, and as such, they became the prototypes for more than 120 new YMHAs established around the country in the next fifteen years.[37]

The active role of the rabbi in the YMHA was not introduced during this period, only reinforced. What, then, was the innovation of the "classical" YMHA? The answer: its tendency to unify. More than any other institution or organization of the late nineteenth century, the YMHA served as a unifying, integrating, and synthesizing agency in Jewish life. This implies, of course, that the American Jewish community of the time was particularly conflicted, at odds with its environment, and divided within. Let us examine three such conflicts and their attempted resolutions by the YMHA. In the order we shall treat them, these were (1) unifying Jewish communities in a national movement; (2) unifying Jewish communities across denominational and ethnic lines (for example, Sephardim and Germans); and (3) unifying Jewish religious and secular life.

1. *Unifying Jewish communities in a national movement.* As early as 1868, Rabbi Max Lilienthal declared that "a perpetual correspondence should spring up between the associations of the various cities. He gloried in the recent organizations of Jewish Young Men's societies . . . and trusted they would persevere and form a more extended union throughout the west." Like his colleague Isaac Mayer Wise, Lilienthal sought to unite disparate Jewish communities into one national movement. Wise succeeded in 1873 through the organization of the Union of American Hebrew Congregations (UAHC), but Lilienthal's initiative was taken up by others.[38]

In 1869, the Washington, D.C.–based communal leader Simon Wolf wrote to the editor of the *Jewish Times* to recommend the formation of a "National Young Men's Hebrew Association." He made certain to distinguish this movement from the "sectarian" (read: religious) YMCA, suggesting instead a YMHA formed "on a rational basis, progressive and social . . . to show our social and intellectual condition as citizens and Israelites." Thus, not only did Wolf recommend the formation of a national movement, he also stressed the desire for cultural uplift. Jews should not only unite with each other, but integrate as well with modern culture, and of course, with America. The theme of Americanization, which will persist throughout the history of the YMHA and Jewish center, may be seen as another form of synthesis—bringing together immigrant Jews and their new environment. It will become especially relevant in the following discussion of the settlement house activity of the YMHA. Prior to 1881, however, the need for unity was felt most of all among the far-flung communities of American Jewry; and thus, the drive to unify via a nationwide movement.[39]

In 1875, the newly formed New York YMHA attempted to create a national body for "the protection of Hebrew interests." According to Rabinowitz, such a defensive objective expressed the "desire to establish the YMHAs as a central Jewish agency." A committee was "appointed to consider the feasibility of organizing a Central Board of the American Jews to take cognizance of any and all matters affecting the welfare of our co-religionists." In its stead, the Board of Delegates of American Israelites merged with the UAHC in 1878. Had it succeeded in bringing in the YMHAs as well, the combined organization might have been the first truly representative central body in the American Jewish community. Though not realized for several years, the above motion was the first time a YMHA sought to extend its influence and ally itself with other YMHAs in a national movement.[40]

Another such attempt was made in concert with the appearance of a lively new Jewish periodical called the *American Hebrew*. It was created in 1879 by several of the leaders of the New York and Philadelphia YMHAs, who joined together in order to broaden their sphere of influence. In its pages and elsewhere, proposals began to appear for a "Union to be composed of Young Men's Hebrew Associations and kindred societies of whatever title." In 1880, the Philadelphia contingent succeeded in its attempt to form a national organization of YMHAs, which became known as the American Hebrew Association (AHA). However, the New York YMHA soon withdrew, in part due to their refusal to accept congregational societies as "real YMHA's." Their absence led to the demise of the national association in 1883. In 1890, the United YMHA of America (UYA) was organized at a convention in Cincinnati; it too lasted only three years, failing due to the financial panic of 1893. A permanent national coordinating body only came into existence when the Council of Young Men's Hebrew and Kindred Associations was formed in 1913. Nonetheless, the unifying tendency of the YMHA as a national movement was apparent from the earlier period.[41]

2. *Unifying Jewish communities across denominational and ethnic lines.* Earlier we observed how the New York YMHA united members of different congregations in common purpose. In this period, YMHAs everywhere would respond to the problem of Jewish communal fragmentation by constructing an institution—a Jewish *center*—to which all members of the community might belong. The problem arose following the initial breakup of the Sephardic-dominated synagogue-community in the 1820s and 1830s. As the decades passed and Jewish immigration increased, multiple new congregations were formed whenever immigrant Jews of a different ethnic background (for example, English, Dutch, German, Polish, Lithuanian) became sufficient in number to constitute their own subcommunity. Ethnic and class tensions between Jews came to be expressed as congregational schisms, which therefore seemed to pose the greatest threat to Jewish unity and survival. In response, religious and quasi-religious institutions began to be reconfigured as unifying agencies. Both the Reform movement and the fraternal lodge were at one time construed as answers to the problem of communal disintegration. But the YMHA, as a broad-based Jewish center, was the most likely institution to deliver its promise of unity. Foreshadowing the later synagogue-center, the classical YMHA was in this sense an attempt to reconstitute the comprehensive synagogue-community.

On the social level, for example, the new YMHA "filled a genuine gap. The [social] Club existed for a restricted group, the congregations had a certain life of their own, but there was no general organization for personal social contact where everyone might mingle." In Philadelphia, wrote the historian of its YMHA, "the Spanish-Portugese Jews constituted a group distinct from the Germans, and the 'Y' was probably the only organization where the youth of both met freely and mingled in common endeavor." Within Mikveh Israel, the original congregation of Philadelphia, tensions between the Sephardic and Ashkenazic members plagued *Hazan* Sabato Morais as they had Isaac Leeser before him. In 1875, the counter-Reform leader Morais followed the earlier lead of Isaac M. Wise and issued a call to unify the American Jewish community by creating a common ritual. But the problem of disunity had become far more urgent since Wise's proposed "Minhag America."[42]

In the pages of his fellow conservative rabbi Samuel M. Isaacs' periodical, the *Jewish Messenger*, Morais declared:

A floodtide of emigration [has] set in during the last quarter of a century. Men of all nationalities and languages came to our shores, and brought along not only the liturgies of the different countries, but local usages, around which they cast a halo of sanctity and to which they would still raise high altars. A seething mass of Minhagim effervesced in our midst and "Reform" so called also bubbled up. . . . Portugese and German, Polish and Hollander, in connection with the manner of worshipping Israel's God, are names that should, long ere this, have been erased from our nomenclature.[43]

Like the earlier initiative of his Reform opponent, Morais's proposal for an Americanized synagogue ritual did nothing to unite the left and right wings of American Judaism. It was ritual preference—the remnant of ethnic attachments—that divided them. Thus, some context other than the synagogue was called for if unity was to be achieved. This context would be the YMHA. Indeed, the YMHA provided a meeting ground that the synagogue could not, and a unifying potential not to be found in the prayerbook. In its founding year, 1874, the *Jewish Messenger* editorialized: "One of the missions of the YMHA is to unite on a common platform the young men of the different synagogues and nationalities." And, after a few years' experience (in 1877), the same editor wrote: "It is absolutely a novelty in American Judaism to see all classes united on a broad platform from which all doctrinal differences are rigidly excluded, to have all nationalities merging together in a general movement."[44]

The unity was both symbolized and actualized by the combination of liberal Reform rabbis and their more conservative colleagues within the classical YMHA; for example, Gustav Gottheil, Frederick de Sola Mendes, and Sabato Morais all sat on the board of directors of the New York YMHA. The classical YMHA continued to bring rabbis together and by extension, their congregants. In 1902, the New York YMHA engaged the following diverse group of rabbis as lecturers: Samuel Schulman, I. S. Moses, Kaufmann Kohler, Stephen S. Wise, Emil G. Hirsch, David Levine, Leon Harrison, Herman Abramowitz, Henry Pereira Mendes, and Rudolph Grossman. But the YMHA did more than invite such men at different times. In its *Monthly Bulletin* of October 1902, the following announcement appeared: "The New York Board of Jewish Ministers have requested the use of one of the rooms in the [YMHA] building for a meeting place, and the Board of Directors have gladly consented to their request. We welcome our rabbis to the building, and orthodox, conservative, and radical can now meet on neutral ground." The YMHA had brought them together.[45]

In Boston, a traditionalist rabbi had urged the revival of the YMHA in 1881. Rabbi S. S. Cohen of Mishkan Israel failed in his attempt, but the cause was soon taken up by Raphael Lasker, the rabbi of the moderate Reform congregation, Ohabei Shalom. Thus, in 1882, the YMHA of Boston was organized by a conservative and a reform rabbi working in tandem. Two decades later, the religious community had polarized further still, and once again, the YMHA provided common ground. In 1905, the Boston YMHA sponsored a "Rabbi's Night" that joined the ultra-Orthodox chief rabbi of Boston and the radical Reform minister of the classical Reform temple on the same program. In any other setting, the meeting of the RaMaZ (Moshe Zevulun Margolis) and the Reverend Charles Fleischer would have been an absurd proposition; but in the nondenominational, "catholic" YMHA, the novelty was not only possible but programmatic. As the president of the new YMHA, lawyer Edward Goulston wrote in 1883:

It goes without saying—that an Association like ours is a great desideratum to the community; and it also goes without saying, that in order to make it progressive in the highest sense, it naturally requires a combination of all the elements of our people to raise it above that of a Lodge or a Club-room. It appears now, in my judgement, that it is a difficult task in Boston to make a fusion of all the elements of our people,—I mean by that a complete union that shall destroy—and destroy inevitably, whatever antagonism or prejudice may exist in regard to nationality.[46]

Goulston thus associated communal unity with the Progressive ideal. As Jewish immigration increased to mass proportions in the 1880s, the YMHA was more and more construed as an agency of relief to the new immigrants. Rather than being influenced by the settlement house movement, however, the philanthropic role of the YMHA was a natural outgrowth of its own earlier preoccupation with communal unity. Thus, when the New York YMHA established its downtown branch in 1883, it preceded by three years the founding of the first settlement house in America. The downtown YMHA has been called "the first neighborhood center in America for the immigrant groups"; it was not, however, a settlement house in the sense of the University Settlement or Hull House. These were institutions established by patrician social workers for the purpose of Americanizing new immigrants. Like the settlements, the YMHA of the Lower East Side sought to Americanize the newcomers; but at the same time its intention was to create a *Jewish* center downtown analogous to the one uptown, and thus to maintain unity in the entire Jewish community.[47]

A typical YMHA of the 1880s combined the interests of the Jewish and general communities. For instance, Rochester's Young Men's Jewish Association of 1887 was formed to provide: "Education in its pleasantest form—voluntary. . . . A free and pleasant intercourse with the representatives of the different Jewish classes . . . a culture and delicacy of refinement . . . the destruction of race prejudice," and concludes, "Everyone who has the true interests of Judaism at heart, will prove it by aiding the new organization to the extent of his ability. The young men of the community have broken down the gates of the old Ghetto and have desire to mingle with the world, as men among men." Thus the YMHA would simultaneously serve the "interests of Judaism" and enable its members to "mingle with the world."[48]

When the United YMHA of America was founded in 1890, its statement of

objectives reflected the same dual purpose. It reflected the typical YMHA program of the time, and in addition, reflected the growing attention of the YMHA
to the problems of Jewish immigrants. At the second convention in 1891, President Alfred M. Cohen recommended an "annual entertainment for the benefit of
a Manual Training School Fund to be used for the education and Americanization of poor immigrant Jews, and others." Resolutions were passed recommending the establishment of "industrial schools for the children of all persecuted
people who seek our shores for protection [and] night schools for immigrants to
teach [them] the language of the country." Once again, this was not a case of
philanthropic outreach from one class to another, but rather the response of a
community to the plight of its own.[49]

In 1887, the *American Hebrew* editorialized:

The society [the YMHA] may not be needed as much as at first as a means of levelling congregational distinctions, but many of our people have freed themselves from synagogue and temple influences, so that those who adhere to the congregation, and as at one time were likely to
pass into narrow grooves, and raise barriers between themselves and their brethren of other
congregations, are in the minority. It is where the pulpit fails to reach that this society must
lend its aid. It must supplement the pulpit, co-operate with it, and vigourously strive not only
to Judaize the Jew, but to Americanize the Jew.[50]

This leads us to the next aspect of the classical YMHA, from having been "a
means of levelling congregational distinctions" to getting "where the pulpit fails
to reach."

3. *Unifying Jewish religious and secular life.* The third unifying tendency was
reflected by the integration of the religious sphere (represented by the rabbis and
the synagogue) with the secular sphere of the lay-led YMHA. During the Civil
War era, the process of American acculturation, and hence secularization, of the
German-Jewish immigrants and their children proceeded apace. By the 1870s
and 1880s the need for Jewish reacculturation became apparent, and the organized Jewish community began to respond in one of two ways. The first was the
introduction of "secular" social activities into the "religious" congregational
realm (as described in Chapter 1); the second was the interpolation of Judaism
into secular settings such as the YMHA. Both of these strategies were conceived
of in educational terms, and both, it should be emphasized, entailed the secularization of Judaism—a central theme of modern Jewish history. The process was
slow, moving through numerous stages of integration, from the first hesitant attempts in the early years to the more self-confident "Jewish" YMHA of the turn
of the century.

As noted earlier, the first president of the New York YMHA was also the president of New York's leading Reform temple; ostensibly, the two institutions
shared other members as well. In keeping with its upper-class pretensions, therefore, the first social "entertainment" of the New York YMHA was held in October 1874. For the occasion, "the parlor walls were graced by three choice paintings, which received due admiration, and several chromos and engravings that

were pleasing to the eye." The scene would smack of a typical Victorian soiree were it not for one of the highlighted paintings, one entitled "Interior of a Polish Synagogue"! It was a subtle intrusion perhaps, but significant nonetheless, as the presence of "Jewish Art" reflected both the modern aspirations of Jewish culture and the beginnings of the Judaization of the YMHA.[51]

A similarly minor intrusion with far greater potential impact occurred in Philadelphia in 1876. Mayer Sulzberger, serving as executor to the estate of the Reverend Isaac Leeser, had deposited Leeser's private collection of books, "one of the best Hebrew libraries in America," in the library rooms of the Philadelphia YMHA. (Volunteering in the YMHA library, the young Cyrus Adler was inspired to catalogue the collection, and so was started on his illustrious career in the Jewish community.) The presence of a prestigious collection of Judaica helped the YMHA to transcend the nonsectarian character of the literary society and athletic club and established the YMHA in Philadelphia as a center of Jewish culture. It presaged the eventual inclusion of Jewish content in other YMHAs as well.[52]

But the transition from a young men's association to a Jewish center did not occur without some internal contradiction. Often, the secular activities and religious nature of the YMHA came into direct conflict, as when the New York YMHA installed a gymnasium in 1877. From the start, the question arose of whether the gymnasium should be kept open on the Sabbath. A compromise was reached in which the gymnasium would be open on the Sabbath for "lighter exercises" only, with no one allowed to practice on the trapeze and horizontal bars on the day of rest. We see here a classic case of secular-religious tension in American Jewish life, of the sort that is repeated to this day in Jewish institutions and organizations. The compromise reached was typical of the YMHA, and broadly speaking, is characteristic of American "folk" Judaism.[53]

The YMHA would continue to proffer such an informal brand of Judaism. The first YMHA periodical, the *Association Review* (published from 1877 to 1879), its public successor, the *American Hebrew* (published from 1879 and edited by YMHA leaders), and the *Association Bulletin* (edited by Solomon Solis-Cohen from 1881 to 1883) all contained articles of Jewish content and interest, often submitted by rabbis. The publications on the whole were unaffiliated with any Jewish religious body and officially secular, yet as Philip Cowen reminisced, "the position of the paper [the *American Hebrew*] was strong for traditional Judaism." Likewise, the names appearing as editors and contributors in the *Association Bulletin* were a veritable Who's Who of conservative rabbis and Historical School leaders. Many of the articles were thus derived from lectures delivered to various YMHAs on Jewish subjects. For example, in the January 1883 issue, the Reverend Dr. Frederick de Sola Mendes published a ten-page article entitled "An Hour in a Beth Hamedrash." Like the painting described above, it was a sentimental depiction of Orthodox Jewish life; yet its setting—the YMHA periodical—was rather unorthodox for the time. The paradox exemplified a new factor in American Jewish life: the enlightened presentation of traditional Judaism in a form that was simultaneously secular and Jewish. The context was the classical YMHA, a Jewish center in the making.[54]

It comes as no surprise, therefore, to find that the program of the classical YMHA included much of a secular Jewish nature. Thus, when the YMHA began to engage in Jewish education, it focused on Hebrew literature and Jewish history. Beginning in 1875, the New York YMHA began to conduct an annual Hebrew competitive examination for students all over the city; within the YMHA itself, classes in Hebrew language and literature were conducted from 1876 by the Reverend Drs. G. Gottheil, F. de Sola Mendes, and Henry P. Mendes. At the Philadelphia YMHA, classes in Jewish history and literature were offered by the Reverends Sabato Morais and George Jacobs. In 1879, the annual competitive examination of the New York YMHA was on the subject "Post-Biblical History: From Ezra to the Fall of Jerusalem." Not religion but literature, and not Bible but postbiblical history were the topics of study, though they were being taught by rabbis. Apparently, the secular and nondenominational setting of the YMHA required a change in the role of the rabbi and in the very character of Judaism.[55]

Thus the secular sphere of the YMHA incorporated religious content. The more radical step of institutional merger nearly came about when, in 1884, the Commission on the State of American Judaism of the UAHC suggested the possibility of admitting YMHAs to membership. The initiative had come from the YMHA movement. Though favored by Jacob Schiff, Simon Wolf, and most others on the executive committee, the recommendation was opposed for a number of reasons: the UAHC was conceived as a congregational body only, the fear that the YMHAs would outnumber and overwhelm the congregations, and that the YMHAs were largely social organizations. Though the UAHC rejected the YMHA, the fact that it was considered at all reveals the Y's denominational pretensions, and demonstrates the tensions created by the religious aspirations of a secular insititution.[56]

The tension decreased when religious elements intruded upon the secular YMHA. Thus, the 1890 convention of the United YMHA of America was held in Cincinnati with several young Reform rabbis in attendance including Maurice Eisenberg, Alexander Geismar, Charles Levi, Edward S. Levy, David Philipson, and Joseph Silverman, most of whom became permanent officers. As they undoubtedly did in their home YMHAs, they invested a religious note into the proceedings of the convention. The constitution adopted stated a newfound "desir[e] to improve the mental, moral, social and *religious* condition of the Jewish youth of this country" (emphasis added). As above, the 1890 statement of objectives reflected the typical program of the contemporary YMHA; as exemplified by the Louisville YMHA of that year, whose statement of purpose read: "the objects of which shall be the moral, *religious,* educational, social, and physical advancement of its members" (emphasis added). The word "religious" in both statements was a new addition to the YMHA platform and reflects the growing acceptance of religious work in the secular YMHA.[57]

Jewish Holidays at the YMHA

The best example of the secularization of Jewish religious practice is the YMHA approach to the holidays. Understandably, the historical holidays with the least religious and ceremonial baggage were emphasized, those considered to be the most fun for the younger set: Hanukkah and Purim. In 1878, the New York YMHA began its annual tradition of sponsoring a Hanukkah festival. First held in the Academy of Music and later at Madison Square Garden, the festival consisted of tableaux and pageants based on the story of the Maccabees, and numbered several hundred participants. Furthermore, the pageants were prepared and supervised by leading local rabbis. Similarly, the Philadelphia YMHA held an annual Purim ball from 1879 to 1910. Operettas and cantatas on Jewish themes were featured at the Purim balls of both the leading YMHAs.[58]

Both holiday celebrations had some degree of outside inspiration. Purim had long been the holiday of choice for the Jewish version of the American charity ball, and Hanukkah was destined to become the American Jewish equivalent to Christmas. But the YMHA exploited the holidays for specifically Jewish purposes as well. Historian Jonathan Sarna has described the annual Hanukkah festival as one of the YMHA's "most notable achievements"; it rescued the holiday from obscurity, and raised it above the status of a minor festival. Furthermore, the "grand revival" of Hanukkah exemplified the growing secularization of Judaism in America. The element of secular Jewishness was made explicit by the description of the Hanukkah festival as a "Jewish *National* Celebration," and once again, Hebrew and Jewish history were stressed.[59]

As the 1879 playbill advertising the celebration gushed:

GRAND REVIVAL of the *Jewish National Holiday of Chanucka.* . . . The greatest Jewish event chronicled in Post-Biblical History, the recollection of which ever awakens the true Jewish spirit and patriotism, will be celebrated by the YMHA, in a manner and style never before equalled, and worthy of the subject and occasion. Living representations of the stirring scenes and glowing events of the Maccabean war and triumph will be vividly protrayed [sic], concluding with a grand procession of the return of the victorious heroes. . . . Costumes new and original, historically correct, and specially designed to illustrate the Maccabean period. Choruses of Hebrew Melodies will be rendered by 100 children of the Hebrew Orphan Asylum.[60]

In a development analogous to the rise of secular Jewish movements in Europe—for example, the Jewish Enlightenment (*Haskalah),* modern Jewish studies (*Wissenschaft des Judentums),* Zionism, and Jewish socialism—the YMHA played a central role in the construction of an ethnic Jewish identity in America. It did so by substituting modern, secular, "national" elements such as Hebrew, Jewish History, and youth-oriented holidays for the traditional elements of Judaism such as Torah, Talmud, and Mitzvot. Foreshadowing the ethnic emphasis of Conservative Judaism, the transposition was legitimated by the participation of Historical School rabbis.

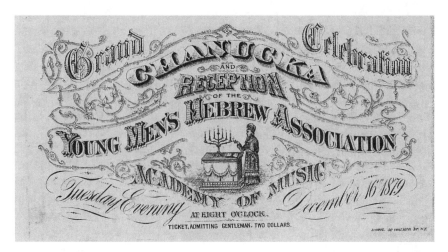

Fig. 7. Ticket to the "Grand Chanucka Celebration and Reception of the YMHA," 1879. Courtesy of the 92nd Street YM-YWHA Archives.

The trend continued into the next era of YMHA history when the classical YMHA—its period of gradual Judaization—culminated in 1900 and a new era began when the New York YMHA moved into its new flagship building on Lexington Avenue and 92d Street. The sponsor of the new facility was Jacob Schiff, Jewish philanthropist extraordinaire, and soon to be the patron and founder of the Jewish Theological Seminary. Significantly, Schiff chose as his architect Arnold Brunner, author of the article on synagogue architecture in the *Jewish Encyclopedia* (1902) and designer of many prominent turn-of-the-century synagogue buildings. The modern YMHA would be, in its architectural effect at least, a "synagogue" for the new century. Looking to the future, the newest YMHA building was equipped as a full-service Jewish community center, including religious, recreational, and educational facilities to accommodate thousands of young people.[61]

To direct the expanded religious activities of the new YMHA, a new department was created as a standing committee of the board of directors, called the Committee on Religious Work. The first chairman was Frederick de Sola Mendes, the rabbi of Temple Shaaray Tefila. The committee's initial responsibility was to plan High Holy Day services, an activity that was so successful that it became a permanent part of the Y's program. Just as the new building established the permanence of the institution, the new department institutionalized the inclusion of Jewish religious content in the YMHA program.[62]

The first "High Holy Day services" were held in the fall of 1900. The announcement of September 10 invited the "members and the friends of the Association" to the newly instituted "Divine Services" for the two days of Rosh Hashana and for Yom Kippur. The services were offered without charge, and were advertised as a "Free Synagogue." The invitation concluded, "A competent

Cantor has been engaged and prominent Rabbis will preach. —F. de Sola Mendes, Chairman, Committee on Religious Work."[63]

Of course, "prominent rabbis" tended to have prior engagements on the high holidays and so younger, less established rabbis were hired instead. This served two purposes: the younger officiant was well received as the peer of the "congregants," and the YMHA services thus became a training ground for student rabbis. For the "Holy-Day Services" of 1902, it was later announced that "Mr. Rudolph I. Coffee will officiate at all the services and deliver the lectures. Rev. J. D. Sapir will be the cantor and will be assisted by a trained choir of male voices. Miss Henrietta Micholson will act as organist. Those who attended the services last year know how inspiring they were. We hope to do just as well this year." At the time, Rudolph Coffee was a student at the newly reconstituted Jewish Theological Seminary. The relationship between the YMHA and JTS would continue to develop thereafter.[64]

The success of the holiday services inspired the institution of Friday evening religious exercises. As reported in the YMHA monthly (the *Bulletin*) of June 1902: "All who are interested in the religious work of the YMHA must rejoice at the noteworthy progress which was achieved during the past season. Not only do we attract a large attendance each week, but what is more, there is a steady and growing body of young people who now make it their Sabbath duty to join us each week. Next winter we hope to enlist a still larger number of earnest Jews and Jewesses in the work of upbuilding our faith." The success of the Friday night service was indicated by the growth in attendance. In 1901, the average attendance was 172; in 1902, some 231; and in the early part of 1903, more than 400.[65]

In August 1902, the *Bulletin* reported:

Fri. Eve. Religious Exercises. "The fact that last season the attendance had increased 100% over that of the former year proved conclusively that this movement had come to stay, and we confidently expect that this season will show a similar increase over the past. It is unfortunately true that many of our people do not observe the Sabbath owing to the stress of our present-day life, but most are only too anxious to attend service on Friday evening. Those who come to our religious exercises will find here that Sabbath quietude and religious tone that 'maketh glad the heart.'"[66]

And, in November:

Notes & Comments. A very graceful compliment was paid the Association by Rev. Dr. G. Gottheil a short time ago for its religious work. Dr. Gottheil had spoken at one of the Fri. Eve. religious exercises, and was so well pleased with the large audience and the real religious feeling displayed by it that he made public mention of it in a sermon delivered on the Day of Atonement at Temple Emanu-El. Coming from so high an authority, encomiums such as these are indeed very pleasant and very encouraging.[67]

Following the example of New York, YMHAs around the country began to see the necessity for religious programming. By 1915, regular Sabbath services were conducted by twenty-eight YMHAs, and in addition, some forty-five associations sponsored religious schools. In 1917, YMHA leader I. E. Goldwasser described the movement's aims in the *Communal Register* of the New York Kehillah. Based on his experience with YMHA activity, he strongly suggested "that if the Association is to win the confidence of the neighborhood, provision must be made for religious services." He especially noted the growing popularity of the "Friday night service or forum," and described the event as follows: "In a number of our buildings, groups of young men and women flock to the buildings on Friday evening, and after participating in a brief service and listening to a short sermon, discuss with the speaker, the subject matter of the address."[68]

It must be added that religious services were not always the most popular activities of the YMHA. In New York, out of a total March 1902 attendance of 15,728, "Religious Exercises" drew only 919; other activities were far bigger draws, such as the "Library" (3,342), the "Gymnasium" (2,217), "Entertainments" (2,230), and "Free lectures" (2,184). Similarly, class attendance in the Educational Department reflected the popularity of various subjects: "Bookkeeping—71 (highest), Hebrew—8 (lowest), Jewish History [taught by R. Coffee]—19, Elocution—22, Arithmetic—59." To bolster the popularity of the two lowest drawing classes, new instructors were engaged: "Mr. B. Russell Throckmorton has been appointed instructor of the class in elocution, and Mr. M. M. Kaplan in Hebrew." At the time, the arrival of the young Mordecai Kaplan was but a minor event in the life of the Y's fledgling religious department; later, his presence in the YMHA would prove auspicious indeed.[69]

In order to increase members' participation in the religious program, the Jewish holiday cycle was exploited to the fullest. As in the earlier period, holidays were celebrated in the American style, festively and fashionably. Now, however, Jewish holidays besides Purim and Chanukah were observed. Thus, the festival of Sukkot was revived in 1902:

Our Religious Work . . . many of those present were attracted by the desire to visit our Succah. Mr. Rudolph I. Coffee delivered the sermon and preached on the "Royal Palm." During the past summer Mr. Coffee had been to the Hawaiian Islands. His sermon that evening was based on the growth of the palm tree, which he saw there. The topmost branch of the royal palm is the Lulav. . . . Succoth was celebrated in the building with all its old-time enthusiasm. On this occasion over 400 people were entertained in the Succah which had been built by the Association, and many exclamations of surprise and delight were heard when they entered the commodious and beautifully decorated structure. . . . Despite the crush nothing occurred to mar the pleasure of the festive occasion.[70]

A similar problem of overcrowding occurred in October 1908, when "a commodious Sukkah was built for the purpose of accommodating at least 200 people." When four hundred showed up instead, the problem was solved by dividing the assembly into two sections, and "dismissing the first before admitting the second." Thereafter, the Sukkah "was also used by the children of the Sabbath School who partook of the good things offered and who were instructed as to the meaning of the festival."[71]

In 1905, a Sukkot celebration in Boston brought "over 1000 people to the

Fig. 8. The YMHA Sukkah, 1908. Courtesy of the 92nd Street YM-YWHA Archives.

YMHA. . . . [It was] the first time in the history of Boston Jewry that any lay organization observed the holiday and also the first time that any organization erected a booth." It has been observed that the biblical holiday of Sukkot was the inspiration for the American holiday of Thanksgiving. This connection was not lost on the religious leaders of the YMHA, as when in 1902 the New York YMHA sponsored "Thanksgiving Day Services": "the services consisted of selections from our Friday night service book and songs. . . . Mr. Rudolph I. Coffee spoke on the 'Meaning of Thanksgiving Day to the Jews.' He spoke of the fact that although this is an American institution which originated on American soil, it nevertheless is taken from the spirit of our Jewish religion."[72]

Even American holidays with no apparent Jewish connection were celebrated and given some Jewish educational content. For instance, in 1902:

The last monthly social was held on New Year's night and was a most enjoyable event. Very nearly 300 members were attracted to the building. . . . The feature of the evening, however, was an excellent address by Rev. Dr. H[enry] P[ereira] Mendes, who spoke on the physical, mental, and spiritual development of young men, and in a heart-to-heart talk lasting about 20 min. made a deep impression upon his hearers, and was rapturously applauded at the end of his address.[73]

As in the earlier period of the YMHA, the "Joyful Occasion" of Purim was observed: "The Association, this year, carried out the old-time Jewish custom of celebrating Purim happily and joyously . . . through the means of the Minstrel

Fig. 9. Passover Seder, 1906. YMHA Superintendent William Mitchell (holding round matzah) officiated; a rather glum looking Rabbi Rudolph Coffee (wearing caftan) sits at left. Courtesy of the 92nd Street YM-YWHA Archives.

Show. . . . While the aim of the Association is educational, we should not over-look the social side of our work, and the coming of Purim gave us a good ex-cuse." At the new YMHA, the Purim festival had become more than an excuse for a charity ball, however; it was now an "old-time Jewish custom," which had its educational aspect as well: "On March 21 [at a Friday evening service] Rev. S. Greenfield spoke on the meaning of Purim . . . the message of Purim: not re-venge, but charity."[74]

The quintessential American Jewish holiday is Passover, and the YMHA was no exception. In spring 1904, the Y held its first Community Seder—for mem-bers only—on Passover, which would become an annual tradition lasting until World War II. New York's English-language Orthodox newspaper, the *Hebrew Standard*, described the original event in the most approving terms:

For the first time in the history of the YMHA a Seder service for young men was held in its building on the first night of Passover. It was intended for all members in whose home the Seder service is no longer given, or who, on account of being alone in the city, had no oppor-tunity of witnessing one. About thirty young men [attended]. . . . The service was conducted by the superintendent, Mr. William Mitchell, who attended with his family, and was host of the occasion. . . . It was carried on in the old-fashioned style, and was indeed an inspiring oc-casion. The majority of the young men had never before witnessed a Seder service and were so well impressed with the event that in all probability the association will make the service an annual feature on a larger scale.[75]

One is struck first of all by the ignorance of the Seder on the part of the young men and hence the nonobservance of Passover by their families. By offering its own Seder service, the YMHA construed itself as a substitute for the Jewish home, its superintendent standing in for the father, his family serving as family for all. Since the German-Jewish home was no longer enlivened by Jewish tradition, the YMHA stood ready and willing to become the center of Jewish life. The idea was carried forward when in 1912, "Eighty young men gathered around the table for the Y's first public Passover seder."[76]

The YMHA continued to inspire "private" Seder dinners as well. One was the outgrowth of a singles' group formed at the YMHA. As Philip Cowen, editor of the *American Hebrew,* recalled, "One of the finest fruits of the YMHA was . . . a unique society that we called the Celibates. The idea was to have an occasional gathering and when any married they had to pay the penalty of a dinner." As the group matured, Mrs. Cowen suggested "having a Celibate Seder. We invited the group to bring with them any or all of their children to celebrate the Passover." Cowen felt the need to defend the revival of Jewish tradition by comparing Passover to American holidays: "We have always looked upon the Seder service as in the nature of a Thanksgiving or Fourth of July celebration."[77]

The "Celibate" society was a friendship circle brought together by the YMHA. Like the Havurah groups of today, the YMHA society found it natural and desirable to extend their group sociability into the realm of religious celebration. While outside the province of the YMHA, it should be added that the "Celibate Seder" inspired Philip Cowen's wife to edit "a book for the Passover with an adequate English translation. [Mrs. Cowen] kept her word and a few years later published 'The Seder Service' which, because of its fine English and musical arrangement was instrumental in bringing about a revival of the Passover celebration in the United States."[78]

In general, YMHA holiday "revivals" had a salutary effect on the state of American Judaism, as for example, the holiday of Shavuot. In 1902, "On Tues. eve., June 10, religious exercises were held to commemorate the festival of Shevuoth. The sermon was preached by Mr. Rudolph I. Coffee, on 'The Book of Ruth.' Mr. Coffee also announced that, because of the success of the past winter's work, it has been decided to expand the scope of the religious work, and this Shevuoth service, which was the first of its kind in the building, which will be held yearly."[79]

And finally, what of the "Grand Revival of Chanucka" so lauded in the earlier period? In 1910, discussion of the "Chanukah Play by the children [was] tabled. Mr. Younker proposed a Chanukah Play to be given by the children of our Hebrew School under the direction of Mrs. Morgenroth, as in former years. These religious plays (he explained) were introduced a few years ago, and are always eagerly looked forward to by the children, their parents and relatives, and others who frequent the building." Apparently, the celebration of Hanukkah had not matched the high expectations of the earlier period, having become an excuse for children's theater and little more. But the innovation it represented, that of the YMHA employing a Jewish holiday to fullest advantage in promoting its religious program, did succeed; only now the strategy was extended to every holiday on the calendar.[80]

Women and the YWHA

By the first decade of the twentieth century, then, the YMHA had become thoroughly Judaized, including religious services and holiday celebrations as a matter of course. The next phase in the development of the YMHA movement would incorporate Judaism even more integrally. This was to be the contribution of Jewish women, who would now achieve some measure of independence. Judging by the name alone, it might seem that the Young Women's Hebrew Association was the women's version of the Young Men's Hebrew Association and nothing more. But just as the YMHA was no mere knockoff of its Christian namesake, so too was the idea of the YWHA both a borrowing and an innovation at once. As a communal agency run entirely by and for women, the YWHA provided an important political arena for Jewish women in the early part of the twentieth century. As a pioneering Jewish institution combining social and religious services, the YWHA became one of the principal sources of the Jewish community center movement.

The immediate precursor of the YWHA movement was the participation of women in the life of the YMHA. Early on, women were admitted to some YMHA activities on a limited basis, such as the "musical and dramatic corps which included young ladies" at the YMHA of Lafayette, Indiana, in 1868, and likewise, the class in elocution and English literature of the Philadelphia YMHA, which permitted women to join in 1876. Whereas the New York YMHA voted against the admittance of women in 1874, other YMHAs proved more liberal. The YMHAs of Chicago and Philadelphia voted to admit women as full members in 1877 and 1880 respectively, and in 1878 a YMHA in Wisconsin changed its name to "Madison Hebrew Association" in order to include women. Following the 1888 establishment of the YWHA auxiliary in New York, similar women's auxiliaries were organized in cities around the country, including Louisville, Denver, New Orleans, Columbus, Birmingham, and Washington, D.C. Women's participation in YMHA activities soon expanded, as when the Louisville YMHA instituted gymnasium classes for women in 1891.

An early Young Womens' Hebrew Association had been founded in 1888, but as an auxiliary to the New York YMHA. In 1889, the downtown YMHA joined with two other educational agencies to form the Hebrew Institute. Soon renamed the Educational Alliance, it was to become the premier Jewish settlement of the Lower East Side and the flagship institution of a nationwide movement. The YMHA thus played a significant role in the emerging settlement movement, an institutional trend largely led and staffed by women. Thus, the first Young *Women's* Hebrew Association was founded in New York City in 1888 for the purpose of immigrant education. Under the presidency of public school educator Julia Richman, this early YWHA—the first time the name appeared—only remained in existence for a few years and was never more than an auxiliary to the YMHA.

The first independent YWHA was established in New York on February 6, 1902, for the purpose of "promoting Judaism among young Jewish women and of instilling in them principles of kindness and benevolence and of improving their mental, moral, religious, social, and physical condition." By the end of the year, the YWHA had rented a building at 1584 Lexington Avenue and established itself as a Jewish community center, now self-consciously religious in orientation.[81]

Its principal founder and guiding spirit was Bella Unterberg (née Epstein), the wife of shirt manufacturer and Jewish philanthropist Israel Unterberg. Born in 1868 to a Russian Jewish immigrant family (her father had arrived in 1855 and fought in the Civil War), Bella Epstein received both a New York City public school education and a sound Jewish upbringing. As a young woman in her twenties, she was profoundly affected by the efflorescence of Jewish women's social activism during the 1890s. Supporting and supported by the parallel efforts of her husband, Mrs. Unterberg became a communal leader in her own right, directing campaigns for the Ladies' Fuel and Aid Society and the Women's Committee of the Council for National Defense. But it was the YWHA which became her foremost concern and "favorite child." She became so closely identified with the YMHA, in fact, that her biographer could quite rightly state: "the story of the Y.W.H.A. is from the beginning the story of Mrs. Unterberg, its record Mrs. Unterberg's record, its triumphs and achievements, her triumphs and achievements."

The institution had its beginnings in a meeting held by Mrs. Unterberg in her home at 143 West 77th Street. The eighteen women present elected Mrs. Unterberg as president, Mrs. Henry Pereira Mendes as vice president, and Mrs. Simon Liebovitz as treasurer. Mrs. Mendes was the wife of the *hazan* of the Spanish and Portugese Synagogue, Shearith Israel, and in addition to the vice presidency was also elected "religious guide" of the organization. Regarding its mission, the newly elected president recommended "that the Society establish an institution akin in character to the Y.M.H.A. but combining therewith features of religious and spiritualizing tendencies." The minutes conclude: "After considerable discussion on the question of the Society's name, it was agreed that it be called and known as the Young Women's Hebrew Association."

So the new institution would be modeled after the YMHA as a community center dedicated to the uplift—both social and spiritual—of young Jews. In Bella Unterberg's view, the best way to reach young people was "by thoroughly fraternizing and associating with them and by placing before them opportunities of pleasant and refined social pleasures to attract them gradually to better, nobler and more spiritual ideals." By the beginning of 1903, the YWHA had rented a

Fig. 10. Bella Unterberg. Portrait presented at the dedication of
the new YWHA building, 1914. Courtesy of the 92nd Street YM-
YWHA Archives.

building at 1584 Lexington Avenue and soon established itself as a vital community center in the burgeoning Jewish neighborhood of Harlem. From the start,
its primary aim was to provide social and recreational activities for Jewish working girls. As such it was an immediate success, recording a total attendance of
more than twenty-one thousand in its first year alone. Mrs. Unterberg soon recognized the need for larger quarters and in 1906 rededicated an expanded and
renovated facility. The building could now house eighteen female residents and
would henceforth become a boarding home as well as a community center. At
the dedication, Unterberg asked those assembled: "Can you imagine doing a
greater good than supplying hundreds of hard working girls with a chance of bet-
tering their condition and of helping them, in many cases, from a condition of
want and necessity to a place in the world where they can become independent
and self-supporting?" Under her beneficent direction, the new YWHA was a
kind of social settlement house for young working Jewish women.

The essential factor setting the new YWHA apart was its pronounced Jewishness. While the YMHA movement had begun to pay greater attention to the observance of Jewish religion and the preservation of Jewish identity, its guiding

Fig. 11. The YWHA building on 110th Street, 1918. Notice the signs to the left, advertising both a swimming pool and Friday evening services. Courtesy of the 92nd Street YM-YWHA Archives.

ethos was still Americanism, not Judaism. Following the turn of the century, many Jewish women would rebel against this emphasis and make their version of the settlement house a positive force for Jewish life. This was part of a general backlash against the assimilationist tendency of the first quarter-century of mass immigration, but must also be seen as a women's movement for the "Judaization" of American Jewry.

In her address at the dedication ceremony of the YWHA building in February 1903, for example, Rebeka Kohut "laid stress upon the necessity of having religion as the foundation stone of the new organization, and paid a tribute to the religious work now being done by the YMHA." The president of the YMHA added: "I wish right here to lay stress upon what I deem to be the cornerstone of success of such work, and that is the religious nature of it. . . . I do not mean that all we wish of the young woman who may come or be attracted, is religion— prayers. . . . But I mean that the various activities of the Association must all be leavened by [religion]." Likewise, a 1912 newspaper article quoted Miss Sophia Berger, superintendent of the YWHA, as saying, "Back of all that we do, is the thought of preserving the essential Jewishness of our people. As Jews we want to save our Judaism. As Jews we bring these girls in here that they may find shelter and help and find, too, the God of their fathers."[82]

The YWHA, even more than the YMHA, was therefore defined as a Jewish center from the start. The program was further expanded in 1912 when the

Fig. 12. YWHA Auditorium as a Synagogue. Courtesy of the 92nd Street YM-YWHA Archives.

YWHA conducted a "two weeks' whirlwind campaign to raise $200,000 for a new dormitory and headquarters for the YWHA." Intriguingly, the director of the campaign effort was Louis Allen Abramson, later to become a leading architect of the synagogue-center building boom. Abramson succeeded in raising the money for the YWHA "to construct its own building. The cornerstone at 31 West 110th Street was laid on April 26, 1914, and the building was dedicated and its Synagogue consecrated on November 22, 1914." In his journal entry for August 1914, Mordecai Kaplan lauded two female acquaintances "for their painstaking efforts in helping to erect such a useful and wonderful edifice." And at the dedication exercises of the new YWHA building, "Miss Augusta Wolf, representing the younger members of the organization, urged that the new home be made distinctly a centre for the propagation of Jewish ideals, Jewish traditions, Jewish culture and Jewish religion. The special care of the association, she declared, was to make Jewish girls grow up into Jewish women."[83]

Since its keynote was Judaism, the YWHA had included a synagogue on its premises from early in its history. The YWHA synagogue functioned as an independent congregation catering to the surrounding community, not a women's congregation as such. To suit the constituents of that highly Americanized immigrant neighborhood, it offered a modernized Orthodox service—the traditional liturgy, but with an English sermon, mixed seating, and choral music—a new religious mix that soon would be called Conservative Judaism. Apparently, such innovation could be accepted more readily in a women's institution. In the new building of 1914, the auditorium doubled as the synagogue and services were

Fig. 13. Same Auditorium (see Fig. 12) converted to "secular" purpose—a Purim play! Courtesy of the 92nd Street YM-YWHA Archives.

conducted every Friday night, Saturday morning, and on Jewish holidays. The other major Jewish aspect of the YWHA was its curriculum consisting of classes in Hebrew, Bible, and Jewish history. This was coordinated with an Experimental Hebrew school for girls conducted at the YWHA by the Bureau of Jewish Education (of the New York City Kehillah).

But the new building was not yet complete. "Additional funds subsequently were raised so that a swimming pool was added to the facilities by October 1916. In addition to the Synagogue (which also could function as an auditorium) and the pool, the building included a dining room, library, gymnasium, rooms for classes and clubs, and residential accommodation for about 150 young women." The new YWHA of 1914–16, replete with a "shul and a pool," was in fact a synagogue-center! What had been implicit in the functioning of the YMHA was now explicit in the building plant of the YWHA.[84]

Of course, the YWHA offered far more than religious services and swimming lessons. In 1917, a few years after the completion of its new eight-story facility on 110th Street overlooking Central Park, the New York YWHA was described as "the only large institution of its kind in America." The description of the "modern social center" continued: "Besides being a most comfortable home for one hundred and seventy girls, the building is also a true center for the communal interests of the neighborhood; it houses a Commercial School, a Hebrew School, Trade Classes in Dressmaking, Millinery, Domestic Science, classes in Hebrew, Bible Study, Jewish History, Art, English to Foreigners, Advanced English, French,

Spanish, and Nursing. There is a completely equipped modern gymnasium and swimming pool." Serving both its residential population and the larger community, the YWHA had become a full-service Jewish center. Housing both a synagogue and a swimming pool, the YWHA was an early exemplar of the synagogue-center movement (Mordecai Kaplan's Jewish Center did not appear until three years later).

Additional amenities included "musical salons" held on Sunday evenings and weekly dances for young women and men on the outdoor Roof Garden that proved to be especially popular. The roof was also used during the summer for day care programs for "anaemic and cardiac children, and the children of poor families." The YWHA also sponsored summer camping including hiking, canoeing, and all manner of sporting activities. Back in the city, athletics was fostered in classes in swimming, tennis, fencing, and so on. Dance was especially popular, being offered in several varieties. An employment bureau was provided for young women in need of a job, and during the First World War, the YWHA cooperated extensively with numerous efforts for war relief. Finally, the earlier emphasis on immigrant adjustment was retained, but from a more sympathetic point of view: "An important work to which a great deal of attention has been paid is the formation of Americanization Classes for Aliens, to help lessen the tragedy in the social evolution of the immigrants."

Rabbis and the "Jewish" YMHA

The new era of the "Jewish" YMHA was ushered in not only by the women of the community, but, as always, by the rabbis. As described above, the Boston YMHA held a special "Rabbis' Night" during the Sukkot holiday of 1905, bringing together Orthodox and Reform rabbis for the same occasion. A third rabbi on the program, the Reverend Dr. J. H. Landau, was also the organizer of the event. Like the others, he delivered a "sermon" that night; as did Rabbi Margolis, Landau spoke on the return of Jews to farming, referring to the Jewish colonies in Palestine. Rather than being a congregational rabbi like the others, however, Landau worked as the "superintendent" of the YMHA. More remarkable than the visitation of rabbis to the YMHA, therefore, was the new role represented by Landau, hired by the YMHA as its director and in-house rabbi. The phenomenon would later be repeated elsewhere, but in the meantime, rabbis increased their general participation in YMHA life during the early 1900s.[85]

As the centrist rabbi of the YMHA, Landau was able to bring together the religious extremes. Though not a graduate of the new Jewish Theological Seminary, Landau was thus solidly within the unifying tradition of the "United Synagogue," or as Solomon Schechter expressed it, "Catholic Israel." For this reason, the Conservative movement soon took the lead in YMHA activity. For example, in 1911, Rabbi Phineas Israeli (Jewish Theological Seminary, 1902) of Boston's Blue Hill Avenue Synagogue linked Conservative Judaism and the

YMHA: "Religiously, we may feel encouraged by the new impetus that has recently been given to conservatism, as well as by the awakening of our young people, evidenced by the reorganization of the Boston Young Men's Hebrew Organization, . . . [and] the remarkable growth of the Dorchester YMHA, thanks to its leader, is carried on in a decidedly Jewish spirit." And in the same year, Charles Hoffman (Jewish Theological Seminary, 1904), a prominent Conservative rabbi in Newark, New Jersey, suggested that "something will have to be done, and done quickly, to organize these young people and surround them with a Jewish atmosphere before they are completely lost to us. United effort by the various congregations of our city ought to enable us to build and maintain a YMHA, where amidst innocent amusement, social intercourse and occasionally religious instruction . . . these young people could . . . grow up imbued with care for their faith."[86]

Besides the centrist position of Conservatism, at least one other factor contributed to its pro-YMHA attitude: the location of its seminary college in New York City. As we saw earlier, rabbinical students often worked part-time at the New York YMHA; these were almost all students at the reorganized Jewish Theological Seminary. Most active among them was Rudolph Coffee (class of 1904), who during his student days was also an assistant instructor in education at Teachers College and superintendent of the Hebrew Orphan Asylum. At the same time, "he also organized and headed the religious branch of the YMHA of NY." In 1916, Coffee moved to Pittsburgh to take the pulpit of the Tree of Life Congregation. There, he continued his YMHA work as one of the founders and later honorary president and member of the advisory board of the Pittsburgh YMHA. Nor was Coffee alone. The "Alumni Notes" of the *JTS Student's Annual* of 1915 reveals much YMHA activity among early seminary graduates. For example, Moses J. S. Abels organized YMHAs in Wilmington, Delaware, and in Altoona, Pennsylvania, and Louis M. Epstein organized both a YMHA and a YWHA in Dallas, Texas. Moses Eckstein served as the president of the YMHA in Kingston, New York, C. David Matt joined the board of directors of the YMHA in Minneapolis, and Elias L. Solomon became the director of the Bronx YMHA. Aaron L. Robison made his career at the YMHA, beginning in 1911 as a teacher of religion at the YWHA, later the rabbi of the New York YMHA, and eventually becoming the director of the Newark YMHA.[87]

At the same time, significant developments were taking place within the leadership structure of the New York YMHA. During the years 1911–13, two rising young rabbis joined the Y hierarchy. In 1911, Judah L. Magnes, chairman of the New York Kehillah, was elected to the Y's board of directors and became chairman of the Committee on Religious Work. Two years later, Mordecai M. Kaplan was elected to the board to "fill a long-felt want in the work of the Religious Department." Kaplan then became chairman of the committee with Magnes as vice-chairman. Magnes and Kaplan, soon to be the two most influential rabbis of the contemporary New York Jewish community, served a common purpose in the YMHA. As aspiring communal leaders, they joined the board of directors of the YMHA and from that position were instrumental in its religious affairs. In 1911, Magnes instituted the "YMHA Congregation" with Kaplan's help, thus contributing the idea of a congregation under YMHA auspices. In the following year, they recommended a young rabbi, Adolph Coblenz, to serve as the Y's first full-time religious director.[88]

Kaplan, it should be noted, saw the achievement as somewhat dubious, allowing his colleague full credit:

Magnes became the chairman of the religious work in the Association, and he raised the hopes of Warburg and one or two others that he would revolutionize conditions at the YMHA and bring new life into its activities which had already been lagging for some time. In consistency with his shutting down the organ at the Madison Ave. Congregation [B'nai Jeshurun] which he then held, Magnes insisted upon its exclusion from the services at the Association. He attempted to organize a congregation out of the young men but failed, because he had neither the patience nor the tact to handle them properly.[89]

Kaplan's cynicism aside, we see here several significant aspects of Magnes's involvement with the YMHA. As noted above, the organization of a religious congregation within the social precincts of the YMHA was an innovative idea, one that Magnes hoped might "revolutionize conditions" there. As part of his new program, Magnes eliminated the organ so as to replace the Reformist elements of the service with his brand of Jewish traditionalism. Acting in a joint capacity as pulpit rabbi at B'nai Jeshurun and as religious director at the YMHA, he personified the cooperative possibilities of the disparate institutions. Of the two innovative rabbis, however, it was Kaplan whose involvement—and whose negative view of the YMHA—proved to be the most propitious for the future of the Jewish center and synagogue-center movements.

As noted above, Mordecai Kaplan was introduced to the New York YMHA as early as 1902, when as a rabbinical student at the Jewish Theological Seminary he was employed there as an instructor of Hebrew. In 1910, his first year on the faculty of the seminary, Kaplan was asked by Felix M. Warburg to speak at the high holiday services of the YMHA; thus began his participation in the religious life of the Y.[90]

Of his first experience with YMHA services, he would later write: "I accepted [Warburg's invitation] only on condition that the organ be removed. . . . Although I personally had no strong objections to an organ, I felt that I would shock my friends and folks if I would consent to officiate at the YMHA so long as they retained the organ." When, after helping Magnes initiate the YMHA congregation in 1911, Kaplan complained of being pressed into further service: "I was expected to help him conduct the services; and as the A[ssociation] had no one to take charge of them, I was expected to do most of the work. I tried various means to arouse an interest, but it was of no avail. With the exclusion of the organ the services grew even more dull than before."[91]

Characteristically, Kaplan felt that his more worthwhile contribution to the

YMHA lay not in the religious realm of the congregation but in the social sphere of personal interactions:

My work that year in the Association that to my mind was of any value was that which I did when I would meet in an informal way a number of the leading young fellows. . . . I succeeded in winning a hearing at least for Judaism, among men who had conceived a prejudice against it. One of these fellows is [Harry] Gluckesman [*sic*], who has in the meantime become assistant superintendent. Ever since then Jewish questions are no longer pooh poohed, and are referred to with a certain amount of respect.[92]

While Jewishness was becoming a more natural part of the YMHA, Judaism, as embodied by the religious services of the Y congregation, remained anathema to the young members of the Association. To better relate to the clientele, Kaplan recommended a series of young rabbis to direct religious activities at the Y. The first, Adolph Coblenz, "turned out a total failure. He had not the least conception of social work." His successor, Leo Mannheimer, fared no better. Rather than instituting new social and educational programs, the rabbis simply rehashed the same old strategy of making the service more attractive.[93]

Yet inattendance remained a problem. The cancellation of weekly religious services at the YMHA was discussed at a meeting of the Religious Committee on September 15, 1913. Reform Rabbi Samuel Schulman "declared himself strongly opposed to any plan that would involve the giving up of services. He maintained that it was the duty of the Association to give the young men an idea of what constituted Jewish religious life, as it was to furnish them with gymnasium, educational classes and club facilities." Judah Magnes now joined Kaplan as a naysayer, arguing "that since a vast number of young men refused to attend services of any character, be they orthodox or reformed, it might be best to dispense with the services." Magnes, however, offered an alternative, suggesting "to have in their stead, a Friday Night Meeting with addresses by eminent speakers on live Jewish topics, not necessarily of a religious or theological character. These addresses might be preceded by the reading of a chapter from the Bible and followed by Jewish songs." The chairman of the committee, Mordecai Kaplan, then concluded: "After considerable discussion, the Committee came to the conclusion that for the year 1913–1914 the Friday Night Services be continued and every effort made to render them attractive and well attended."[94]

Once again, the intractable problem of religious apathy plagued the rabbis. Besides tampering with the service, they asked themselves, how else to meet the dilemma? Two weeks after the meeting, Kaplan wrote to Felix Warburg, the president of the New York YMHA (and shortly, of the YMHA Council):

In my opinion, all YMHA work, which at present is still to a large extent a mere fumbling in the dark, would be rendered more definite and effective, if ranged about a religious, rather than a purely social or philanthropic ideal. By this I mean, that, instead of confining ourselves to holding out such distractions as might compete successfully with the dangerous distractions that tempt young men, we should seek to stimulate in them a positive enthusiasm for Judaism. . . . It must be borne in mind, however, that it is futile to expect YMHAs to adopt this course without leaders who unite in themselves the qualifications of social worker as well as those of the religious worker. That there are no such leaders at the present time is due to the fact that the YMHA movement has only begun to assume the proportions necessary to call them forth. Instead, however, of leaving it to chance for these leaders to arise, it were advisable that the National YMHA get into touch with the two Seminaries in this country, which prepare men for the ministry, and urge them to encourage some of their students to prepare themselves for a career of YMHA leadership.[95]

Kaplan's solution was the training of a new type of Jewish leader, one who would combine the talents of the rabbi and the social worker, an individual who could effectively function as leader of both synagogue and center. Such individuals did in fact arise, exemplified by Conservative rabbi and Jewish Center leader Aaron Robison. Having succeeded Coblenz and Mannheimer as religious director in 1914, Robison assumed the new title of director of religious and social work of the YMHA, reflecting both an expanded responsiblity and a new emphasis on religious-social integration. As he wrote at the time, "Not only has it become necessary that Jewish social work be made religious, but it is equally important that our religious work be socialized."[96] In 1918, Robison ascended to the highest position in the YMHA bureaucracy, executive director. He resigned after one year to take the same position at the Newark YM/YWHA, being replaced in New York by another rabbi, Lee Levinger. Both continued to exert their influence beyond their local YMHAs through active participation in the Jewish Center movement.[97]

On November 2, 1913, the period of the "Jewish" YMHA reached its climax when a new national movement was formed, the Council of Young Men's Hebrew and Kindred Associations (CYMHKA). The name, with its evocative acronym (*simcha* is Hebrew for "happiness" or "a celebration"), was proposed by Louis Marshall. At the founding convention, held in the New York YMHA, a board of "experts" was appointed, including Mordecai Kaplan and Judah Magnes. Magnes was responsible for "the problem of building up in every existing institution the feeling that it should not be alone a center for educational and religious work as such, but that it shall become a center for Jewish communal life [in the city] in which it is located." With the founding of CYMHKA, the YMHA was officially designated a Jewish center, and the Jewish center movement was officially begun, shepherded by none other than Magnes and Kaplan.[98]

Conclusion

By the end of the First World War, the YMHA was a thoroughly Judaized institution, a Jewish center in every sense. It had therefore evolved considerably from the combination literary society and young men's [sectarian] association of the nineteenth century. This was implied by the chairman of CYMHKA's advisory committee to the NYC Kehillah when he wrote: "The YMHA of today differs so completely from what was known as the Association thirty years ago, that it is almost impossible to consider the problems of the two types of institutions in connection with each other." Yet, as we have demonstrated, the religious seed was planted from the very beginning of the history of the social Jewish center. Only in the last period, however, was the social-religious dynamic fully expressed.[99]

We have already seen the construction of a synagogue within the precincts of the YWHA; we have also seen the creation of a YMHA congregation. In some instances elsewhere in the country, an entire YMHA was actually converted into a synagogue! This was the case with the YMHAs of Galveston, Texas, and of both Waltham and Milford, Massachusetts. In a later era, YMHAs and congregations would sometimes merge into one institution, as in the case of the YMHA Temple of Aurora, Illinois (1927), and the Jewish Community Center of Norristown, Pennsylvania (1936), which was the merger of Congregation Tiferes Israel and the local YMHA. These examples are but the ultimate extension of the earlier evolution of the YMHA from a purely social agency into a religious institution.[100]

In most of these cases, however, the religious function had been introduced into the social institution; but rarely did the two spheres combine thoroughly and equally. In 1916, "a Boy's Synagogue was organized [in the New York YMHA] for Saturday afternoon services, under the direction of the Director of Boys' Clubs, in an attempt to integrate the religious and social components of the Y's program." Aaron Robison, who likely was responsible for the innovation, had referred earlier to the necessity of merging the religious and social functions. As discussed above, that goal was pursued in the YMHA before; but never consciously and intentionally as now. The new ideologists of the Jewish center movement would make much of it.[101]

However, while the two strands of Jewish life were successfully woven together in some quarters, they began to unravel in others. In Baltimore, for instance, a new YMHA was proposed by William Levy in 1916. Though the popular response was enthusiastic, Rabbi William Rosenau objected to the idea. As he wrote to Levy: "I am opposed to the formation of a YMHA in this city or anywhere else because these deflect the interests of young people from the synagogue." Rosenau, an active member of the earlier synagogue-center movement of Reform Judaism, centered his hopes in the synagogue alone. Yet as Isaac Fein, the historian of Baltimore Jewry, points out, "the people who wished to establish a "Y" did not oppose the synagogue. They did not, however, consider the two institutions mutually exclusive."[102]

In the following year, as if to answer Rosenau, Cyrus Adler (then president of the United Synagogue of America) wrote, "I am aware of the fact that in some communities the Congregations and the Rabbis rather hold aloof from the YMHA's, considering them antagonistic to the young people's association of the Congregation." He disapproved of their segregation, however, and declared that "every opportunity which the Synagogue has to hold and interest young men should be utilized and all existing agencies which are not distinctly anti-religious or non-religious should be employed. The YMHA movement is one with which the members of the United Synagogue should heartily cooperate in every way."[103]

The leader of Conservative Judaism, having grown up in the Philadelphia YMHA, endorsed the full integration of the religious synagogue and the social center. He lamented the fact that the synagogue was no longer the "center of the entire Jewish communal life"; thus, lacking the vision to see what was implicit in the Judaized YMHA (or, for that matter, in the recently expanded synagogue), he recommended that rabbis devote their energies to "all of the Communal organizations" as well as to their synagogues. Like the earlier recommendation of Mordecai Kaplan to train rabbis as social workers, Adler's suggestion related to the individual. Certainly, one way to mend Jewish life was to integrate the various aspects of Judaism within the Jewish person. However, both Adler and Kaplan missed seeing the institutional solution as it had developed throughout the history of the Jewish center.

Kaplan would later write that it is "erroneous to trace an historical connection between the [Jewish] center and the movement to establish YMHAs. . . . Not even as late as 1900, when the New York YMHA issued a call to a number of similar institutions, do we discern an interest in the furtherance of Jewish life." We have seen differently. The first "Jewish centers," the fraternal lodges and literary societies, were not explicitly Jewish but provided German-Jewish immigrants with some means of Jewish identification. The early YMHA began to exploit this potential through the active participation of Reform rabbis. Well before the turn of the century, the YMHA began to function as a Jewish center in the sense(s) of unifying the Jewish community nationally, ethnically, and denominationally; and in healing the breach between the secular and religious aspects of American-Jewish life. When the Jewishness of the YMHA was made explicit after 1900, the groundwork was firmly in place. The increasing Judaization of the YMHA was not due simply to the backlash against Americanization (which Kaplan suggests, and which is further explored below), but also to the Jewish center itself, an institution that by its very nature combines religious ends with social means, and pragmatic goals with spiritual pursuits.[104]

Max Dimont, the popular author, once observed that "Kaplan got his inspiration for Reconstructionism from the Young Men's and Womens' Hebrew Association. In them he saw a model for the future synagogue as a Jewish center for the integration of all Jews into one organization . . . [and for the] unification of all activities—cultural, civic, charitable, social, religious." The idea that Kaplan's religious philosophy was inspired solely by the YMHA is simplistic to say the least. However, the connection between the YMHA and the synagogue-center is correct. As we shall explore in later chapters, Mordecai Kaplan's personal experiences certainly had some bearing upon his role in the creation of the synagogue-center and its ideology. Yet aside from Kaplan, the YMHA and synagogue-center are linked by a more wide-ranging development: the rise of the Jewish center movement from the earlier Jewish settlement movement, the subject of the following chapter.[105]

3

SETTLEMENT
A "Department Store" of Jewish Life

Most people conceive of the Center in terms of geographic location, a department store with all merchandise under one roof to save the customer expenditure of energy, and to provide the management greater economic efficiency. No, my friends, the Center, the saving institution of Jewish life in America, is much more than that.

—RABBI ABRAHAM M. HELLER, 1946[1]

As COMMONLY OBSERVED, American Jews such as Isidor Straus, Abraham Abraham, and Julius Rosenwald pioneered in the development of the "department store idea." Less well known is that all three were instrumental in the founding and support of a new type of Jewish communal institution: the Jewish settlement. Straus (of Macy's fame) was the moving force behind the Educational Alliance of the Lower East Side, Abraham (Abraham & Straus) was the trustee of the Baron de Hirsch Fund who led the drive to create the Hebrew Educational Society in Brooklyn, and Rosenwald (Sears) served as president of the Chicago Hebrew Institute. On one level, these "merchant princes" were simply contributing to the Jewish community to help speed the Americanization of the East European immigrants. But there is another, far more significant, connection: the Jewish settlement itself would become a "department store" of education and social activity! In fact, the development of both the mercantile and educational centers proceeded along similar lines, each having emerged from the consolidation of smaller, more specialized outlets of retailing and social service. In the spirit of the industrial age, the trend toward centralized planning and organization was applied by German Jewish philanthropists such as Abraham and Straus to their efforts in Jewish community building just as surely as to their more pecuniary pursuits. Later, the departmentalized settlement would become one of the principal sources of the Jewish center movement. When the synagogue-center was later deprecated as "a department store of religion," the accuser did not know how accurate an assessment it was.[2]

Like the YMHA before it, the Jewish settlement was paralleled and to some degree inspired by a contemporary Christian movement, and yet the Jewish

Fig. 14. From the *Official Souvenir Book of the Fair—In Aid of the Educational Alliance and the Hebrew Technical Institute*, 1895. The Executive Board of the Alliance was headed by Isidor Straus, owner of Macy's, and Joseph Bloomingdale, also a department store magnate. From the archive collection of The Educational Alliance.

institutions developed in their own distinctive way. Both the YMHA and the settlement began as social and educational centers for Jews and grew progressively
more religious in orientation. Both were the creations of the established Jewish
community of Central European descent, the first intended for its own younger
generation, and the second for the newly arrived immigrant population from
Eastern Europe. By combining social activity with Jewish culture, the settlement,
like the YMHA, was meant to resolve certain conflicts in Jewish life. The YMHA
attempted to resolve the tension between religious Judaism and social Jewishness
by merging the functions of the synagogue and the social club. The settlement
would seek to bridge the gaps between all the various elements of the Jewish
community. It would bring all together by offering something for everyone, becoming an emporium of social, educational, and religious programming. As such
a locus of multiple Jewish activities, it provided an essential model for the later
development of the Jewish community center.

In its earlier days, the primary tension addressed by the settlement would be
that between Americanism and Judaism. Arising side by side with the settlement
house of the 1880s and 1890s, Jewish settlements were likewise intended to help
the immigrant adjust to the conditions of American life; that is, to advance the
process of "Americanization." But the Jewish settlement, as distinct from its nonsectarian neighbor, had a double purpose. The Jewish settlement would combine
the goal of Americanization with that of preserving and harmonizing Jewish
communal life—thus seeming to some observers to be at odds with itself. The
combination of American and Jewish agenda was not merely a dual track program, however. In an apparent paradox, the Jewish settlement would market Judaism—that is, Jewish education and religion—as a form of Americanization.

The historical contexts that gave rise to a Jewish settlement movement were
twofold: first, the mass influx of Jewish immigrants from Eastern Europe that
began in the 1870s and accelerated after 1881; and second, the American movement of Progressivism, which was in part a response to conditions created by the
mass immigration. Falling in the heart of the Jewish immigration period, the
Progressive Era (approximately 1890–1915) was characterized by an optimistic
and pragmatic spirit of social reform. American Jews—Jewish women especially—were also activated by the Progressive impulse. For many, the problems
posed by the rising tide of immigration were thought to be surmountable
through the creation of rationally planned social institutions. American Jewish
Progressivism thus directed its energies toward the immigrant ghetto and
spawned a wide variety of philanthropic agencies, most notably, the Jewish settlement. As the settlement evolved into a Jewish center, the Progressive spirit never
abated. Such institutions were consistently understood to be modern, progressive, and above all, American to the core.[3]

The Progressive temper influenced Jewish communal life in less obvious ways
as well. To meet the perceived threat of the immigrants' foreignness and diversity,
Progressive ideologues posited a theory of cultural integration that came to be

known as Anglo-conformity, or more popularly, the "melting pot" ideal. America would serve as the great unifier, absorbing the foreign cultures into its own, and creating one from the many. Only after World War I, when ethnic separatism acquired greater legitimacy, did the ideology of "cultural pluralism" pose an effective challenge to the earlier conception. The emergence of the Jewish center is often related to the newer pluralist model. But this conventional explanation ignores the earlier influence of liberal Progressivism and its melting pot idealism. On a smaller scale, the same theme of ethnic merging was applied by Jews to themselves.[4]

Hence in 1905, at the height of the immigration period—and on the 250th anniversary of Jewish settlement in America—the American Hebrew voiced the concern of many: "What will be the future of Judaism on American soil? . . . Will there be 'confusion worse confounded' out of the mingling of nationalities and ideas?" The arrival of so many foreign Jews from so many points of origin posed the threat of communal breakdown. The editorialist's solution was a Jewish melting pot: "Out of the blending of divine elements, the crossfertilization of types, views and principles, a Jewish renaissance may be witnessed on American soil, springing from conviction and shaped by our stirring life." The idiom was American Progressivism, but the intent was the making of an American Judaism.[5]

The settlement was thus intended, like the YMHA, to be a unifying institution: a Jewish community "center." More pointedly than the YMHA, however, the settlement would attempt to bridge the social divide between "German" and "Russian" Jews. Speaking at the founding of the New York Kehillah, Judah Magnes described the sharp division between the two communities as the "invidious distinctions between East European and West European, foreigner and native, Uptown and Downtown Jews, rich and poor." In essence, the conflict was symmetrical: the native-born "Yahudim" scorned the foreign Jews for not being properly American (as they themselves were); while the immigrants viewed their predecessors with disdain for no longer being authentically Jewish (as they were themselves). In some quarters the mutual enmity ran deep. When "uptown" extended its philanthropy, "downtown" often resented the seeming condescension. The Jewish settlement, especially the exemplary Educational Alliance, has been described by some historians as such a paternalistic agency, at odds with the very people it meant to serve.[6]

The truth is that as early as the 1880s the two groups began to come together in common purpose and shared interest. In his classic study of New York's Jews, Moses Rischin portrayed in sensitive detail the process of reconciliation between the two communities, heralding the "dawn of a new era" in intra-Jewish relations. Yet even Rischin underplayed the crucial role of the Jewish settlement movement. In fact, the settlement house provided a key meeting ground for the two groups. Through the medium of philanthropy, the settlement gave the two communities opportunity for social contact and common endeavor. Within its bounds, the immigrants came to know their benefactors as something apart from the stereotype of the pompous "Yahudi." At the same time, many assimilated up-town Jews—especially women and youth—were exposed firsthand to the rich-ness of Jewish culture and to the charm of the East European Jewish personality.

The settlement house movement enabled some well-known Jewish figures to make the trip downtown, both literally and figuratively; Lillian Wald became a settlement house founder and worker, while Louis Marshall learned Yiddish. Working in a settlement house during college, Horace Kallen encountered Jew-ish immigrant culture, and later went on to become the champion of cultural pluralism. But many more unheralded Jews were equally affected by their settle-ment work experience. One young woman in Denver would write in 1906: "The neighborhood house is a meeting ground where we hope to get close to our [im-migrant] brethren. While we bring to them Americanism we may at the same time be inspired with some of the spiritual passion which glows in the breasts of these ardent Jews, who are after all the rock which is the foundation of the House of Israel."[7]

Yet the immigrant community had an even more pressing concern than the social divide between themselves and the German Jews. The tension between up-town Americanism and downtown Judaism was replicated by the cultural gap between immigrant parents and their rapidly Americanizing children. Immi-grants and settlement workers alike were acutely aware of this problem and sought to heal the rift. As Hutchins Hapgood observed of the Educational Al-liance in 1902, "its avowed purpose is to combine the American and Hebrew ele-ments, reconcile fathers and sons by making the former more American and the latter more Hebraic, and in that way improve the home life of the quarter."[8]

Thus, almost from the start, the American Jewish settlement had dual goals: to Americanize and to Judaize. The common denominator of both these aims was education; hence the Jewish settlement was primarily an educational institu-tion. Indeed, it was this quality more than any other that marked the settlement as Jewish. As a contemporary non-Jewish observer of the ghetto would remark: "Of all immigrants, the Jews run most distinctly to educational organizations, in which, although social and recreational features are present, first place is given to immediate instruction through classes, text books, lectures and debates. In every Jewish neighborhood of any size educational societies which are really local in character spring up, usually in great profusion."[9]

The "Educational Side of Charitable Work": Origins of the Jewish Settlement

As noted, the Jewish settlement appeared on the scene simultaneous with a gen-eral movement of philanthropic "settlement" in the urban ghetto. Though it was called a settlement too, and was naturally associated with its nonsectarian neighbor, the Jewish settlement was derived as well from paradigmatic Jewish values: the duty of philanthropy (*tzedakah* in Hebrew) combined with the duty of universal Jewish education *(talmud torah)*. Both are essential religious responsibilities in Judaism, and both are therefore primary functions of Jewish community. In late nineteenth-century America, however, philanthropy and education were each becoming public charges—hence an American rather than a Jewish province. But in cases where philanthropy and education remained in combination (such as the settlement formed by Jews for their fellow Jews) they remained a Jewish specialty. The merging of Jewish education and philanthropic work was especially pronounced in three related phenomena: the Hebrew free school, the Jewish orphanage, and the occupational training school—all educational agencies of Jewish philanthropy, and together laying the groundwork for the rise of the Jewish settlement.

The first Hebrew free school was established in 1864 to combat the Christian missionary schools then operating in the Jewish neighborhoods of the city. It was to be a new type of Jewish school: all-day and free to all. By drawing immigrant children to a such a Jewish-sponsored school, they would be kept Jewish, and proselytization would be thwarted. At the same time the Hebrew free school was intended to "exert a refining influence" upon the Jewish children of the immigrant ghetto. Overlaid on the original Jewish educational intent of the school was the newer goal of refinement, that is, Americanization. With this dual mission, the Hebrew free school movement flourished. The principal connection between the Hebrew free school and the later settlement movement was their common program of Americanization with Jewish content. Another link would be the active participation of rabbis, often in collaboration with the Jewish women of their congregations. For much of the nineteenth century, the rabbi and the Jewish woman had been the primary supporters of religious education in the Jewish community (think of Isaac Leeser and Rebecca Gratz as prototypes) and together became intimately involved in both the Hebrew free school and settlement movements.[10]

As part of a complete Jewish education, Hebrew free schools even organized religious services for the children. Philip Cowen's evocative description of the New York scene reveals that not only children attended such educational services: "Reverting to the Hebrew Free Schools, I must tell of the Sabbath afternoon services that were held by them. The superintendent, Rabbi Isaac C. Noot, was in charge, but the children conducted the service, and they drew a considerable number of adults. Mr. [Jacob] Schiff was especially interested in the children attending these schools. He offered prizes for essays that were read at the anniversary of his parents' death, and at these times he usually visited the schools and said Kaddish, the anniversary prayer for the dead. Often he himself read the evening service. Schiff knew his Hebrew."[11]

Another early arena of philanthropic Jewish education was the orphanage, which had its earliest appearance in the 1801 Jewish Orphans' Home of Charleston, South Carolina. Three decades later, the Jews of New York City formed the Hebrew Benevolent and Orphan Asylum, and in 1855 the New Orleans Jewish

Orphans' Home was established. By the end of the century, similar institutions in Philadelphia, Cleveland, Brooklyn, Milwaukee, and elsewhere housed approximately six thousand Jewish orphans. As at the Hebrew free school, religious services were provided. Philip Cowen recalled that when the Hebrew Orphan Asylum moved up "to 137th Street, in 1884, then the outskirts of the city, many adults were attracted to the [Sabbath] services regularly in spite of its comparative outofthewayness."[12]

Like the Hebrew free school, the first Jewish orphanages were founded due to the fear of Christian proselytizing. Both institutions thus shared a commitment to the education of the Jewish unfortunate. Orphans, like immigrant Jews, were considered by the established community to be culturally deficient, sorely in need of "uplift" and "refinement"; thus the orphanages of the time, like the settlements, became educational laboratories. Since the orphans who came to these institutions were young children, without family influence, the prospects for their "improvement" seemed unlimited; the rawest of material, they could be turned into model American Jews. Speaking at the 1873 dedication of the Baltimore Hebrew Orphan Asylum, William S. Rayner pointed out that "a fatherless and motherless child, especially when left in poverty, is almost an entirely a creature of circumstances" and can be molded "like the clay in the hands of the potter" for "right or for wrong, for virtue or for crime." Most tellingly, Rayner described the orphans as "children of our faith, [whom] we intend to raise in our own way to become good American citizens as well as true Israelites."[13]

Rayner's description of the orphanage as both an agency of Americanization and of Judaization helps us make sense of the heavy involvement of American rabbis in orphan education. In fact, it was not uncommon to find Jewish orphanages directed by rabbis. The first superintendent of the Baltimore Hebrew Orphan Asylum was Rabbi Abraham Hoffman (1873–76), who was later succeeded by Rabbi S. Fruedenthal (1885–1910). In Boston, the Leopold Morse Home for Aged and Infirm Hebrews and Orphanage opened in 1889, due in part to the social activism of Rabbi Solomon Schindler. To aid the fund-raising campaign, Schindler published a short history of the Boston Jewish community, and after leaving Temple Israel in 1893, became superintendent of the orphanage (as well as of the United Hebrew Charities, soon to become the pioneer of the Federation movement). And similarly, the Cleveland Jewish Orphan Asylum remembers the dominant influence of Rabbi Samuel Wolfenstein, superintendent from 1878 to 1913.[14]

In Cleveland as elsewhere, the connection between Americanization and Jewish education was clearly established. In his 1883 report, Wolfenstein explained how modern educational methods were having their effect: "Our children are preserving order and decorum, not through coercion or military drill, but because they have learned to love order and have acquired a sense of propriety. . . . Religious feelings are fostered in their young hearts by regular exhortations and the tenets of our faith are practically imbued in them by our mode of living and upholding a strictly Jewish household." In order to turn his young charges into model American citizens, it seemed necessary to rear them in the tradition of classical Reform Judaism, of which he was an ardent proponent. Jewish orphanages even served as recruitment houses for the Reform rabbinate; Rabbis Michael Aaronsohn, Edward Calisch, William S. Friedman, M. P. Jacobson, and Joseph Krauskopf all started life as orphans.[15]

A national movement for vocational education had its start at the Philadelphia Centennial Exposition of 1876 where an exhibit of a Russian technical school inspired John D. Runkle of the Massachusetts Institute of Technology and Calvin M. Woodward of Washington University to promote "manual training" as a way of educating young people for "all spheres of usefulness." The Jewish counterpart began in the mid-1870s as well, when the United Hebrew Charities (UHC) opened the first vocational school for Jewish girls in New York City. Significantly, the UHC had its origins as an orphanage. In 1860, the Hebrew Benevolent Society, until then a fund of minor importance, established a "little home for children," and in 1870, changed its name to the Hebrew Benevolent and Orphan Asylum Society. Four years later, shortly after the 1873 depression and in the same year as the founding of the New York YMHA, the society proposed a "plan of union" that became the charter for the United Hebrew Charities of New York. Among its first projects was the establishment of an industrial school in 1875, later known as the Hebrew Technical School for girls.[16]

Both the United Hebrew Charities and the Hebrew Free School Association thus established agencies of Americanization—in the form of vocational preparation—prior to the advent of the social settlement. Philip Cowen relates the role of the *American Hebrew* and of one of its better-known contributors in the establishment of the new movement:

Emma Lazarus, who had developed a great interest in the refugees, visited them in their new homes, and soon discovered that, unless the people were given something to occupy them, there would be trouble. . . . The more Miss Lazarus went into the matter the more she was satisfied that, for the refugees as a class and for their children, it was necessary that they be given technical instruction. Her articles in the *American Hebrew* emphasized this need, and led us to form a committee that met frequently to discuss the idea. . . . Manuel A. Kursheedt and I went to Boston to look into the work of the Massachusetts Technical Institute, to Philadelphia to study the work of the Franklin Institute, and we got considerable advice from Charles Godfrey Leland who was especially interested in industrial education. . . . The result was the establishment of the Hebrew Technical Institute.[17]

Other Jewish communities soon followed the example of New York. In Saint Louis, the Hebrew Free and Industrial School was organized in 1879 and conducted both religious and industrial classes for the children of immigrants. Similarly, the Hebrew Education Society of Philadelphia opened an industrial school for girls in 1880. And in 1889, Mrs. Lina Hecht of Boston persuaded the leading Russian Jewish congregation of the North End to allow her to open a Sunday School for girls on its premises. From this beginning, Mrs. Hecht and Golde

Bamber founded the Hebrew Industrial School for girls in January 1890. Teaching its charges to be "wage earners, breadwinners, and self-respecting intelligent citizens," its motto was "a good Israelite will make a better citizen."[18]

We thus return yet again to the theme of Jewish education. While purveying manual and vocational training (neither were features of the later center) the new schools did continue the "tradition" of Americanization with religious content. As always, religious education was promoted by the rabbis. In 1880, the first annual "Report of Committee on Industrial School" (of the UHC) stated: "The Jewish clergy have taken commendable interest in our undertaking. The school has been visited by Rev. Drs. G. Gottheil, H. S. Jacobs, F. De Sola Mendes, and A. S. Isaacs and Rev. H. P. Mendes and D. H. Nieto. Rev. Dr. Jacobs afforded the pupils much valuable instruction by delivering a series of addresses on Monday afternoons. Rev. Dr. Mendes has kindly offered a medal to be awarded to the girl who is most neat in her habits." A modest beginning, to be sure, but the influence of the rabbis would increase with time.[19]

Beginning in 1881, Bible classes were added to the curriculum of the Industrial School of the UHC. Religious instruction came to be seen as complementary to vocational training. By 1894, Henry S. Allen, the chairman of the industrial school committee, would report that "experience forces other problems upon us for solution. . . . We are forced to consider the religious problem, . . . as well as the ability to earn an honorable livelihood." Allen cited the troubling rise of Jewish prostitution as reason enough for "the legitimacy of religious education as part of charity work." More important, he displayed the contemporary understanding of religious inculcation as a form of Americanization: "We claim that this is true charity, wide charity, scientific charity. For it means self-helpfulness, refinement, uplifting out of poverty's surroundings, and above all, religion or reverence for God, which is the crown of human character, for poor as well as for rich." Like the orphan asylum, the industrial school would educate its charges in American ways through the medium of progressive religion. The idea particularly appealed to American Reform Jews, for whom the deficiency of the Jewish immigrant consisted in large part of a "backward" religious expression: Orthodox Judaism. At the same time, it revealed the modern Jewish tendency to conceive of religious affiliation as patriotism. Since every good American goes to church, the socialization of the Jewish immigrant required the element of religion as a matter of course. Jewish education thereby joined the cause of Americanization.[20]

Allen also referred to another feature of the industrial school that foreshadowed the settlement movement: the functioning of the Jewish institution as a neighborhood center. "On certain evenings, the Literary Circle, Emma Lazarus Club for Working Girls, and other societies hold meetings, so that our building is almost constantly occupied in the cause of religion, industrial education, the intelligent training of young children, or the mental and moral education of young men and working girls." Similarly, in 1882, the Boston YMHA relocated to Minot Hall in the South End, becoming a center of activity. Besides the full range of "Y" offerings, "various fraternal orders and the Hebrew Women's Sewing Society used its assembly rooms as their meeting place." In the following year, the New York YMHA established its downtown branch, "the first Jewish neighborhood center in America for immigrant groups." Its activities included Americanization classes, an employment bureau, lecture forums, entertainments, and a library. And in 1885, the *American Hebrew* stated that "the idea of a central building for the Hebrew Free Schools, to contain at the same time executive offices for the Charities beneath its roof, together with room for a Free Synagogue, is an excellent one." Such developments adumbrated the Jewish center idea: to bring all the various functions of Jewish life together under one roof. Although a fully unified Jewish communal institution—one that included a synagogue—would not appear until after the turn of the century, its antecedents were clearly in evidence by the 1880s, when several significant developments took place.[21]

The Emergence of the Jewish Settlement Movement

The Jewish settlement movement was most immediately preceded by the example of the nonsectarian (though often religiously inspired) settlement house. In the summer of 1886, a young idealist named Stanton Coit organized a working-men's club in a tenement house on the Lower East Side of Manhattan. The founding of the Neighborhood Guild (later reorganized as the University Settlement), inspired by precedents in England, is often cited as the origin of the settlement house movement in America. A Jewish version of the settlement house would soon appear, though with some significant distinctions. The Jewish version would tend to be a larger institution than the homelike settlement; it would often be founded by another philanthropic organization rather than by individuals; and it would be clearly identified as Jewish in both sponsorship and character (if not in exclusivity of clientele). For these reasons, the origins of the Jewish settlement cannot be attributed to the general settlement house movement alone. But it is clear that the success of the Jewish settlement movement would owe much to the rapid spread of the settlement idea.[22]

After Coit's initiative, the movement seemed to respond most readily to the liberated energies of the Victorian-era woman. In 1889, Jane Addams and Ellen Gates Starr founded Hull House in Chicago, another oft-cited origin of the settlement movement. In that same year, in a separate development, Vida Scudder and several fellow Smith graduates founded the College Settlement in a tenement nearby the Neighborhood Guild. Four years later, fellow nurses Lillian Wald and Mary Brewster stayed at College Settlement while organizing a health clinic for immigrants—later to become the Henry Street Settlement. Besides its primary functions, Henry Street provided sanctuary and community for numerous women social workers of the time. According to Linda Gordon Kuzmack, "the Wald circle agreed with feminist social reformers' claims that women were particularly suited to undertake social reform because they were morally superior to men and were filled with a gentleness, sensitivity, and responsiveness to human needs." Women were closely associated with the rise of the settlement movement for good reason.[23]

Since settlement work emphasized education as well as social reform, it comes as no surprise to find that Jewish women (other than Lillian Wald) gravitated to settlement work within the Jewish community. In Philadelphia, for example, young Fanny Binswanger led thirty of her friends—the unmarried contingent of the Women's Auxiliary of the Hebrew Educational Society—in opening a kindergarten for Jewish immigrant children. The school was opened in the winter of 1885, with the declared intention "to make of the children good American citizens, [and] to imbue them with the best American ideals." The informal group was reorganized as the Young Women's Union and soon expanded its activities to include a "Household School" for girls aged ten to thirteen. In subsequent years, other services were added, including evening classes for working girls (for example, in 1896, Henrietta Szold taught an evening course in American literature), a day nursery and shelter, a bank (the Penny Savings Bank), an art school (the Graphic Sketch Club), and a women's clubhouse (the Working Girl's Club). When, in 1918, the Young Women's Union changed its name to the Neighborhood Center, it was simply opting for a more accurate title, better descriptive of its role as a pioneering settlement house/Jewish center.[24]

Similarly, German-Jewish women innovated in social work elsewhere around the country. In Baltimore, the young Henrietta Szold established a night school for Russian Jews in 1889 in cooperation with the Hebrew Literary Society; the school was described as "among the pioneers of its kind in America." As mentioned earlier, Lina Hecht, married to Boston's leading Jewish philanthropist, founded the Hebrew Industrial School for girls in 1890. Hecht installed Golde Bamber as superintendent, who had previously taught elocution at the YMHA. In the same year, the "Daughters in Israel" of Baltimore opened a home for girls. Later on, many of these early efforts would blossom into Jewish centers.[25]

Yet the greatest impact of women on the Jewish settlement movement did not derive from individual effort but from the group activity of a new institution: the temple sisterhood. The first "Sisterhood of Personal Service" was founded in 1889 by Rabbi Gustav Gottheil of New York's Temple Emanu-El. Writing in the 1905 edition of the *Jewish Encyclopedia,* Hannah Einstein described the sisterhood as an association of "female charity-workers who devote time to the care of the needy and the distressed." Attributing its origins to "a sermon delivered by Dr. Gustav Gottheil in 1887," Einstein noted the innovativeness of a charity group based on the direct involvement of its membership—hence the name, sisterhood of "personal service." As she explained: "The work contemplated was to be done by the members themselves. Every sister was to devote a certain portion of her time to a definite task, and attend to it personally." Moreover, the essential goal of such active participation was "to overcome the estrangement of one class of the Jewish population from another and to bring together the well-to-do and the poor, in the relation, not of patron and dependent, but of friend and friend."[26]

The idea was timely. The Emanu-El Sisterhood example was soon "followed by congregation after congregation, until almost every organized place of worship in the upper portion of New York city has a part of its communal work in charge of such a sisterhood." The settlement idea was thus taken up by the women of the leading Jewish congregations, and put into practice in the form of sisterhood "homes." The Emanu-El Sisterhood home, located at 318 East 82d Street, was the pioneer in this respect. Soon, every sisterhood in New York City had its home outpost, a fortuitous situation that attracted the attention of the United Hebrew Charities. Sisterhood members, displaying "great initiative and ability," were drafted as "friendly visitors" (that is, volunteer social workers) by the UHC, and sisterhood homes came to serve as its branch offices. After the founding of the Federation of Sisterhoods in 1896, "the city was divided into districts, specific territory was assigned to each sisterhood, and the whole city, from the New Bowery to Harlem, was covered in this way."[27]

As might be expected, the development was quickly imitated throughout the country. Besides the New York sisterhoods, mission schools and other social service centers were established by sisterhoods in Chicago (the Jewish Training School of Sinai Temple, founded in 1888), San Francisco (Emanuel Sisterhood, 1894), Saint Paul (Neighborhood House founded by Mount Zion Temple in 1899), and Buffalo (Zion House, later the Jewish Community Building, organized by the sisterhood of Temple Beth Zion in 1893). In Buffalo, as elsewhere, the rabbi of the congregation played a key role in the organization of the sisterhood: "In 1891, Rabbi Israel Aaron urged the organization of the Sisterhood of Zion, and it proved to be the most lasting work of his ministry."[28]

Historical circumstance as well as psychological need promoted this close relationship between the rabbi and the sisterhood. The decade of the 1890s fell midway between the awakening of the social impulse in classical Reform Judaism (exemplifed by the eighth plank of the Pittsburgh Platform of 1885) and its realization in the early 1900s as the Jewish analogue to the Social Gospel movement (exemplified by the Free Synagogue founded by Stephen S. Wise in 1906). His social consciousness raised, but not yet "free" to commit his own office or the temple he represented, the rabbi of the 1890s inspired the women of the congregation to take up the progressive cause outside temple bounds. The establishment of a sisterhood by the rabbi was thus a strategic compromise that helped ease the transition from "creed to deed." On a symbolic level, the relationship cut even deeper. When the "emancipated" Jewish woman transferred the focus of her energies from the family home to the public sphere of the settlement house, she may have felt the absence of a male authority figure in the reconstructed "home," a role naturally filled by the rabbi. Just as the rabbi needed a temporary surrogate for his social activist ambitions, the sisterhood required a father figure to give its public role legitimacy. The rabbi-sisterhood relationship was symbiotic to say the least.

The idea is borne out by an exchange in the 1903 winter issues of *Jewish Charity,* the periodical of the United Hebrew Charities. To start, Joseph Jacobs, scholar of English Jewry and editor of the *Jewish Encyclopedia,* wrote the following critique of "Jewish Clergy and Jewish Charity":

Without taking any account of religious exhortation, in which naturally we have no concern, there is much that a clergyman can do which may prevent his clients from falling into the class which Jewish charity has to cater for. . . . If the modern Jewish clergyman would *pasken* about hygiene and savings banks he would be performing a function as useful and honorable as answering the old order of questions about kosheriety of sturgeon, or the trifah-like quality of peacock. . . . The only way to overcome these evils [referring to the uptown-downtown schism] would be to apportion out the city into districts which would be regarded as peculiarly belonging to one particular Rabbi for charitable purposes. . . . The late Dr. Gottheil evidently intended his system of sisterhoods to take the place of the clergy to some extent, because he saw the difficulties indicated above. No one would suggest that the work of the sisterhood is an adequate substitute for the ministerial advice which the members of other sects get from their clergy. Is there no means by which similar assistance can be obtained by the Jewish poor through the Jewish clergy?[29]

What, after all, ought the relationship to be between the rabbi and the charity worker, between the synagogue and communal philanthropy? It is one of the persistent questions of American Jewish life. In response to Jacobs, one rabbi defended the status quo, claiming that "the only organization that at all mediates between the congregations and communal work is the sisterhood." He continues, "As a matter of fact every sisterhood in its district, so to speak, creates a parish for the minister of the synagogue to which the sisterhood belongs. . . . The sisterhood is the connecting link between the synagogue and the larger community in philanthropic matters."[30]

In 1893, the same year in which Lillian Wald moved to the Lower East Side, the National Council for Jewish Women (CJW) was organized and immediately began to organize mission schools and settlement centers. Local chapters of the council quickly became nondenominational versions of the sisterhood. For example, in Denver, the local Council of Jewish Women led the way toward creating an "Americanization program" through settlement work. This included a kindergarten, night schools with Americanization classes, a settlement house, a "mission Sunday School," and provisions for free baths. In Pittsburgh, a local chapter was formed in 1894, named the Columbian Council. One year after its founding, the Columbian Council established a Sisterhood of Personal Service, and on the advice of Rabbi Lippman Mayer, opened a religious school for the children of immigrants in 1896. Similar settlement projects were founded by local CJW chapters in New York (the Council House, est. 1894), Nashville (the Fensterwald Settlement, 1894), Pittsburgh (the Irene Kaufmann Settlement, 1895), Portland, Oregon (the Neighborhood House, 1896), Milwaukee (the Jewish Mission, 1896), Seattle and San Francisco (1900).[31]

Alongside Jewish women, there was one other important group that began to initiate settlement activity: the immigrants themselves. As early as 1890, "branches of the Jewish Alliance of America were formed in various cities by the

Russian-Jewish immigrants in an effort to solve by themselves the host of prob-lems involved in the settlement of the Jewish immigrants." Though the move-ment foundered on the national level, local initiatives such as that of Saint Louis succeeded. Using a public school donated by the municipal school system, the St. Louis Alliance conducted English classes and established an employment bu-reau. Likewise, the Benoth Israel Association of the North End of Boston was successful in the 1891 creation of a Sheltering Home for newly arrived immi-grants. As historian Barbara Solomon described it: "The Sheltering Home not only gave temporary lodging and food, but provided many personal services cherished by the orthodox. During the season of Passover, the poor and lonely newcomers were welcomed with a *seder*." The Home was the pride of the immi-grant community. As noted by contemporary rabbi Raphael Lasker, "this great charity was not established from above," but by the immigrants themselves. Not surprisingly, it was the women of the immigrant community who led the way.[32]

As had German Jewish women, the immigrants thought of themselves as es-pecially qualified to serve the needs of the Jewish needy. Certainly, those immi-grants who had arrived at an earlier date were uniquely situated to bridge the gap between the American and immigrant Jewish mentalities. Perhaps the best exam-ple of the type was David Blaustein, who arrived in the United States in 1886 at the age of twenty and would later become the director of the two leading Jewish settlement/centers of New York and Chicago. The young Blaustein was academ-ically ambitious, and just two years after arrival was to be found studying at Har-vard College. The seeds of his later settlement work were sown during his stu-dent days in Boston. In 1891, Blaustein organized the B'nai Zion Educational Society, a reading room and literary club that combined Americanization activi-ties with Jewish education. About the same time, he also opened "a modern German-Hebrew school—the first of its kind in the United States," and was one of the founders of the Sheltering Home for Immigrants as well. But it was the B'nai Zion Educational Society that best represented the union of American so-cial settlement forms with Jewish education and culture—in this case, the culture of Jewish nationalism. The Society rented a building on the main avenue of the North End, and renamed it, "Zion Hall." Though all but forgotten, Zion Hall has one significant claim to fame. For the 1891 dedication, a member named Jacob Askowith designed a special banner: the same design later adopted as the Zionist flag, ultimately becoming the "star and stripes" of modern Israel![33]

Similar syntheses of Zionism and the Jewish settlement appeared in city after city, reflecting both the secularism and the visionary quality of Zionist ideology. When the Knights of Zion fraternal lodge of Chicago agitated for a social center to embody their program and to extend it to the greater community, they were acting as Zionist emissaries. Inasmuch as Zionism represented the secularization of Judaism, its ideological adherents tended naturally to expand the activities of Jewish communal life. And just as the Zionist enterprise entailed the creation of a new society and infrastructure, Zionist activists in the diaspora tended to think big. In Philadelphia, the Zion Institute was dedicated in 1902 to house the activities of ten Zionist societies. The new building, which included lecture and classrooms, a gymnasium, and a library containing more than five hundred volumes, immediately became the city's Zionist center.[34]

Such central clubhouses soon came to house activities of all kinds. The need for an adequate physical plant would lead to the construction of new Jewish settlement/center facilities, with New York and Philadelphia leading the way. The first buildings specially erected as Jewish settlement houses were the New York Hebrew Institute and Touro Hall in Philadelphia, both opened in 1890–91. The buildings immediately became centers of a variety of activity. Touro Hall, for example, housed "the Southern Branch of YMHA, University Extension Society Courses, Hebrew School, Sunday School, Night School, Trade Schools, Employment Bureau, Agent of Immigrant Society, auxiliary charities conducted by the United Hebrew Charities, and the Baron de Hirsch Fund. . . . The facilities included a swimming pool."[35]

Clearly, the new building was more than merely a settlement house. Touro Hall, as Rabinowitz notes, was also the home of Gratz College, which had been inaugurated as a lecture series held "in the synagogue hall of Cong. Mikveh Israel," the historic Sephardic congregation of Philadelphia—this, in a structure built expressly to serve the immigrant community. The existence of an all-purpose facility served to unify the entire community. Elsewhere, the construction of new buildings would quicken the consolidation of diverse organizations and agencies. For example, "In 1899, the St. Louis Jewish Alliance, the Hebrew Free and Industrial School [1879], and the United Jewish Charities were merged and, two years later, were housed in the new building of the Jewish Charitable and Educational Union. The building, however, was known as the Jewish Alliance . . . a new building was purchased in 1920, and the name changed to the Jewish Community Center." In New York City, a merger of Jewish institutions was the beginning of the most famous and most influential Jewish center of all, the Educational Alliance.[36]

The Ambivalent Settlement/Center: The Educational Alliance

Though once described as a "curious mixture of night school, settlement house, day-care center, gymnasium, and public forum," the Educational Alliance program was not curious at all, but rather the logical culmination and consolidation of the Jewish institutional trends of the late nineteenth century. By establishing the ideal settlement house, the German Jews of uptown Manhattan channeled their integrationist desires for the immigrants and projected themselves into the downtown world. As such, the Alliance was the quintessential Jewish settlement. More than a settlement, however, it was also the first true Jewish center to emerge from the settlement movement. Despite its uptown origins and backing, it quickly became a people's institution, known to all as the "Palace of Immigrants." Notwithstanding the intentions of its uptown sponsors, the Alliance tended to the needs of the immigrant community from the start, and soon took on the intensely Jewish colorations of the Lower East Side. The Educational Alliance was therefore an ambivalent institution, representing both uptown and downtown, fostering both Americanization and Jewish life, and thus encapsulating the internal conflicts of American Jewry.[37]

The Alliance traces its origins to the 1889 amalgamation of the East Side activities of the YMHA, the Hebrew Free School Association (HFSA), and the Aguilar Free Library Society. Prompted by Jacob Schiff's pledge to donate $30,000 if the competing groups would only unify, the organizations decided to form an "alliance" under the name Hebrew Education Aid Society and called their new location the Hebrew Institute. The names are significant, as "Hebrew" was the sectarian signifier typical of the German Jewish community (but soon to fall out of fashion); "education" refers to the common denominator of the three cultural/literary societies; "aid" alludes to its philanthropic intent; and "institute" places the new agency squarely within the modern institutional trends of the progressive era.

A new building was planned beginning in 1890. In March of that year, a plot was purchased at the corner of Jefferson Street and East Broadway, Jewish architect Arnold Brunner was hired, and construction was soon under way. The building was erected during the course of the summer and fall, and the Hebrew Institute opened its doors by the end of the year. The excitement of the opening was marred, however, by the withdrawal of the YMHA from the merger of organizations. Yet the women's arm of the "Y" remained involved, with Julia Richman as its representative on the board of directors. The involvement of educator Richman—held in low regard by many in the immigrant community for her Americanization activities—raises the question of the educational intent of the institute. Certainly it would be an educative institution, but education to what end?[38]

Despite some Jewish content, the overarching purpose of the original Educational Alliance was Americanization. According to the reorganization agreement of May 4, 1893, the objectives of the new institution were to be "of an Americanizing, educational, social and humanizing character." In fact, despite its Jewish provenance, the Educational Alliance was conceived as a settlement for the entire immigrant community. In 1897, the first president of the Educational Alliance, Isidor Straus, stressed the point: "At first blush our work may seem sectarian; it is nothing of that sort. It is educational, humanitarian, philanthropic and patriotic in the broadest sense. It is true that we have reached chiefly Jews, but this is due to the fact that the neighborhood in which the Alliance is situated is inhabited principally by Jews. The library, the reading room, the gymnasium, and the entertainments of every sort, are accessible to any and all who choose to avail themselves of them."[39]

Fig. 15. The Educational Alliance building at 197 East Broadway, built 1890. Collection of the New York Historical Society.

Nevertheless, Straus and his fellow sponsors would shortly be influenced by the changing times, and the Alliance would respond more directly to its Jewish milieu. By 1902, Hutchins Hapgood could describe the Alliance as a bastion of American Jewish education: "The Educational Alliance is a still better organized and more intelligent institution, having much more the same purpose in view as the best Hebrew schools." Hapgood's perspective, advocating a "synthesis of the old and the new," may be counted as an early example of cultural pluralism. As he further explained, "The ideal situation for [the] young Jew would be that where he could become an integral part of American life without losing the seriousness of nature developed by Hebraic tradition and education."[40]

Not everyone agreed with Hapgood's positive assessment, however. Perhaps the most vitriolic attack came from Abraham H. Fromenson, the editor of New York's *Jewish Daily News–Jewish Gazette*. Writing in 1904, Fromenson ridiculed the claim of the Educational Alliance and other settlements to be serving the masses: "When all is said and done, however, when every claim made for them by their most enthusiastic admirers and workers is conceded, the fact remains that as far as the overwhelming majority of the East Side residents are concerned, it is as if these institutions did not exist at all." Moreover, he declared, "they are regarded by a very large number with absolute antipathy and by another very large number with mistrust." Such suspicion related to the most often heard criticism of the Alliance: its lack of true Jewishness. As proof, Fromenson pointed to the change of name from the proudly sectarian Hebrew Institute to the "noncommittal" Educational Alliance. He accused the Alliance of doing more harm than good: "It would not be going too far to say that what good they have accomplished has been offset by the harm they have wrought. Cleavage of the home tie, depreciation, if not outright repudiation, of parental authority, contempt for the religious opinion of elders, the creation of an unbridgeable chasm between parents and children—all this may with perfect propriety be charged against the non-Jewishness of Jewish institutions on the East Side."[41]

Yet most contemporary observers were rather more laudatory. In 1906, Edward Steiner called the Educational Alliance "the one great Jewish intellectual and ethical centre of the Ghetto," and noted its superiority to a Young Mens' Christian Association, "inasmuch as it ministers to all, from childhood to old age." He testified to its popularity by describing the "gigantic building, covering a block and containing forty-three classrooms, [which] is entirely inadequate to meet the demand. The main entrance is always in a state of siege, and two policemen are stationed there to maintain order and keep the crowding people in line. I visited it on a hot Sunday afternoon in July, and I found the large, well-stocked reading-room uncomfortably filled by young men. The roof-garden is a breathing-place for thousands, and is always crowded by children, who are supervised in their play and who enjoy it eagerly." Philip Cowen concurred: "So great a beehive was it, and such masses of people entered the building, that within twenty years of its construction the marble steps were worn so thin that they had to be replaced." And finally, Boris Bogen described the situation just prior to the turn of the century: "The Alliance was the real educational and social center [on the East Side]—no one could deny its influence; some thought it was for the good, others for the bad, but all agreed that the work of the Alliance counted in the life of the Ghetto."[42]

Simply put, if the observer was Americanized and thus inclined toward the Americanization of the immigrant, then his view of the Alliance was likely to be positive; if, however, one was first and foremost a Jewish survivalist, then the Alliance was likely to be seen as detrimental to the immigrant's true interests. Such differences aside, all historians agree that the hallmark of the Alliance was its emphasis on education, which marked a key distinction between Jewish and non-Jewish settlements. Describing the settlement houses of New York, social worker J. K. Paulding noted that "except among the clubs of the youngest there is little direct instruction in any settlement with which I happen to be acquainted." The Educational Alliance, by contrast, soon evolved into an "immigrants' university," both to feed the Jewish immigrants' intellectual hunger and to quench their thirst for acculturation. Serving the entire community, young and old alike, the Alliance offered "classes for nearly every grade of culture, the subject-list including languages, literature, history, civics, mathematics, natural science, music, cookery, book-keeping, drawing, millinery, typewriting, philosophy, gymnastics, and religion." And above all, the Alliance taught the immigrant English.[43]

Nevertheless, as should be apparent by now, the Educational Alliance program was not focused upon Americanization to the exclusion of Jewish culture; Jewish schooling and even religious services would take place on its premises. But neither was the Alliance an institution solely committed to the preservation of Jewish tradition. Instead, the immigrants' original culture would serve as a means to the end of Americanization. For example, the apparent antithesis of English-language instruction—the use of Yiddish—was in evidence from early on. Jacob Riis reported in 1892: "The Declaration of Independence half the children knew by heart before they had gone over it twice. To help them along it is printed in the school-books with a Hebrew translation and another in Jargon, a "Jewish-German" [Yiddish], in parallel columns and the explanatory notes in Hebrew."[44]

The main factor that kept the Educational Alliance from becoming a paternalistic agency of Americanization was its key personnel: figures such as Isaac Spectorsky and David Blaustein, consecutive directors of the Alliance between 1893 and 1905. Immigrants themselves, they were clearly sympathetic to the needs of the neighborhood. Whereas the founders of the Alliance had been uptown Jews of German extraction, these were East Europeans who had immigrated earlier and had attained some degree of acculturation. When such men became settlement workers, they were able simultaneously to represent the concerns of the uptown sponsors and to create programming more attuned to their fellow immigrants. The trait they shared was an integrated personality combining Jewish immigrant origins with an acculturated sense of the benefits of Americanization. By translating their own experience into their work at the Alliance, they would serve as the essential mediators between the worlds of uptown and downtown.

David Blaustein and the "Peoples Synagogue"

The person most responsible for introducing "an Americanized version of Judaism" to the Educational Alliance was its second superintendent, David Blaustein. Blaustein had left Lithuania for the United States in 1886, settled in Boston and after just three years in the country, entered Harvard University as a special student in Semitics; receiving his Bachelor of Arts degree in 1893. While a student he remained active in the immigrant Jewish community; as noted earlier, his activities in the North End prepared him well for his later forays into settlement work. But a fortuitous circumstance had "prepared" him in another way. At Harvard, Blaustein befriended Jesse Straus, the eldest son of Isidor Straus, owner of Macy's department store—and, it so happened, the president of the board of the Educational Alliance. Thus, after six years as the Reform rabbi of the German Jewish congregation in Providence, Rhode Island (1892–98), Blaustein came to New York under the aegis of the Straus family. As superintendent of the Alliance, moreover, he would occupy a position far better suited to his

Fig. 16. David Blaustein. *Memoirs of David Blaustein* (1913), courtesy of the author.

unique combination of immigrant background, educational achievement, and organizational abilities.[45]

As a former rabbi, Blaustein had an abiding concern with Judaism. He later recounted: "About ten years ago, when I came to live in New York, I visited a Jewish settlement, and I found a club of young girls studying the religion of Zoroaster, and I asked them whether they had ever studied the religion of Moses. They were horrified. Horrified, because they were given to understand that anything that is Jewish did not belong to settlements, for were they not to become Americanized? Were they not to become cultured? And to be cultured meant to them not to be Jewish." One of David Blaustein's most important contributions to the settlement movement would be the correction of such perverse attitudes toward Judaism. In his new task, Blaustein also proved to be the ideal intermediary between uptown and downtown, and thus personified the mediating qualities of the Educational Alliance. A later commentator would describe "the tragic struggle and martyrdom of David Blaustein, a man who had an unusually fine insight into the problem and whose dream of a 'People's Palace' might be regarded as the bridge between the older humanitarian conception of the 'Settlement' and the modern democratic notion of the 'Community Centre.'"[46]

In a somewhat better known tale of martyrdom, Isidor Straus died aboard the *Titanic* in 1912. Rather than join the other women and children aboard a lifeboat,

Ida Straus insisted upon staying with her husband as the boat went down. In a moving eulogy for his benefactor, Blaustein recalled his arrival at the Alliance fourteen years earlier:

When I was called to the Alliance, it was not yet fully organized. There were different bodies working in the building for the betterment of the conditions of the neighborhood. The central body (the Alliance itself), however, was not yet clear as to what its real aim and object was, and it was therefore a house divided against itself. The directors, under the leadership of Isidor Straus, at last succeeded in uniting the different elements . . . [allowing] the people, through the different committees, to develop freely in accordance with their own inclinations, their hopes and aspirations. When the Educational Alliance took up one of its most important questions—that, since it is a Jewish institution, it should have a Jewish aspect, there were men and women who, in good faith, thought differently. The Jewish ideas have prevailed at last, Mr. Isidor Straus giving his approval and encouragement to the new era of the Alliance.[47]

With characteristic modesty, Blaustein attributed his own accomplishments to Isidor Straus; the "new era" for which he lauded his benefactor had resulted from his own indefatigable efforts. Blaustein's achievement was due in large part to his scientific approach. He first surveyed the neighborhood, and in accordance with his findings, developed "new conceptions" of Jewish social work. As he saw it, the major social problem of the Jewish ghetto was its divisiveness: "He soon realized that the East Side is not a homogenous body, and he also learned, to his great concern, that the leaders of the East Side were . . . divided into factions, groups, constantly fighting, constantly quarreling." He therefore saw it as his mission to seek unity through the agency of the Educational Alliance: "He proposed to find a ground where people with different views and tendencies could meet—he proposed to make the Alliance the melting pot of ideals—he wanted the orthodox to come nearer to the reformers, the socialists to come in contact with the Zionists, the radicals to mingle with the conservatives." The unifying institution should not stand for any particular ideology, therefore, but should rather "introduce educational and social features that would exert a wholesome influence and in their sum, reach every possible group of the entire East Side."[48]

The most important group in need of education was, of course, the children. Blaustein therefore fostered Jewish education at the Alliance, as he described in *Charities & Commons* in 1903:

At half past three, when the [public school] closes, the Educational Alliance becomes a regular beehive of youngsters. They come for various purposes, chiefly for religious and industrial instruction. Most of the people of the neighborhood being Jewish of the more conservative element, the desire of the parents is that their children should receive a religious education. . . . The children are taught biblical history, the ethics of Judaism, and the Hebrew language.[49]

The absorption of the HFSA by the Alliance in 1898 further abetted Blaustein's plan to inject religion into the Alliance. The corporation charter of the new union "authorized and empowered" the two institutions "to consolidate into a single corporation under the name Educational Alliance, for the purpose of promoting the education, religious and civic training, moral and physical culture, the amelioration of the condition and social advancement of the residents of the City of New York, and its vicinity, and especially of those professing the Jewish religion, and of maintaining and conducting for that purpose schools, synagogues, libraries, laboratories, reading, class and club rooms, gymnasium, music and lecture halls." The 1899 charter provides an interesting contrast with the founding statement of a decade earlier. For one, the Jewish constituency of the Alliance is now expressly mentioned; and more critically, the element of Jewish religion has now been added, both in the realm of education and in the provision of religious services. While the Hebrew Free School had pioneered the use of religious services as an educational device, the Alliance would elevate the form to new heights. The introduction of a "people's synagogue" into the program of the Educational Alliance marked the beginning of a new era in the history of the Jewish center: now including a synagogue on its premises, the center would henceforth become a "pool with a shul."[50]

The People's Synagogue of the Educational Alliance was primarily influenced by two indigenous factors. First was the "civilizing" ethos of the Jewish settlement. Julia Richman, director of education at the Alliance, would claim that the purpose of the People's Synagogue was to "remedy the evils of the East Side and better the morals of the people." Thus, "the People's Synagogue evaluated the doctrine of traditional Judaism in terms of good citizenship." Second and more important, the new synagogue was inspired by the people themselves, by the *amcha* (folk) of the Lower East Side; indeed, it was the direct outgrowth of the Russian American Hebrew Association, an immigrant organization founded by Adolph Radin in 1890.

Radin's group had a membership of approximately six hundred, and after being instituted at the Alliance, nearly one thousand began coming "on Friday evenings to hear sermons by the noted orator Rabbi H. Masliansky." Blaustein had brought Zvi Hirsch Masliansky to the Alliance in 1898. Masliansky had immigrated from Russia in 1894, and "immediately began to speak out for Zionism and for the Jew's need to acculturate to America short of abandoning tradition." This familiar stance—for Americanization but against total assimilation—is what recommended Masliansky to the directors of the Educational Alliance. Transcending the ineffectual Americanization of the HFSA, the new People's Synagogue thus offered "a strictly and rigorously orthodox service . . . under decorous and dignified conditions with services both seemly and orderly." Simultaneously "American" and "Russian," the People's Synagogue pioneered the modern Orthodox service, forming what might be called a "progressive shul." Jointly ministered by Radin and Masliansky, the new institution met with the full approval of the immigrant community.[51]

In 1899, the Educational Alliance added "religious work" to the responsibilities of the Committee on Moral Culture whose report proclaimed that "this Institution shall, for all time, plant itself on the Rock of Judaism. . . . This will necessitate a continuation of the People's Synagogue, which has proven a most successful

Fig. 17. Illustration of Zvi Hirsch Masliansky, depicted as a fiery Yiddish orator and ardent defender of the Zionist cause. Courtesy of YIVO.

undertaking." That year, the new synagogue was officially instituted at the Alliance, and Adolph Radin was officially appointed rabbi. In 1900, the eighth annual president's report of the Alliance stated: "The People's Synagogue has become an established institution showing a total attendance of 51,910 or an average of over 700. The services are beautiful and impressive and remarkable for the decorum and devoutness of the worshippers. Without departing from the essentials of the ritual to such an extent as to offend the most conservative, there had been a modernization of procedure which augurs well for the future of religious services in lower New York. This result is largely owing to the intelligent and zealous labors of the Rev. Dr. A. M. Radin, the Rabbi of the Synagogue, and we take this opportunity of expressing to him our acknowledgment of his faithful services. It is expected that the Synagogue will prove practically self-supporting."[52]

The religious life of the Alliance was carefully compartmentalized. As Blaustein described it in 1903, the Alliance entirely shut down on the Sabbath, "for everything except for religious work." On Friday evenings, there was first a traditional religious service for the older generation, and at eight o'clock in the evening two options for the younger: either "an address in Yiddish on a moral topic of the day," or "in the social rooms a gathering of young people where religious and moral topics are discussed." On Saturday morning, there were two services, again divided between old and young. According to Blaustein, the difference consisted in the first's being "of a conservative nature, all the prayers being read in Hebrew, while the service in the afternoon is more progressive and most of the prayers and the sermon being in English." Blaustein also instituted a "young people's service" that sought to strike a balance between the extremes. The service he introduced was a set of compromises: "It was a kind by which the parents were not offended, and yet the young people were attracted. There was no instrumental music but there was congregational singing. The sexes were separated, but the young women were not sent to the gallery. The young men had their heads covered, but there order and decorum prevailed. There was no English read as far as the prayers were concerned, but there was an address in English." It was Blaustein's hope for the future that "services should be orthodox in spirit and modern in form."[53]

Although some have disparaged its activities, the People's Synagogue must be judged a success. Even after the departures of David Blaustein and Adolph Radin (in 1907 and 1909 respectively), the Alliance synagogue continued its active role. The *Annual Report* for 1911 claimed "that we have what is probably the best attendance on Friday evenings and Saturday mornings of any in the city. . . . It is, of course, difficult in speaking of a matter of this kind to demonstrate just how far we have influenced the neighborhood, but the fact that our services at all times are so well attended, speaks for itself." Significantly, the People's Synagogue functioned both as a regular congregation and as a community-wide service. Like a congregation, the People's Synagogue had its ladies' auxiliary and board of trustees, both of which "served their organization splendidly." To combat the phenomenon of "mushroom synagogues," free services for the high holidays were offered attracting nearly three thousand people (thus necessitating the charging of a nominal fee of ten cents). In balancing the demands of congregation and community, the People's Synagogue was one of the first synagogue-centers.[54]

The Educational Alliance Movement and the Emergence of a "Jewish" Center

The Jewish settlement taught immigrant Jews to live as Americans; the Jewish center would teach their children to live as Jews in America. As we have seen, the Educational Alliance attempted to do both, in the end proving to be a transition between the two phases. The actual transformation of the settlement into a center was the result of three Alliance-related developments in the years following the turn of the century: (1) the widespread acceptance of the Educational Alliance idea, forming a national movement; (2) the simultaneous rejection of the uptown-sponsored institutions in favor of "self-help" agencies formed by East Europeans for their own use (for example, new YMHAs, "kindred associations" and other communal centers); and (3) the decline of Americanization as the raison d'être for the center, the consequent search for a new ideological rationale, and finally, the birth of the Jewish center.

1. *The Educational Alliance movement.* When, after the turn of the century,

American Jewish communities sought to improve their earlier initiatives in settlement work, they seized upon the precedent of the Educational Alliance of New York. The appealing idea of "alliance" was actually twofold: first, the reconciliation of disparate subgroups of the Jewish community, especially the German and East European Jews of uptown-downtown fame; and second, the consolidation of competing social and educational agencies into one institution and in one building, for greater efficiency as well as broader appeal to the community. It was the very same impulse toward unification that had inspired both the Jewish Federation movement and the short-lived Kehillah experiment. Like the Kehillah, the Educational Alliance never quite fulfilled its potential; yet, despite its limited success in New York, the Alliance formula caught on around the country. Earlier settlements were redesigned as Alliances or analogous institutions were created anew. The early Jewish center movement was thus largely due to the intoxicating effect of the Educational Alliance idea, which, like old wine decanted into new bottles, was to find form in Jewish community centers throughout the United States.

One of the first Alliance-inspired institutions was founded by the Cleveland branch of the National Council of Jewish Women (NCJW) in 1897, known as the "Council Educational Alliance" (CEA). Not only was its name inspired by the New York institution, but none other than Isaac Spectorsky was hired as director (1900–1906)—the same position he had earlier occupied in New York (1893–98). Predictably, the activities and facilities offered by the CEA were nearly identical to those of the East Side original, including English classes, a library, a gymnasium, social clubs, a Sabbath school, a People's Synagogue, and so forth. As described in 1905: "The Alliance is the natural center for the people of the neighborhood. It interests itself in all the interests of the neighborhood. . . . The emphasis of our work is educational."[55]

The source of that description was Rabbi Moses J. Gries, encountered earlier as the "prophet" of the classical Reform synagogue-center. As a driving force behind the CEA Gries provides a significant connection between the Jewish center movement and the development of the synagogue-center idea. While transforming his own congregation into an institutional synagogue, Rabbi Gries was simultaneously involved in the CEA and remained so throughout his life. The CEA and the "Temple" were therefore parallel institutions, one serving the Jewish immigrant community and the other serving the established German Jews of Cleveland—but both conceived as all-encompassing Jewish communal centers.

Another direct offshoot of the Educational Alliance was the Hebrew Educational Society of Brooklyn (HES), formed to serve the rapidly growing Jewish neighborhood of Brownsville. Organized by the Baron de Hirsch Fund in 1899, the HES "began by proudly calling itself the "younger sister" of the the Educational Alliance in New York and since its creation it has, in many vital respects, duplicated the effective efforts of the East Side institution." Rabbi Alter Landesman, historian of the Brownsville community and longtime executive director of

Fig. 18. The Hebrew Educational Society of Brooklyn. *Jewish Communal Register, 1917–18.* Courtesy of the Library of the Jewish Theological Seminary of America.

the HES (1922–62), notes that the name first suggested for the HES was the Hebrew Educational Alliance. Despite the alteration of the name from Alliance to Society, the program and purpose of "the first Jewish Community Center in Brooklyn" was virtually identical to that of its sister institution of the Lower East Side.[56]

The Alliance movement continued to grow. In the early years of the century, Alliance-styled settlements were established in Albany (Council House, 1900), Detroit (Hannah Schloss Memorial and Jewish Institute, 1900), Boston (West End Educational Union, 1903), Indianapolis (Nathan Morris House, 1904), Newark (Jewish Day Nursery and Neighborhood House, 1905), Columbus (B'nai B'rith House, 1906), Pittsburgh (Columbian School and Settlement, 1906), and Des Moines (Jewish Settlement Association, 1907). All of these institutions were founded as settlement houses and soon evolved into Jewish centers. To take just one example, the Nathan Morris House was established in 1905 by a group of Reform women as a social settlement to serve the Jewish community of the south side of Indianapolis. Its original program included vocational training (such as courses in dressmaking, typing, and cooking) and Americanization classes (not only English instruction but dancing classes too). In subsequent years, other Jewish organization began to make use of the Nathan Morris House: the Zionist organization Banner of Zion, in 1905, and the Workmen's Circle from 1908. In that year, a "School in Jewish History," later called the Council Religious School, was established as well.[57]

Fig. 19. The Jewish Educational Alliance of Savannah. Collection of Peter Schweitzer.

The turning point for most of these institutions was the moment they changed their names, most often, to something approximating "Educational Alliance." The change in nomenclature is significant as it reveals the functional evolution of the centers as well as the process of communal consolidation. In 1899 Saint Louis, for example, the "German" Hebrew Free and Industrial School of 1879 merged with the "Russian" Jewish Alliance of 1890 to form the Jewish Charitable and Educational Union. Two years later, in a brand-new building, the organization became popularly known as "the Alliance." Under the direction of Philip Seman, from 1904 to 1910, the institution came to be called the Jewish Educational Alliance. In subsequent years, the same name was applied to institutions in Atlanta (1908), Baltimore (1909), Columbus (1910), and Savannah (1912). Approximations of the name included the Jewish Educational Institute in Kansas City (1909), the Educational Alliance in Los Angeles (1910), and the Jewish Educational League in Toledo (1913).[58]

The addition of the modifier "Jewish" made clear that these institutions were to be unabashedly sectarian; but the popularity of "Educational Alliance" nevertheless reveals their still transitional quality; they were not yet Jewish centers in the sense of having a positive Jewish program. Benjamin Rabinowitz identified the year 1910 as the high point of the Alliance movement. In that year, more than seventy-five "Jewish neighborhood centers and settlement-type agencies" were in existence around the country. Together with some fifty-seven nonsectarian centers serving a Jewish clientele, these represented "nearly one-third of the total number of settlement houses in existence at the time." Within the following decade, many if not most of these institutions would abandon their original philanthropic stance and become something new: a Jewish community center.[59]

Furthermore, Rabinowitz stressed the importance of the construction of new buildings in the development of the Jewish center: "One important result of this trend [to Federation] was the merger of functions and the erection of buildings to house several organizations. These buildings frequently afforded facilities for federation headquarters, the Hebrew School, the YMHA, the YWHA, the B'nai B'rith and other lodges, and similar communal activities. In many respects they functioned as community centers." He cites as early examples the Saint Louis Jewish Charitable and Educational Union—also known as the Jewish Alliance (1901)—and the Detroit Hannah Schloss Building and Jewish Institute (1903). The tendency acclerated in the following decade, as in the case of the Atlanta YMHA (1902), which, after merging with the Jewish Educational Alliance (1908), had a new building erected in 1910 as "a community building, a social center for all Jewry."[60]

Indeed, we have already seen the importance of a centralized location and all-encompassing facility in the precedents of the Educational Alliance in New York and Touro Hall in Philadelphia. In the years following the turn of the century, the urge to centralize in one building appeared in community after community. At the 1909 convention of the New York Kehillah held at the United Hebrew Charities headquarters on East 21st Street, Judah Magnes suggested that "this beautiful building, moreover, or some other such building, might be made into a *bet am*, the Jewish Communal House, and here Jewish communal activities might find a center."[61]

Another important example was the 1913 Jewish Communal Building of Indianapolis. Rabinowitz quotes from the building campaign of 1911, whose stated purpose was "to erect a communal building for a Jewish Center and for educational activities." The move away from philanthropic motives and toward the principle of self-help was evident in the stated desire "to combine all Jewish activities, as lodges and all other organizations in this movement, so as to build up an institution on democratic principles and to eliminate all charitable phases." In order to entice "every Jewish citizen" to "become a member of the institution," the planned facilities included "a library, gymnasium, swimming pool, lodge-rooms, and auditorium, kitchen facilities, dining room, and play-grounds."[62]

Morris Feuerlicht, the Hungarian-born Reform rabbi of the Indianapolis Hebrew Congregation, completes the picture of the Jewish Communal Building, explaining the significance of both the "communal" name and the "central" building:

Shortly before the Jewish Federation was formally organized in the fall of 1904, about a dozen members of the community met to establish the Nathan Morris House, a local equivalent of the neighborhood settlement movement then growing in popularity. . . . [In 1913] the federation was able to purchase a large wooden structure that had been used previously as a sort of public assembly and gymnasium for the general neighborhood and called it the Jewish Communal Building, to house the activities of both the federation and the Nathan Morris House. It was insisted that the name *Communal* be emphasized, because, rightly or wrongly, we in

Indianapolis held the notion that much of the social service being rendered by the neighborhood settlements of that day was inspired and consciously motivated by a feeling of social superiority on the part of rich to poor, of privileged to underprivileged. We wanted to avoid every semblance of any such condescending or patronizing attitude. We sought to make our settlement house as realistically democratic as possible in the purely communal sense of the term. *All* members, rich and poor, privileged and underprivileged alike, were to be full and equal participants in all its various and manifold activities.[63]

In like manner, the desire to ally the factions of the community was realized by Jewish settlements throughout the country. Adopting the Educational Alliance format of comprehensive communal service (but not communal control), the revamped settlements finally moved into new buildings, completing the process of transformation into community centers. As Selig Adler and Thomas Connolly wrote of Buffalo, "the Jewish Community Building [dedicated in March 1914] served as the transition between Zion House, which had the single aim of charity, and the Jewish Center with a program designed for the entire population." Still, the institutions were financed and ultimately controlled by the upper-class establishment and not quite so "democratic" as they imagined themselves to be. The next stage, therefore, was brought about when the East European immigrants began to engage actively in the development of Jewish centers of their own.[64]

2. *The Immigrant Center.* Often, centers originally established to create an "alliance" between uptown and downtown had the unintended effect of giving the immigrant community an arena of their own, and eventually, the upper hand in communal affairs. Communal hegemony would thus be transferred through the Jewish center. The process began when immigrant-led institutions—especially Talmud Torahs—were welcomed into the constellation of activities at the settlement/center. The next step was to bring the two communal forces into equilibrium. In Atlanta, the Jewish Educational Alliance served both subcommunities simultaneously, and also provided neutral ground for cooperation and contact between the two groups. A true alliance of uptown and downtown, the JEA was founded as the result of parallel initiatives. In 1906, the Russian Jewish immigrants of Atlanta held a "mass meeting" to organize a "Hebrew Institute" that would offer educational and recreational amenities. A few months later, a group of German Jews began to raise funds for a building for the Free Kindergarten and Social Settlement. After two years of separate activity, the two groups agreed to join forces. The Jewish Educational Alliance, founded in 1909, was the result, and soon became the center of Jewish communal life. "It is a school, recreation center, club and shule for our people," explained a spokesman in 1915. "You can not explain it on paper. You must see it and catch the spirit of the hive."[65]

To make such multiple activities possible, it was necessary to have a substantial constituency, and this the East Europeans provided. Thus, the simple fact of population size led to the dominance of the center by the former immigrants. Even when built by German and Russian Jews together, the center was mostly frequented by the immigrants—there were simply more of them—who soon predominated overall. Also worth noting is the effect the Alliance had on the various subdivisions of the immigrant community. Isaac Fein described the case of Baltimore and the Jewish Educational Alliance of 1909, which "brought together East European Jews stemming from different countries. *Landsmanshaftn* remained strong, but the beginning of an amalgam was made within the walls of the JEA; it was a melting pot of its own for East Baltimore Jewry. It would certainly make possible another and much more difficult task, the consolidation of this group with the German Jews."[66]

The first center to be established by the immigrant community for its own use was the Chicago Hebrew Institute (CHI) of 1903. Chicago makes an interesting case study in the development of the Jewish center, as the several stages are clearly marked by distinct institutions, having no transitional body such as the Educational Alliance. In 1892, the Maxwell Street settlement house was established in the west side of Chicago as a Jewish version of its famous neighbor, Jane Addams's Hull House—in fact, the Maxwell Street Settlement was organized at a meeting held at Hull House, with Jane Addams in attendance. Like the pioneer settlement house, Maxwell Street was intended to bring American refinement and culture to the immigrant masses; like Addams, the resident workers of the Jewish settlement were well-bred young men and women who had "descended into the Ghetto . . . to help the "poor Russian immigrants." While Jewish-sponsored with all good intentions, the Maxwell Street Settlement failed to win the heart of the Jewish immigrant community—a problem also experienced by Hull House. Expressing their dissatisfaction with the settlements, the Jewish immigrants of Chicago began to form their own institutions. In 1894, the Self-Educational Club was founded "as a direct reaction to the Settlement."[67]

Having rejected the established settlement houses, a group of immigrants nevertheless looked to them as models and created an institution identical in function; the phenomenon revealed the degree of their own Americanization. Although the Self-educational Club solved the problem of settlement condescension, it entirely bypassed the problem of intercommunal tension. Not only did Germans and East Europeans remain separate, but the Chicago Jewish community remained torn between the competing demands of Orthodox and Reform Jews, Zionists and radicals, and the old and new generations. A new institution was called for, one that could unite the factions and unify Chicago Jewry. Such a center was the Hebrew Institute, founded "as an alternative to American institutions of the Hull House type and American Jewish institutions of the Self-educational Club type." Its guiding principle would be "self-help," entailing, finally, escape from the unwanted support and influence of the uptown establishment. The founding of the Chicago Hebrew Institute in 1903 was thus a declaration of independence for the Jews of Chicago's west side, and heralded the beginning of a new era for the Jewish immigrant in America.[68]

Yet despite its claim of uniqueness, the Chicago Hebrew Institute had much in common with the Educational Alliance of New York, the original "Hebrew Institute." The first point of comparison is the name—in all likelihood, the founders of the CHI chose it to differentiate themselves from the Educational Alliance in the belief that the Alliance name represented nonsectarian neutrality and that "Hebrew Institute," on the other hand, would confer Jewish legitimacy—ironic, considering the original intent of the name. Certainly, the word "Hebrew" meant something very different to the organizers of the Chicago Institute in 1903 than it had to the founders of the New York Institute in 1889. Second, and despite its claim to self-reliance, the CHI came to depend on the backing of German-Jewish financiers, most notably the department store magnate Julius Rosenwald. Third, the CHI charter sounded very much like that of the original Hebrew Institute, stating as its purpose, "the promotion of education, civic training, moral and physical culture, the amelioration of the condition and social advancement of the Jewish residents of Chicago . . . and maintaining and conducting for that purpose schools, libraries, laboratories, reading classes and club rooms, gymnasium, music and lecture halls . . . all to be conducted under Jewish auspices."[69]

The CHI also duplicated the Alliance in its incredible range of activities and broad popularity. Due to its commitment to 'self-help,' however, the CHI followed a different course of development than the Alliance and grew into a distinctive institution. In his 1917 *Jewish Philanthropy*, Boris Bogen emphasized its uniqueness, describing the CHI as a "new departure" in Jewish social work: "In Chicago, the Hebrew Institute is a representative type of an institution of somewhat different principle from those of the Educational Alliance. Its motto is 'Self-Help.' It asserts that the establishment of charitable institutions by patronizing lodges or societies in the midst of the Russian Jewish community is a detriment to the people whom it is introduced for, rather than a blessing. . . . What is the institute? It is not a settlement. It is not a school. It is not a social center. It is not a club. It is not a charitable institution. It is—Unique. It cannot be readily classified because it is the spontaneous outgrowth of the demand of the Jewish community of two-thirds of Chicago. . . . What is the institute? Well—it is just *The* Institute."[70]

The institute may have stood for "self-help" and "education, refinement, and decorum," but toward what end? Bogen's vague statement of the institute's purpose was due to the vacuum created by the absence of that old reliable, Americanization. In fact, the institution would require some new rationale to supplant the former call to Americanize, an agenda that had become a dead letter. For one, it was associated with uptown condescension; second, it was no longer seen as the necessity that it once had been, since so many immigrants had gone through the natural process of acculturation and proved that Americanization took care of itself. Moreover, Jewish institutions themselves had "Americanized," changing from the British-inspired, patrician-led settlement house to the more indigenous and democratic alliances, institutes, and centers. The settlement-type institution therefore needed a new motivating purpose, a new ideology to replace the old. The Americanized Zionists who founded the Chicago Hebrew Institute provided just such a raison d'être for Jewish group life in America: the principle of *klal yisrael*, the unity of the Jewish people. It was a principle on which the various elements of the community could agree—even Reform Jews—and an idea that would enable the Hebrew Institute to become the center of Jewish life in Chicago.

The CHI thus became the first communal institution to be inspired by and infused with the new American Jewish ideals of cultural Zionism and ethnic Jewishness—the very ideas that define the "Jewish" in Jewish center. Yet it is important to note that the ideals mentioned were never adopted as explicit ideologies by the Hebrew Institute. Though founded by Zionists, the CHI was a non-ideological institution, a neutral position it had to occupy in order to serve effectively as an all-inclusive communal center—the same compromise that has been employed by the Jewish community center ever since. Paradoxically, its lack of ideology was legitimated by the ideology of Zionism; but only a Zionism of the watered-down, nonpolitical variety that defines the Jews as an ethnic group based on peoplehood and culture, a status that as easily legitimates life in the American diaspora as in the "holy land" of Israel. Such a Zionism was palatable to all in the community, including the Reform rabbis who supported the Institute wholeheartedly. Thus symbolizing the unity of Jewish peoplehood, the Hebrew Institute became the Jewish center of Chicago.[71]

The "Zionist" ethos of peoplehood would serve the Jewish center in a general sense by uniting all the various elements of the community; but more particularly, by bringing religion back into Jewish community life. As in Chicago, most center organizers were cultural Zionists who, under the influence of Ahad Ha'am, were intent on the modern revival of Judaism. Hence, in the 1905 compilation *The Russian Jew in the United States,* Jeanette Isaacs (Mrs. Benjamin Davis) could describe the immigrant Jewish community of Chicago as follows:

The Zionist movement is also one of the causes which has led to a religious awakening, and has resolved itself into an educational revival, chiefly on matters of Jewish interest. . . . In fact, wherever a Zion organization is formed some kind of religious study is introduced, and the seeds sown will undoubtedly bear fruit in the future, for the Jewish consciousness has been aroused. . . . The young people are aroused to the importance of action. This is evidenced by their interest in a movement which is now launched by them for a Chicago Hebrew Institute that shall include synagogue, religious schools, classes, clubs, gymnasium, and the various forms of modern culture and entertainment, physical, moral and intellectual, under Jewish auspices, with the doors open for worship, study, and recreation. The time is ripe for such a movement.[72]

In 1908, David Blaustein arrived in Chicago to become the new superintendent of the CHI. He soon discovered that the problem there was different from that in New York. "The process of Americanization," he would say of Chicago, "is taken care of by itself. But it is their Judaism that the people lose too rapidly."

At the CHI, therefore, Blaustein redoubled his earlier efforts to inject Judaism into the Jewish center. The modern synagogue program he introduced in Chicago was brought with him from New York, of course, as was the innovation of a periodical publication. The latter idea did not derive from the Alliance, however, but from the model of the Lower East Side community. He had observed the powerful moral influence of the Yiddish press in the immigrant community, and even secretly aided his friend Masliansky in the publication of the *Jewish World*. In Chicago, he was freed of the restrictions imposed by an uptown board, and felt no such compunctions. The device of an in-house publication, tying together the community and "spreading its influence," had been pioneered by congregational rabbis in the late nineteenth century—including Rabbi David Blaustein in Providence—and would later be widely adopted by the synagogue-center as well.[73]

The new synagogue, on the other hand, was not so well received. In fact, Blaustein found himself in the center of new disputes at the CHI, as when "he prohibited the speaking of Emma Goldman, and the Radicals boycotted the institute. He organized a modern Orthodox congregation, and the Reform element found fault with him." Apparently, the unifying intent of the Jewish center did not succeed so well in the metropolis of Chicago. Yet despite the fallibility of the Chicago model, "self-activity" in Jewish center development became the norm elsewhere around the country. Boris Bogen reported on the subject of "neighborhood self-activity": "The self-activity of the masses has lately received expression in institutions administering to certain groups only and having a definite program of propaganda. Thus, in a number of cities, we find Radical Centers, Zion Institutes, Labor Lyceums, and so forth. All these institutions are still in the experimental stage, and have great difficulty in raising sufficient funds. The management is rather crude. It is difficult to predict their future."[74]

Just as the earlier Jewish settlement philosophy reflected the progressive ideal of the melting pot, such specialized Jewish centers reflected the new ideal of cultural pluralism, expressed internally, within the Jewish community. Other cities besides Chicago experienced such communal differentiation and witnessed "institutions administering to certain groups only." The first Zionist organization in Philadelphia, for example, created a center in the same year as the founding of the CHI, whose "object was to serve the ten Zionist societies which had been sired by the *Ohavei Zion*. A lecture room, school room, a gymnasium and a library which contained more than five hundred volumes became the city's Zionist center. It was called the Zion Institute and was dedicated on *Hanukah, 1902*." More common and more significant, however, were centers that, like the CHI, aimed to serve the entire Jewish community.[75]

In Boston, Zionism played a role as well, although the Jewish centers were never construed as Zionist per se. The key personality here was Jacob de Haas, the British Jewish journalist notable in Zionist history as the link between Theodore Herzl and Louis D. Brandeis. In 1906, de Haas left the Zionist movement in New

York for Boston and immediately began to involve himself in Jewish community life and center activity. For four years, de Haas served as superintendent of the YMHA of Boston where he "emphasized the values of communal participation." Inevitably, the former journalist also became involved in the affairs of the local Jewish newspaper, the *Boston Advocate*. The *Advocate* had at one time been the official organ of the YMHA. De Haas reestablished the connection after taking over control of the paper in the summer of 1908, and shortly changed its name to the *Jewish Advocate*. He would later recall the controversy evoked by the name change; some feared it would sound "too Jewish." But de Haas was adamant in his intentions to "Judaize" and to unify the Jewish community of Boston. In 1927, he recalled the beginning of his involvement with the paper: "We re-dedicated the paper to the unification of the Boston community. A little less of German and a little less of Russian, and a good deal more of Jewish."[76]

In the pages of the new *Jewish Advocate*, editor de Haas began to advocate his favorite causes, such as the establishment of Jewish "centers" both in Palestine and in Boston. In January 1908, the front page of the *Advocate* announced a new movement to establish a "People's Institute," describing it as "a move to have the YMHA make its headquarters in the West End." The neighborhood of the YMHA building on East Concord Street was nearly empty of Jews, whereas the new in-stitute would be located "in the centre of the largest Jewish community" in Boston, and would be available "for the general use of all Jews and Jewish Associ-ations in the North and West Ends." Significantly, it was an attempt to integrate a "German" Jewish institution into the life of the East European immigrant com-munity. De Haas was, again, deeply concerned with unifying the competing fac-tions of the Jewish community of Boston, whether through the medium of a newspaper or a Jewish center. By April, the editor lamented the delays in the es-tablishment of the "Jewish People's Institute," and enumerated its objectives as including both the Americanizing of the immigrant and Jewish education to counter Christian proselytizing. Finally, in October of that year, the "Jewish Peo-ple's Institute" was opened in the West End, sponsored by both the Educational Union settlement house and the YMHA of Jacob de Haas.[77]

At its opening ceremonies, none other than David Blaustein showed up to give his blessings to the project. The featured address of the evening was given by Samuel Straus of the *New York Globe* who was, like de Haas, a Zionist, a progres-sive, and a journalist. His speech, described as "markedly Orthodox religious" (read: Jewish survivalist), included the following exhortation: "We need to check these tendencies [of assimilation]; and in every Jewish community there should be a home and a centre, where the young men and women of today may congre-gate and learn how to solve these problems of extricating themselves from these influences. . . . All this can be done by a Jewish Educational Institution, and all this could not be done, and was not done, because of its absence."[78]

After a few years' experience, de Haas wrote: "[the Jewish People's Institute] was organized four years ago. It was opened by the Jewish community as an educational centre and as a home for those who the community felt needed such a centre. The opening of the institution was an important event in the communal work of this city. It was the first practical attempt at an institution which should be of the people who were to derive benefit from it." The "self-help" institution did not last very long, however, as the younger and more upwardly mobile Jews of the West End began to help themselves by leaving the immigrant ghetto for the newer Jewish neighborhoods of Chelsea, Roxbury, and Brookline. As in Chicago, the Americanizing aspects of the center no longer held any appeal for second-generation American Jews, and their institutions would reflect instead the social and recreational emphasis of the YMHA. In fact, the formation of YMHAs by East Europeans became the new trend in center activity and thus the first center to be established by the second-generation "Russian" Jews of Boston was the Roxbury YMHA of 1917. In the following year, the president of the West End YMHA submitted an article to the "YMHA News" section of the *Advocate* entitled, "The YMHA Must Specialize in Jewishness." It was a sentiment that had originated a decade before, however, at least as early as 1908.[79]

3. *Judaization replaces Americanization.* Both of the trends inspired by the Educational Alliance and the Chicago Hebrew Institute thus led to the replacement of the ideology of Americanization by that of "Judaization." The first, the spread of the Alliance idea to Jewish communities around the country, created Americanizing agencies in a period when it was becoming more and more evident that immigrant adjustment to America was no longer the issue. The call for Americanization was supplanted by "the demand for an affirmative Jewish program," which "became pronounced in the early 1900s, and was due in large measure to the opposition of immigrant groups to the assimilation policies of the philanthropically administered agencies." The second trend, the creation of new centers ("Hebrew Institutes," "Jewish People's Institutes," and YMHAs) by the immigrants themselves, led more directly to the same conclusion: that the first obligation of the Jewish center was to perpetuate Jewish life in America; the integration of the Jew into American life was being accomplished with or without the center.[80]

The would-be "Americanizers" of the previous generation had vastly underestimated the power of the American environment to socialize the immigrant; they mistakenly believed the process needed their help and intervention. Little did they realize that they could neither speed it nor impede it in any way; the process of Americanization was inexorable. Thus, institutions set up to Americanize came to realize that they must find some other rationale for their existence. At the same time, the predicament of the Educational Alliance, a sectarian institution saddled with an ideology of nonsectarianism, begged for help. The obvious solution to both problems would be, in the words of David Blaustein, "that since it is a Jewish institution, it should have a Jewish aspect." But what aspect of Judaism would appeal to the German Jewish supporters of these institutions?[81]

It was at this point that Jewish philanthropists discovered the "Social Gospel" ideal of Reform Judaism that identified Judaism with social justice. Whereas

Reform rabbis had begun to stress the *tsedaka* connection at least a decade earlier, the community at large only seized the idea after the turn of the century when faced with the problem of philanthropic rationale. Thus Boris Bogen wrote in 1916: "Social service was par excellence the medium of religion in the Reform Jewry of Cincinnati; it was religion. In the Hebrew Union College there was established a social-service course for the instruction of the embryonic rabbis and I was the teacher. This was a new thing in theological seminaries; since then social service has been put into the curricula of most seminaries, non-Jewish and Jewish as well." Social service was not only introduced into the Reform seminary, but into congregational life as well. Whereas the philanthropic impulse of the rabbis had manifested itself in the 1890s in the extracurricular activity of the sisterhoods, it was not until after 1900 that such activities were brought into the "main" (that is, male) body of the congregation. In 1903, the Brotherhood of Temple Emanu-El in New York founded its settlement house as an explicitly "religious center."[82]

Rabbi Stephen S. Wise—religious Reformist, social Progressivist, and leading Zionist—established the Free Synagogue in 1907, and was soon called upon to open a branch on the Lower East Side. As he later described it: "Within a year thereafter many requests came to me to found a Free Synagogue branch on the East Side. These requests were fortified by a meeting held at the Henry Street Settlement, suggested, if not called, by Lillian Wald, a meeting for the most part of young people under Henry Street Settlement inspiration. . . . We found a meeting place, namely, Clinton Hall near Grand Street, for Sabbath Eve services, and we conjoined with this a religious school to provide a pleasant and friendly meeting place for young people, who were all but compelled to find their social life amid places unfit for the young intellectuals of the East Side."[83]

The founding of the downtown branch of the Free Synagogue came at a pivotal moment: 1908 was also the year in which David Blaustein moved to Chicago, and the year when Jacob de Haas established the Jewish People's Institute in Boston. It was the year that saw Israel Zangwill's play *The Melting Pot* celebrate the triumph of Americanization. The same year witnessed a course of events that marked a watershed in American Jewish history and a turning point in the gradual transition from Americanization to Judaization. In the spring of that year, word began to spread that a new movement was afoot in New York. An April editorial in the *Boston Advocate* announced the advent of "REJUDAISING," simply the idea "that Jewish institutions must endeavor to do specific Jewish work." The editorialist, probably Jacob de Haas, continued by lauding the efforts of Louis Marshall and Cyrus Sulzberger for "propagating the gospel of Judaisation in institutionalism," and by excoriating the opponents of the idea, notably Julia Richman who "is to be forced out of the Educational Alliance." A new era was dawning, the editor implied, as "New York is about to repent assimilation and seeks to be conservative in all things Jewish." The public debut of the new philosophy was scheduled for the following month.[84]

The Fifth Biennial Session of the National Conference of Jewish Charities in the United States was held in Richmond, Virginia, in May 1908. One session of the conference entitled, "The Unification of Jewish Communal Activities," signaled the beginning of the Kehillah movement and the trend to communal federation. (Note: this discussion took place four months before the infamous Bingham incident, which is usually cited as the impetus for the Kehillah.) Another session, "The Need of a Distinctly Jewish Tendency in the Conduct of Jewish Educational Insitutions," served notice that the time of Judaization had arrived. A conference paper under that title was prepared by Louis Marshall, and the several discussants included David Blaustein and Boris Bogen. Marshall's paper was a spirited defense of Jewish sectarianism, religious education, and cultural pluralism. In unequivocal terms, he offered a fresh perspective on the "Jewishness" of Jewish communal life:

A Jewish educational institution must be one which is, presumably, organized for the purpose of functionalizing Jewish conceptions and of promoting Jewish tendencies, otherwise there would be no reason for establishing Jewish educational institutions or for conducting orphan asylums, institutions for dependent or delinquent children, settlements or even hospitals under Jewish auspices. . . .

Unless, therefore, our educational institutions shall create for themselves a Jewish atmosphere, and a distinctly Jewish tendency, they have no reason whatever for existing. It is only the presence of such a tendency, which makes them Jewish; not the fact that they are constructed with funds contributed by Jews, that they are officered by Jews, that Jews alone support them, and that Jews alone are their beneficiaries. . . . The effort should be, not to strive for a minimum, but for a maximum of Jewishness.[85]

Not unexpectedly, David Blaustein agreed "with everything that Mr. Marshall has said." He added, however, the admonition that in addition to religion, Jewish social life must also become the responsibility of the Jewish center, for the following reason: "I am going to make a bold statement, which may be surprising to some. Inter-marriage among the children of the immigrants or better the poor classes is surprisingly large . . . social life should, therefore, be in the settlements with the end in view of the preservation of the Jew." The statement was an early and prescient commentary on the threat of intermarriage to Jewish survival in America. Besides providing religious education, Blaustein recommended, the Jewish center must provide a place for young Jews to have social intercourse with other Jews. The innovation here was the use of Jewish religious and educational resources for explicitly social purposes, implying that Judaism is a means, not an end. Similarly, the secularist Boris Bogen complained that Marshall's address had stressed Jewish religion over the social amelioration of Jews as the purpose of Jewish philanthropy. The general consensus of the discussants seemed to be that in addition to the important social work being done by "educational institutions," the infusion of Jewish content—however vaguely defined—was a desirable goal. The survival of both Jews and Judaism would thus find common cause in the Jewish center.[86]

The very career of David Blaustein encapsulated the dual purpose of the Jewish center. We have already reviewed some of his manifold roles as Jewish educator, Zionist organizer, Progressive rabbi, professor of Semitics, settlement house director, founder of a model synagogue, and community ombudsman. In 1904, while still superintendent of the Educational Alliance, he made a study of the conditions of Jewish life in smaller communities throughout the United States. While reporting a general sense of malaise, he also ascertained "a revival of interest in Jewish matters; and this is not so much a religious revival as it is one of interest in all that pertains to Jewish brotherhood which has always been the characteristic relation of Jew and Jew." His main recommendation therefore was "the need of some social or religious center" to replicate the intensive community life of the larger cities.[87]

Blaustein was able to act upon his own suggestion when, in 1910, after returning to New York from Chicago, "he undertook a special investigation of the scattered Jewish population in the smaller communities throughout the United States. His purpose was to determine on a plan for establishing social centers to attract the Jewish population from the large cities and thus increase their distribution among the small communities by the organization of centers for educational and communal endeavor." Thus, one conclusion Blaustein had drawn from his years of experience at the Educational Alliance and the Chicago Hebrew Institute was the importance of social life in the maintenance of Jewish community. Within such centers of social work he also introduced religious activity, establishing religion as a central aspect of Jewish communal life. But what of the synagogue itself? In his 1904 report, Blaustein had lamented the existence in New Orleans of nothing but synagogues to serve as Jewish centers.[88]

In 1911, one year before his untimely death, Blaustein returned to Providence for the dedication ceremony of the new temple for the congregation whom he had served as rabbi from 1892 to 1898. After first reiterating his commitment to Jewish life in small communities, Blaustein "then urged the members of the Congregation to make their new temple, not only a place for religious services, but that it should become the center of the Jewish community of Providence. He further urged the members to make their new House of Worship the center of all communal activities of the Jews of Providence. Dr. Blaustein impressed his audience with the fact that a House of God should always be open to the 'stranger within the gates.' He said that the vestry-room of a synagogue should be a common meeting place for people in all walks of life and different shades of opinion."[89]

Blaustein was concerned that the new temple might serve to divide the community rather than unite its diverse elements. Just as the "people's synagogue" had been a central, unifying feature of the Jewish center, so too would the synagogue be the central, unifying component of the Jewish community. The purpose of the synagogue was, as always, to serve God; in Blaustein's vision, however, it would also serve Jews as a center of Jewish community. This vision would later constitute the definition of the synagogue-center.

Blaustein died in 1912 at the age of forty-six. Though he did not live to witness the final demise of the settlement agenda of Americanization, he had done much to bring it about. In 1913, a new umbrella organization, the Council of Young Men's and Kindred Associations, was formed which merged the YMHA and settlement movements. The following year saw the onset of World War I and the cessation of mass Jewish immigration. Thus the Jewish center movement came to realize that in the future it would no longer administer to immigrants but to their children. Many of those young Jewish men soon joined the armed forces and found themselves in the quandary of providing for their Jewish needs—both religious and social. The communal response was the formation of the Jewish Welfare Board (JWB) in 1917, whose major activities were the provision of rabbis during wartime and the creation of "*Jewish* Welfare Board *Centres*" as social centers for the Jewish troops. These centers were largely inspired by the example of the YMHA. The JWB centers served all Jews, regardless of religious affiliation or social status. When, after the war, the JWB came to parallel the CYMHKA, the organizations merged and gave birth to the Jewish Center movement of the 1920s.[90]

Yet even with the rise of the Judaized center, the settlement had not disappeared. In his 1917 doctoral dissertation (published in 1918 as *Jewish Education in New York City*), Alexander Dushkin described the three principal educational settings of the contemporary Jewish community—"the Synagogue, the Settlement and the School"—each of which, he claimed, was then competing "to become the [primary] unit of organized Jewish life." In common, their tendency was to broaden their range of activities to "reach more effectively . . . all the members of the Jewish family" and thus to become a Jewish communal center. The ultimate goal was nothing less than the "reintegration of Jewish communal life." Because the trend entailed the merging of social, educational, and religious functions, the three distinct institutions—religious synagogue, social settlement, and educational school—began to undergo a process of cross-fertilization and even unification. Social settlements became educational centers, Jewish schools incorporated synagogues, and Reform temples began to engage in settlement work. The synagogue, as Dushkin later admitted, was on its way toward becoming "the inevitable unit of American Jewish life," and it too was prone to the tendency to unify. This "department store" mentality in Jewish life ultimately led to the movement for the creation of synagogue-centers—yet first, there would appear on the scene a movement to modernize, centralize, and "departmentalize" the Jewish school.[91]

4

SCHOOL
Jewish Education at the Center

It may take some time before our influential Jews recognize that the Jewish educational problem is the most serious problem that confronts American Jews as Jews, and that upon its solution depends the future of Judaism and the Jews in this country; and then we must first find the few educational leaders with the necessary ability who will devote themselves to Jewish education . . . [and above all], we must have recourse to the establishment of a number of model schools or educational centres. —SAMSON BENDERLY, 1908[1]

THE LIFE STORY of Samson Benderly (1876–1944) is somewhat of an anomaly in Jewish history. A native of Safed, Palestine, he emigrated to Baltimore, Maryland, in 1898. He was a promising young physician who left the practice of medicine to enter the field of Jewish education. A descendant of famed rabbis and passionately devoted to Judaism and Jewish learning, he was an acculturated Zionist routinely denounced as an atheistic "Bolshevik." And most puzzling of all: though Benderly was the key figure in the development of modern Jewish education in this country, few American Jews have ever heard of him. No schools are named for him, no chairs of higher learning are endowed in his honor. Despite his own prodigious efforts on behalf of Jewish education, he is remembered only tangentially, in association with those he mentored. Perhaps the sole testament to his name, though an appropriate one at that, is the fond nickname given the corps of young disciples who carried his teachings across the land: the "Benderly boys."

Benderly intended nothing less than to place Jewish education at the center of the communal agenda. Knowing that he would not succeed alone, he planned to train a select group of young men and women as the leadership cadre of a new Jewish educational system. As he foretold in 1908: "Let us suppose that we have in the United States half a dozen young men who are willing to champion the cause of Jewish educational reform and devote themselves to it exclusively. . . . The six young men concentrate all their experience and financial help on the establishment of a number of model schools. These schools are situated in the heart of Jewish centres, and are connected with model [teacher] training schools.

Fig. 20. Samson Benderly, circa 1910, at a Zionist conference in Tannersville, N.Y. Courtesy of the Library of the Jewish Theological Seminary of America.

. . . The people have found out that the model schools know the secret of combining Jewishness with Americanism, and they are flooding the schools with their children. The training schools are working overtime, and the model school system is expanding rapidly. Thus, in the course of a generation a substantial school system is established."[2]

Benderly began to put his plan into action immediately following his move to New York City in 1910 to head the new Bureau of Jewish Education of the Kehillah. With the aid of Israel Friedlaender and Mordecai Kaplan, he combed the colleges of New York to find likely candidates and soon discovered Alexander Dushkin, Isaac Berkson, Israel Chipkin, Leo Honor, Barnet Brickner, and Rebecca Aaronson (later to become Mrs. Brickner). These, and a few dozen others, went on to become the organizers and directors of Jewish schools and citywide bureaus of education around the country, effectively spreading the gospel of progressive Jewish pedagogy. Acknowledged as Benderly's protégés—hence the "Benderly boys"—they collectively instituted their mentor's modern system of Jewish education in America. For this achievement alone, Benderly deserves the title of "father of American Jewish education."[3]

In their teacher's image, the Benderly boys combined intense Jewish learning with progressive educational theory. Benderly's plan, in cooperation with Mordecai Kaplan (in his capacity as principal of the Teachers Institute of the Jewish Theological Seminary), was to train his young charges along a dual track. While taking courses in Jewish studies at the Seminary, they would simultaneously pursue graduate work in education at nearby Teachers College of Columbia University. Kaplan the rabbi expressed some reservation that their religious education would suffer, and he was right. Under the spell of Benderly, the group became entranced by two modernist, secular worldviews: the cultural Zionism of Ahad Ha'am and the progressive *paideia* of John Dewey. As the "agnostic rabbi" whose writings inspired the movement of cultural Zionism, Ahad Ha'am provided an intellectual foundation for Benderly's group. And as the leading light of American educational philosophy, Dewey was an especially potent influence. Both were progressive thinkers oriented to the new century, and each in their way attempted to replace traditional religion with a modern "civil religion" of humanistic education and democratic culture. Just as Mark Twain jokingly called himself the "Shalom Aleichem" of American literature, John Dewey might be thought of as the "Ahad Ha'am" of American education. The net effect of the dual program, therefore, was to bring the best of contemporary thought into the sphere of Jewish educational discourse.[4]

Together, Benderly and his "boys" would bring Jewish education into the modern age. One of their main achievements—and there were many, including the communalization of Jewish education and the invention of Jewish educational camping—was the transformation of the Jewish school. In the campaign to place Jewish education at the center of communal concern, they employed the *klal yisrael* ethos of cultural Zionism as the foundation of a new Jewish curriculum. Applying Deweyan principles to the traditional communal school of the Jewish community, they reinvented Jewish schooling in the image of the progressive public school and recreational youth facility. In short, they turned the Talmud Torah into a Jewish center. Through the intervention of the new Jewish educators, therefore, a third source of the Jewish center phenomenon must be added to the YMHA and the Jewish settlement: the Talmud Torah.

The Jewish Center–Talmud Torah Connection

The connection between Jewish schooling and the Jewish center concept came about in two distinct ways. The first originated in the spontaneous association of the immigrant Talmud Torah with early Jewish center trends. As the Talmud Torah was adapted to American circumstances around the turn of the century, it began to evolve into a kind of Jewish center itself. In the process of its Americanization, that is, the traditional school of the Jewish community was modernized, feminized, Hebraized, and ultimately reconceived explicitly as a "Jewish center." This reconceptualization was effected through the second link between Jewish school and center, the philosophical connection described above. At the very moment that Jewish immigrants were busy modernizing the institution, Jewish intellectuals were refining the concept of a "center" in Jewish life. The two trends dovetailed when Benderly and other like-minded progressives applied the theoretical concept to the practical movement. We first briefly examine the course of intellectual influence, and then in some greater detail, the popular movement. The two will coalesce in the final section describing the "Jewish school center" experiment—conceived and led by Benderly boys, of course.

Alexander Dushkin was among the first of the Benderly boys and perhaps the best known. In his 1917 study of Jewish education in New York City, Dushkin categorized the principal educational settings of the contemporary Jewish community: the synagogue, the settlement, and the school. As he described them, the three institutions were then in competition "to become the [principal] unit of organized Jewish life"; hence, each one was evolving into a multifunctional Jewish communal center. Dushkin believed that of the three, "the Jewish School as a Communal Center" held the greatest potential for the future of the Jewish community. He thus echoed the sentiments of Samson Benderly, of course, but also those of his teacher at Columbia University, John Dewey, the famed philosopher of Progressivism and champion of the centrality of the school in modern society.[5]

Dewey, the prime mover of progressive education in America, began his career at the University of Chicago in 1894, joining a teaching staff that sometimes included classical Reform Rabbi Emil G. Hirsch. In Chicago, he was exposed (as was Hirsch) to the settlement house work of Jane Addams, which influenced his conception of the school as a social institution. He soon became identified with the movement to convert public schools into neighborhood centers, a movement begun by James K. Paulding of New York's University Settlement in 1897. In 1898 Paulding published an article entitled, "Public Schools as a Center of Community Life," which was followed by Dewey's "The School as Social Center" in 1902. Dewey's article in particular influenced the creation of numerous community centers on public school premises over the next decade. Initiated by settlement workers and carried forth by reform-minded educators, a national movement to turn schools into social centers was under way by 1910—the very same historical moment in which Jewish communal institutions (YMHAs, settlements, schools, and synagogues) began to be turned into Jewish centers.

Dewey's direct influence in Jewish circles commenced with his move to New York City in 1904 to join Teachers College of Columbia University. There, as described above, he served as a primary intellectual mentor for a coterie of American Jewish educators under the tutelage of Mordecai Kaplan and Samson Benderly. The Benderly boys would often cite John Dewey as their mentor, a kind of secular "rebbe" from the Progressive academic tradition. Many of their educational experiments would bear the distinct imprint of Deweyan ideas—as, for example, the transformation of the Jewish school into a social center. Dewey therefore exerted influence upon the Jewish center movement both through his personal contact with Jewish educators as well as through his broad prescription to turn schools into centers.[6]

While the idea of a central Jewish institution encompassing all aspects of community life was largely inspired by John Dewey and the school social center movement, we cannot neglect specifically Jewish sources. Here, the word "center" is key to unlocking the course of intellectual influence. As discussed in Chapter 1, the 1896 publication of Israel Abrahams's *Jewish Life in the Middle Ages* popularized the term early on. In modern Jewish historiography, the word is more often associated with the work of Abrahams's contemporary social historian, Simon Dubnow, whose *Jewish History—An Essay in the Philosophy of History* was first published in English in 1903. Dubnow depicted Jewish history as "a succession of changing autonomous *centres*—Babylon, Spain, Germany, Polish-Lithuania." He utilized his sociological conception of Jewish life to fashion an ideology of "Diaspora Nationalism," in which organized Jewish communities were urged to "overcome their limitations as religious bodies and become *Volksgemeinden,* i.e. secular national autonomous communities." Dubnow suggested that Jews in the United States were particularly well positioned to create such a center, but first they must "advance beyond the confines of the 'religious community.'" In Jewish intellectual discourse, therefore, the word "center" came to be associated with a Jewish corporate existence whose rationale was social and political rather than religious.[7]

Obviously, therefore, the primary use of the term "center" was in connection with Zionism. In this regard, Ahad Ha'am (1856–1927), the father of cultural Zionism, is the relevant figure. Born Asher Zvi Ginsberg, his nom de plume means literally, "one of the people." Best known for his conception of Zion as "spiritual center," Ahad Ha'am wrote in 1897: "[The] Jewish settlement, which will be a gradual growth, will become in course of time the center of the nation, wherein its spirit will find pure expression and develop in all its aspects to the highest degree of perfection of which it is capable. Then, from this center, the spirit of Judaism will radiate to the great circumference, to all the communities of the Diaspora, to inspire them with new life and to preserve the over-all unity of our people." Ahad Ha'am's American follower, Samson Benderly, would thus write in 1908: "The Zionists have an additional fact which is of great significance [to Jewish education]—the establishment of a Jewish centre in Palestine"; and in the year of Ahad Ha'am's death: "Palestine as a Jewish spiritual centre is an indispensable force in the production of that resultant which we call the American Judaism of tomorrow."[8]

Besides Benderly, Ahad Ha'am's principal disciple in America was Rabbi Judah L. Magnes. So it was not incidental when Magnes described his own congregation in early 1911 as "a Jewish Center." Just six months before, Ahad Ha'am had written to Magnes to recommend that "the Synagogue must be the center to which those who want to learn about Judaism resort every day." In "Ahad-Ha'amist" terminology, the word "center" could only echo the call for a Jewish center in Palestine. Thus, in a 1912 speech, Magnes would assert that "the idea common to both" Zionism and his own Kehillah movement "is that of the Jewish

Centre." On the one hand, the Kehillah was positioning "itself as the Jewish Centre of the million Jews of New York City." On the other hand, the Zionist movement was "endeavoring to establish the Jewish Centre for the Jewish people in the Jewish land." Echoing Ahad Ha'am again, Magnes applied the term to the synagogue as "the only Jewish Centre which the Jews had" in the past; he noted that the current "idea of having a single Jewish Centre, in which should be gathered all kinds of Jewish activities is again becoming fashionable."⁹

In Judah Magnes's formulation, the phrase ranged in connotation from Jewish corporate existence to Jewish national home to Jewish community to Jewish institution. His Kehillah experiment (a comprehensive communal organization for the Jews of New York, in operation from 1909 to 1922) was the attempt to unite all these levels of Jewish group life; the Kehillah was also, of course, the sponsor of Samson Benderly's Bureau of Jewish Education. The main staff members of the Bureau were, in turn, Benderly boys. When we add the outside influence of Deweyan discourse, is it any wonder that the words "Jewish center" turned up embedded in phrases such as "Jewish school center" and "Central Jewish Institute"? The phrase was in the air, and was most famously adopted by Mordecai Kaplan for his first synagogue-center experiment, the "Jewish Center" of the West Side. As we shall soon see, however, it was a Talmud Torah that first employed and helped to popularize the term.

The connection between the traditional Jewish school and the nascent Jewish center was established on the popular level well before the influence of elite educational theorists was felt. Native-born American Jews, for example, tended to view the Talmud Torah as the immigrants' version of the 'Hebrew Free School, the philanthropic "mission" school of the established Jewish community. Of course, the Hebrew free school itself was originally conceived as an analogue of the Talmud Torah. Therefore the terms were often employed as synonyms, the one used to "translate" the other; as when Philip Davis described "the Talmud Torah, or Hebrew Free School" of Chicago. In 1883, the name of the Chicago Talmud Torah was officially changed to the Moses Montefiore Hebrew Free School, and three years later, an institution of the same name was founded in Cleveland. As Lloyd Gartner points out, however, the school was still colloquially referred to as the Talmud Torah. In New York, a pioneering American Orthodox synagogue established The Hebrew Free School of Congregation Zichron Ephraim in 1890, adopting the term Talmud Torah some twenty years later. Reform Rabbis Maurice Harris and Kaufmann Kohler described the Uptown Talmud Torah of 1892 as a branch of downtown's Hebrew Free School. The names were used interchangeably in Baltimore as well, but most telling of all is the case of Boston, where the Talmud Tora Hebrew Free School was founded on April 12, 1887. Located at 4 Baldwin Place in the heart of the Jewish North End, the institution was also identified on a 1902 map by settlement worker Robert Woods as the "Hebrew Talmud & Torah Free School," thus entangling the terms together. On the facade of the former school building (now an apartment house) one may still see the Hebrew initials of Talmud Torah superimposed over the English initials "H.F." (for "Hebrew Free"). As time passed and Americanization proceeded, "Talmud Torah" would be translated into American terms in more ways as well.[10]

For the immigrants themselves, the Hebrew Free School was nothing new at all; in their eyes, it was simply the American description for their old familiar Talmud Torah. But the Talmud Torah was primarily a religious school whose traditional curriculum was its essence. In its content, therefore, it was clearly distinct from the Hebrew Free School, which rarely tutored its charges in Hebrew, much less Torah and Talmud. Yet despite their differences, an analogy was drawn between the institutions from which two practical effects emerged. First, the Jewish center movement absorbed the function of the Talmud Torah. As described in the previous chapter, the settlement-type school turned into a Jewish center, and began to include more programming along the lines of Jewish religious instruction. When the East European immigrant communities began to take over the administration of the former settlements, it seemed only logical to unite the indigenous American institution with their own educational center, the Talmud Torah.

In 1905, for example, the "flourishing Jewish centre" of Hoboken, New Jersey, boasted that its communal center, "The Hebrew Institute," was "almost next in rank to the Educational Alliance, a sister institution of the city of New York." Unlike the New York model, however, it maintained a "Talmud Torah, [as] a branch of the institute." Similarly, in 1912, the Jewish settlement of Kansas City "cordially extended to the Talmud Torah the privilege of maintaining a school in its main institute." In Portland, Oregon, the local Council of Jewish Women was inspired by the newly arrived Rabbi Stephen Wise to organize a settlement house called the Neighborhood Guild. Besides the usual array of settlement services, the Neighborhood Guild housed a Talmud Torah under the direction of Russian Jewish educator Morris Ostrow. The secular settlement and the religious school existed side by side until 1905, when a new building was erected to house the joint endeavor.[11]

Similarly, in 1912, the Jewish Educational Institute of Kansas City responded to "the formation of a Talmud Torah, financed largely by the Russian Jewish element of the community," by seeking to incorporate the religious school into the body of the settlement. "Realizing that such work forms an integral part of the Jewish settlement, the Board of Directors of the Institute cordially extended to the Talmud Torah the privilege of maintaining a school in its main institute." While still condescending in tone, the intention was constructive: to broaden the scope of the "settlement" to better serve the community, that is, to turn it into a "center." The inclusion of a Talmud Torah in the settlement particularly recommended itself due to the similarities between the two institutions.[12]

The opposite tendency was also common, in which the Talmud Torah itself began to turn into a Jewish center. Thus, the historians of Buffalo Jewry described its Talmud Torah building of 1906 as being "the first non-synagogal edifice of the Orthodox Jews, [which] served, in its day, as an embryonic Jewish Center." At first merely a pragmatic combination, the idea soon spread on its own merits. Hence in 1910, Louis Levin (editor of Baltimore's *Jewish Comment* from 1899 to 1916) wrote: "Given a Talmud Torah with its Jewish population from one hundred to one thousand, why should it not be possible to make it also the center of the best activities of the settlement house? Has it not graduates and alumni, organizable into clubs or classes for further improvement? Cannot the Jewish year, rich in incident, in story, in pathos, in joy, be used to give point to the teachings of national, religious, and domestic loyalty, which is now being sought in many other ways? Would not parents and preachers find it easy to sympathize with and participate in such settlement work?"[13]

Following Levin's suggestion, the Talmud Torah of Baltimore extended its activities along settlement lines, including in its program a library, a printing press, children's clubs, and entertainments and lectures for adults. Similarly, in 1914, the Minneapolis Talmud Torah began planning to incorporate recreational facilities. The new educational and recreational combination became known as the Talmud Torah Social Service Department of the Associated Jewish Charities. Boris Bogen would later remark that "the widespread tendency among Orthodox Jews for religious instruction suggests the possibility of utilizing the Talmud Torah as a center of different social activities." By 1917 (the date of Bogen's *Jewish Philanthropy*), however, the suggestion was already widespread in practice. In the course of its Americanization the Talmud Torah was reinvented as a Jewish center.[14]

The Early Americanization of the Talmud Torah

Hence, the idea of the Jewish school as communal center had a specifically Jewish precedent: the Talmud Torah. In the shtetls and cities of Eastern Europe the Talmud Torah was but one of several forms of Jewish schooling which offered the traditional menu of religious education: Hebrew, *Tefila* (prayer), Torah, and Talmud. Since these subjects were understood to be required of every male member of the community, the kehillah (the community organization) provided a communal "charity school" that provided the requisite education to all who could not afford the more desirable *yeshivot* (religious schools). In the New World, however, the Talmud Torah would gain in prestige, eventually providing the model for all subsequent forms of Jewish education in America.[15]

The traditional version of the Talmud Torah made its way to these shores as early as 1857, when Pesach Rosenthal opened a communal school in New York City for the free instruction of poor children after school hours. Rosenthal's school was later reconstituted as the Machzike Talmud Torah, a leading Jewish institution during the early 1880s—the time coincident with the advent of the mass immigration of East European Jewry. Following that historical watershed, new Talmud Torahs were founded in New York, Chicago, Cleveland, and Boston. Eventually, such schools were organized in every immigrant community to respond to the numerous entrepreneurial "heders" that had sprung up to provide an old-fashioned Jewish schooling for a fee. The Talmud Torah, on the other hand, intended to serve the entire community economically and efficiently. Rather than perpetuate the modes of an earlier time and place, therefore, the new Jewish schools quickly became the settings for communal and educational progress. As opposed to the other archetypal schools of traditional Jewish life (the heder and the yeshiva), the Talmud Torah proved far easier to translate into American terms. In Cincinnati, for example, a Talmud Torah Society was formed in 1887 for the purpose of teaching "poor children the Jewish religion according to the Orthodox traditions in order that they may become good American citizens, and loyal to the Orthodox faith." The American ideals of civic duty and patriotic pride thus became objectives of the Jewish school.[16]

Furthermore, rather than providing a comprehensive education to the Jewish poor of the European shtetl, the American Talmud Torah became more limited in its curriculum; its demands on the time of its pupils would be reduced, becoming supplementary and subsidiary to the American public school. It now offered several hours a week (in the afternoons, after a day spent in public school) of instruction in the rudiments of Jewish knowledge, and became more expansive in its scope, opening up its doors to the community-at-large. The Talmud Torah was not only intended to provide a more efficient and affordable alternative to the heder, but also to substitute for congregational schools. Sometimes a community school was founded by a group of Orthodox synagogues who could not have afforded a school individually. Talmud Torahs were thus founded as communal endeavors, often generating their own auxiliary support society or "Talmud Torah Association." As a sovereign institution, the Talmud Torah became open to changes that would not have been countenanced by the synagogue. As further examined below, the tendency to improve the state of Jewish education in America was influenced and paralleled by a similar development in Europe, the Heder Metukan of the Russian Haskalah.[17]

The movement to Americanize the Talmud Torah had its start in New York City, the major center of both transplanted Orthodoxy and Haskalah. The beginning of the movement may be placed in 1886–87, the years of the public appearance of the Lower East Side's leading Talmud Torah. 1886 saw the Machzike Talmud Torah acquire a building of its own on East Broadway, the main artery of the Jewish Lower East Side (the same year, incidentally, in which the landmark Eldridge Street Shul was constructed). In the following year a young rabbi named Moses Weinberger published a short work entitled *Jews and Judaism in New York*. Its publication was not intended to benefit the author, however; the proceeds from the book "were dedicated to the Machzike Talmud Torah Institute, a Hebrew Free School," one of the first of the communally sponsored Talmud Torahs in America. Weinberger's essay was published by the directors of "the Machzike Talmud Torah [Support of the Religious School] Society" to raise funds for "the coming expansion of our Talmud Torah." The fund-raising technique itself demonstrates the public nature of the Talmud Torah enterprise. In making their appeal, the directors' constant refrain is a desire for improvement— of the facilities, of the teachers, of the efficacy of the school in any way possible. The future of the Jewish people was at stake, after all. Pained by what they saw as the widespread and single-minded devotion to the building of new synagogues, school supporters boldly countered that the Talmud Torah "completely over-shadowed" the synagogue in importance. Attention to one at the expense of the other was seen as a waste of communal resources. From the beginning, therefore, the Talmud Torah stood in competition with the synagogue.[18]

Due in part to their competitive relationship, the synagogue and Talmud Torah developed in remarkably similar ways. Both the immigrant synagogue (shul) and the immigrant school (the heder) began as small, informal, and unruly affairs. In both cases, the effect of America would be to enlarge, formalize, and *modernize* the institution. In the case of the immigrant shul, the modern Ortho-dox synagogue soon emerged to replace it. In the case of the heder, the modern Talmud Torah provided the solution to its widely acknowledged faults. One pro-totype for the new and improved Jewish schools would be the Machzike Talmud Torah, which Weinberger called the "first school of its kind in the history of Or-thodox Judaism in America." Though the statement was somewhat exaggerated, the Machzike Talmud Torah was certainly emblematic of the modern Talmud Torah institution by virtue of its desire for better facilities and more efficient functioning.[19]

As Arthur Goren points out, the Talmud Torah was the first of the East Euro-pean Jewish institutions to have "transcended, at least in part, the rampant partic-ularism of the immigrant ghetto." Whereas immigrants tended to create numer-ous small societies to serve their own needs—the various *hevrot, landsmanshaftn,* and shuls of Jewish life—they were less inclined to divide into such small units for their children's education. Goren further described the Talmud Torah's attrac-tion to the leaders of the New York Kehillah: "The Talmud Torah association as a communal body owed an accounting to its supporting members; hence some de-gree of form and order was inevitable. This, in turn, implied rational, institutional management. Popular support, public accountability, and communal direction, Kehillah leaders believed, would lead to the modernization of the Jewish educa-tional structure. Modernization would bring graded classes, a stable teaching staff, pedagogical supervision, decent salaries, textbooks and, eventually, even proper physical plants. In short, the charity school of the Russian-Jewish town would now become the supplementary Jewish public school." Supported by the findings of Mordecai Kaplan's survey of Jewish education, the Kehillah would take up the cause of Talmud Torah modernization from its inception.[20]

Yet the Talmud Torah had entered its period of modernization well before 1909, the year in which the Kehillah was founded. Like the Machzike Talmud

Torah, most Talmud Torahs occupied an entire building, which implied two "modern" elements in particular: its means of financial support and the form of its political organization. The construction and support of a building required relatively large sums of money, and necessitated a fund-raising apparatus sophisticated enough to reach the broader community. It was a communal enterprise in other ways as well; serving a broad constituency, the Talmud Torah was planned, organized, and supervised by a bureaucratic board of communal leaders. At the same time, the wide-ranging support and the varied needs of the neighborhood constituents required a democratic decision-making process. As Goren put it, the Talmud Torah "owed an accounting to its supporting members." The modern Talmud Torah would be run as a bureaucracy and as a democracy, becoming a characteristically American institution.[21]

In this regard, one other quintessentially American institution must be mentioned: the public school. Whereas the initial model for the Talmud Torah had been the philanthropic free school, founders of Talmud Torahs soon began to see their institutions as analogues of the municipal public schools. Their influence should not be underestimated for, as is well known, the immigrant Jew idealized the public school as the gateway to American identity, acceptance, and success. The parallel (though at the time, lesser) quest to preserve Jewish identity understandably took its cues from the American public school system; for example, in 1911, the Hebrew Literary Association of Cambridge and Somerville announced the purchase of a new school building, and boasted that "now the Jews of Cambridge and Somerville will have as fine a Hebrew school as any of the regular public schools." (The quote continued: "Besides, all the Zionist organizations will now have a proper place to meet in.") When Mordecai Kaplan was granted his proposal to survey the Jewish school conditions of New York City in 1909, a public school principal named Bernard Cronson was assigned to help him. One year later, when the principals of New York's leading Talmud Torahs met to coordinate their activities, they noted that their institutions had "a public communal character" and called them "the public Jewish schools."[22]

Alexander Dushkin described the Americanization of the Talmud Torah in more concrete terms: "it came to be housed in special school buildings, which the school laws of the state required to be sanitary and safe. Because of its situation in congested quarters of the city, it reached many pupils, and was therefore capable of developing a system of grading and school management similar to that of the public schools." The public school contributed more to the Talmud Torah than a new standard of modern facilities, however. As noted above, the progressive educational movement of John Dewey envisioned an expanded role for the public school, incorporating social clubs, education, and athletics. The New York Board of Education instituted a series of popular lectures in its school buildings in 1889, and further expanded recreational opportunities eight years later when boys' club work was allowed into the schools for the first time. James K. Paulding, in his 1898 article entitled, "Public School as a Center of Community Life," promoted

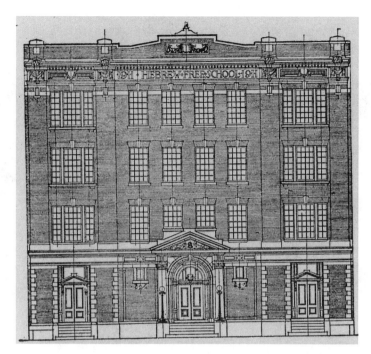

Fig. 21. The Hebrew Free School of Brownsville, more familiarly known as the Stone Avenue Talmud Torah—exemplifying the transformation of the traditional communal school into a modern "public school" for the Jewish community. *Jewish Communal Register, 1917–18.* Courtesy of the Library of the Jewish Theological Seminary of America.

the "use of [the] school as a center of neighborhood social life," and helped initiate the school center movement. Further experiments were undertaken in Boston and Chicago (in 1903 and 1905 respectively), and in 1907, Edward Ward aroused national interest in the school center with his well-publicized project in Rochester, New York.[23]

What was the degree of Jewish participation in such initiatives? In the ethnically mixed areas of second settlement of Boston, neighborhoods such as Cambridgeport, Roxbury, and East Boston, Jewish immigrants and their children were said to be the most enthusiastic participants in the evening programs of the public school centers. Describing a recreational program that typically included "an orchestra, a band, a choral club, debating societies, dramatic clubs, classes in folk dancing, athletics and sewing, games, lectures and entertainment," settlement house worker Albert Kennedy added, "The Jews are perhaps the chief patrons of the municipal recreation facilities." On another such experiment in East Boston, Kennedy concluded: "As was expected the complexion of the center has been predominantly Jewish." Besides the Jews' general love affair with the public school system, another reason for their overrepresentation was that other ethnic immigrants (especially Irish and Italians) could satisfy their social and recreational

Fig. 22. Downtown Talmud Torah. *Universal Jewish Encyclopedia,* courtesy of the Judaica Collection, Florida Atlantic University Library.

needs in the Catholic church, whereas the immigrant synagogue had yet to be turned into a community center. In the earlier period, therefore, Jews flocked to the welcoming confines of their local school center.[24]

So enthusiastic were they that sometimes the creation of a school center was a Jewish initiative. In Philadelphia, for instance, the Junior Congregation of Rodeph Shalom organized "a section for social service organizing various clubs for boys and girls in one of the most congested sections of the city," that is, in the Jewish immigrant ghetto. This settlement activity continued to develop to the point that a professional social worker was engaged to "centralize" the work. Finally, "under the auspices of the Board of Recreation a community center was opened at the Kearney Public School. In a section of which perhaps 80 per cent are Jewish people social, civic, educational and recreational opportunities were provided." Americanizing Jews who had never heard of Dewey, Paulding, or Ward, put their progressive theories into effect with aplomb.[25]

Thus influenced by the American milieu, the Talmud Torah clearly departed from the European model well before 1910, the year in which the progressive Bureau of Jewish Education was established by the New York Kehillah. As we have seen, the Machzike Talmud Torah became a "public" school in 1887. Two years later, a group of Jewish women in Williamsburg (Brooklyn) established the School of Biblical Instruction, more familiarly known as the Meserole Street Talmud Torah. Both its initial founding by women and its curricular emphasis on Bible implied a progressive orientation. Other Talmud Torahs founded in early

Fig. 23. Uptown Talmud Torah. *Jewish Communal Register, 1917–18.* Courtesy of the Library of the Jewish Theological Seminary of America.

1890s New York City included the Hebrew Free School of Brownsville (also known as the Stone Avenue Talmud Torah), the First Austrian Talmud Torah (later renamed the Downtown Talmud Torah), the Montefiore Talmud Torah, and the Uptown Talmud Torah—each of which later developed into a model institution. Yet in the 1890s, it must be remembered, the Talmud Torah was still primarily an Old World, traditionalist institution, as revealed by the fact that Yiddish remained its language of choice. It was not until 1899, when Jacob Schiff first became involved with the Machzike Talmud Torah, that "English began to replace Yiddish as the language of instruction," signaling that the "movement towards the Americanization of the Talmud Torah" had begun in earnest. (Note the paradox: it was the same historical moment in which the Educational Alliance began to accept the use of Yiddish.)[26]

The Downtown Experiments of Albert Lucas, 1903–1908

In most cases of Talmud Torah modernization, being housed in a physical structure was key. But even without a building of its own the Talmud Torah purported to be a modern American institution, as exemplified by the "Religious

Classes" and "Jewish Centres" established by Albert Lucas in New York City. Lucas, an emigrant from England, became one of the lay leaders of the Union of Orthodox Jewish Congregations of America (UOJC, founded in 1898). Once established, he waged a one-man campaign to provide the children of the Lower East Side with traditional Jewish schooling that would replace the unsuccessful heder system. Citing the urgency of combating Christian missionary work in the area, he convinced several synagogues and other local institutions to provide free housing for his educational programs. Seen within the context of the Talmud Torah movement, however, the "Albert Lucas Religious Classes" were part of the general trend toward modernization in Jewish education. Throughout the period of his activities, Lucas grappled with the greater enemy of assimilation as well as the more immediate threat of proselytization.[27]

In early 1903, Lucas organized free religious classes, which were held in the newly constructed Kalvarier Synagogue on Pike Street. The new school was funded by public functions such as a "Purim entertainment held at the Educational Alliance" and was soon lauded as "one of the oases in the desert of irreligion at the present time." Lucas later reported to the UOJC "that my classes are the only instance on record of an independent effort to impart religious instruction in the vernacular." In September 1903 he announced that yet another downtown synagogue (the First Roumanian-American Congregation) had granted the use of its premises to conduct classes, open to all children of the neighborhood and free of charge. The following month, the B'nai B'rith Building on Forsyth Street joined the expanding list of Lucas's educational centers. By mid-1905, the *Hebrew Standard* would include the Albert Lucas Religious Classes in its series on significant Jewish communal institutions.[28]

At that time the original impetus of anti-missionary work became important by providing a model for the new institution(s). In July 1905, Albert Lucas wrote to the *Hebrew Standard* to publicly warn of rampant missionizing and to challenge the community to respond. Later that year, the same newspaper suggested emulating the example of the Emanu-El Brotherhood, which had recently created "the first Jewish settlement on the East Side." The editorial continued: "The Emanu-El Brotherhood House will be the bright spot in a neighborhood sadly in need of some Jewish sunshine. More than one Jewish settlement is needed and those who always deprecate Reform Judaism might for once bestir themselves and put their teaching into practice. We know Mr. Albert Lucas is desirous of establishing a number of Jewish centres and we shall watch with interest the amount of material support he will receive, now that the practical example has been afforded."[29]

In the spring of 1906, Albert Lucas founded the Jewish Centres Association, becoming superintendent of the enterprise. The name "Jewish center" was a logical choice; like the concurrent school center movement, the intention was to combine educational programming with the recreational activities of the neighborhood center and social settlement. In Lucas's formulation, however, the program would be uncompromisingly Jewish. The first public meeting of the new organization was held at the Educational Alliance with several communal leaders and rabbis in attendance; the latter included Israel Davidson, Hyman Shoher, Zvi Hirsch Masliansky, Henry Pereira Mendes, Bernard Drachman, and none other than Mordecai Kaplan. On August 1, 1906, Centre No. 1 was opened on the Lower East Side. In his first report on the new institution, Lucas reviewed its objects: "to provide a centre where the Jewish children and youth shall receive, under Jewish influence, the advantages of religious, physical and moral training, that are now too often held out to them only as allurements to stray from our ancestral faith." Its program included a kindergarten, a sewing class, a ladies' auxiliary, a choral society (for ritual service and music), boys' and girls' clubs, and a literary circle. Lucas added: "These activities have been fully organized. Our entire quarters are already a hive of social and true Jewish work. . . . Jewishness is ever our watchword." In short, it was a Jewish traditionalist version of the settlement house, evolved directly from the educational endeavors of Albert Lucas.[30]

Shortly thereafter, a movement was launched to create similar centers elsewhere in the city, especially uptown. In a letter to the *Hebrew Standard* regarding the "Need of Jewish Centres in Harlem," S. P. Frank cited the example of the downtown institution and claimed that "there should be as many similar Centres as there are synagogues in this metropolis. In fact the Centres, properly conducted, are more vital to Judaism than the synagogues." He thus repeated the earlier grievance of the founders of the Machzike Talmud Torah; more important, however, he took his lead from Albert Lucas. Inadvertently, Lucas had supplied the necessary ingredient to energize the Talmud Torah movement. Make the educational institution more like a settlement, he implied, and have it incorporate what he called "all the advantages of . . . 'modern social work,' under Jewish auspices." Whereas his own initiative faltered—due in part to the rise of the Kehillah and its emphasis on constructive Jewish work rather than anti-missionary negativism—Lucas's pioneering activities set the precedent for the modern Talmud Torah to follow.[31]

Cultural Zionism and Hebrew Schooling in America

Another likely reason for the failure of Albert Lucas's school system was its inattention to a blossoming ideology of the immigrant Jewish community: cultural Zionism (including the related literary movement of Hebraism), ultimately the most effective force in the modernization of the Talmud Torah. In its campaign to win the hearts and minds of Jews the world over, the Zionist movement in Europe first attempted to win control of the Kehillah and synagogue, and when that proved impracticable, to "conquer the schools." The new strategy was suggested by Ahad Ha'am in a speech to the 1902 Zionist Conference, inspiring his followers to launch a new educational project, a system of improved schools (in

Hebrew, *hadarim metukanim*) that would follow the Zionist program for the modernization of Jewish life. Hence a model "reformed *heder*" that had been established in Pinsk in 1895 was soon imitated all over.[32]

Besides the *heder metukan,* notes historian Ehud Luz, "the Zionists schemed to take over another educational institution—the Talmud Torah." Under their influence, "the Talmud Torah gradually metamorphosed into a true "public school" where both religious and secular subjects were taught." The Zionist movement thus posited two new types of Jewish school, the *heder metukan* and the "Zionist Talmud Torah." Both ideas soon took hold in America, following the immigration of *maskilim* (adherents of *Haskalah,* the "Jewish enlightenment") and *hovevei zion* (a group of early Zionists; literally, "lovers of Zion") who often gravitated to the teaching profession upon their arrival. Committed above all else to the revival of Hebrew language and literature, they translated the ideals of cultural Zionism into their educational curricula, introducing the new pedagogical technique known as *ivrit b'ivrit* (literally, "Hebrew in Hebrew"; also known as the Natural Method, it was pioneered by progressive Zionist educators in Palestine, Eastern Europe, and America), and redefining the Jewish school as a *Hebrew* school.[33]

In 1893, two years prior to the Pinsk experiment, Zvi Hirsch (Sundel) Neumann established the Shaare Zion school in Brooklyn, called "the first Jewish school in America to reflect the spirit of the new Jewish nationalism." Neumann had previously conducted a *heder metukan* in his native Latvia, and intended just such a modern school in America. His opening announcement declared it to be "a model school" in which Hebrew would be "taught as a living language." In 1905, the year in which a conference of Hebrew-speaking clubs resolved to introduce *ivrit b'ivrit* into Jewish education, a second Hebraist school was established in Brooklyn by Ephraim Kaplan, called the National Hebrew School. (Note: the term "Hebrew School," the translation of "bet sefer ivri," has since come into universal usage for Jewish schools, especially of the congregational variety.)[34]

Kaplan's school succeeded by opening to female students only, a stratagem that both ensured enrollments and reflected Zionist ideals. Leo Honor explains that "a girls' school had a twofold advantage; it provided greater leeway for the experimentors and it concretized a new concept for the Jewish immigrants from Eastern Europe that girls as well as boys were in need of Jewish education." Elazar Goelman adds: "The results were phenomenal. Instead of a dismal little school, there were three thriving branches consisting of many classes, full to capacity. Its spirit was a three-fold combination of Hebrew, nationalism and tradition." The popularity of these innovative schools thus set into motion a nationwide movement for Hebrew (and by implication, cultural Zionism) in Jewish education.[35]

The premier figure in this movement was, of course, Samson Benderly. In his native Safed, Benderly had probably come under the influence of Izhac Epstein, principal of the local public school during the 1890s and subsequently the inventor of the *ivrit b'ivrit* method (though it was later called the "Benderly method," Benderly was merely its leading proponent in the United States). Benderly came to Baltimore in 1898 at the invitation of Aaron Friedenwald and soon abandoned his medical career to devote himself entirely to Jewish education. In 1903, he opened a new type of Hebrew school in which he introduced the innovations of cleanliness, recreation, educational games, and above all, the use of the Hebrew language. In addition, he paid attention to the problems of teacher training and curricular goals. In 1909, Benjamin Henry Hartogensis reported on the progress of the "Talmud Torah" in Baltimore, and commented that "Dr. S. Benderly, the superintendent, has achieved national distinction for conducting at this building a model school in which, beginning with children at tender ages, Hebrew is taught as a living language." Benderly would later move to New York to head the Bureau of Education of the Kehillah, a position from which he would exercise broad influence and pioneer the modern profession of Jewish education.[36]

Following Benderly's 1903 experiment by one year was an *ivrit b'ivrit* class opened in Boston by two brothers, Israel and Meyer Abrams. Due to limited finances and interest the school faded, only to be revived in 1907 by the recently formed Jewish People's Institute. Although "an immediate success" with the West End community, the new "Evrio" school was plagued throughout its quarter-century existence by Orthodox suspicions of "epikorsut" (heresy). Nevertheless, the *ivrit b'ivrit* movement spread to other cities, including Philadelphia where "there were already three schools in 1906 which used Ivrit Be-Ivrit textbooks. They were *Safa Brura, Bet HaSefer HaLeumi,* and *Bet Sefer Ivri.*" Ivrit b'ivrit schools were also established in Detroit (1906), Chicago (1906, at the Chicago Hebrew Institute), Buffalo (1906), Cleveland (1907), Indianapolis (1911), Minneapolis (1910), and Pittsburgh (1913). One of the best publicized was the Bet Sefer Leumi, or National Hebrew School for Girls (after the school of the same name in Brooklyn), founded by eighteen-year-old Hayyim Abraham Friedland in 1910 and located on Madison Street in New York City. The "Madison Street School," as it was familiarly called, "became one of the best known of the Hebrew nationalist schools in America." Its success was due largely to the ambience created by Friedland "of joyous educational activity," highlighted by an extracurricular program of clubs in "literature, drama, newspaper, singing, dancing, drawing, Zionism, and more."[37]

The Hebrew nationalist schools soon influenced the more traditional Talmud Torahs. Of course, the distinction between nationalist and religious schools was not so rigidly drawn as we might believe; the immigrant constituents of the communal school called it a "Talmud Torah" regardless of its level of religiosity. As in the case of the Hebrew free schools, the National Hebrew Schools were popularly understood as Talmud Torahs despite the fundamental differences between them. So the lines were blurred from the start. Soon however, the underlying ideology and new pedagogical techniques of the Hebrew schools began to influence the traditional Talmud Torahs more explicitly. Ben-Horin has called this phase of the movement "the Hebraic-nationalist-Zionist transformation of the American Jewish school [read: the American Talmud Torah]." A 1911 editorial entitled "The New Education" acknowledged the connection with the following statement: "To the zealots for Hebrew as a living tongue must be given credit for the evolution of a Jewish system of education. . . . Then some of the Talmud Torahs began to arouse themselves. Model Talmud Torahs, at least as far as the buildings are concerned, made their appearance."[38]

One of the earliest examples was the Religious School of Congregation B'nai Jeshurun in New York. At the turn of the century, the historic Conservative congregation elected to its pulpit Joseph Mayor Asher, a young British rabbi who had helped organize the Manchester Talmud Torah School system. At B'nai Jeshurun, he promptly introduced the *ivrit b'ivrit* system into its congregational school. More in the mainstream of American orthodoxy was the Uptown Talmud Torah of Harlem. From the moment that Hillel Malachowsky became principal in 1903 he immediately set about introducing "the spirit of the Hebrew language" by replacing its old-style *melamdim* (traditional teachers) with "highly competent teachers capable of imbuing the pupils with love for our language and our literature." Similarly, the Hibat Zion leader Joseph Bluestone was able to influence the Machzike Talmud Torah to adopt modern methods through his position on the board of directors. In 1905, he persuaded the board to make the school coeducational, a reform that had previously been associated with the nationalist schools. One other important Zionist-inflected Talmud Torah was the Tifereth Israel Hebrew Institute of East New York, founded in 1907, and known popularly as the Pennsylvania Avenue Talmud Torah. Of its influence, Edward Orentlicher wrote: "It became a model to be imitated and envied by many other Talmud Torahs in the country. This may be attributed to the fact that throughout its existence it stood for a maximum Jewish educational program in the Ivrit be-Ivrit method. Its entire curriculum, methodology, and philosophy were imbued with the Hebraic spirit."[39]

By World War I, both the pervasive influence of Hebraism and the configuration of the Jewish school as a social center had become commonplace. For example, Dr. George J. Gordon reorganized the Minneapolis Talmud Torah as a modern Hebrew school in 1910, and began to plan for social extension in 1914. There were several reasons cited for the incorporation of social services: to organize the numerous clubs of the Talmud Torah, to provide recreational facilities for students and alumni, to raise funds for the Talmud Torah, to combat juvenile delinquency, to maintain a social center for the local Jewish community, and to centralize the activities of disparate agencies such as the Gymal Doled Club (a Jewish fraternity), the Associated Jewish Charities, and the YM/YWHA. No matter the motive, the Talmud Torah became the hub of Jewish life on the North Side of Minneapolis. When Mordecai Kaplan visited the "Talmud Torah and Social Center" in 1917, he reported that it deserved its "reputation of being one of the very best of its kind in the country." "In all my experience," he continued, "I had not seen anything on so large and well organized a scale." Kaplan reported the then unusual practice of importing teachers from Palestine and also noted the swimming pool then under construction. Dr. Gordon, who had been "the prime mover of the undertaking to establish a modern Hebrew school," objected to the addition of a swimming pool, fearing that it "would drown the Talmud Torah." Kaplan appears to have disagreed.[40]

The Bureau of Jewish Education of the New York Kehillah

The year of Gordon's reorganization in Minneapolis also marked an important turning point for the Talmud Torah movement in New York City. Soon after the Bureau of Jewish Education of the New York Kehillah was formed in 1910, all major Talmud Torahs were brought together under its aegis. The first attempt to coordinate Jewish education in New York had occurred five years earlier, when Joseph Bluestone, H. B. Isaacson, and Hillel Malachowsky called a meeting of Talmud Torah representatives together to form a central agency. Finally instituted in 1909 as the Central Board of Jewish Education, with Bluestone as president and Samuel Abelow as secretary, it included the Downtown Talmud Torah, the Uptown Talmud Torah, the Meserole Street Talmud Torah of Williamsburg (the School of Biblical Instruction), the Pennsylvania Avenue Talmud Torah of Brownsville, and, belying the Orthodox nature of the union, the Educational Alliance. Though the Central Board would be absorbed by the soon to be formed Kehillah, it marked the appearance of a new group of Talmud Torahs whose forward-looking administrators were open to centralization, modernization, and in general, the influences of American society.[41]

Jacob Schiff's involvement with the downtown Machzike Talmud Torah may be seen as part of the trend of Talmud Torah Americanization. As noted above, the uptown philanthopist became involved as early as 1899; in 1905, however, he actually paid the school an unpublicized visit and, apparently, was very impressed by both its structure and content. He thereupon offered to donate $25,000 for the construction of another branch of the school, an amount he doubled four years later in an endowment to the general field of Jewish education. The first installment of Schiff's 1909 donation of $50,000 went to the training of teachers at the new Teachers Institute of the Jewish Theological Seminary, with Mordecai M. Kaplan as principal. Significantly, for the first seven years of its operation the Teachers Institute held its classes in the Uptown and Downtown Talmud Torahs, and its students received their practical training in the classrooms of these and other Talmud Torahs around the city. The secondary use of Schiff's endowment was for the establishment of the Bureau of Jewish Education, which would similarly have an impact upon the Talmud Torahs of New York. In September 1909, the newly created Kehillah's executive committee approved a proposal by Mordecai Kaplan to survey the conditions of Jewish Education in New York City, and in February of the following year, the Kaplan-Cronson Report was delivered to the board.[42]

The report harshly criticized the current state of Jewish schooling, yet found one cause for optimism: the Talmud Torah, being communally sponsored, might serve as an agent of change. The pivotal figure here was not Kaplan but Samson Benderly, who arrived in New York in 1910 to become the founding director of the Bureau of Jewish Education. According to Goren, the Bureau's major contribution was the introduction of "communal responsibility for Jewish education." Though communal responsibility and central organization were certainly the hallmarks of the Kehillah, the new agency also helped transform the public image of the Talmud Torah from one of old-fashioned inefficiency to one of up-to-date institutionalism. As implied above, the transformation was largely effected by the Hebraist movement; a movement embodied, at least in New York, by the Bureau of Jewish Education. Led by Samson Benderly and fellow cultural Zionists Magnes, Kaplan, Friedlaender, and so forth, the Bureau attempted to impose the modern, nationalist Hebrew school program upon the more traditionalist Talmud Torahs. Though they did not succeed in winning over every Talmud Torah initially, they exerted a profound effect on the Talmud Torah movement over the course of subsequent decades.[43]

One of Benderly's first actions was to bring together the principals of the major New York City Talmud Torahs. Remarkably, the conference in the fall of 1910 was the first time most of the men had met. The newfound colleagues eagerly shared their concerns and aired their grievances, finding not only common cause but common background; nearly all were Russian *maskilim* ("enlightened" Jews) sympathetic to the modernization schemes of Benderly. Convening thirty more such meetings over the next ten months, the new Hebrew Principals' Association agreed upon a standardized curriculum, common educational goals, and the introduction of the Hebraist program. Thus the *ivrit b'ivrit* method of teaching Hebrew was officially adopted by the largest Talmud Torahs of New York City.[44]

Benderly also succeeded in introducing many of his pedagogical innovations through the teachers' training, model schools, and extension programs instituted by the Bureau. His young disciples, the Benderly boys, formed a corps of American-born teachers who introduced the novelties of educational play and the arts to the Talmud Torahs and model schools where they were student teachers. Their willingness to experiment was reinforced by their exposure to the educational theoreticians at Teachers' College, especially John Dewey. Through his Jewish graduate students, Dewey's gospel of a child-centered pedagogy—as well as a school-centered society—was spread to the Talmud Torah of the American Jewish community.

Of course, most traditional Talmud Torahs would not countenance such radical innovations. Instead, the earliest experimenting took place in the model schools established by the Bureau (which catered to girls alone) as well as in the

Fig. 24. "A Class in Jewish History—In Girls' School No. 2 of the Bureau of Jewish Education." Note the stereopticon (slide projector). *Jewish Communal Register, 1917–18.* Courtesy of the Library of the Jewish Theological Seminary of America.

"extension centers" formed to reach the unschooled. Concerning these, Dushkin wrote: "The Bureau clearly realized that it would be impossible to create sufficient school facilities in the immediate future for the 150,000 Jewish children who were outside of the Jewish schools. . . . In order to deal with this problem, the Bureau of Education saw that Extension work must be organized, as an educational *movement,* with as wide a scope as possible." In place of text study, holiday celebration and life-cycle events were conceived as the focus of the less intensive curriculum of extension classes. Along these lines, the Bureau of Jewish Education organized several such "Extension Centers."[45]

The centers, by offering informal educational activities, were intended to reach those Jewish children who were not enrolled in a Talmud Torah or other school program. Although the extension centers evolved into youth groups and were themselves short-lived, the tendency to incorporate pleasure and recreation into Jewish education began to influence the mainstream Talmud Torahs. From 1910 on, the Bureau of Jewish Education supported the ambitions of Talmud Torahs to construct their own buildings, new structures that would invariably include recreational facilities. For example, in 1911 the Stone Avenue Talmud Torah of Brownsville (see fig. 21) constructed its new home, a sturdy four-story brick building, containing nineteen classrooms and other facilities. In its new premises, the Talmud Torah served both as a model school (conducting a Hebrew High School under the auspices of the Bureau of Jewish Education) and as a Jewish

Fig. 25. "In Their Own Synagogue—Little Jews and Jewesses at the Downtown Talmud Torah." *Jewish Communal Register, 1917–18.* Courtesy of the Library of the Jewish Theological Seminary of America.

center with numerous clubs. Eventually, therefore, the extension activities of the Bureau came to be housed within the Talmud Torahs themselves.[46]

Still another "extension" activity was taken on by the modern Talmud Torah: the sponsoring of a community synagogue. In many of the earlier Talmud Torahs, religious services were provided as an ad hoc communal service and as an income-producing expedient. Typically, in the early years of the century, the Talmud Torah of Beth Jacob Joseph in Brooklyn held religious services every day. The expanded and modernized Talmud Torah institution would incorporate a synagogue as a matter of course. The new Stone Avenue Talmud Torah, for example, included a synagogue large enough to seat eight hundred, in which services were held daily. Samuel Abelow, the historian of Brooklyn Jewry, adds that "it [was] a very effective agent in spreading Judaism in Brownsville." Thus combining educational, social, and religious functions, we may add that it did so as an early version of the synagogue-center.[47]

Likewise, the Pennsylvania Avenue Talmud Torah dedicated its new building in 1914 with a large synagogue of its own. A major feature of this leading Talmud Torah was its in-house "Junior" Congregation, which included not only the current students but also many older alumni. The "youth" congregation persisted for half a century and was well known for its wide variety of educational and social activities. In addition to the Junior Congregation, which was instituted for educational purposes, the Pennsylvania Avenue Talmud Torah also conducted a "Synagogue for Adults" for the more pragmatic purpose of providing financial support.

Nevertheless, the inclusion of a synagogue on Talmud Torah premises became a common phenomenon and helped lay the groundwork for the institutional expansion that would eventually evolve into the synagogue-center. But first, with or without a synagogue, the Talmud Torah was converted into a Jewish center.[48]

The history of the Uptown Talmud Torah is a case in point. Founded as a small heder in 1899, the Talmud Torah joined the modernizing trend with the hiring of Hillel Malachowsky as principal in 1903 and the subsequent fund-raising campaign for a new building. At the same time, another group headed by David and Elias A. Cohen was attempting to establish an analogue to the Educational Alliance in the same neighborhood, but found itself stymied by the competition. In early 1905, therefore, the would-be organizers of the "Harlem Educational Institute" joined with the fund-raisers of the Talmud Torah to form the Uptown Talmud Torah Association. Their merger exemplified the Talmud Torah–Jewish center connection.[49]

In March 1906—just months before the experimental "Jewish Centre" of Albert Lucas—principal Malachowsky published his vision for the future of the Uptown Talmud Torah: "In all sections of New York, as well as in other parts of the country, there is a great movement towards the establishment of large, modern, Hebrew Institutions. In New York, Brooklyn, and Baltimore and other large cities there are commodious, convenient and large 'Talmud Torahs.' The 'Uptown Talmud Torah' is at present contemplating the erection of a veritable Temple of Learning in the heart of Harlem, a large Hebrew School to contain 20 classes for boys and girls, with an auditorium, lecture hall and library. Naturally they will adopt the most modern, up to date system." In November of that year, the *Hebrew Standard* published a drawing of the planned "Educational Institute of the Uptown Talmud Torah," whose actual building was dedicated in March 1909.[50]

But rather than stressing the Jewish educational aspect of the new Talmud Torah, the dedication announcement listed the goals and activities of the Educational Institute as:

broadening the mental, moral, physical and religious instruction of our Jewish boy and girl. The problem in Harlem is the more acute because nothing had been done for that section of the city thus far, and there are over 20,000 Jewish boys and girls growing up without the slightest conception of Judaism or the history of their race. The new building is splendidly fitted to cope with this situation, as there is an auditorium and gallery, seating over 900, where Friday evening and Sabbath services are held for young people, lectures given during the week. There are 21 classrooms, a library and social room, a gymnasium as large as any in Harlem, a roof garden and kindergarten . . . thus being in the foreground of modern and intelligent teaching of the young. . . . 3000 children whose names are registered, ready to be taught the tenets of the Hebrew faith. There will also be classes in Kosher cooking for girls, typewriting, stenography, manual training and first aid to the injured. The building will be the civic centre which Harlem has needed so long.[51]

As if the Machzike Talmud Torah had suddenly amalgamated with the Educational Alliance, the Educational Institute of the Uptown Talmud Torah was an awkward combination of the two institutional types. The new Talmud Torah/

Institute thus became a crucible for conflict between the traditionalist and modernist factions of the community, as well as the setting for attempts at reconciliation. As opposed to the downtown agencies of Americanization, the Harlem Educational Institute showed greater sensitivity to the Jewishness of its constituency, for example, shortly changing its name to the Harlem *Hebrew* Institute. However, Malachowsky soon left the Uptown Talmud Torah (in June 1907, replaced by an English Zionist named Ephraim Ish-Kishor), perhaps indicating his resistance to the Americanizing tendency. Despite a period of early growth, therefore, the tensions inherent in such a hybrid institution proved to be a source of continual dissension, as when Jacob Schiff and the more traditional board members engaged in a dispute over the course of modernization.[52]

The contentiousness abated temporarily when Harry Fischel, "the well-known Jewish builder and philanthropist," assumed the presidency of the Uptown Talmud Torah in 1911. Fischel was a unique personality in the Orthodox world. Frustrated in his youthful ambition to become an architect (he could not find an architectural firm that would allow him to work only five days and thereby keep the Sabbath), he became a builder and real estate developer instead, made a fortune at an early age, and devoted much of his life to the erection of Jewish communal institutions. Formed in his own image, his creations always exhibited two characteristics: they would adhere strictly to Orthodox standards of Kashruth and Sabbath observance, and they would adopt the most up-to-date methods of construction and planning—including the multiple usage of space. The combination, for example, of a synagogue and a gymnasium within one institution seemed only natural to this progressive Jewish builder. Fischel personified modern Orthodoxy in a way that no rabbi could, and his building projects embodied that commitment.[53]

In 1911 he joined forces with Schiff, Magnes, and Benderly, by committing the Uptown Talmud Torah to the progressive programs of the Kehillah's Board of Jewish Education. He purchased a stereopticon (slide projector) for their Jewish history lessons and created a children's synagogue whose congregation numbered more than four hundred boys and girls. Reportedly, the children felt empowered by the opportunity to run synagogue life and instituted a modern Orthodox service; that is, they, introduced decorum into the traditional service. Despite such innocuous innovations, Fischel still met with opposition. The more traditionalist members of the board apparently feared the modernizing implications of placing a piano in a synagogue and showing motion pictures in a religious institution. Fischel remained adamant. At the annual meeting of February 1914, he asked for a vote of confidence from the board, did not receive support, and resigned his post.[54]

Fischel's opponents also objected "to the Uptown Talmud Torah being made a 'social centre' as well as a school for the teaching of Hebrew." In 1913, the year prior to his resignation, Fischel had initiated and funded two new recreational centers: an annex to the Uptown Talmud Torah on East 111th Street, and a West

Side Branch, intended as a "rich man's Annex" to serve the children of the wealthier benefactors of the school, who were then moving to a more upscale area of Harlem. The branch was located on West 115th Street near Lenox Avenue, a few blocks away from both Temple Israel and Temple Ansche Chesed, the leading congregations of the "better" Jewish neighborhood. The new premises, dedicated in November 1913, included a school accommodating more than six hundred children, clubrooms, a gymnasium, and a children's synagogue that doubled as an auditorium. Once again, the Talmud Torah had evolved into a Jewish center and thus become an embryonic synagogue-center.[55]

The new "Harry Fischel West Side Annex of the Uptown Talmud" also provided the setting for the founding of a new youth organization, the Harlem Young Men's Hebrew Orthodox League, in April 1915. Expanding upon the example of the children's synagogue, the league instituted model youth synagogues at the annex that emphasized decorum, congregational singing, and services conducted by the young people themselves. The league also sponsored social and cultural activities in the club rooms, library, and gymnasium of the West Side Annex. Paralleling the downtown development of the Young Israel movement, the league was born as a social organization, began to incorporate religious services for young people, and as we shall later see, grew into one of the first bona fide synagogue-center experiments (the Institutional Synagogue of 1917).[56]

The Ideal "Jewish School Center": The Central Jewish Institute of Kehilath Jeshurun

The transition from the Talmud Torah–Jewish center to the synagogue-center is most clearly revealed in the history of the Central Jewish Institute (CJI), the uptown educational center created in 1916. Though heir to the Uptown Talmud Torah in many respects, the CJI was also a new departure, a bold experiment that has few (if any) parallels in American Jewish history. According to Jeffrey Gurock, "The CJI represented the first major attempt at amalgamating Jewish social, cultural, and recreational programs with religious educational activities under the auspices of an established Orthodox congregation." The congregation was the leading East European synagogue of New York City, Kehilath Jeshurun of Yorkville on the Upper East Side. Its new adjunct institution was to be a "Jewish school center," combining the progressive American features of the Jewish center with the positive Jewish emphasis of the modern Talmud Torah. It was intended to serve the entire Jewish family and community as a neighborhood center, but in a *Jewish educational* capacity. As Meir Ben-Horin emphasizes, "the Institute's *central* activity was the school," making it unique as a Jewish institution. The CJI was therefore the "missing link" in the evolution from Talmud Torah–Jewish center to synagogue-center.[57]

Though it remained a separate organization de jure, Kehilath Jeshurun (KJ) provided its daughter institution with the political base and religious center lacking in earlier Talmud Torah–Jewish Center experiments. Originating as a congregational movement to create a communal Talmud Torah, the CJI was to be administered by the young Mordecai Kaplan, who had been hired by KJ in November 1903 to superintend the congregational school just established in their new synagogue building on East 85th Street. In 1907 Kaplan initiated a movement to expand the school into the "Yorkville Talmud Torah"; although he left the congregation in 1909, his influence lived on in the person of Samuel Hyman, who became the guiding force behind the establishment of the Talmud Torah and its first president. In late 1910, buoyed by the success of the Kehillah's first model schools, Kehilath Jeshurun purchased the adjoining buildings to the synagogue and in May 1912 voted to establish a Talmud Torah school center of its own. From 1912 to 1916, both the Kehilath Jeshurun school and the Yorkville Talmud Torah were in operation, under the direction of new assistant rabbi Herbert Goldstein. The cornerstone-laying ceremony for a new school building took place in the spring of 1915, and during the course of construction it was renamed the Central Jewish Institute.[58]

Herbert Goldstein (1890–1970) had been invited to assist Rabbi M. Z. Margolies ("Ramaz") at Kehilath Jeshurun while still a rabbinical student at the Jewish Theological Seminary. He succeeded Kaplan as "minister and superintendent of its religious school" on November 29, 1913. Among his early activities was the organization of various clubs and circles for the youth and women of the congregation—similar to those popular in Reform temples of the day. As Kaplan pointed out, Goldstein was particularly prone to borrowing forms from other contexts. Nevertheless, the "all-embracing Social Welfare Circle" and Goldstein's "all-pervasive" role in its activities marked the evolution of Kehilath Jeshurun into a synagogue-center. Similarly, he developed the idea of a Sabbath service conducted by the pupils of the Hebrew School. Rabbi Goldstein thus integrated school and synagogue, two-thirds of the synagogue-center synthesis. In the new CJI, Goldstein saw further potential for such integration, later priding himself that he had succeeded in moving "the Hebrew School of the Congregation . . . from the basement of the synagogue into the light and airy rooms of the Central Jewish Insitute."[59]

In addition, the new building was to include all sorts of "gadgets and sophisticated equipment" for the use of its progressive Jewish educational program, as reported in 1916: "The institute's auditorium can be converted into a synagogue by opening doors at the back of the platform, thus revealing the tablets of the Ten Commandments and the scrolls. It can be then be turned into a dancing floor by folding up the chairs and packing them into drawers which slide under the platform, making it possible to have a stage for theatricals, and a complete moving picture outfit lurks behind the wall opposite the platform, ready for use."[60]

Through such flexible arrangements, Goldstein showed his interest in integrating Jewish religion with Jewish education—ironically enough, an ambition that would be thwarted by the CJI. During his three years at KJ, Goldstein worked closely with Samuel Hyman to create the new institution, and he fully expected to be named its first administrator. Yet his positions as assistant rabbi and school superintendent must have given pause to the board of directors of KJ who were adamant about maintaining its independence from the settlement-like educational institution. Though Goldstein's biographer trumpets his multiple roles as testament to "his uncanny ability to jockey successfully for maximum latitude and authority," it is more likely that he found his overlapping duties enormously frustrating, influencing his decision to leave KJ and CJI in early 1917.[61]

During the same period, Mordecai Kaplan recorded his impressions of the CJI in his journal. At the "cornerstone laying of the 85th St. Yorkville Jewish Institute and Talmud Torah" in May 1915, he gave an address, "the main point of which was that the laying of the cornerstone marked the inauguration of a new method in Jewish life." When the Central Jewish Institute building was completed in the spring of 1916, Kaplan lauded Samuel Hyman for the accomplishment, but complained that Hyman had subverted the purpose of the institution by "developing it into a central meeting place for all sorts of Jewish organizations instead of making it into a social Jewish centre for the people of the neighborhood." In March, Kaplan, Friedlaender, and Benderly were invited to confer with the CJI directors on their choice of superintendent for the new institute. Kaplan writes, "Of course, it would have been foolish to advise them to take anyone else than Goldstein who is now the English-speaking rabbi of 85th Street [Kehilath Jeshurun]."[62]

When later that year Goldstein indicated his intention to leave the CJI, Kaplan was offered the job by director Edward Kaufman. He declined so as to concentrate on his West Side affairs, and because, as he told Isaac Cohen, "the only condition on which I would consider taking the position after Goldstein would give it up, is that the Institute change its form of organization from a philanthropic to a congregational institution." He even suggested the possibility of "taking charge both of the Central Institute and of the West Side Centre." Clearly, Kaplan saw the two in similar terms. There can be little doubt that the Jewish Center was intended to be analogous to the CJI, with these differences: it was to be inward in its scope (that is, congregational, not communal); it was to be centered about the synagogue, not the school; and it was to be Kaplan's conception, not Benderly's. Both the Jewish Center and the Institutional Synagogue, therefore, were directly derivative of their lesser known predecessor, the Talmud Torah–Jewish center synthesis called the Central Jewish Institute. In all likelihood, had Mordecai Kaplan and Herbert Goldstein not been involved in the creation of the CJI, their synagogue-center experiments—or others like them—would have appeared regardless. But the two were there from the beginning, observing its operation and absorbing its lessons; lessons such as the importance of a modern physical plant, the idea of a neighborhood center, the pivotal role of the rabbi, and most critically, the advantages of combining institutional functions.[63]

The CJI opened its doors in 1916 amid high hopes and expectant enthusiasm. As Jenna Joselit recounts, its opening marked "the culmination of more than five years of trial and error at both the Uptown Talmud Torah and the Bureau of Jewish Education"; and hence "the institute represented the most polished embodiment of the modern talmud torah ideal." Thus the CJI was not only the creation of Kehilath Jeshurun and its young rabbis, but was simultaneously the brainchild of Samson Benderly and the Bureau of Jewish Education. The new school incorporated the *ivrit b'ivrit* system, of course, and drew heavily from the teaching pool created by Benderly and Kaplan. They adopted progressive teaching methods such as the use of pictorial slides in the teaching of the Bible; although such innovations aroused the ire of the traditionalists at first, their "revolutionary" methodology was eventually accepted across the board. Indeed, the Benderly boys became the dominant force in American Jewish education throughout the interwar period.[64]

Two of the Benderly boys in particular became associated with the Central Jewish Institute and the "Jewish School Center" idea: Isaac B. Berkson and Alexander M. Dushkin. Succeeding Herbert Goldstein, Berkson was appointed executive director of the CJI in 1917 after submitting a new policy statement to the trustees. The published plan appeared in the journal of the Bureau of Jewish Education under the title "The Community School Center"[65] and recommended the following guidelines:

> The underlying idea of The Central Jewish Institute is "Talmud Torah," as is indicated by its sub-title. The preservation of Jewish spiritual life is the idea which gives point and purpose to all the activities of the institution. With all its strong insistence on a Jewish purpose, it nevertheless recognizes the need of adjusting to the conditions of American life and thought. The harmonization of Jewish purpose with American life is the institution's *raison d'être*. . . . In addition to specifically Jewish work, the Jewish center must carry on activities which make for the physical and social well-being of the people who live in the neighborhood. . . . Just as the activity of the Institute should not be limited to one aspect in the life of the individual, so, too, it should not be limited to one age in the population. . . . In fine, the Central Jewish Institute hopes to make a contribution to the solution of the problem of creating the educational institution that will be potent to preserve a vital Jewish life in America.[66]

In 1918, Alexander Dushkin published his dissertation as *Jewish Education in New York City*, in which he discussed the various recent attempts that had been made by "five or six of the larger schools . . . in fully becoming a real Community School Center. The Central Jewish Institute, under Mr. I. B. Berkson, at 125 East 85th Street, is the clearest indication of the efforts that are being made along these lines." Dushkin further claimed that the ideal Jewish school center was more than a school; it was also a neighborhood house, recreation center, forum and lecture hall, meeting place (both for local societies and for citywide organizations), charities headquarters, neighborhood synagogue, and American civic center. In short, it would become a sort of local branch of the Kehillah and fulfill all the needs of Jewish communal life under one roof—the ideal Jewish center. To provide an example of such a comprehensive Jewish institution, Dushkin

Fig. 26. Central Jewish Institute, built 1916. *Jewish Communal Register, 1917–18.*

reprinted the CJI's program of activities for December 1917. The program included fifteen graded Talmud Torah classes for boys and girls, special classes for High School students, lectures of the Jewish Communal School (of the Kehillah), youth group meetings (the League of Jewish Youth and the Circle of Jewish Children), club events, meetings of Jewish communal organizations, Hanukah celebrations, religious services, and meetings of the governing and auxiliary bodies of the institute.[67]

While serving as director of the CJI, Isaac Berkson followed Dushkin's lead by publishing his dissertation in 1920. *Theories of Americanization: A Critical Study with Special Reference to the Jewish Group* described the various "theories of ethnic adjustment" that arise in a democratic society and became a classic in the literature of cultural pluralism. The discussion culminates with his own ideal, which he referred to as "the Community theory." To demonstrate how the pluralist theory would work in practice, he added a final chapter on "The Central Jewish Institute—A Jewish Community Center." As had Dushkin, Berkson emphasized the importance of the school building, and cites the CJI, in which "the structure is itself a vital part of the plan." He continues:

The Central Jewish Institute is a thoroughly fire-proof four story building, standing on a lot 60 × 100 feet. It contains, in addition to ten classrooms, two kindergarten rooms, two social rooms, a sitting and reading room, an auditorium, gymnasium, kitchenette, and two roof-gardens, one adjoining the kindergarten room, the other on top of the building. Such a combination of facilities has hitherto not been associated with a Talmud Torah. In recent years the need of facilities for general work has begun to be recognized. Talmud Torahs have included an assembly hall for lectures and for synagogue purposes. One Talmud Torah has even added a gymnasium. But the Central Jewish Institute is the first Jewish educational institution in New York City that has combined all facilities for social work with thoroughly adequate accommodation for school work.[68]

In the CJI, therefore, the Talmud Torah and the Jewish center were synthesized both in theory and in concrete form. Berkson furthermore suggested architectural principles that should inform the planning of future centers. They were "variety of usage" through "convertible units" (seen above in the convertible auditorium/synagogue/theater); an "organic relationship" to give "a unity of character" (or, Mordecai Kaplan meets Frank Lloyd Wright); "a warm and intimate rather than institutionalized atmosphere" (the Jewish school metaphorized as *home*); and "the unique character of the ethnic group embodied so far as possible in architecture and decorations." With this last idea Berkson confronted the lack of a Jewish style of architecture; nonetheless he recommended that a Jewish Community House ought to look Jewish. It was, after all, American in nearly every other way, in its flexibility, organicity, and utility. For Berkson, this was the hallmark of the ideal Jewish center: its embodiment of the American-Jewish duality, paying equal attention to both sides of the equation. The CJI may not have met that ideal in every way, but it was as close to a full-blown American Jewish school center as there had been to date.[69]

With the dissolution of the Kehillah in 1918, the ambitious schemes of the Benderly group were curtailed. Modern Talmud Torahs and Jewish school centers continued to be formed around the country, often on the model of institutions such as the Central Jewish Institute. Like the CJI, they were communally sponsored projects aspiring to be "the [primary] unit of Jewish communal organization," as Dushkin intended. Most Talmud Torahs, however, remained identified with Orthodox Judaism and failed to compete with Jewish centers as comprehensive social centers serving entire families and communities. Other communal schools were formed along the secularist lines of Labor Zionism and Yiddishist Socialism and further contributed to the failure of the modern Talmud Torah idea to unite the community. Finally, a separate Jewish Community

Center movement evolved a secularist ideology of its own, failing to retain the commitment to a comprehensive *Jewish* program and Jewish educational content of the CJI. Thus it was neither the settlement-center nor the Talmud Torah but the synagogue that soon emerged as the preeminent institution of the American Jewish community.[70]

The Synagogue–Talmud Torah synthesis

As Dushkin suggested, the synagogue triumphed by co-opting the educational function of the Talmud Torah and turning into the ideal Jewish center itself. We have seen, however, that prior to the emergence of the Talmud Torah–Jewish center many Talmud Torahs often provided the services of a synagogue. In fact, during the same period in which the Talmud Torah evolved into a center, Talmud Torahs and synagogues were undergoing an uneasy courtship themselves. From their encounter, therefore, three possibilities emerged: (1) the Talmud Torah–sponsored synagogue, (2) the synagogue-sponsored Talmud Torah, and (3) a synthesis of the two institutions, the so-called Talmud Torah Congregation, serving both functions at once.

The rise of the congregational school was an important by-product of the Americanization of the Orthodox synagogue, the process by which the insular *landsmanshaft shul* blossomed into a modern institution oriented to the entire community (to be fully explored in the next chapter). A common feature of this second stage of the synagogue's development was a communal school, a Talmud Torah. The development flew in the face of the Benderly group who had staked the future of Jewish education upon the noncongregational communal school.

One early example of such a synagogue-sponsored Hebrew school was that of Congregation Zichron Ephraim. Rabbi Bernard Drachman recounted that, from the start, "the congregation established a school for the instruction of children in the Hebrew language, Biblical history, and the principles of the Jewish faith." Called "The Hebrew Free School of Congregation *Zichron Ephraim*" (only later renamed the Talmud Torah), the school was housed in the basement of the synagogue and was attended by approximately two hundred and fifty students. The women of the Orthodox congregation, denied involvement in most other areas of synagogue life, devoted themselves to the support of the Talmud Torah. Drachman continued: "Shortly after the opening of the synagogue [in 1890, the year following the establishment of the first temple Sisterhood by Temple Emanu-El] a Sisterhood or Women's Society was organized by some zealous and devout women. . . . Early in its career it took upon itself the responsibility of maintaining the Talmud Torah, thereby freeing the congregation from the entire burden of its upkeep."[71]

Following the turn of the century, the establishment of a Talmud Torah by a new congregation became standard practice—especially when a new synagogue building was constructed. In 1905, Congregation Agudath Sholom of Stamford, Connecticut, announced: "As soon as the Beth Hammidrash will be completed, a 'Talmud Torah' will be organized in accordance with modern ideas and principles." When synagogues began to establish Talmud Torahs catering to the entire community, the competitive relationship between synagogues and independent Talmud Torahs experienced earlier in the ghetto district grew even more contentious. Contention became especially common in areas of second settlement, for the creation of a Talmud Torah was an eminently logical way for the synagogue to attract the membership of young families in the new areas.[72]

Congregational Talmud Torahs were prevalent in second-settlement areas of New York City such as Harlem and Brooklyn. In 1898, the Talmud Torah of Congregation Sons of Israel was formed in Bensonhurst, Brooklyn, and in 1905, the Talmud Torah of Congregation Baith Israel Anshei Emes. Samuel Abelow, the historian of Brooklyn Jewry, recalls his own involvement in one such enterprise, the Congregation Tiphereth Israel School, which

bought a cottage on the southeast corner of Throop and Willoughby Avenues and converted it into a synagogue. This was in 1907. One of the organizers, Joseph Prensky, asked Samuel P. Abelow, who was active in Jewish social work at that time, for a plan that would make the synagogue a vital force in that community. Mr. Abelow suggested that the building should be opened every Sunday afternoon for the boys and girls, and that he would lecture to them on Jewish history gratis. The plan proved satisfactory . . . within a short time, the attendance at the meetings filled the synagogue. The boys and girls were organized into a group called Young Israel, and pins were awarded to the most deserving members.[73]

The formation of Talmud Torahs by congregations and their rabbis continued even after the war, as when, in 1918, Rabbi Jacob A. Dolgenas left the pulpit of a Harlem congregation (Shearith B'nai Israel) for one in Brooklyn (B'nai Israel). The *American Hebrew* reported that, in his new job, "one of his chief activities will be to interest the neighborhood in the establishment of a Talmud Torah." And so the synagogue continued to compete with the nonaffiliated Talmud Torah. The tension would eventually be resolved during the interwar era when the Talmud Torah went into decline and the synagogue school emerged victorious—as part of the synagogue-center program, of course.[74]

The more surprising development during the prewar years was the transformation of Talmud Torahs into synagogues. Oftentimes, the pioneer Jewish institution of a new area of settlement was not a synagogue but a school; this was the case of the Hebrew school organized in 1895 by Philip Cowen and others for an emerging Jewish community in the Tremont section of the Bronx. As Cowen recalled: "There was a fine teaching staff; Mordecai M. Kaplan, Leon Elmaleh, Arthur Dembitz, Miss Kaplan and Miss Baum. The final outcome was the present Temple at Burnside and Jerome Avenues." Similarly, the "final outcome" of many a Talmud Torah would be a synagogue. Introducing his discussion of the Talmud Torahs of Brooklyn, Abelow stated plainly: "A third group of schools is the Talmud Torahs. These schools are connected with the synagogues or they form the

Fig. 27. Congregation Shaari Israel Talmud Torah. Courtesy of the Library of the Jewish Theological Seminary of America.

nuclei around which the synagogues are built. The number of Talmud Torahs is growing. The boom period following the World War marked a golden era."[75]

Synagogues and Talmud Torahs often shared the same quarters in part because of the efficiency of space sharing, but primarily because of the shared purpose of the two institutions: to perpetuate Judaism among the children of the immigrants. The combination of synagogue and Talmud Torah is therefore indicative of a progressive orientation, of an Americanized congregation concerned with the future of the Jewish community. In Youngstown, Ohio, for example, the Youngstown Hebrew Institute of 1908 was housed within the building of the Emanuel Congregation, founded three years earlier. In Denver, Colorado, both the Congregation Beth Hamedrosh Hagodol and the Denver Hebrew School were to be found at the same address, with the same rabbi (C. E. H. Kauvar) in charge. Often, the two agencies would take the next step and amalgamate into one, and thus the synthetic Talmud Torah–synagogue arose, a hybrid institution that was both a school and congregation at once: for example, the Talmud Torah Beth Jacob Joseph, in which "religious services are held in the Talmud Torah every day."[76]

The phenomenon appeared as early as 1868 in New York City with the formation of (Congregation) Talmud Torah Chevrah Kadisha, and in more obscure locations such as Altoona, Pennsylvania, where (Congregation) Talmud Torah was formed in 1873, and Charleston, West Virginia, where the B'nai Israel Hebrew Educational Society was founded in 1874. Between 1880 and 1900, such combination school/congregations were established in locations as farflung as Elmira, New York; Waco, Texas; Washington, D.C., Lincoln, Nebraska; and Boston. Following the turn of the century—as immigrants began to transcend the self-orientation of their *landsmanshaftn*—more and more such forward-look-ing institutions were established. Such hybrid institutions as Tiphereth Achim Talmud Torah (1909) flourished by the dozens in New York City, but were by no means relegated to the metropolis. In nearby Philadelphia, Talmud Torah con-gregations included Strawberry Mansion Talmud Torah–Kerem Israel Synagogue (1911), Hebrew Free School Congregation, and Talmud Torah Adath Jeshurun. Further afield, we find the Hebrew Educational School and Chapel in Quincy, Massachusetts (1909), the West Denver Hebrew School and Synagogue (1910), Congregation Talmud Torah of Asheville, North Carolina (1911), Congregation Talmud Torah of the South Side of Pittsburgh (1914), the Talmud Torah of Los Angeles (1915), and Congregation Hebrew Free School of Tampa, Florida (1917).[77]

As the communal Talmud Torah went into decline, it became further inclined to amalgamate with other Jewish institutions. We have seen the Talmud Torah merge with the Jewish settlement and with the synagogue. Following the war, it was even sometimes absorbed by the YMHA: for example, "the Bronx YMHA Talmud Torah, established in 1919 as part of the YMHA which came into being ten years earlier." It was only to be expected, therefore, that the synthesis of syna-gogue, Talmud Torah, and YMHA would appear. In 1908, for example, the Tal-mud Torah Congregation of Tacoma, Washington, was founded at the same ad-dress as the Young People's Hebrew Association. In Reading, Pennsylvania, the YMHA (founded in 1909) was the location of the founding of Congregation B'nai Zion in 1912, and five years later, the Hebrew Institute was added. The re-sult was an ad hoc synagogue-center.[78]

Conclusion

Transplanted from the Old Country, the Talmud Torah became the primary ed-ucational institution of the East European immigrant Jewish community. On American soil it was transformed into a supplementary school attempting to pro-vide all the children of the community with an affordable Jewish education. Its first American model was the philanthropic free school, and its second, the mu-nicipal public school. In the first case, the Hebrew free school linked the Talmud Torah with the settlement movement, an association that later would bear fruit in its reconfiguration as a neighborhood center. In the second, the example of the public school provided a model of modern American efficiency in terms of "light and airy" school environments, graded curricula, scientific methods of pedagogy and school organization, and perhaps most important, the idea of an in-school social center for the neighborhood. Both models helped set the process of mod-ernization into motion, a process fostered by individuals such as Albert Lucas and Samson Benderly; the former responsible for the creation of anti-missionary "Jewish Centres" on the Lower East Side, the latter for the spread of the He-braist method in Jewish education in America. Around the turn of the century, a number of "Hebrew Schools" were founded that were nationalist rather than religious. These too would exert a profound influence on the Talmud Torah. When Benderly arrived in New York in 1910, the trends began to coalesce under the auspices of the Bureau of Jewish Education of the Kehillah. Benderly and a group of progressive Talmud Torah principals joined forces to Hebraize and modernize the Talmud Torahs of New York. A group of Benderly's protégés, trained in modern educational theory by John Dewey and his circle at Columbia, also influenced the Talmud Torah movement by introducing Deweyan ideas such as reconfiguring the school as a community center. Their ideal "school center" was to be the Central Jewish Institute, a notable experiment that ultimately influenced the synagogue-center movement more than either the Talmud Torah or Jewish center movements. For this reason perhaps, the period of Americanization of the Talmud Torah—beginning in the 1880s and culminating with its development into a "Jewish school center" in the second decade of the twentieth century—has been, heretofore, a lost chapter in the history of the American Jewish community. The next logical step would be to create a combination Talmud Torah, Jewish center, and synagogue; that is, a true synagogue-center. It was this synagogue-center of the post–World War I period that would be the true heir of the modern Talmud Torah, "Judaized" Jewish center, and their exemplar, the Central Jewish Institute.

5

SHUL
The Orthodox Synagogue in Transition

The tales of the New York ghetto were heart-breaking comedies of the tragic conflict between the old and the new, the very old and the very new; in many matters, all at once: religion, class, clothes, manners, customs, language, culture. . . . We saw it everywhere all the time. Responding to a reported suicide, we would pass a synagogue where a score or more of boys were sitting hatless in their old clothes, smoking cigarettes on the steps outside, and their fathers, all dressed in black, with their high hats, uncut beards, and temple curls, were going into the synagogue, tearing their hair and rending their garments. . . . It was a revolution. Their sons were rebels against the law of Moses; they were lost souls, lost to God, the family, and to Israel of old. . . . Two, three thousand years of devotion, courage, and suffering for a cause [were] lost in a generation.　　　　　　　　　　　　　　　　　　—LINCOLN STEFFENS, 1931[1]

THE SYNAGOGUE—or "shul" in colloquial Yiddish—was an especially noteworthy feature of the turn-of-the-century Jewish ghetto, for it symbolized the basic duality of immigrant Judaism: both the persistence of the old and the encounter with the new. Outside observers often took note of this dilemma, as when Lincoln Steffens recalled passing a Lower East Side synagogue. The muckraking journalist interpreted the generational divide he saw there in the starkest terms, as a spiritual "revolution." In hindsight, however, Steffens's observation was over pessimistic; neither the fathers nor the sons were to remain very long at opposite ends of the spectrum. In the early decades of the century, immigrant fathers themselves began to Americanize, and many of their sons would seek a path back to Judaism at the same time. Jewish women, who tended to neither extreme in the first place, would enter the sphere of the synagogue in force. In consequence, the traditional synagogue—the immigrants' old familiar shul—would be transformed.

Changes in the air were evident in the winter of 1909, when the *Boston Advocate* provocatively asked its readership: "Can the Synagogue Do Anything to Attract the Younger Generation? If So, What?" The underlying assumption, of course, was that the synagogue as constituted was not attracting the young. In their varied responses, the youthful correspondents vented a litany of complaints against the immigrant shul, some logical, some laughable. One suggested "a single method of ventilation for the synagogue," recalling Alfred Kazin's pungent description of the "permanently stale smell" of the shul. Another advised that "the synagogue be made as beautiful as possible in physical appearance. . . . Then only could the young Jew be made to feel the inner meaning and beauty of the synagogue." Both criticisms reflected the decrepit conditions of most immigrant shuls, which often were housed in the poorest quarters of the community.

Still other responses referred to the character of synagogue life, especially regarding the importance of Jewish social activity. Saul Shore wrote: "Our rabbis should get at us, organize us into national clubs, religious clubs, if you please. . . . Large vestries, nay, even the smallest chamber of the synagogue should be converted to meeting rooms, gamerooms, Sunday Schools, religious classes, and public libraries." Daniel Bloomfield suggested that "clubs for social purposes, and to study Jewish questions and ideals as well as clubs for Bible study should be organized by every synagogue." Apparently the social emphasis of the immigrant shul was lost upon the next generation, for whom its premises seemed open only to the fathers and off-limits to the sons. A North End social worker named Philip Davis (*né* Feivel Chemerinsky) offered the sharpest critique, writing that "the synagogue will never interest the younger generation until it is taken out of the hands of the older generation which now manages it exclusively. Apparently those now in charge care very little about attracting the younger generations. They decide everything solely from the standpoint of their own tastes and needs. The services, ceremonies, sermons, everything that the synagogue stands for are conducted for sake of the old."[2]

Davis's recommendation was to emulate the institutional church with "its Sunday school, its young men's clubs, its parties and socials," and like the church, make an effort "to accommodate itself to the needs and interests of the young generation; to make the church the centre of all neighborhood activities. . . . Just as soon as the synagogue becomes, by an extension of function in all the spheres of life, a physical and spiritual centre of growth, by an attempt to cover all the cycles of life, just so soon will it win over the younger generation and no sooner." He had hit upon what many perceived as the core problem of the immigrant synagogue: its seeming unwillingness to reach out, to the younger generation in particular, to the greater world in general. Ultimately, the shul would open up to the "outside" in several ways, including: outside influences, such as the Reform temple; outside constituencies, such as women; and outside ideologies, such as Zionism. The factor uniting all these innovations would be the expansion of the scope of synagogue activity. Yet as we shall see, the idea of sociability was inherent in the Orthodox synagogue all along.

In the second installment of the symposium, editor Jacob de Haas reiterated Davis's recommendation to expand the scope of synagogue activity; rather than drawing on the example of the church, however, he cited the historical role of the synagogue to reach the same conclusion:

Up to our own times the synagogue was the congregational pivot . . . because the life of the congregation was conducted within its four walls. . . . It was a house of learning, house of worship, meeting house, all rolled in one, with a court of justice in an ante-room and a school in another. It was not a place to which a Jew went on occasion, it was the place in which every Jew passed quite a large portion of his life. It was the headquarters of a tiny Jewish municipality. The break begun by Reform, was widened by the lodge movement, but there is nothing repugnant historically to such development within the synagogue structure as the housing of a social settlement, library, gymnasium."[3]

De Haas not only provided a Jewish rationale for the synagogue-center, but was one of the first to offer the "house of worship, study, and assembly" formula. As he implies, that was always the function of the synagogue. Whether historically accurate or not, it was certainly true of the Orthodox synagogue in America. Nevertheless, most historians of American Judaism have described the modern Orthodox synagogue as the antithesis of the immigrant shul. Their assessment mirrors those earlier critics of the shul who were repelled by its antiquated appearance and unruly ways, so lacking in the dignity and decorum of a "proper" religious institution. The orderly, modernized synagogue is thereby understood as the very opposite of its predecessor. Yet the fact remains that the modern synagogue had its roots in the ghetto shul, which was a kind of synagogue-center from the very beginning. The innovations of later years were not so much a reversal of earlier patterns as they were a restatement, or "reconstruction," of those same Jewish communal traditions in American terms. Within a single generation, during the thirty-year span from 1885 to 1915, the social basis of the *bet knesset* (literally, house of assembly) would be rediscovered—and the immigrant shul would be transformed into a modern institution.[4]

Shuls of the Immigrant Ghetto

The East European immigrant synagogue, or "shul," was a product of the mass immigration of the late nineteenth century. Whereas earlier Ashkenazic immigrants to America often joined the established synagogue-community, the East European Jewish immigrants of the post–Civil War era were neither welcomed by the native Jewish community nor in the least inclined to join its religious fold. The gap between their respective religious cultures was simply too wide. Rather than joining the established synagogues of the earlier settlers, the immigrants formed their own synagogue-community to fulfill both their religious and social needs. At first a small, intimate, men-only conclave, the shul was intended to provide social solace as much as to fulfill religious obligation. Jewish immigrants were sorely in need of such solace as they arrived in an America unprepared for their mass arrival. Through the 1870s, 1880s, and 1890s, therefore, small shuls proliferated, evoking the stereotypical ghetto portrayal of "a shul on every corner."

The first East European congregation in any given city was usually established

Fig. 28. "The Synagogues Are Everywhere—Imposing or Shabby-Looking Buildings," engraving by Abraham Phillips, depicting the Warshawer Shul, Rivington Street, built 1903. Lillian D. Wald, *The House on Henry Street* (New York: Holt, Rinehart and Winston, 1915; repr. Dover Publications, Inc., 1971).

by Jews from a particular region. This is apparent in their designations as "Russishe" (Russian) or "Litvishe" (Lithuanian) synagogues in contrast to their German Jewish predecessors. Sometimes, the contrast would be denoted by the congregational name chosen: in Boston, for example, the first East European shul was founded by Lithuanian Jews and called, "Shomre Shabbes" (literally, Sabbath observers). Next to be formed were Galician, Hungarian, Rumanian, and/or Polish congregations, arising in competition with the original shul. Finally, when masses of immigrants arrived after 1880, smaller and smaller locales provided the basis for the new "*landsmanshaft* shuls," often named after the members' *shtetl* of origin. By the 1880s, the German Jewish community had moved "uptown," and the immigrant neighborhood was fast turning into an East European "ghetto," recognizable by the Yiddish hubbub in its crowded streets, the ubiquitous pushcarts and Hebrew-lettered signs, the teeming tenements and alleyways, and not least, by its multitude of immigrant shuls.[5]

To the outside observer, all shuls seemed remarkably similar. Following the East European model, the ritual observance of the shul conformed with traditional (Ashkenazic) Judaism—the pattern we now commonly refer to as "orthodoxy." Religious norms such as daily services (*shachrit* and *mincha/maariv*), the traditional Hebrew prayerbook (*siddur*), Yiddish homilies (*drashes*), separation of the sexes (often women were excluded entirely), Talmud study groups and other auxiliaries (*hevras;* e.g., the burial society, or *hevra kadisha*) characterized all synagogues of the immigrant period. Similarly, the Yiddish language and a homogeneous composition of adult males were common features of the first-generation synagogue. Shuls varied widely in size, however. Though always begun on the smaller scale, immigrant synagogues would later range from the bare minimum of a ten-man quorum (minyan) to large congregations of several hundred members.

For the purpose of this discussion, I shall divide the wide variety of sizes and shapes into two categories, or types: the small, private conventicle and the large communal synagogue. The first type has alternately been known as a "landsmanshaft shul," "anshe," "hevra," or "shtibl." Like the purely secular landsmanshaft, the shul formed by immigrants from the same hometown was a microcosmic substitute for the community they had left behind. The second type, often named the "Bet Hamidrash Hagadol" (literally, "the great house of study"), was the central showpiece synagogue of the immigrant community. There is no commonly accepted term for this type; I must therefore invent a phrase, and can do no better than "community synagogue." The word "community" encapsulates both the traditional role of the main communal synagogue as well as the new institution's orientation to a rapidly Americanizing populace. The American community synagogue both replicated the "stadt shul" of the European Jewish community and at the same time aspired to public prestige in the New World.[6]

The two types of immigrant synagogue make an interesting comparison. The essential distinction between the two lies in their communal reference point. The landsmanshaft shul, "an institution defined by and oriented toward the Old World," linked its members to their former communal home, whether it was a *shtetl* or a major East European city. The community synagogue was oriented to the community it found itself in at the moment, whether the immigrant ghetto or an area of second settlement. The shul was thus backward-looking and transitional, while the synagogue had settled in for the duration, looking toward a more permanent future. Furthermore, the small shul luxuriated in its inner-directed intimacy, while the larger synagogue revelled in its outer-directed showiness. Paradoxically, the former fulfilled all the functions of a community, while the latter was somewhat curtailed in function as a congregation. The landsmanshaft shul was located in rented quarters (a tenement flat or a storefront window), whereas the community synagogue was housed in its own synagogue structure, purchased or built. Yet the impermanent shul provided shelter from a hostile environment, while the permanent sanctuary flung open its doors to the outside world. Though different in many ways, both types perpetuated the European

Jewish past in the new American context. Both would also provide models for the modernized synagogues of the following generation, establishing institutional precedents that ultimately influenced the development of the modern Orthodox synagogue-center.[7]

The "Landsmanshaft Shul" as Synagogue-Community

While the earliest shuls were small by necessity—the numbers of East European immigrants remained few through the 1870s—the small shul continued to predominate long after the burst of mass immigration of the 1880s. Perhaps the most striking aspect of the small Orthodox synagogue is the sheer number that were founded during the immigrant period. To open his 1901 history of the first "Russian-American" shul, J. D. Eisenstein made the following observation:

History is indeed stranger than fiction, yet stranger is the history of the Jews, and that of the Russian-American Jews the strangest. . . . Neither the dreamer nor the prophet, however, could reasonably imagine or predict their remarkable growth and development in that short period—from the sparse few of their humble congregation to the present mighty army of numerous synagogues, *shules* and *hebras* with the fervor of religious activity. . . . The lowest estimate credits this locality [the Lower East Side of New York] with 300,000 Russian Jews, and nearly 300 congregations including *Minyanim,* making it probably unique in the world. And yet it is but fifty years since, in that whole neighborhood, not a single congregation of Russian Jews could be found.[8]

The phenomenon of shul proliferation is most often related to the voluntaristic foundations of American society: when dissatisfied with his church, the individual may simply go out and establish a new one; hence, the rampant denomi-nationalism of American religious life. In Jewish life, the principle led to the founding of numerous synagogues. Yet Eisenstein would later allude to another critical factor in the immigrants' willingness to establish breakaway congregations: the schismatic experience of the Hasidim in Eastern Europe. Referring to the "Forsyth St. congregation," he wrote:

another split was imminent between two factions of the congregation, who became more distinct and more divided as each increased in numbers, namely the *Hasidim* and their opponents. As a rule the former are socially religious, they combine piety with pleasure; they call their *shule* a *stuebel* or prayer-clubroom; they desire to be on familiar terms with the Almighty and abhor decorum; they want every one present to join and chant the prayers; above all they scorn a regularly ordained cantor, whom they are not allowed and cannot follow in his "foreign" melodies. On the other hand, the reformed element wanted to introduce decorum and a musical cantor.[9]

In this light, the increase of immigrant shuls would seem to be a "Hasidic" phenomenon. In the late eighteenth and nineteenth centuries, the Hasidic movement set the precedent of creating small prayer conventicles in opposition to the established kehillah hierarchy. The existence of multiple synagogues within the same Jewish community had thus become the norm in Eastern Europe. To take but one example, the city of Biala in southern Poland boasted four major congregations and fourteen Hasidic *shtiblach*. The principle of congregational diversity would later be carried to the New World, even when the founders of shuls were not true Hasidim. Furthermore, as Eisenstein points out, the Hasidim were "socially religious," combining the function of the prayer-room with that of a "club-room." The combination virtually defines the landsmanshaft shul! Thus, both the principle of shul proliferation and the social emphasis of shul life may be related to an East European model, the Hasidic *shtibl*.[10]

Far more significant, the immigrant shul owes its special character to its origin as a "landsmanshaft." As Charles Liebman has suggested, the proliferation of synagogues did not necessarily indicate an overwhelming religious urge on the part of the immigrants, but was rather the result of "social and cultural needs." Familiarity, not spirituality, was the immigrant's most pressing need (obviously, they are not mutually exclusive). The immigrant synagogue was thus almost always founded as a landsmanshaft, "an organization of *landslayt*—of Jews who emigrated from the same town or locality." The landsmanshaft shul was a community reconstituted in the form of a synagogue, a "synagogue-community" serving both the religious functions of the synagogue and the social needs of the community.[11]

Despite some confusion in the literature, it seems clear that the majority of immigrant synagogues founded between 1880 and 1900 were formed by groups of *landslayt;* and that the majority of landsmanshafts formed in the same period also functioned as shuls. That is to say, before 1900, there did not yet exist the clear distinction between landsmanshaft and shul that later emerged. Of course, the functional distinction can always be blurred, as when Deborah Dash Moore draws a parallel between the two: "the chevra [that is, the landsmanshaft shul] filled religious and social welfare needs through membership in a meaningful community. What secular Jews found in *landsmanshaftn* and fraternal lodges, religiously observant immigrants obtained in their chevras." Both the religious and the nonreligious immigrant felt the same need for community, the one fulfilling it in religious terms, the other, in secular fashion. The function of the landsmanshaft remains the same.[12]

How, then, to understand the variety of landsmanshaft forms? While many pre-1900 landsmanshafts may be identified as distinctly religious and many as distinctly secular, most fell between the two extremes. Following Nathan Glazer's suggestion to view the observance level of immigrants along a continuum, we may similarly see the variety of landsmanshafts as lying along a continuum between religious shuls and secular societies. Just as most Jewish immigrants were neither ultra-Orthodox traditionalists nor atheistic radicals, the typical landsmanshaft shul hewed to the center, somewhere between the religious and social extremes.[13]

Though the landsmanshaft shul was criticized in its day for its lack of decorum, crass commercialism, and narrow-minded parochialism, we are not here concerned with its acknowledged faults. Nor are we overconcerned with its socio-logical characteristics, which would describe its intimate scale and social homo-geneity. Instead, the elements most relevant to the present discussion are those that reveal the small shul to have been an early version of the synagogue-center. Such characteristics include its synthesis of social and religious functions, its multifunctionality, and its centrality for the immigrant community. These are all related ideas inasmuch as they all derive from the same principle of organization: the landsmanshaft.[14]

The landsmanshaft shul exhibited religious and social characteristics simulta-neously. For example, the sheer number of synagogues in the immigrant neigh-borhood ensured a "religious" atmosphere. While many immigrants avoided the shul altogether—except on the high holidays when they came in droves—the shuls' ubiquitous presence served as a constant reminder of the religious under-pinnings of Jewish life. The shul was a visible symbol of Jewish tradition and identification, a communal mnemonic reminding the immigrants who they were and whence they had come. Parallel to its role as religious exemplar, the shul was an "ethnic church," a religious form with social content. The landsmanshaft shul was a synagogue whose major purpose was to tie Jews to other Jews. One's rela-tionship to God was expressed as well, of course, but no longer was it central to the enterprise; not because religiosity was unimportant, but because Jewish com-munality had attained equal importance. Since the same equivalence between so-cial and religious ends lies at the heart of the synagogue-center concept, the shul may be considered a significant forerunner of the later institution. The difference between the immigrant shul and the modern synagogue-center is only the degree to which they openly acknowledge their social ends. Rather than having been "the antithesis of the immigrant chevra," therefore, the synagogue-center was the shul-idea fully realized. As we shall explore below, it may even have been the sec-ond generation's re-creation of the fondly remembered synagogue from the old neighborhood, a landsmanshaft shul for "landsleit" from the immigrant ghetto.[15]

Documentary sources often testify to the dual nature of Jewish institutional life. In *The Russian Jew in the United States,* for example, I. K. Friedman was asked to describe the "amusements and social life" of Jewish immigrants in Chicago, but could not ignore the religious dimension. As he put it: "I found it difficult to draw a hard and fast line between the diversion afforded by the syna-gogue and its festivals, and the pastimes which are purely secular. I am not sure that a comprehensive paper should not include both; so intimately do the beth hamedrash (house of learning connected with the synagogue) and the religious rites and festivals enter into the amenities of the confines of Ghetto life, so much does religion contribute to the mere pleasure of the orthodox Russian Jew—pleasure which his less orthodox brethren seek in the secular world without."[16]

Similarly, it is possible to emphasize the religiosity of the landsmanshaft shul while describing its social life. Even the most secularist sociological observers such as Louis Wirth and Nathan Glazer are apt to celebrate its religious spirit.

Wirth wrote that "these *shuls,* most of which were merely private rooms or storefront synagogues, were places that glowed with the familiar, intense religious enthusiasm of old." Glazer states with surprising hyperbole that "figures [of numbers of immigrant shuls] cannot suggest the intensity of the Judaism of the East European Jews, which not only was unique in world history, but represented something of a peak even in Jewish history." Somewhat more soberly, Gerard Wolfe, the synagogue historian of the Lower East Side has written that "the single most important institution to the immigrant Jews, however, was the *shul,* or synagogue. While not everyone was a passionate follower of the traditional Orthodox rituals, the *shul* was the center for most immigrants of Jewish life."[17]

Alternatively, one may emphasize the social side of the equation. Irving Howe's description of the secular landsmanshaft provides the the key to understanding the landsmanshaft shul: "As if to re-create in miniature the very world from which they had fled, the immigrant Jews established a remarkable network of societies called *landsmanshaftn,* . . . in the main, the *landsmanshaftn* were jealous of their self-contained character—that impulse to social inwardness which brought a member to the monthly meeting in an East Side hall. . . . What they wanted was the closeness of familiars, the pleasures of smallness regained." The Old World, best represented by the shtetl, was self-contained, social, inward, close, familiar, and small—the attributes of *gemeinschaft.* The New World encountered in America was exactly the opposite—*gesellschaft.* The formation of an immigrant landsmanshaft was the natural response to the trauma of entering modern society.[18]

Why, one might ask, did East European Jews create landsmanshaft-type organizations in disproportionate numbers to other immigrant groups? The degree to which an immigrant population had come from a traditional society raised the likelihood of forming landsmanshaft-type institutions. If that society had been located in a region without its own state government and national body politic, than the immigrants' identification with the provincial locale would be greater, again raising the chances for such an organization. The likelihood was still greater if the immigrant group lacked a formal "church" hierarchy in the New World. More than any other immigrant group, therefore, Jews from Eastern Europe tended to form small groups based upon place of origin.[19]

The communalization of the American synagogue thus had its antecedents in the landsmanshaft shul. This meant that not only would the synagogue be social in emphasis, but multifunctional as well; that is, serving all the various functions of community. In this regard, Moses Weinberger wrote in 1887: "The purposes and aims of most Orthodox congregations are to meet twice daily or every Sabbath for group worship; to visit and succor their sick; to bury and give last rites to their dead; and to extend financial aid in an hour of distress to loyal members." Louis Wirth would later add: "Each of these congregations constituted a little world by itself, but a full world, in which were gathered all the interests of the people, religious, educational, social."[20]

Since the shul had originally been intended as a replication of the European Jewish community, it included many of the communal functions of the kehillah structure, now reconfigured as synagogue hevrot. Moses Rischin could thus describe the shul as "many-sided, . . . uniting the features of the Old World burial, study, and visitors-of-the-sick societies." And, as Irving Howe later noted: "In principle, the *shul* claimed the whole of its members' attention, quite as it had in eastern Europe. It tried to provide a range of activities to rival that of the immigrant culture itself, for the believers feared, reasonably enough, that this culture was a threat to their hegemony." Arthur Goren specified that of some 365 Lower East Side congregations surveyed in 1917, "90 percent owned cemetery plots, nearly half had free-loan societies, a third had sick-benefit societies, and nearly half sponsored traditional study groups."[21]

To further illustrate the point, Howe quotes from *The Russian Jew in the United States*. But he does not quote nearly enough from that wonderful anthology, for nearly every contributor has something to add concerning the multifunctionality of the shul. Abraham Cahan, an immigrant who became famous as a journalist, editor, novelist, socialist leader, and Americanizer, described the immigrant synagogue as "not merely a house of prayer," but also, "a mutual aid society, . . . and a literary club, no less than a place of worship." Cahan's approval of the multifunctional shul seems to make sense, perhaps having been a projection of his multifaceted self. Louis Lipsky, a pivotal figure in American Zionism, and like Cahan an immigrant turned journalist, similarly described the shul as nothing less than an "institutional church"! He was right, in a sense, but inadvertently revealed the great difference between the Christian and Jewish institutions by pointing to the "chevra kadisha" and the "chevra shas" as evidence of the parallel. We may rest assured that the Orthodox shul, with its traditional Jewish elements, was not at all influenced by the American Christian example. The reference is nevertheless significant in that Lipsky perceived a potential in the shul that later would be fulfilled by the multifunctional synagogue-centers created by the immigrants' children.

Charles Bernheimer pointed to the "social celebrations" of the shul, and Mrs. Benjamin Davis stressed its philanthropic role. But differences aside, all four commentators held one idea in common: the synagogue as a "centre." Cahan referred to it as an "intellectual centre," Bernheimer as a "social centre," Lipsky as the "centre" of Judaism, and Davis as both "the religious and social centre" of the community. The reader may infer that the synagogue ought to be central to any Jewish community. The second generation would do more than draw inferences; they would create the synagogue anew. After the related contributions of social-religious synthesis and multifunctionality, therefore, the idea of centrality constitutes the principal legacy of the immigrant shul to the synagogue-center.

At the same time, the small shul could be criticized for lacking precisely this attribute. Following his earlier statement, Louis Lipsky wrote: "Communal pride of a petty sort impresses the foreign Jew with the necessity of joining a synagogue,

but he finds very soon that the necessity is not so forceful as he had at first supposed. The effect of this change in standards is to be seen in the medley of congregations that may be found in the city of New York, each with its limited territory and its ignorance of the others. Instead of one compact Jewish community
with an organized centre we see group after group forming on the basis of
democracy, with a steady defiance of all ecclesiastical authority beyond its own
boundaries." Lipsky's critique reflected an attitude that had become common
among the more enlightened immigrants. By the turn of the century, the proliferation of landsmanshaft shuls came to be seen as a gross duplication of effort
and a disintegrative force in the Jewish community. The ready solution, a unifying institution, was already in evidence: the community-wide synagogue,
founded by immigrant Jews both as an echo of the old country "stadt shul" and
as a foreshadow of the synagogue-center to come.[22]

The Shul as "Community Synagogue"

Like the small landsmanshaft shul, the larger immigrant synagogue was founded
by a homogeneous group of Jewish men; like its predecessor, it was social, multifunctional, and "central." In fact, the community synagogue was in many ways
simply a re-creation of the original shul in larger and more permanent form.
Even the minyan-sized intimacy of the shul was transferred to the large synagogue in the form of the basement "bes medrash," an auxiliary room below the
main sanctuary upstairs, but an increasingly important space as it served all three
of the classical synagogue functions of prayer, study, and assembly. The immigrant synagogue thus continued its traditional communal role.

Yet the community synagogue also innovated in many areas; as East European
Jews transformed themselves from "greene" immigrants into Americanized ethnics, their institutions began to change as well. In contrast to the landsmanshaft
shul, the second type of immigrant synagogue was a much larger congregation
open to any Jew (willing to pay its membership dues), and was housed in its own
building. The community synagogue saw the beginning of significant changes in
Orthodox religious life, including the introduction of decorum in the service,
cantorial and choral music, women's sections, assigned seating, the professionalization of its personnel, and the creation of a synagogue bureaucracy. It was
outer-directed, open to the influences of the majority culture, and thus initiated
the trend toward greater participation for women in synagogue life. Above all, it
was conceived as the central synagogue of the surrounding community.[23]

Community synagogues were most often the result of the growth and/or
mergers of smaller congregations, as for example, the Beth Hamedrash Hagodol
of New York City. Its origin was a small shul named Beth Hamedrash (literally,
"house of study," but in the context of the New World Jewish community, a
synonym for synagogue), founded in 1852 as the "first Russian-American Jewish

congregation" in America. It had been organized by Rabbi Abraham Joseph Ash
and several others who rejected the reformist tendencies of the German Jewish
congregations. The new "Russian" shul occupied rented quarters until 1856,
when some wealthy Sephardic Jews, who sympathized with the traditionalism of
the newest immigrants, helped them to purchase an old Welsh chapel on Allen
Street, where Beth Hamedrash "rapidly became the most important center for
Orthodox Jewish guidance in the country." In the following years, disagreements
within the group led to the formation of new congregations, including one organized by Rabbi Ash in 1859, who renamed the offshoot Beth Hamedrash
Hagodol (the great synagogue), indicating his ambitions for the future. Its first
home was the top floor of a building at the corner of Forsyth and Grand Streets.
In 1865, the congregation moved to a former courthouse on Clinton Street, and
in 1872, a synagogue was built on Ludlow Street.[24]

Once in the new building, the younger members soon "gained the upper
hand" in synagogue affairs, "and introduced improvements and innovations"
such as changing the title of *parnas* to president. Religiously radical they were
not. The Ludlow Street Synagogue, for example, still sponsored both a *hevra shas*
and a *hevra mishnayot* (societies for the study of Talmud and Mishnah, respectively) and continued to train young men for the Orthodox rabbinate. The most
significant innovation of those years was the addition of a cantor, whose hiring in
1877 followed the expressed desire for greater decorum in the shul's religious
"services." More pressing than internal change, however, was the desire to gain
public attention. In 1885, the congregation sold its Ludlow Street property and
purchased a Methodist church on Norfolk Street (where it remains to this day).[25]

The dedication ceremonies for the newly renovated synagogue were praised in
the Jewish press for setting a new style and tone:

DEDICATION OF THE BETH HAMEDRASH HAGODOL. Hundreds of coreligionists from Upper and
Lower Manhattan, were pleasantly surprised to see the order of things prevailing at its dedication last Sunday. From the very outer gates which were strongly guarded against any disorderly
intruders, down to the end of the ceremonies, the usual noise and hubbub were conspicuous
by their absence. Inside the audience were furnished with handsome programmes consisting of
hymns and psalms which were pleasantly chanted by the chazan and a fully equipped choir.
The orators of the occasion were Dr. Lieberman, who delivered a subtle DROSHE in German,
and Dr. A. S. Isaacs, in English who imparted to his listeners a piece of common sense advice.
Adolf Cohen Esq. gave a history of the congregation, the exercises were concluded by Dr. D.
Brekes in German. A book was placed on the reading desk for anybody who wished to donate.
In this mode, they realized nearly 300 dollars. Too much praise could not be lavished on the
Committee of Arrangements for their sound judgement in showing the outer world that event
the dedication of a Beth Hamedrash could be performed in a quiet, respectable way which
mode formerly used to be monopolized by the reformers temples. Let us hope that this true
Jewish spirit will be perpetual.[26]

The moment was a turning point in American Orthodoxy. At the 1885 dedication of the new Beth Hamedrash Hagodol, the modern elements of decorum, choral music, and vernacular addresses were introduced into the Orthodox

Fig. 29. Beth Hamedrash Hagodol, Norfolk Street, former church building acquired in 1885. *The Jewish Encyclopedia* (New York: Funk & Wagnalls, 1905).

synagogue, all in order to show "the outer world" that the Jews of the Lower East Side were no less civilized than the uptown "reformers." The editorialist further recommended the addition of "a benevolent association and a school for children," but these were innovations that could wait. Instead, caught in the "hazan craze" of the 1880s, Beth Hamedrash Hagodol next imported a well-known— and thus highly paid—cantor named Israel Michaelowsky. Both the hiring of a famous hazan and the acquisition of an impressive new building were intended to raise the prestige of the congregation, and thereby surpass its competitors in the marketplace. It was, after all, the American way.[27]

Historians have explained the "hazan craze" in various ways. Jeffrey Gurock relates it to the new emphasis on the "maintenance of order" in the newly formalized synagogue service: "Decorum, always the first demand of acculturating groups in making their religious regimen more intelligible and respectable to the world around them, was strongly emphasized." While Jonathan Sarna points to the hazan's role as a mediating device that "met some deep-seated immigrant need": "What the *chazan* represented, I think, was the ultimate synthesis of the

Old World and New—a synthesis most immigrants sought to achieve but few succeeded. The *chazan* was an ideal role model: observant yet rich, traditional yet modern. He formed a bridge between East Europe and the East Side. . . . In short, a cantorial performance simultaneously served both as an exercise in nostalgia and as living proof that in America the talented could succeed handsomely."[28]

The "hazan craze" went hand in hand with another mania, the so-called edifice complex. As complementary fund-raising devices, the star hazan and new synagogue building were materialistically motivated and thus came under heavy criticism for subverting the true functions of the synagogue. As early as 1887, Moses Weinberger lambasted "the unworthy generation that has merited to bask in the light of America, [who] prefer a sweet singing *chazan* [cantor] to all the rabbis, judges, preachers, and expositors in the world"; he further complained that beside the usual "purposes and aims of most Orthodox congregations, . . . their more exalted aim is to build beautifully adorned synagogues. Every congregation that succeeds in doing this is boundlessly happy. Its members think that in this way they have fulfilled their every duty to Judaism." Beth Hamedrash Hagodol exemplified the synagogue that both scrambled for a famous hazan and purchased a new building at the same time, a phenomenon that Eisenstein ascribed to "the competition of other Russian congregations which were then building large synagogues in the same vicinity."[29]

To counter the disintegrative effects of synagogue competition, Beth Hamedrash Hagodol initiated a movement for the centralization of religious life, first forming the Association of American Orthodox Congregations (1887) and next bringing over famed scholar Jacob Joseph of Vilna to serve as chief rabbi (1888). Though neither the rabbi nor the synagogue ever quite achieved the goal of creating a central religious authority, the association of the venerable rabbi with the Norfolk Street Shul at least created the impression of its being the leading religious center of the East Side. The question of hegemony aside, the essential function of Beth Hamedrash Hagodol maintained throughout its history was as a synagogue serving the immigrant community. As late as the 1970s, its rabbi could still describe the synagogue as "recreating the role of *shul* in the "old country," which cared for the poor who huddled on the synagogue steps and which served as a center for religious learning and inspiration."[30]

Beth Hamedrash Hagodol had not survived as a tiny *shtiebl*, however, but as a "great synagogue" (not only the translation of Beth Hamedrash Hagodol, but also commonly employed to distinguish the largest, most prestigious synagogues from the rest). Contrary to popular wisdom, the monumental synagogue was not the sole domain of wealthy German Jews and second-generation East Europeans, but was also built by upwardly mobile immigrants while still living in the ghetto neighborhood. Of the great synagogues of the Lower East Side enumerated by Gerard Wolfe, four were renovated church edifices, two were former German Jewish temples, and two were built by the immigrants themselves. They either built or bought architectural showpieces for several reasons: to accommodate a growing membership, to make conspicuous their material success, to assert their equality with other American denominations, to emulate the uptown temples, to compete with other leading synagogues, to create a communal center, and simply to "build up" the congregation. Whatever the motive, the enthusiasm for "bigger and better" synagogues was remarkable.[31]

In his insightful introduction to Weinberger's *Jews and Judaism in New York*, Jonathan Sarna emphasizes the "outer-directness" of synagogue-building, and suggests some other causes and effects of the trend. "East European Jewish immigrants," he writes, "like their Jewish predecessors in America, wanted synagogues that they could proudly show off: both to Jews from other backgrounds and to Christian visitors." An impressive synagogue building "raised immigrant self-esteem, and even brought East Europeans some of the outside respect they so sedulously sought. By building modern ostentatious structures, newcomers demonstrated their Americanization." Moreover, "the large new buildings led synagogue officials to enlarge their own frames of vision. They now had vast new expenses and required equally vast memberships. No longer could they afford just to appeal to *landsmen*. Instead they had to welcome East Europeans from different homelands into their midst. They had to begin to cater to more varied religious needs. They had to become more tolerant of different customs and traditions. As a result synagogues unconsciously joined with schools, newspapers, and Gentiles in ethnicizing Jews. By joining Jews together into a more solidly unified community, they helped them to forget their old destructive internal divisions." Sarna thereby indicates the messages sent by a new synagogue structure to the greater community: We have arrived, we are Americans now, and just as America was open to us, we are open to all Jews; we are, in short, a community institution. No longer directed backward to a world gone by, the immigrant synagogue would henceforth relate to its new milieu and become a communal focus—the shul as "community center"! A building was as essential, therefore, as it was to the YMHAs, Educational Alliances, and other Jewish centers of the time.[32]

The immigrants' eagerness to move into larger quarters engendered a willingness to acquire houses of worship formerly used by "goyim" (derogatory term for non-Jews)—a slur even applied to the German Jews whose temples, replete with organs, family pews and stained-glass windows, seemed as *treif* (unkosher) as the Christian churches. The immigrant soon learned, however, that in contrast to the Old Country, churches were not really so foreign and forbidding in this land of equality of religion. The move into a church building (almost always a "democratic" Protestant meeting house as opposed to a "hierarchal" Catholic cathedral) was a demonstration of that powerful idea: in America, Judaism was as much at home as any Christian denomination.[33]

While Jewish law allows the conversion of a church building into a synagogue (although not the other way around), the practice was nearly unheard of in the Old Country; in America, however, it became commonplace. B'nai Jeshurun, the first Ashkenazic synagogue in New York, foreshadowed the later wholesale

Fig. 30. Lower East Side street scene, by Lewis Hine, 1912—looking east on Rivington Street, across Orchard Street. Visible at center, in the distance, is the synagogue of the First Roumanian-American Congregation, a former church building acquired in 1902. The photograph captures the imbalance within the immigrant community between the life of the synagogue—receding into the background—and the life of the marketplace—dominating everyday existence in the foreground. Lewis W. Hine Collection. United States History, Local History and Genealogy Division, The New York Public Library; Astor, Lenox and Tilden Foundations.

conversion of churches into synagogues when it purchased an African Methodist church in 1826. As we have seen, both the Beth Hamedrash and the Beth Hamedrash Hagodol occupied church buildings. Similar Lower East Side church conversions included Beth Haknesseth Mogen Avraham (church purchased in 1884), the Mishkan Israel Suwalki Synagogue (1886), the First Roumanian-American Congregation (1902), and the Bialystoker Synagogue (1905). Interestingly, the "Rumaynishe Shul" on Rivington Street had been constructed a few decades earlier as a Methodist mission church, intended to serve the immigrant population of "Kleindeutschland." The building was well suited to its new purpose: "after remodeling the church building, the Rumanian congregation converted the adjacent rectory into a *Talmud Torah*." In this case, therefore,

Louis Lipsky's description of the downtown synagogues as institutional churches was somewhat accurate.[34]

Gerard Wolfe's description of the renovation of Mogen Avraham is typical of the conversion process: "To adapt the former church sanctuary to synagogue use, a *bimah* was installed in the center, the walls and ceiling were repainted with zodiac symbols and scenes of the Holy Land, and the *Mogen David* (Star of David) was set into the stained-glass windows above the small gallery." As at the Rumanian Synagogue, Mogen Avraham "converted" its adjoining structure, originally the parsonage, to synagogue use. Orthodox congregations thus became accustomed to having multiple buildings, and former church buildings exercised some influence on the religious life of their Jewish reincarnations.[35]

Besides purchasing and renovating church structures, many congregations moved into vacated German Jewish temples; they therefore inherited many of the combined temple and schoolhouses discussed in Chapter 1. Yet the synagogues erected by the East Europeans themselves are the most revealing of the builders' motivations. Three elements of the new buildings need concern us. First, the architectural style of the exterior of the buildings (surely a good indicator of the "outer-directed" values intended to be expressed); second, the elaboration of the sacred furnishings of the sanctuary reveals something of the religious attitudes of the Orthodox congregants; and third, the interior arrangement of spaces reflects the new and varied uses of the modernized synagogue institution. Each of these architectural aspects of the community synagogue building adumbrated the later synagogue-center.

The first East European congregation in New York to erect its own synagogue was Khal Adas Jeshurun, which built the famed "Eldridge Street Shul" in 1886. The building is striking in its contradictions. Though designed by the Herter brothers (not the uptown design firm of the same name) on a grand scale and in fanciful style, the new shul fit easily into its immigrant milieu. The facade is dominated by the oversized rose window of a Gothic cathedral, and yet the overall effect is one of compactness, much like the rows of tenements along narrow Eldridge Street of which it was a part. In that cramped environment, the rose window was an exuberant note of self-importance. The architectural style integrates Moorish, Gothic, and Romanesque elements—each foreign to Judaism on its own, whereas together, they neatly express the cosmopolitan origins of Jews from around the world. The new shul was, after all, a community synagogue, open to all Jews no matter where their place of origin. Inside, the main hall was sumptuously appointed, especially the beautifully carved wooden Ark dominating the eastern wall of the sanctuary. Such lavish decor expressed the economic success of the immigrants as well as their continued commitment to religious tradition.[36]

Gerard Wolfe also describes the division of the immigrant synagogue into two distinct parts: "It was customary for the larger synagogues to have two rooms for worship, an upstairs main sanctuary, called in Yiddish the *aybershter* (upper) *shul,* and the downstairs *untershter* (lower) *shul,* often called the *bes medrash* (house of

Fig. 31. Artist Unknown. Khal
Adas Jeshurun Synagogue,
12–16 Eldridge Street, built
1886. Watercolor, 21.8 × 17.14.
Museum of the City of New
York. The J. Clarence Davies
Collection.

Fig. 32. View of interior of Khal Adas
Jeshurun, the Eldridge Street Synagogue,
1892. Courtesy of the Eldridge Street
Project.

study)." He characterized the downstairs space, where weekday services were held as well as "weddings, important functions, and social events," as "a miniature synagogue." Anyone familiar with Jewish life will immediately recognize the description as typical of such subsidiary synagogue spaces. Yet in 1886, the basement *bes medrash*—a synagogue within a synagogue—was something of a novelty. On the one hand, it perpetuated the intimacy and the social functions of the landsmanshaft shul; on the other, it created a spatial division between weekday services and Sabbath or holiday services, allaying the embarrassment of the disproportionate numbers attending.[37]

The *bes medrash* also provided a setting for the congregational meeting, according to some observers the central function of American synagogue life. As Moses Weinberger described it in the year of the Eldridge Street Synagogue's dedication (1887):

At congregational gatherings in the meetinghouse, people bring before their ruling throne all quarrels and contentions. . . . They prefer one hour of contentment in the community hall to all the joy, satisfaction, and spiritual pleasure that their fathers found in studying the Torah, Prophets, and commentaries all together. . . . The best of our people, who in their homelands went to the *bes midrash* to hear classes and pass their spare time, as well, on the other hand, as the most rotten who used to gather in the pubs and banquet halls to while away their time, find that all such things are unnecessary here. Both those who traditionally sat idle and those who traditionally sat learning run to the congregational meeting and find just what they have been seeking: merry fellowship. Night turns into day with them as they debate, split hairs, argue, and battle, make peace and compromise, all the while enjoying themselves immensely.[38]

Insofar as the congregational meeting was about politics and power, its prominence in synagogue life represented an outer-directed, New World orientation. One must keep in mind, however, that such shul "power brokers" were still immigrants. They had Americanized to a degree, as revealed by their "conspicuous construction" of synagogues and other communal institutions; on the other hand, they were still insecure enough to kept their contentiousness behind closed doors, sheltered by the cool quiet of the basement *bes medrash*. In its internal political aspect, the American synagogue would continue to play such a role: as a social sanctuary, a safe place apart from the greater society.

The frequent meetings in the *bes medrash* also set a precedent for the use of synagogue premises by outside organizations. In 1905, Mrs. Benjamin Davis of Chicago reported that "the use of the synagogues is given freely for meetings, religious, charitable, or educational." The *bes medrash* of the Eldridge Street Shul, for example, housed an independent Talmud Torah from 1901, while the main sanctuary was used for public gatherings, such as that reported in the *Reform Advocate* in 1900: "A Newspaper dispatch tells us that a remarkable mass meeting was held in the Eldridge St. Synagogue, NY, to organize for effective action against the vice which has been grown so flagrant in that vicinity. Among the speakers, Felix Adler repeated a portion of a conversation he had with a high police official who attributed the bad moral condition of New York to the Jews."

Even the founder of the heretical Ethical Culture movement was welcome in the synagogue when community interests were at stake. Certainly, Jewish organizations of all kinds were at home there. This "institutional" attribute of the community synagogue would later become a formal feature of the synagogue-center program.[39]

Nothing revealed the public aspirations of the shul better than the architecture of the building. By the early 1900s, enough time had passed for substantial numbers of immigrants to have "made it" in America, and the grandiosity of their new synagogues would reflect their new status. They selected architects and architectural styles by looking to the synagogues of uptown; accordingly, their choices revealed interrelations within the greater Jewish community. In this regard, the Moorish Revival details of Khal Adas Jeshurun (1886) may be read as a reference to the synagogue styles of uptown's most prestigious temples, such as Temple Emanu-El on Fifth Avenue (1868), Ahavath Chesed on Lexington Avenue (1872), and B'nai Jeshurun on Madison Avenue (1885). Whereas the first was a radical Reform temple, the latter two were both moderate Reform congregations recently taken up by the counter-Reform trend under their respective rabbis, Alexander Kohut and Henry S. Jacobs. Not coincidentally, the year of the new Eldridge Street Shul was also the year of the founding of the Jewish Theological Seminary and the beginning of the "Conservative" movement. When the Jews of Eldridge Street chose the lavish look of their new synagogue, they were emulating the religious style of American Judaism, made palatable by the counter-Reform trend. By its choice of architectural style, therefore, the downtown congregation made the statement that Lower East Side Jews could be as progressive *and* as conservative as their uptown coreligionists.[40]

As the East European community rose in economic stature, moving "uptown" both literally and figuratively, they were correspondingly more apt to be influenced by their uptown brethren. We have seen this process earlier in their adoption of the Educational Alliance–Jewish center idea; likewise, the community synagogue would be modeled indirectly on the temple. In 1898, Kasriel Sarasohn, editor of New York's *Yiddishes Tageblatt* (Jewish Daily News), had occasion to peruse the annual report of a Reform temple in Philadelphia and described it for his readers:

The Report of the Congregation Rodeph Shalom, of Philadelphia, is on my desk. . . . I have been filled with admiration for the splendid work achieved by this Congregation, which is so ably guided by Rev. Dr. Henry Berkowitz. . . . More than anything I have read in a long time has it made me feel with painful keenness, the difference between the works of Russian Polish Orthodox congregations and the American congregations. Let me give you an idea of the work of the Congregation Rodeph Shalom, as described in the booklet. A school-house is maintained by the Congregation . . . there is a Young Folks Reading Union. . . . The boys and the girls of the Congregation are united under the banner of "Rodeph Shalom Juniors." . . . It is a synagogue after my own heart! It stands a brilliant example for my orthodox brethren to emulate. It is time truly, that all the accumulated filth of the Russian, Polish, Roumanian and Galician Ghettos be swept out of the orthodox Synagogues. It is time that American enlightened methods came in. It is time that the young men and women, the boys and girls who have had the benefit of American training in their secular affairs, become factors in the spiritual life of the orthodox community.[41]

The winds of Americanization had begun to blow. To find their way, Ortho-dox Jews would look to Reform rabbis like Henry Berkowitz and American con-gregations like Rodeph Shalom for guidance. First, the exterior of the immigrant synagogues would show this influence (for example, Rodeph Shalom was housed in one of the finest examples of Moorish Revival architecture in America); and soon the internal life of the synagogue would be affected as well. But first, the building of new synagogues became the order of the day. In the same year of 1898, another editorial writer (probably J. P. Solomon, editor of the *Hebrew Stan-dard,* "America's Leading Jewish Family Paper" [Orthodox]) lamented that "there are in the City of New York in comparison to its Jewish population but a very small number of imposing Temples or Synagogues. There are, it is true, innu-merable chevras and small places of meeting in which religious services are held, but these are mere makeshifts. They satisfy the demands of those who sustain them, but they add nothing to the perpetuation of Judaism. It is not necessary that in order to worship the Deity, structures costing hundreds of thousands of dollars be erected, but it is desirable that for worship a dignified building, com-porting with the object sought, should hold the worshippers. We reiterate that we have too few of these edifices."[42]

In the decade to come, the *Hebrew Standard* frequently printed photographs of synagogue buildings on its front page, some from Central Europe, and some Reform temples from America; the immigrant building boom of those years would have ample example for imitation. More often, however, the builders of synagogues simply looked around town; again, they responded most readily to prestigious kindred congregations. After the Eldridge Street Shul became the first East European synagogue to adopt the Moorish style, many other upwardly mo-bile immigrant shuls would follow its example. The first and perhaps the best known was Zichron Ephraim, the American Orthodox synagogue founded by Rabbi Bernard Drachman and his father-in-law Jonas Weil in 1889. Their stated intention was to have a congregation representative of "all the various elements of the Jewish community," that is, a community synagogue in conscious rejec-tion of the landsmanshaft principle. Its ornate and picturesque building on East 67th Street, designed by architects Schneider and Herter (perhaps the same Herter that had designed Eldridge Street), was said to be "the most beautiful structure devoted to Orthodox Judaism" in New York (remaining in the posses-sion of the congregation to this day), clearly influenced by the Moorish Revival precedent of the Lower East Side.[43]

Moreover, one of Zichron Ephraim's more prominent early members was Sender Jarmulowsky, the famed Jewish banker and former leader of the Eldridge Street Shul. Fascinatingly, Jarmulowsky went so far as to design his own office building in the Moorish style in 1903: the famous Jarmulowsky Bank Building on East Broadway, heralded in the Jewish press as "A Jewish Temple of Finance." The landmark building, "a conspicuous monument of the Jewish community," even had its own *bes medrash!* "The hall below the bank is devoted for public meetings." Other examples of the Moorish Revival synagogue in New York City include Shaare Zedek of Harlem (1900), Ohav Sholom of Brownsville (1906), Tiphereth Israel of Bedford-Stuyvesant (1912), and Montefiore Hebrew Congregation of the Bronx (1912). The community synagogue of the immigrant settlement thus became a "mother church" to shuls in the newly developing areas. The ghetto may have been left behind but its social intensity and religious panache would be well remembered, and through the medium of the community synagogue, created anew.[44]

The Community Synagogue in New Areas of Settlement, 1900–1915

The heyday of the community synagogue fell during the years 1900–1915, a period bridging the "classical" eras of the immigrant shul (1885–1900) and the synagogue-center (1915–30). By 1900 the mass immigration had been under way for two decades, sufficient time for many immigrant Jews to better themselves economically and escape the ghetto. In cities all over the country, Americanized Jewish immigrants established new neighborhoods, later labeled by sociologists "areas of second settlement." When they resettled, the former immigrants tended to be in their thirties or forties, having found success in light manufacturing such as the clothing industry and in entrepreneurial enterprises such as real estate. Often, their places of business remained in the older neighborhoods (for example, Jarmulowsky's bank), as did family members and cherished institutions. Strong connections, therefore—economic, social, and religious—were maintained between the areas. The new communities were populated rapidly, becoming in effect "second ghettos." Furthermore, a new infusion of immigrants in the peak years of 1904–8 (during which time more than 640,000 Jews entered the country) ensured both the persistence of the ghetto areas and ongoing intercourse with the new communities. They also gave synagogue builders the legitimate hope that more members would always be on the horizon.[45]

Just as the immigrants had re-created shtetl life in the New World in the form of shuls and landsmanshafts, the Americanized group transplanted the institutions of the ghetto to their new locales; most notably, the community synagogue. Around the turn of the century numerous large synagogues began to spring up in the burgeoning communities, in numbers reminiscent of the shul proliferation of years past. In the Borough Park neighborhood of Brooklyn, New York, for example, twenty new synagogue structures were put up by 1918. As early as 1908, the *New York American* incredulously reported there to be fifty new synagogues in Brooklyn overall (in an article entitled, "Every Seventh Brooklynite a Jew"). In

that same year, the *Boston Advocate* editorialized: "We are still building synagogues, and building them better and larger than ever. If buildings were a test we
are becoming more religious year by year. If expenditures be a test, we are five-
fold as religious as we were twenty years ago. It is a fact, which all those who
study Jewish problems have to face, that the individual willingness to sacrifice for
synagogues still outdoes the willingness to sacrifice for any two other causes, even
charity and education."[46]

The settlers were so eager to build that their new community synagogues
often preceded a community; that is, the synagogue was established before large-
scale migration had even begun. They then served as magnets for Jewish population movement and as incentives for community development, trends encouraged by real estate agents[47] and rabbis alike. For example, Rabbi Louis Epstein of
Roxbury's Beth Hamidrash Hagadol recalled its genesis as follows:

One foolish plan called for another, this time the most daring one, namely to erect a modern
up-to-the-moment house of worship that shall be a credit to Boston Jewry. Little did the small
group of men then think that that most daring undertaking shall leave room for regret that it
was not even more daring. Little did they think that in a measure Roxbury Jewry would build
itself around the Crawford Street Synagogue, that its seating capacity of eleven to twelve hundred would only meet half of that need. It was beyond human powers to look ahead ten years
and to see what the synagogue would mean to the community. . . . The Crawford Street Synagogue is an illustration of the fact that not always is a synagogue built where the Jewish community is, but that sometimes the community is built where the synagogue is. Our Synagogue
has in a great measure been the making of the Roxbury Jewish community.[48]

Once again, the architectural record has much to tell us concerning the rise of
community synagogues in the new Jewish neighborhoods and their continued
relationship with the ghetto community. In 1902, the Orthodox congregation
Kehilath Jeshurun built its new building on East 85th Street in the fashionable
Yorkville district of New York. Eschewing the outdated Moorish style, the uptown shul commissioned architect George Pelham to copy the design of a prominent temple, the West End Synagogue (Congregation Shaaray Tefila on West
88th Street), designed by Arnold Brunner in the Renaissance Revival style in
1894. As above (regarding B'nai Jeshurun and Ahavath Chesed), Shaaray Tefila
was an uptown liberal congregation, yet it had strong ties to downtown Orthodoxy. The upwardly mobile immigrant Jews thus revealed their social ambitions
through their choice of architecture. They had moved from the Lower to the
Upper East Side and wanted the world to know it.[49]

Once Kehilath Jeshurun had set the precedent, other immigrant congregations were able to imitate the American Jewish architecture as well (though most
did so secondhand by claiming their inspiration in the first copy). Thus, the pala-
tial facade soon reappeared when Congregation Sons of Israel Kalwarie, known as
the "Kalvarier Shul," built its grand Pike Street synagogue on the Lower East Side
in 1903. It was an exact replica of Kehilath Jeshurun, in all likelihood designed by
the same architect. In this instance, the downtown Jews emulated an uptown shul

Fig. 33. Kehilath Jeshurun, East 85th Street, built 1902. Photo by Geo. D. Chinn. Collection of the New York Historical Society.

rather than a temple, thereby proving their own good taste by copying an Orthodox institution. The fact that "the Kalvarier Shul was the East Side's favorite synagogue for large ceremonies and affairs" (that is, for public, communal events), comes as no surprise, for the architectural setting was appropriately upscale. When Judah Magnes came downtown to deliver a series of Friday night lectures in 1913, he spoke at the Pike Street Synagogue and there inspired the founders of the Young Israel movement. Just as Magnes had journeyed from the uptown Reform environment to the world of Lower East Side Orthodoxy, the architecture of the synagogue had traveled downtown as well.[50]

Nor was this imitation the end of the matter. In 1905, Congregation Beth Jacob Anshe Sholom in the Williamsburg section of Brooklyn hired George Pelham and, once again, "instructed [him] to take his plans from those of the West End Synagogue." Like the modern assembly line, a prototype was duplicated repeatedly. The newspaper account of the projected synagogue describes the scheme in glowing terms and sheds further light on its attractions: "The seating capacity of [the main] auditorium will be nearly one thousand. In the basement will be the 'Talmud Thora' for the education of the children in Hebrew. There

Fig. 34. Kalvarier Synagogue, Pike Street, built 1903. *The Jewish Encyclopedia* (New York: Funk & Wagnalls, 1905).

Fig. 35. Beth Jacob Anshe Sholom, Williamsburg, as projected in 1905. Courtesy of the author.

will be meeting rooms for the societies of the younger element. The entire building is to be illuminated by electricity, and will be steam heated during the winter
months. When completed the new structure will be an 'architectural beauty,' and
well may the Jewish race be proud of it. It will mark the great strides of progres-
sion which the Hebrew community of the Eastern district has made in the last
twenty-five years."[51]

The immigrant Jews of Brooklyn were justly proud of their Progressive community in the "Eastern district" and looked toward a glorious future. They saw
the West End Synagogue–Kehilath Jeshurun paradigm as a model Jewish institution enabling them to move forward into the modern age. Of all its modern appurtenances, the "Talmud Thora" most clearly indicated their orientation toward the future. Where the earlier community synagogue only provided space
for a *bes medrash* and perhaps for additional meeting rooms, the new synagogues
would almost universally include space for schooling of the young. As Abraham
Karp has written: "Commitment to progress led to interest and labors for a
school and a new synagogue to serve the requirements of the present but also to
prepare for the future." Thus, despite the rise of the communal Talmud Torah in
the same era and in the same neighborhoods, all of the new community synagogues incorporated schoolrooms in their plans. The addition of such an annex
was perceived as being de rigueur for a "modern synagogue," and was implicitly
intended to ensure the future membership of the congregation. This Progressivist orientation was reflected in the choice of an architectural model.[52]

While the modernization of the synagogue was intended to attract the young
and ensure the future, it could look backward for inspiration as well. In 1905,
Rabbi Joseph Mayor Asher of Congregation B'nai Jeshurun addressed the "Cornerstone Laying of [a] New Synagogue and School" on West 35th Street in New
York City, and declaimed: "Make the synagogue a house of gathering as well as
of prayer, where as of old the Jewish democracy comes together to care for its
poor and look after its communal affairs. There is more religion and real spirituality in the downtown synagogue for the poor foreign Jews who cherish the religion of their fathers than in all the marble temples of Fifth Avenue. Make your
temple such a sanctuary of the old time faith." By "old time faith," Asher was
not promoting traditional Jewish religion per se, but the old-time Jewish social
life that centered in the synagogue. Thus would past and future unite in the
modern shul.[53]

The same architectural design as before, therefore, could stand for traditional
as well as for modern values. In 1906, members of Congregation Shaarai Torah of
Worcester, Massachusetts, traveled to New York to consult with the Ramaz on
their planned synagogue, and came away deciding to create yet another replica of
Kehilath Jeshurun—intended, this time, to express adherence to "Torah-true"
Judaism. In the span of a few years, therefore, the synagogue design of a single
Reform temple was chosen by Orthodox shuls from New York City to Worcester,
Massachusetts (and as discussed below, it would reach Boston as well). More

than mere flattery, architectural imitation was the physical expression of social aspiration, religious loyalty, and educational progress—all ideals of the community synagogue.[54]

One other aspect of the design deserves attention. The stoop, flanked by dual staircases, created a two-tier entrance: a main entry on the second floor leading to the main sanctuary, and a street-level doorway to the auxiliary spaces below. The much-copied architectural scheme thus provided for the essential feature of the community synagogue, the *bes medrash*. The two-tier entrance was incorporated into the designs of the West End Synagogue, Kehilath Jeshurun, the Kalvarier Shul, Beth Jacob Anshe Sholom, Shaarai Torah, and countless shuls and synagogue-centers to come.

A similar process occurred in Boston, where several shuls emulated the leading Reform congregation, Temple Israel. Its 1886 building on Columbus Avenue [see fig. 38] was designed by Jewish architect Lewis Weissbein in the *Rundbogenstil*—the Romanesque "round-arched style" characteristic of Central European synagogues—thereby expressing the congregation's cultural and religious ties to their German homeland. Yet for a different reason entirely, the design was copied by numerous East European immigrant congregations and thereby became the dominant synagogue style of the Boston area. The imitative immigrant shuls included Beth Israel on Columbia Street in Cambridge (1901), Ahabat Sholom on Church Street in Lynn (1905), Adath Jeshurun on Blue Hill Avenue in Roxbury (1906), and Agudas Sholom on Walnut Street in Chelsea (1908). All were pioneer immigrant congregations in new areas of Jewish settlement and all aspired to leadership status in their growing communities. Such ambitions entailed the construction of a monumental synagogue, inspired in both concept and form by the leading Jewish congregation of Boston, the radical Reform Temple Israel. Unconsciously influenced by the Reform institution, the Orthodox Jewish immigrants of Boston would often lapse into calling their shul "temple."[55]

In their histories of Kehilath Jeshurun (New York) and Shaarai Torah (Worcester, Massachusetts), Jenna Weissman Joselit and Norma Feingold clearly demonstrate how the new Orthodox synagogues were intended to be improvements over the older immigrant shuls; in Joselit's phrase, "bigger and better," and in Feingold's, "modern, up-to-date and beautiful." The immigrants established the new synagogues in order to create a religious life for themselves and their children that would achieve two simultaneous ends: to preserve traditional Judaism and to harmonize with their new respectability as middle-class businessmen and American citizens. Like Kehilath Jeshurun and Shaarai Torah, all community synagogues of the area of second settlement were founded by upwardly mobile Jewish immigrants who sought to reestablish the community synagogue from the "ghetto" in their new neighborhood. Just as many Kehilath Jeshurun members had previously belonged to the Eldridge Street Shul on the Lower East Side, and several founders of Shaarai Torah had been leaders at Sons of Abraham, the founders of the new community synagogues usually had been associated with the leading shul(s) of the immigrant ghetto.[56]

As Joselit points out, a sure sign of the shift from immigrant ghetto to American neighborhood was the change in nomenclature from the "Khal Adas Jeshurun" to "Congregation Kehilath Jeshurun." Yet despite this formal distinction, the popular perception was of continuity between the successive institutions; both were still colloquially called "Shuls." Just as the Lower East Side landmark was most often called the "Eldridge Street Shul," the uptown institution was just as surely referred to as the "85th Street Shul." (Note: the more Americanized members of the community would have said "85th Street *Synagogue*" instead, as was always the case in print). The same was true of the "Blue Hill Avenue Shul," the "Providence Street Shul," and so forth. The popular usage of "———— Street Shul" first appeared in the East European *shtetl*, was re-created in the immigrant district and reached its zenith in the area of second settlement (only beginning to fade in the interwar period, though one may still hear echoes of it today). The phrase was used to distinguish the various synagogues of a neighborhood (or of a city) from one another and furthermore reflects the role of the institutions as communal signposts, each defining its own "turf," or subcommunity. Collectively, the "Street Shuls" defined the overall Jewish community. For example, former residents of Chelsea, Massachusetts, will nostalgically enumerate its synagogues as the "Walnut Street Shul," the "Elm Street Shul," the "Orange Street Shul," the "Chestnut Street Shul" (note: another shul on Chestnut Street was distinguished as the "Carpenter's Shul"), and so forth; as if each were a fondly remembered room in the home of their youth. Communal identification of this sort typified the era of the community synagogue, a time when synagogues were expanding, communities were consolidating, and the two were fast becoming synonymous.[57]

Together with the many continuities from the earlier immigrant shul, the community synagogues of 1900–1915 also exhibited many innovations. Perhaps the most striking difference between the old and new shuls was the inclusion of women and youth in the latter. In the landsmanshaft shul, women had been excluded entirely (though many secular landsmanshafts had womens' auxiliaries). In the early community synagogues, women's galleries were added to the sanctuary; and in the community synagogues of the new areas of settlement, the secular women's auxiliaries reappeared in the form of "temple" sisterhoods and other such women's groups. Similarly, children were excluded from the original shul and relegated to the heder. The community synagogue was the setting for the introduction of synagogue-sponsored Hebrew schools, at first hesitant and disorganized, and as we have shown, later incorporated formally into the body of the new synagogues in the new neighborhoods. However, these new functions were only innovative on the surface. The social activity and organizing introduced by the women had been part of synagogue life earlier, but engaged in by men only. Likewise, the synagogue function of schooling was formerly expressed by the men in their study *hevras*. In the community synagogue, the same function was taken over by the youth of the community. The synagogue had always been a "house of worship, study, and assembly," but only men had occupied the house. Transcending its role as a men's club, the new community synagogue would be occupied by the entire Jewish family.

The inclusion of women and youth was but one aspect of the modernization of the Orthodox synagogue. Second-settlement community synagogues exhibited the many internal conflicts characteristic of such change. Jenna Joselit notes that "friction and intrasynagogue dissent were often the companions of change, especially on the part of the more Europeanized old guard, which found it difficult to adjust to some of the innovations." In some of the larger and wealthier congregations, generational tensions could be alleviated in part through the hiring of two complementary rabbis, one traditionalist and Yiddish-speaking for the older group, and the other progressive and English-speaking for the younger (earlier we saw a similar compromise made by reforming German congregations). More often, however, one or the other path was followed. Where a rabbi of the old school was employed, the traditional patterns prevailed until the congregation either faded or was transformed at a later period. Where an American rabbi was chosen, conflict ensued, and the synagogue began the painful process of transition into a modern institution.[58]

Most of these young rabbis were graduates of the Jewish Theological Seminary of America, the rabbinical training school of the Conservative movement. During the period at hand, JTS rabbis took pulpits in community synagogues around the country, and more often than not succeeded in creating early versions of the synagogue-center. This development, it must be kept in mind, largely occurred prior to the formation of the United Synagogue of America in 1913 and the subsequent emergence of Conservative-affiliated synagogues in the 1920s. Before community synagogues openly identified with Conservativism, therefore, they had already become synagogue-centers—often under the guidance and supervision of a Seminary-trained rabbi. The role of the rabbi should not be overestimated, however. Some particularly effective leaders were able to convert their synagogues into centers single-handedly and pull their congregations into the Conservative movement behind them. Most, however, were simply the agents of a change that was already in the air, having been hired for that very reason. And as we shall see in the following chapter, sometimes their efforts were stymied by congregational intransigence and the transition aborted.

There were two principal routes by which traditionalist Jewish congregations arrived at the synagogue-center solution: the evolution of an older "German Orthodox" congregation, and the formation of a modern synagogue by the younger generation of the East European community. Because nearly all of these emergent synagogue-centers were led by Conservative rabbis and most would eventually identify with the Conservative movement, we might describe them as "early," or "emerging Conservative." Whether old or new, the early Conservative congregations all shared two features. First, they conformed to the type we have described as the community synagogue: congregations interested in gaining public notice and attaining social status in new areas of Jewish settlement. Like the Orthodox shul, their religious stance was traditionalist; departing from the ghetto precedent, however, they were inclusive of the entire family and fostered Jewish education and social activity. As always in the development of the synagogue-center, youth was the key.[59]

Young People's Synagogues

Thus, during the same period in which community synagogues were being formed in areas of second settlement, young people in the ghetto districts began to create their own alternatives to the immigrant shuls of their fathers. As early as 1899, Rabbi Henry Pereira Mendes urged the establishment of "a young people's synagogue" on the Lower East Side. Experimental synagogues soon began to appear, formed by downtown youth in partnership with forward-thinking rabbis like Mendes. Their shared concern was the widespread religious apathy of the new generation of American Jews. Preceding the emergence of the Orthodox synagogue-center, therefore, the youth movement produced a series of tentative though innovative steps that challenged the hegemony of the immigrant shul, and at the same time, perpetuated its traditionalist values. The new youth services would abolish the oriental hubbub of the immigrant synagogue while retaining its sense of *havershaft* (camaraderie). Control of the synagogue would pass from the European *landsmen*—for whom the shul had been a clubhouse and political domain—to the American youngsters. Yet even with the empowerment of youth, traditional Judaism would remain the unquestioned ideology of the congregation. In Orthodoxy, the process of modernization was influenced less by the American milieu than by the Jewish value of continuity. Improving the efficacy of the synagogue for that purpose was less a matter of Americanization than of Judaization.[60]

One of the first synagogues geared specifically to youth was attempted by the Jewish Endeavor Society (JES), founded in 1901 and remaining in existence until 1910. Under the auspices of the nascent Union of Orthodox Congregations (1898) and the reorganized Jewish Theological Seminary of America (1902), the JES was planned and directed by rabbinical students committed to the revival of traditional Judaism. The name and idea, however, were borrowed from the Christian Endeavor Society, a Protestant movement formed in 1881 by a Congregational minister in Maine to "revitalize the Sunday schools with a new kind of youth organization." Historian Sydney Ahlstrom relates that "by 1900 'Christian Endeavor,' with its exciting international conventions and good organization, had become not only a significant ecumenical force, but had inspired emulation in almost every denomination not participating."[61]

The young rabbis of the Jewish Theological Seminary were inspired as well. Their goal in creating a Jewish version of the Christian revivalist youth movement was to provide their own young people with religious, educational and cultural programming attractive to a new generation. The idea resonated especially well within the halls of the Seminary, whose mission was to revitalize traditional Judaism for the coming American generation. By the turn of the century, the perception was increasing that immigrant religious life could not meet the needs of the immigrants' children. The acculturated second generation, many then thought, would only respond to an Americanized religious service, requiring the substitution of decorum for shul informality, English for Yiddish, and intellectual stimulation for ghetto sentimentality. To provide the leadership required for such change, the Seminary would train future generations of American rabbis. Its youth wing, the JES, would train future generations of American Jews to be their congregants.[62]

In line with the transitional nature of the enterprise, the JES embodied collaboration between older and younger men. The established rabbis who served as the project's "leading spirits" were Bernard Drachman, Henry Morais, and Henry Pereira Mendes. The young rabbinical students who were its "chief workers" included Charles Kauvar, Elias Solomon, Herman Abramowitz, Leopold Zinsler, Joseph Asher, Arnold Eiseman, Louis Egelson, Joseph Schwartz, Phineas Israeli, and Mordecai Kaplan. Nearly all would later become pulpit rabbis in Orthodox and Conservative congregations around the country, and their JES experience would go with them.[63]

The JES activists' primary accomplishment was the establishment in 1904 of a "young people's synagogue" on the Lower East Side, an idea that had been "the dream of the best minds who [had] entertained the project for some time." In December 1903 the *Hebrew Standard* had editorialized for the need of "A People's Synagogue on the lower East Side that will touch the ranks of those who at present are not reached by existing institutions." Existing institutions included both the landsmanshaft shuls and community synagogues that characterized the immigrant neighborhood. Both were seen by the rising generation as old-fashioned vestiges of Old World Judaism. Rather than establishing yet another segregated immigrant club like "Chevrah Achei Grodno V'anshei [people of] Staputkin," "Anshei [people of] Chasidei Vishnitze Austria," or "First Sokolover Cong. Anshei [people of] Yosher," the American generation would establish synagogues for *all* the people, for the growing majority who were not born in a *shtetl* but in the New York ghetto. Hence, the generic phrase "people's synagogue" contains the implicit messages of democratic inclusion, Americanization, and generational change.[64]

"Existing institutions" may have referred also to several so-called people's synagogues founded earlier on the Lower East Side. One of them was the People's Synagogue of the Educational Alliance, which had been in existence for four years. The Endeavorers were well aware of this institution, as they themselves were accorded space in the Alliance—as, for example, when young Rudolph

Coffee, superintendent of the Hebrew Orphan Asylum, spoke before the JES in their assigned room in the Alliance building. More recently, Rabbi Joseph Silverman of Temple Emanu-El had established a religious settlement house on the Lower East Side: the New York "branch" of the People's Synagogue movement of Reform Judaism. The newest people's synagogue would set itself apart from its competitors as an Orthodox institution appealing to the younger generation, and so the JES was ideally suited to the project. In early 1904, its members set about collecting funds "for the building of a Synagogue for young people."[65]

Beyond fund-raising, the JES intended to call a conference of young people, to consider organizing a congregation. On February 1, the Endeavorers indeed held such a conference to discuss the proposed People's Synagogue; rather than consisting solely of young people, however, the conference was made up of representatives of some thirty-five Jewish organizations. Two days later, Elias Solomon reported on the meeting before the New York Board of Jewish Ministers, which included potential adversaries such as Reform rabbis Joseph Silverman and Samuel Schulman, and social workers Lillian Wald and Henry Moskowitz. Jeffrey Gurock has called this meeting a "landmark moment," in which "a basic consensus was reached in outline form on an approach to worship acceptable to almost all Americanized religious elements in meeting the needs of second generation East European Jews." Their broad agreement was identical to the compromise later characteristic of the modern Orthodox and Conservative synagogue: keeping the traditional content intact, while modernizing its form through decorum and the use of English.[66]

Balancing the traditionalism of the service, JES leaders also incorporated Americanized "reforms" such as supplementary English-language prayers, English sermons, and congregational singing in English and/or Hebrew. In an educational vein, the JES sponsored classes in Hebrew, the Bible, History, Religion, Spelling and Grammar, as well as lectures in various subjects of Jewish interest. Yet beyond its specifically religious and educational aims, the JES also functioned as a social organization. At the February meeting, the society's combination of religious and social elements was reflected in the joint participation of rabbis and social workers. In April, "a unity conference" was called in which the People's Synagogue Association (PSA) was founded through the cooperative efforts of "Jewish congregations *and societies*." Their stated goal was "to maintain a synagogue, religious school, *and other activities*." At a meeting held at Temple Emanu-El to elect a Central Committee of the new PSA, the decision was taken that one-half of the committee must be representatives of congregations, and the other half from societies. The new People's Synagogue would be one part religious, one part social; providing both the traditional activities of the "synagogue" and social activities for the "people"—like the synagogue-center it was to become.[67]

Thus, during the same period in which the JES engaged in synagogue experimentation, the newspaper accounts of its activities include much of a purely social nature. In early 1903, for instance, the *Hebrew Standard* reported that "an open meeting of the Harlem Branch was held in the assembly room of Temple

Israel." Tellingly, the account continues: "Through some inadvertence the Benoth Zine [*sic*] Circle Hadassa had been accorded the use of the rooms for the same evening, and a joint meeting of the two societies was arranged." Similarly, one year later, "The JES gave an informal dance." An important aspect of "Jewish Endeavor," apparently, was the very youthful "endeavor" to meet the opposite sex (which was also a "Jewish" endeavor insofar as the ultimate goal was marriage). This element of the JES should not be underestimated, for what better expedient than social mixing would appeal to young people and draw them to the synagogue? Later synagogue-centers would apply the same principle to great effect, and rationalize the stategy in much the same way—as a countermeasure against the threat of intermarriage.[68]

There is one other overlooked aspect of the JES. The above newspaper item of 1903 continued its description of the meeting in Harlem's Temple Israel: "The Rev. Dr. H. Pereira Mendes spoke briefly. He said that to be a good Endeavorer one must be a good Zionist. He showed that 'Jewish Endeavor' is practical Zionism. . . . The last speaker was the Rev. Mr. [Herman] Abramowitz, president of the JES, who showed that 'Jewish Endeavor' stood for Judaism." Perhaps Dr. Mendes was attempting to further the connection between the Endeavorers and the women's "Zine"ist organization. More likely, the *hazan* of New York's Spanish-Portugese Congregation was implying a new form of Judaism to be propagated by the modern youth synagogue. Mendes's admonition to the JES members was intended to suggest a Jewish "theological" principle upon which the society might be based. He proposed Zionism, the ideology of Jewish peoplehood, and the emerging civil religion of American Jewry. The employ of cultural Zionism as a synagogue ideology was not dissimilar to the populist mix of Judaism and Zionism preached by Zvi Hirsch Masliansky at the People's Synagogue of the Educational Alliance. That it was still a controversial combination was shown by Abramowitz's quick rejoinder that Judaism, not Zionism, was the soul of Jewish Endeavor. Yet for many of its young members, traditional Judaism represented the Old World, while "practical" Zionism was perceived as being modern and up-to-date—the same guiding principles as those underlying the community synagogue. During the same period, therefore, the JES would advance a modern synagogue inspired by a people-centered form of Judaism. The word "people" in People's Synagogue (or, for that matter, in the Jewish People's Institutes of Chicago and Boston) did not refer only to "young people," nor simply to the democratic implications of the term. It resonated as well with the Zionist ethos of Jewish *people*hood.[69]

The Phenomenon of the "Zionist Synagogue"

A more direct connection between Judaism and Zionism was made in the immigrant community of Boston. By the first decade of the twentieth century, immigrant Jews had begun interpolating Zionist sentiment and symbolism into synagogue life. When, for example, the newly acquired church building of Boston's "Vilner Congregation" was dedicated in September 1906, "hundreds crowded into the new synagogue and hundreds were unable to obtain admittance. The Scrolls were taken from the old home of the congregation on Leverett Street [in Boston's West End] to the new synagogue, accompanied by the Knights of Zion led by the Zion band. . . . The reception of the flags, American and Zionist, was attended with great enthusiasm." As above, the combination of American and Jewish patriotism reflected a new synthesis created by acculturating immigrants, a civil religion for newly forged "American Jews."[70]

But a further step taken in Boston would be the wholesale conversion of the religious ideology of the synagogue—to Zionism. On August 31, 1908, the "Yavne Congregation" was chartered in Massachusetts and commenced its activities at 4 Milton Street in the West End. The new venture was described as "the only Zionist congregation in this country," and in 1911 its members were recorded to have "held services Yom Kippur at their synagogue." The *American Jewish Yearbook* of the previous year recorded its existence and listed its rabbi as one Aaron Gorovitz. The Russian-born Orthodox rabbi had attended the 1905 Zionist Congress in Basel, Switzerland, and was again elected as delegate in 1907 when "the Zionists of the New England States chose [him] for this important duty." A vice-president of the Federation of American Zionists, Rabbi Gorovitz was an ardent Zionist and a likely candidate for founder of Boston's 1908 Zionist synagogue, which coincided in both time and place with the formation of both the Jewish Peoples Institute and the Ivrio Hebrew school, both Zionist-inspired institutions in the West End. Many of the area's young Zionists chose Cambridge as their next area of settlement, and it follows that Gorovitz later became "chief rabbi" of the United Orthodox Congregations of Cambridge and Somerville. The 1919–20 *American Jewish Yearbook* lists two congregations: the Yavne Congregation in Boston and the Yavno Congregation in Cambridge under Rabbi Gorovitz.[71]

Beyond this the documentary sources are scarce, but a clue to the genesis of the Zionist synagogue may be found in a letter to the editor of the *Boston Advocate* in December 1908. The correspondent, one Israel Makransky, objected to a recent piece by Horace Kallen in which the Harvard intellectual drew a distinction between traditional Judaism and modern "Hebraism." The latter term referred to an emerging American Jewish synthesis, later identified with Louis Brandeis, in which "Zionism, a secular expression of Jewish nationalism compatible with American ideals, could become a valid replacement for the Jewish theology and rituals which Kallen had rejected." In his letter, Makransky called the distinction a false one, asserting that "orthodox customs and traditions are nothing more than means to form and preserve Jewish life and character." Yet the problem remained that Orthodoxy, like Reform, "fails to keep in its fold the young generation of orthodox Jews . . . [who] are no longer orthodox, but ARE JEWS." He then offered a bold solution to the problem: "The Zionistic and nationalistic movements must be united with the synagogue, making the synagogue a centre—even for the atheist, if you please,—where all the Jewish national forces shall be marshalled—at present the synagogue marshalls only some of those who are already with 'one foot in the grave.'"[72]

Whether Makransky was connected with or even aware of the Yavne Congregation is unknown, but the parallel between them is unmistakable. As the letter indicates, Zionism was attractive as a synagogue ideology for more than one reason. First was its unifying quality. As the unity of the Jewish people lies at the heart of Zionist philosophy, it is necessarily inclusive of all Jews, of all persuasions. How better to unify the fragmented Jewish community than through a Zionist synagogue? Even Jewish atheists would be welcome in such a congregation, and indeed, this was another attraction of the idea. Second-generation Jews were not deserting the synagogue merely because of its lack of decorum or its crass commercialism. Neither can we accept alone the explanation that many young Jews were forced by economic circumstances to work on the Sabbath. Such explanations are the understandable result of the limited perspective of contemporary observers. A more sophisticated view of the mass exodus will take into account the powerful forces of secularization that had swept through modern society and that had profoundly affected the Americanizing Jew. The American-born child of immigrants no longer responded to the authority of Jewish tradition. The synagogue, representing that tradition, could no longer assert an absolute claim upon Jewish loyalty—unless it could find a new rationale, and suggest a new reason for being a Jew. One potential answer was Zionism, an ideology appealing to Orthodox and secular Jews alike.

Ida Uchill, the historian of Denver's Jewish community, suggests yet another motive for the formation of a Zionist synagogue. She relates the founding of the Dorshe Zion Society (in 1909) to the phenomenon of landsmanshaft proliferation: "The Zionists are said to have started their own congregation in 1903. These men left the other synagogues where their relatives and landsmen prayed, to be with those of similar ideals. Many of them were intellectuals, or at least secular-minded enough to take a deep interest in world affairs. Their synagogue is said to have been more peaceful than any of the others." The establishment of such a synagogue was therefore an advance beyond the landsmanshaft principle. Looking around them at the plethora of congregations named for *shtetlach,* more progressive immigrants questioned the practice of perpetuating the memory of an East European homeland. The true Jewish homeland, Zionists asserted, lay further to the east. Hence, instead of the "Roumanian Congregation" or "Anshe Matzover" (other Denver congregations), the new group became "Dorshe Zion." Rather than being joined by the essentially arbitrary ties of geography and/or kinship, the founders of a Zionist synagogue came together as the result of a shared ideological orientation. They tended to be more intellectual and more secular than their fellow shul-goers; hence the service was more sedate (that is, decorous) and they self-consciously expressed their philosophy of Judaism as a

Fig. 36. Temple Petach Tikvah, Brownsville, built 1915. Courtesy of the Brooklyn Public Library—Brooklyn Collection.

form of cultural Zionism. Both decorum and Zionism were elements of the modernization process and foreshadowed the modern synagogue-centers to come.[73]

Though the Jewish raison d'être of peoplehood was essentially a social rather than religious principle, the most enthusiastic proponents of an American Judaism infused with Zionism were often rabbis. In Philadelphia, for example, Bernard Levinthal was both chief rabbi of the city and its leading Zionist. Yet it was left to his son to take the next step and achieve synthesis; as it often happened, American-born Jews exhibited fewer inhibitions when it came to combining the religious and nationalist concerns of the immigrant generation. Israel Levinthal started out in his father's footsteps, pursuing both the rabbinic and Zionist callings. As a youth, he founded and was president of a Zionist youth group in Philadelphia. In his mature years, he would become the founding rabbi of the Brooklyn Jewish Center. In between, however, Israel Levinthal was the rabbi (1915–19) of Temple Petach Tikvah, a modern Orthodox community synagogue named after "the mother of the *moshavot* (settlements)," the Jewish village Petach Tikvah in Palestine (established permanently in 1883). Formed as a young man's offshoot of Brownsville's leading community synagogue, Petach Tikvah would be a new kind of synagogue. Its Zionist-inspired name was a clear indication of its new-age ambitions. Just as the original Petach Tikvah had pioneered Jewish settlement in the Yishuv, Temple Petach Tikvah would pioneer the movement to modernize traditional Judaism. Under the guidance of Rabbi Levinthal, Petach Tikvah joined the United Synagogue of America and evolved into a typical Conservative synagogue-center.[74]

The intent of the name was clear again when, in Boston, a congregation was founded calling itself "Tel Abiv." Other such "Zionist synagogues" formed at the turn of the century included Am Echad of Waukegan, Illinois, Chovevei Zion of Springfield, Massachusetts, Chevrah Chovevei Zion of Harlem, and Herzl Congregation of Seattle. As their names clearly indicate, these congregations were founded by immigrants whose primary Jewish ideology was Zionism. A shared commitment to the Zionist cause and belief in Jewish peoplehood is what bonded them together, and it was only natural to form their religious community on that basis.[75]

Few of these local congregations were likely to have been exposed to the more sophisticated rendering of the idea by up-and-coming young rabbis such as Judah L. Magnes and Mordecai M. Kaplan. As is often the case, the declarations of such intellectuals only echoed developments already in play. Magnes first confided his dream of forming a *bet hak'neset hal'umi,* a "nationalistic synagogue," in May 1907, while serving as associate rabbi of the Reform Temple Emanu-El. In February of 1911, he envisioned his new congregation, B'nai Jeshurun, as "a Jewish Center—a *bet ha'am,* a 'house of the Jewish people.'" In this early formulation, both the terms "Jewish Center" and "Beth Ha-Am" were colored by Zionist sentiment. A Zionist synagogue, according to Judah Magnes, is one in which the ideal of Jewish peoplehood is actualized by the varied activities of Jewish life. Mordecai Kaplan, too, conceived the notion "of a Zionist Synagogue that is to meet the Jewish spiritual needs of the modern man" at the very time he was engaged in the creation of his far better known synagogue-center. Kaplan and Magnes, together with Israel Friedlaender, were deeply influenced by Ahad-Ha'am, the father of cultural Zionism; the rabbinic troika thus became the leading exponents in America of a people-centered Judaism. It was no coincidence, therefore, that these three Zionist rabbis were the guiding spirits behind the next people-centered synagogue initiative to arise.[76]

The Young Israel Movement, 1912–1918

In 1912, as is commonly observed, a new Jewish youth movement arose on the Lower East Side called "Young Israel." Less well known is the fact that Young Israel (YI) was the name of two separate movements that only merged after several years of parallel existence. The first was a Jewish revival movement, inspired by the nationalist rabbis Judah Magnes and Israel Friedlaender, and attempting to win disaffected young Jews back to Judaism. It provided social and educational activities similar in nature to those of the Jewish center movement. The second YI was primarily a synagogue movement, founded by local youngsters dissatisfied with the landsmanshaft Judaism of their fathers. It established a model synagogue intended to modernize and Americanize the old-fashioned shul with an attractive, decorous, and English-speaking context for Orthodox services. The two groups united in 1918, synthesizing their social and religious emphases, and thus turning YI into a true synagogue-center movement.[77]

Like its predecessor, the Jewish Endeavor Society, the first YI was inspired and mentored by a group of rabbis from the Jewish Theological Seminary whose goal was nothing less than "a revival of Judaism" among the growing numbers of second-generation East European Jews in America. Young Israel, however, was a youth movement founded and led by the young people themselves, to serve their own social and religious needs. According to one historian of YI, the three college-age initiators of the movement—Max Grablowsky, Joshua Horowitz, and Ben Koenigsberg—were responding to the challenge of Stephen Wise's Downtown Branch of the Free Synagogue, which, from its establishment in 1908, had been offering Friday night services and sundry clubs and classes at its Clinton Hall location to "the Jewish young men and women of the lower East Side." Perceiving the liberalism of Stephen Wise as a threat to downtown orthodoxy, the young men began to organize a countermovement sometime in 1911. Since Wise's religious settlement house was successful, they understandably envisioned a similar social and educational program, albeit in more traditional terms. In certain respects, therefore, their initiative replicated that of Albert Lucas several years earlier. With six others—Max and Bernard Oxenhandler, Moishe Krumbein, David B. Cohen, Louis L. Cohen, and Moses Rosenthal—Grablowsky, Horowitz, and Koenigsberg formed a group called the "Hebrew Circle," soon to evolve into YI.[78]

In late 1912, the organizers of the movement on the Lower East Side contacted the head of the New York Kehillah for assistance. Meeting with the young men on December 28, Rabbi Judah L. Magnes "agreed to organize revival meetings in the form of English lectures on Friday nights." At that meeting Magnes is believed to have "suggested a name with the word "young" in it." "Young Israel" had been part of colloquial parlance for some time, but as Shulamith Berger notes: "The phrase "young Israel" (with a small 'y') had been used by Dr. Magnes two years earlier in an article in the *Hebrew Standard* explaining his resignation from Temple Emanu-El." In the new context it was the perfect description for the Jewish revivalist youth movement. The succinct and catchy phrase "Young Israel" proved to have lasting appeal, and indeed, it has endured until this day. Furthermore, the name "Israel" was synonymous with Jewish peoplehood, and the movement would succeed by exploiting the communal aspect of Judaism.[79]

Judah Magnes, champion of Jewish peoplehood and darling of the downtown Jewish revival, delivered the first YI lecture in the Kalvarier Shul on Pike Street, on January 10, 1913. The synagogue was packed to overflowing and "with his words [the] movement was born."[80]

Both the *American Hebrew* and *Hebrew Standard* hailed the new movement and printed its founding statement, which included the following:

The appeal is to all Jewish young men and women, whatever be their views of Judaism, whatever be their social or economic status. The movement is not Orthodox or Reform. It is not Zionistic or Socialistic. It intends to awaken Jewish young men and women to their

responsibilities as Jews, in whatever form these responsibilities are conceived. Young Israel believes in the old Jewish doctrine: all Israel are brothers. We are convinced that through a broad,
earnest appeal to the Jewish spirit of our young men and women, the Jewish people will be
strengthened and Judaism made a living force.[81]

The YI spokesman echoed the centrist call for *klal yisrael* associated with
Solomon Schechter and his Seminary circle. Since religion and politics were divi-
sive factors in contemporary Jewish life (especially on the contentious Lower East
Side) the YI platform highlighted the unifying idea of Jewish peoplehood in their
stead. The strategy was calculated to appeal to the widest range of downtown
youth not only for ideological reasons but for practical considerations as well. If,
as both the YI organizers and their Kehillah sponsors sensed, the youth of the
Lower East Side could not be wooed by religious services, then the most effective
method would be to offer social activities instead.

When Magnes's fellow cultural Zionist and Kehillah stalwart Israel Friedlaender became involved with the fledgling organization, he immediately sought a
social context for the group in the premier Jewish settlement on the East Side. In
February 1913, Friedlaender sent Moses Rosenthal—his student at the Seminary
and the president of the Young Israel—downtown to the Educational Alliance to
make arrangements to use space in their building for Young Israel meetings. In
the following month, Young Israel held a mass meeting at the Educational Alliance, presided over by Cyrus L. Sulzberger, vice-chairman of the Kehillah and
board member of the Seminary. As the YI expanded its activities through the
coming years, it tended to avoid explicitly religious activities and instead provided social services such as the employment bureau for Sabbath observers established in July 1913. The summer of 1913 also saw the rise of the second YI movement, although the idea of a young people's Orthodox synagogue had been in
the air for some time. As discussed earlier, several "people's synagogues" had long
operated on the East Side. Because all were imports from uptown, however, an
indigenous Orthodox response was inevitable.[82]

In May 1912, the "Sons and Daughters of Israel of the People's Orthodox Synagogue" held a rally to promote just such an initiative. The *Jewish Advocate* of
Boston reported "a mass meeting of the Sons and Daughters of Israel of the People's Orthodox Synagogue, held last night at the Synagogue Beth Hamedrish
Hagodol, for the purpose of pushing a campaign to raise a fund for the establishment of a modern synagogue in the neighborhood of 2nd & 3rd Streets and 2nd
Avenue and the consolidation of hundreds of small synagogues situated in the
tenement houses." The reference to hundreds of tenement synagogues is the key
to understanding the initiative. The YI synagogue was intended to provide an acceptable alternative to the landsmanshaft shul for the American-born or -raised
Jew; rather than replacing the earlier form outright, however, the East Side group
sought to transform the traditional institution from within.[83]

David Warshaw traces the origins of the new synagogue to the summer of
1913, when some members of the YI group were asked into a storefront shul (at

205 East Broadway) to complete a minyan, and much to their delight, were allowed to lead the service. Drawing on melodies learned at the boys' minyan of
the Downtown Talmud Torah (introduced by Samson Benderly in 1910), the
teenagers were soon leading the service; one need only compare this touching
scene to the gloomy portrayal drawn by Lincoln Steffens to see how far the immigrant community had come. The new youth-led synagogue, formerly an immigrant *hevra,* soon attracted a larger audience. Under the guidance of Israel
Friedlander, it followed YI's lead and moved into the premises of the Educational
Alliance, there becoming known as the Model Synagogue. According to Warshaw, one Rabbi Israel Odes "became president and soon arranged for the historic mass meeting at the Norfolk Street Beth Midrash Hagadol in 1913. The purpose of the rally was to raise funds for the Model." The guest speaker at that
occasion was Jacob Schiff.[84]

The Model Synagogue continued to operate alongside the more secular and
social Young Israel meetings for the next four years. Even so, their goals and constituencies overlapped, they shared quarters in the Educational Alliance, and for
all intents and purposes, they were two parts of the same movement. Yet they remained separate organizations; as Warshaw explains, one group consisted of
"professionals with little religious background or convictions [who] were interested in cultural and social activities," while the members of the Model Synagogue "were primarily concerned with the improvement of the synagogue. Most
of them were from orthodox families and their interests were not solely cultural
or social." It was only a matter of time until the conflicts were resolved and the
natural union of the YI and the Model Synagogue would take place. Such a social-
religious synthesis was in the making elsewhere, most famously in 1916 when
both Mordecai Kaplan and Herbert Goldstein began to agitate for the combination of synagogue and center.[85]

In the *Hebrew Standard* issue of September 15, 1916, Goldstein published his
call to arms entitled, "The Institutional Synagogue." Leaders of the downtown
Model Synagogue recognized their own imprint in the scheme, and in a letter to
the *Hebrew Standard,* Harry Fromberg, president of the Model Synagogue, described his institution as a forerunner of Herbert Goldstein's "innovation":

A similar idea, however, presented itself to a number of young men on the East Side a little
more than a year ago. A model synagogue as the only and effective solution was the dream of
these young men—a synagogue where every atom of our time-honored traditions could be observed and at the same time prove an attraction, particularly to the young men and
women. . . . An institutional synagogue on the East Side is our real aim—a synagogue which
will be a social center as well as a place of worship; a library (Jewish and English), a reading
room, a gymnasium, and auditorium for public functions and dancing, clubrooms, etc.[86]

When Rabbi Odes chose to form his own model synagogue in 1917, the remaining members decided to take a new name: the Young Israel Synagogue. In
January 1918 the two YI groups merged, "realizing that true success . . . would result only through the combination of education and a proper synagogue," and

indeed, the movement began rapidly to expand during the coming years. Reminiscent of the community synagogues of the areas of second settlement, the YI movement was supported at first by "young businessman and professional people." As Jeffrey Gurock relates, it was they who redefined the synagogue "as a Jewish social center, where young men and women could meet," and thereby transformed the early YI program into "the synagogue-center it became."[87]

YI leader Harry Fromberg declared at the time of the merger: "The time has come when the man and woman in America must be taught to feel that he or she need not be deprived of the innocent social pleasures so long as it is done in accord with Jewish rites and principles, it is the aim of the synagogue to make the young people feel that being Jews need not deprive them of their social activities and pleasure." Like its Hasidic antecedent, the revolutionary idea of a pleasurable Orthodox synagogue held tremendous appeal to young Jews and soon spread beyond its place of origin. Branches were soon organized in Brooklyn, the Bronx, Newark, and Jersey City.[88]

In March 1918, the *American Hebrew* announced the formation of the first YI offshoot in Williamsburg: "30 young men and women have formed an organization in Brooklyn called Young Israel, for the purpose of holding strictly orthodox services every Sabbath morning at 9:00 at the YMHA on Clymer Street. Meetings are also held Tuesday evenings at P.S. #50, and those interested are invited to attend." It was no coincidence that the housing for the incipient synagogue-center was the youth-oriented, recreational, and essentially *social* premises of the YMHA—just as the original YI–Model Synagogue had held its services at the Educational Alliance. Alter Landesman adds that "from 1924 to 1957 the Young Israel of Brownsville used the Hebrew Educational Society building as its headquarters for their religious, educational, and social programs." Similarly, before moving into the HES (of which Landesman was executive director), the YI synagogue was housed first in the Tiphereth Zion Talmud Torah building on Prospect Place, and then the Stone Avenue Talmud Torah building. The modern Talmud Torah, as we have seen (in Chapter 4), had itself been influenced by the Jewish center movement and served as a critical link between that movement and the modern Orthodox synagogue. The young people's synagogue of Young Israel was the common denominator of the three.[89]

In the spring of 1918, the original Young Israel Synagogue purchased the old Hebrew Sheltering and Immigrant Aid Society building on East Broadway, and "instituted a rich program of religious, educational and social activities." The YI Synagogue, which had begun as two separate organizations—a young person's social organization whose ideology was Orthodox Judaism and a model synagogue whose rationale was Americanization—had thus evolved into one of the archetypal Orthodox synagogue-centers. As we have implied, however, this was only one of a series of youth-oriented Orthodox synagogue-center experiments occurring at the same time. Most notable among them were the innovations of Mordecai Kaplan and Herbert Goldstein. Both had been involved in the formation of the

Central Jewish Institute between 1909 and 1915, and each would soon thereafter create their own version of the synagogue-center. For this reason, perhaps, neither had shown as much interest in the downtown YI as had Judah Magnes and Israel Friedlaender. In certain significant ways, their experimentation would depart from the contemporaneous example of YI.[90]

And yet, in one important regard, the uptown movements followed the example of Young Israel. Though it was a group of "downtown youths" who originated the YI movement, several rabbis and rabbinical students from the uptown Seminary soon became involved as well. YI was thus a cooperative effort between young rabbis and the idealistic youth of the neighborhood, both groups equally concerned with the rising religious apathy. This exemplifies the cooperation between the rabbinate and the laity that marked the emergence of the synagogue-center. Other examples of this rabbinic-lay connection include Stephen S. Wise and Henry Morgenthau at the Free Synagogue, Herbert Goldstein and Isaac Siegel at the Institutional Synagogue, Mordecai Kaplan and Joseph H. Cohen at the Jewish Center, and Israel Levinthal and Louis Cohen at the Brooklyn Jewish Center. The synagogue-center was a synthetic institution bringing together disparate elements of the community—not only young and old, but rabbi and layman as well—thus responding to the growing alienation between them.[91]

Before we turn to the rabbis and their contribution, it ought to be reiterated that the great distance traversed by the Orthodox synagogue, from immigrant shul to modern center, was largely the result of *lay* activity. As Marshall Sklare explained in his brilliant study *Conservative Judaism,* change in the synagogue was the direct result of Jewish resettlement in new neighborhoods. The modernization of the Orthodox synagogue, therefore, was not always self-conscious and rationally planned, but was most often a form of social adjustment to new environments. Even when ideological movements for the transformation of synagogue life appeared on the scene, laymen often took leading roles, as we have seen. This chapter has argued that ordinary Jews, not rabbis, are ultimately responsible for the creation of American Judaism. The next chapter presents a somewhat different point of view.[92]

6

RABBI

Seminary Men and Synagogue-Centers
in the Making

For the last three or four years I have been urging Joseph H. Cohen to induce his friends to establish an institution that would not only provide a place of worship for the elders and a
school for the children but also an opportunity to all affiliated with it to develop their social
life Jewishly . . .   —MORDECAI M. KAPLAN, 1915[1]

Ask any reasonably knowledgeable American Jew who first created the
synagogue-center, and the unvarying response will be Rabbi Mordecai M. Kaplan (1881–1983). Kaplan, whose public career spanned seven decades, was a figure of major importance in the history of twentieth-century Judaism. Despite
the recent publication of two biographies, he deserves far more attention than he
has yet received. Certainly, there is ample reason for the father of Reconstructionist Judaism to be associated in the popular mind with the synagogue-center
(only partly due to his key role in the establishment of the Jewish Center in
1917). But we are caught here on the horns of a historiographical dilemma. To
highlight Kaplan in the saga of the synagogue-center is to emphasize unduly the
contribution of elites in general, when in fact the Jewish "folk" played an essential part in the development of the expanded, socialized American synagogue.
Moreover, isolating Kaplan as the progenitor of the synagogue-center diminishes
the importance of other rabbis. The challenge of this chapter, therefore, is to
maintain a balance between the achievement of a leading individual and the do-
ings of significant others.[2]

The balance of Kaplan's synagogue-centrality notwithstanding, the assignment of authorship to him alone is clearly mistaken. A case in point is modern
Orthodox rabbi Herbert Goldstein. Having worked with Kaplan as the director
of the Central Jewish Institute, Goldstein created the Institutional Synagogue simultaneous with his liberal colleague's more famous experiment. But neither was
he alone in his efforts. There was in fact an entire cohort of early twentieth-
century rabbis—most long forgotten—who jointly participated in the invention

of the synagogue-center. All but a handful of these young rabbis were graduates of a single institution: the Jewish Theological Seminary of America. In a turn of events that hardly needs repeating, the American Jewish philanthropic elite—themselves Reform Jews—felt the need to provide the East European immigrants with a form of Judaism acceptable to them (that is, not Reform) yet suitable to America (that is, not European Orthodoxy). Their solution was to rejuvenate a moribund institution, the Jewish Theological Seminary (established in 1886), and transform it into a major training center for Americanized rabbis espousing traditional Judaism. In 1902, the new school opened under the direction of Solomon Schechter, the renowned scholar of rabbinics at Cambridge University. The revamped Jewish Theological Seminary of America soon became known simply as "Schechter's Seminary." In an uncanny parallel to Hebrew Union College and Isaac Mayer Wise, the first generation of Schechter's protégés left the halls of the Seminary imbued with a passion for Jewish education and a fervor for the renewal of Judaism in America.[3]

Somewhat less familiar is the fact that during Schechter's tenure (1902–15), there was little agreement on the theological stance of the new institution, and a sometimes deliberate blurring of distinctions among Orthodox, Conservative, and Reformist tendencies. There was, on the other hand, general consensus regarding the need to modernize the American synagogue. Thus, while the Seminary rabbis were often far apart on theological issues—Kaplan and Goldstein being prime examples—they would share near unanimity regarding the conversion of synagogues into centers. As in the classical Reform precedent, the synagogue-center idea emerged from their collective experience as modern rabbis committed to the survival of Judaism in America. In many instances, the idea was borrowed directly from neighboring Reform congregations, but it derived as well from the rabbis' acquaintance with Jewish settlement centers and modern school centers. It also emerged directly out of the social and religious tensions they encountered within their conservative congregations. Sometimes those same tensions were enough to quash the rabbi's attempt to upgrade synagogue life. To demonstrate, let us take the case of one Phineas Israeli of Congregation Adath Jeshurun (Roxbury, Massachusetts), better known as the Blue Hill Avenue Shul—a synagogue that did not become a center despite the best intentions of its rabbi.

Rabbi Phineas Israeli and the Blue Hill Avenue Shul

Phineas (in Hebrew, Pinchas) Israeli was born in Elisavetgrad, Russia, in 1880, had his early education in heder, and immigrated to Hartford, Connecticut, as a youth. He attended the City College of New York and Columbia University, and was ordained a rabbi at the Jewish Theological Seminary of America in 1902, the year of its reorganization under Solomon Schechter. His graduating class of eight

Fig. 37. Student Rabbis at the Jewish Theological Seminary, 1900. The bearded figure in the center is Professor Joshua Joffe; seated to his right is Phineas Israeli, to his left, Mordecai Kaplan (leaning on hand); top row, left to right, are Abraham Herschman, unidentified, Rudolph Coffee (with bowtie), Herman Abramowitz, Charles Kauvar, and sitting next to Kaplan, Israel Goldfarb. Courtesy of the Library of the Jewish Theological Seminary of America.

included none other than Mordecai Kaplan (who became his brother-in-law when Phineas married his sister Sophie). The two were not particularly close as friends, but still supported each other unstintingly. In 1904, Israeli rushed to his brother-in-law's defense when he was slighted by the Slutsker Rov (Jacob David Willowsky), a traditional East European rabbi who refused to share the *bimah* (podium) with Kaplan because he preached in English—foreshadowing a similar incident that would later occur to Israeli. In early 1908, after serving congregations in Des Moines, Iowa, and Williamsport, Pennsylvania, he was called to the pulpit of Adath Jeshurun in Roxbury, a growing Jewish community just south of Boston.[4]

The Roxbury congregation, a typical community synagogue in an area of second settlement, was established in 1900 as an offshoot of the leading synagogue of the immigrant ghetto of Boston's North End. At that time, the "chief rabbi" of Boston was Moshe Zevulun Margolies, better known by his acronym "RaMaZ." The Ramaz had arrived in Boston about 1889 as the first traditional East European rabbi in that city. Legend has it that he disliked it so much at first that he retreated to his native Lithuania, but there he was maligned as an "American rabbi" and was forced to return! Ensconced in his North End home as the communal rabbinic authority of Greater Boston, the Ramaz was perceived as the nominal rabbi of numerous Orthodox congregations, including Adath Jeshurun. Only after building a new synagogue in 1906, and losing the Ramaz to New York in the same year, did the congregation choose to hire an in-house rabbi. Ironically, the Ramaz was called to New York's Congregation Kehilath Jeshurun to serve as senior rabbi to its young American minister, Mordecai Kaplan.[5]

In contrast to the traditionalist Ramaz, Phineas Israeli was chosen as an American-trained, English-speaking rabbi who might appeal to the younger generation. But he would still have to contend with the old guard and their traditional leanings. As reported approvingly in the local Jewish press, he advanced his agenda through frequent sermons in favor of a fully religious and nationalist Jewish culture. In a 1910 address, "The American Congregation [as] the Centre of Religious Activities," he maintained: "It is those congregations which have come to realize that they must become centres of energetic, almost feverish religious activity, having each its spiritual leader, whose business it is to appeal in various ways to the children, to the young generation and to the older generation to return to loyalty to Judaism, which have no doubt contributed most materially toward starting the revival of a Jewish religious spirit in this country." His own congregation, however, would prove to be less amenable to such "modern" notions of synagogue life.[6]

In November 1911, a traditional East European *Rov* was invited to share the pulpit with Israeli. Rabbi Wolf (Velvele) Margolies had succeeded the Ramaz,

Fig. 38. Adath Jeshurun, Blue Hill Avenue, Roxbury, Mass., built 1906. Collection of Peter Schweitzer.

touted by the Orthodox community as the new chief rabbi of Boston upon his arrival in 1907. To the chagrin of the *Jewish Advocate,* he "received considerable support, especially from those who were formerly connected with the North End Congregations." Four years later, however, he was invited to become the "Rav Hakollel" (chief rabbi) of "the Adas Israel Community, the Orthodox Union of the Lower East Side." A movement to keep him in Boston was led by none other than Nathan Pinanski, the president of Adath Jeshurun. Pinanski called an emergency meeting and recommended that Margolies be relocated to Roxbury and reestablish himself there as the chief rabbi of Boston. He likely considered his congregation's young rabbi not up to the task of conserving traditional Judaism. But the effort was to no avail: Margolies moved to New York in September, only to return two months later for a *Siyum* celebration. While he was in town, the *balabatim* (lay leaders) of Adath Jeshurun invited him to their shul for *Shabbes.* Seated on the bimah next to Israeli, Margolies caused a furor when he refused to speak, protesting the innovation of a modern rabbi and his liberal use of English.[7]

The *Jewish Advocate* reported that the incident was only "the culmination of a series of happenings in which Cong. Adath Jeshurun has played a peculiar part. It seems to be a house divided against itself. At one moment it is more than abreast of modern orthodoxy, at another its influence is used to promote a standpattism, which can be of little use." The quote reveals the great divide between traditional and modern Orthodoxy within such transitional congregations. Rabbis like Phineas Israeli were caught in the middle, simultaneously expected to preserve the old and foster the new. Prior to the rise of Conservative Judaism, Zionism offered the readiest synthesis of old and new—epitomized by Herzl's depiction of Israel as the "Old/New-land"—and not surprisingly, rabbis in Israeli's position often became ardent Zionists and Hebraists. Shortly after the above incident, the rabbi surprised his congregation at a Bar-Mitzvah service by spontaneously deciding to deliver "his sermon in pure biblical Hebrew" (that is, the modern revival of biblical Hebrew). The address was "on Chanucah and on Jewish education for the young generation," but after the departure of the Yiddish-speaking Margolies, Israeli was making a subtler point.[8]

The road to an American Judaism down Blue Hill Avenue was thus blocked by generational conflict. Both the disputes and Rabbi Israeli's attempted solutions are recorded in the journals of Mordecai Kaplan, who visited his brother-in-law several times between 1911 and 1918, because, as he wrote, he felt "duty bound to strengthen him in his position at Roxbury which he has been holding for the last seven years in the face of the most trying odds." In December 1914, Kaplan came to the Blue Hill Avenue Shul and observed the first of Israeli's innovations, the "newly organized Junior Congregation." Imitative of Henry Berkowitz's experiment in Philadelphia, it was nonetheless claimed to be the first Junior Congregation in an Orthodox synagogue in America. In addition to the example of Henry Berkowitz, Phineas Israeli's earlier involvement in the Jewish

Endeavor Society and its young people's synagogue may certainly have influenced his creation of a Junior Congregation as well.[9]

After the Friday night service—also an innovation in Orthodoxy—Kaplan spoke to the congregants, observing that "the main auditorium of the synagogue was filled with young and middle aged people, men and women sitting together." At Shabbat services the next day, he was shocked by the contrast: "In the morning the auditorium was half filled with middle aged and old men and a few women of the old fashioned type in the gallery." Apparently, Israeli had organized his congregation into two separate entities, split between old and young, separate seating and mixed, Sabbath morning and Friday evening services. Such a compromise between tradition and modernity was tenable for the time being, but could not and would not last for long.[10]

In his remarks, Kaplan pointed out the error of the immigrant generation for having built "synagogues where their own but not their children's spiritual needs were reckoned with." On his next visit Kaplan spoke again, lamenting the absence of a Jewish parallel to the Christian Revival movement of Billy Sunday. On both occasions, he was responding to the moribund congregational life he observed in the synagogues of his day. Kaplan, like other second-generation critics of the shul, bitterly resented the lingering effects of the past generation and its stifling hold on the present. The following period would be one of spiritual crisis and creative ferment for him, during which time he began formulating various plans for a modern synagogue. In his talks to the Junior Congregation of Adath Jeshurun, he had impatiently recommended the immediate transformation of the synagogue. But Adath Jeshurun was already in the midst of a more gradual process of transition, undergoing precisely the kind of changes Kaplan envisaged. While "General" Kaplan plotted strategy in New York, unsung heroes like Phineas Israeli were busy fighting the (often losing) battles in congregational trenches around the country.[11]

On the occasion of the tenth anniversary of the building of the synagogue, Mordecai Kaplan again came to Blue Hill Avenue and delivered an address on the "ideal synagogue." Once again, he was impressed by the attendance of the Junior Congregation, "four to five hundred people" who arrived on a Saturday evening "despite the heavy snow storm." He also described, in glowing terms, a second subcongregation introduced by Rabbi Israeli consisting of about one hundred children. In addition, Israeli had reorganized "the Hebrew School of the congregation, so that [by 1918 it was] one of the largest in New England [soon to become the Menorah Institute]"; and furthermore "organized a Young People's Culture Circle, which later became an auxiliary to the Roxbury Ladies' Aid and Fuel Society." By the time he resigned from Adath Jeshurun in 1918 to accept an educational post in Chelsea, therefore, the congregation was well on its way toward the utopian ideal that Mordecai Kaplan proposed. It was not Kaplan, however, but Phineas Israeli who had labored diligently in pursuit of the synagogue-center ideal for ten long years.[12]

"Seminary Men"

Although Israeli never fully succeeded in converting his congregation into a synagogue-center, others of his contemporaries would. In fact, the transformation of the community synagogue was most often facilitated by the arrival of a rabbi trained at the Jewish Theological Seminary. In a close parallel to the classical Reform trend of the preceding period, the community synagogues of 1900–1915 began to seek English-speaking rabbis who could better relate to the Americanized generation. This was especially true of the community synagogues established by Americanized East European immigrants, often the secession of younger members of an older Orthodox shul dissatisfied with its unyielding adherence to European norms. These new congregations would often stress their use of English in place of Yiddish as the synagogue lingua franca, and hence, their interest in an Anglophone rabbi. As in the case of the earlier Reform temples, the acquisition of a new rabbi often accompanied the move into a new building. And just as Reform congregations had tapped the Hebrew Union College (HUC) for modern American rabbis, their more conservative neighbors turned to the Jewish Theological Seminary of America for the same reason.

Following the arrival of Solomon Schechter in 1902, JTS entered a period of reorganization that culminated with Schechter's untimely death in 1915—a period coincident with the heyday of the community synagogue. During the Schechter years, most of the eighty-four JTS alumni ("Seminary men" as they were called) spread across the country to serve as new rabbis for the burgeoning community synagogues. Significantly, these early Conservative rabbis were the contemporaries rather than the students of Mordecai Kaplan, who only became a professor at JTS in 1909 and principal of the Teachers Institute in 1910. In lieu of Kaplan, they were largely inspired and influenced by their mentor Schechter, who, while more staunchly traditionalist in temperament than Kaplan, nevertheless encouraged innovation in synagogue life. Furthermore, they followed the job market to locations around the country, far from the liberal New York circle of Mordecai Kaplan (whose sphere of influence would only broaden in later years).[13]

In nearly every instance, they followed graduates of HUC to the same communities. As noted before, community synagogues often aspired to the prestigious status of their contemporary Reform temples. While eschewing doctrinal imitation, they competed in other ways; mostly by acquiring architecturally impressive buildings and hiring oratorically impressive rabbis. Like their Reform counterparts, the young Conservative rabbis quickly set about injecting new life into the congregation by introducing English sermons, special services, modern schools, women's and youth groups, and various social events. The congregations and their new rabbis were influenced by the Reform ritual to some degree, as when they adopted mixed seating and choral music, but for the most part influence was confined to the less controversial areas of social and educational activities. Where

American Reform rabbis had served to channel Protestant example into their congregations, Conservative rabbis and congregations drew upon the example of the Reformers, thus avoiding imitation of the church.

Where association with church practice persisted, as in the case of the organ, the more Orthodox synagogues drew the line. An interesting case occurred in Roxbury, not far from Phineas Israeli and Adath Jeshurun. Congregation Mishkan Tefila, unlike its neighboring community synagogue, was of the older type, founded in 1859 by German and Polish Jews. Resisting the Reformist trend of the late nineteenth century, it had retained its lean toward traditionalism and may be considered "early Conservative." In 1907, Mishkan Tefila purchased the second of its two church buildings, and immediately faced a problem: what should be done with the organ? Some members, it seems, wanted nothing to do with the Christian apparatus, while others favored its use. A compromise was achieved whereby the organ was retained, but used only "during the Sunday night lectures and any entertainment which may be held in the Synagogue." Seven years later, however, a new rabbi named Herman Rubenovitz (JTS, 1908) persuaded the congregation that organ music in Sabbath and holiday services was both permissible and desirable. He himself had become convinced of this by witnessing the effective use of instrumental music in synagogue ritual on a trip to Europe. No matter that it ultimately derived from church practice, Rubenovitz's legitimating precedent was Jewish.[14]

It was Rubenovitz who, in the fall of 1909, first suggested to his colleague Charles Hoffman the formation of "a union of conservative forces in America." At the annual Seminary alumni meeting the following year, the two together with Jacob Kohn and Mordecai Kaplan formed the Committee on Conservative Union to push their agenda. Their goal was nothing less than the creation of a centrist, "modern-traditional," "religious-nationalist" movement in American Judaism. They would therefore organize a congregational union to embody the new trend (which would also serve the practical purpose of helping to match Seminary rabbis with sympathetic congregations). Three years later, now under the leadership of Solomon Schechter, the movement was formalized as the "United Synagogue of America, A Union for Promoting Traditional Judaism." Its official founding took place on February 23, 1913, at a meeting of representatives from twenty-two congregations—almost all from the Jewish population centers of the Northeast: New York City (8 affiliates), Philadelphia (4), New Jersey (3), upstate New York (3), and Boston (2). Later spreading across the continent, the United Synagogue was to become the force behind the emergence of Conservative Judaism, the third major religious movement of American Jewry.[15]

At its founding, it must be remembered, the constituent members were Orthodox synagogues of the transitional type we have called the "community synagogue." A key effect of the United Synagogue would be the coordination of the effort to convert such congregations into full-fledged synagogue-centers. Yet as revealed by the case of Adath Jeshurun in Roxbury, not every community synagogue completed the transition. Two factors most influenced the outcome: the strength of personality of the rabbi (apparently lacking in the case of Phineas Israeli), and the age of the congregation (whether it was established before or during the period of mass immigration). Congregations founded by Americanizing immigrants, like Adath Jeshurun, were less likely to complete the transition than the older congregations. In the more recently established congregations, the founders were still present, insisting that the synagogue belonged to them. Though acculturated to a degree, they tended to be more traditional in matters of ritual and observance, and often battled fiercely with the more progressive elements of the congregation—often led by the very rabbi they had hired to "save" the synagogue.

Yet most of Israeli's Seminary colleagues managed to overcome such intransigency. For example, his classmate Charles Eliezer Hillel Kauvar (who, incidentally, was Mordecai Kaplan's distant cousin), was hired immediately upon ordination by Congregation Beth Hamedrosh Hagodol of Denver. "BMH," as it was called, originated in the 1897 service held in Henry Plonsky's shoe store, and grew into the leading Orthodox synagogue of Denver. Though joining the United Synagogue at its inception, its traditionalist element remained strong, and ultimately (in 1958, with the elderly Rabbi Kauvar's blessings) left the Conservative fold for Orthodoxy. But not before Kauvar had effected its transition into "a model synagogue-center." As early as 1905, for example, he founded the Denver Hebrew School, which functioned both as a congregational and a communal school. Evidently Kauvar was the confident leader that Israeli was not, using his rabbinic post to attain communal leadership. As reward for his efforts, he was elected rabbi for life in 1919, and retired as rabbi emeritus in 1952.[16]

More often, however, the stronger candidates—the rising stars—were hired by better-off congregations, that is, the more established, pre-1880 synagogues. Mordecai Kaplan, for one, was appointed "minister" of Orthodox congregation Kehilath Jeshurun, established in 1872. At the time of Kaplan's appointment in 1904, it was housed in a new (1902) architecturally impressive synagogue building in the fashionable Upper East Side district of Yorkville. But Kehilath Jeshurun was still under the sway of downtown Orthodoxy. Kaplan was not given the title of rabbi there because Seminary ordination was not considered legitimate by downtown authorities. Suffering the subordination of more "authentic" senior rabbis, he lasted but four years (1904–9). Another of Kaplan's classmates, Elias Solomon (officially graduated in 1904, but had been a senior along with Kaplan in 1902), later served under the Ramaz at Kehilath Jeshurun as well (1918–21). Solomon, it will be recalled, was instrumental in the organization of the Jewish Endeavor Society and the founding of its experimental youth synagogue. While at Kehilath Jeshurun (note, the same period that Kaplan was at the Jewish Center across town) he also served as president of the United Synagogue of America. Like Kaplan before him, Solomon left the staunchly Orthodox congregation after four frustrating years.[17]

Two other members of the 1902 class, Israel Goldfarb and Herman Abramowitz, fared far better in their first pulpits. Goldfarb was elected "Hazan and
Teacher" of Brooklyn's second oldest congregation, Baith Israel Anshei Emes (established 1854; also known as the Kane Street Synagogue), in 1905—again, the
same year the congregation dedicated their new synagogue. His first task was the
founding of a Talmud Torah; after continuing to expand the activities of the congregation, he remained its rabbi for over half a century. Similarly, Abramowitz
became spiritual leader of Canada's oldest Ashkenazi congregation, Shaar
Hashomayim of Montreal (established 1846). By enlarging its scope, he turned it
into one of the leading synagogues in the country and in the process became the
most prominent Canadian rabbi of his time.[18]

Some other exemplary figures of the period include Charles Hoffman (class of
1904), Abraham Herschman (1906), Jacob Kohn (1907), Herman Rubenovitz
(1908), Max Drob (1911), Max David Klein (1911), Samuel Cohen (1912), and Eugene Kohn (1912). Every one of these took the pulpit of one of the pre-1880,
German-Polish, "early Conservative" synagogues noted earlier. Hence, Hoffman
went to Oheb Shalom in Newark (established 1859), Herschman to Shaaray
Zedek in Detroit (1861), J. Kohn to Ansche Chesed in New York (1828), Rubenovitz to Mishkan Tefila in Boston (1858), Drob to Beth El in Buffalo (1847),
Klein to Adath Jeshurun in Philadelphia (1859), Cohen to Keneseth Israel in
Kansas City (1878), and E. Kohn to Chizuk Amuno in Baltimore (1871). By the
second decade of the twentieth century, these congregations had undergone several decades of acculturation—a process accelerated by their competition with
neighboring Reform temples—and were ripe for the innovations of their new
rabbis. Moreover, many of the prominent Reform congregations in these cities
had established temple centers a few years earlier, so it follows that all of the
above-named congregations would later develop into full-fledged synagogue-
centers as well.

One excellent example is Congregation Shaarey Zedek of Detroit, founded in
1861 as the traditionalist secession from the original congregation of the city,
Temple Beth El. Abraham Herschman was ordained in 1906 and, following one
year in Syracuse (at Adath Jeshurun, which had been the first pulpit of Joseph
Hertz, the earliest graduate of the Seminary in 1894, and where both Jacob Kohn
and Max Drob were to serve briefly as well), was hired by the Detroit congregation. As its historians write, "it was not long before the congregation felt the impact of [his] forceful personality. The new rabbi established a congregational
school, reorganized the Sunday school, and organized a Young People's Society
and the Kadimah Society for the study of Jewish history." The congregation had
begun to grow even before Herschman's arrival, and by 1908 the membership had
increased to two hundred families. In 1910 a site was purchased for a new synagogue structure, and the cornerstone was laid three years later. Present at both that
occasion and at the dedication in 1915 was Rabbi Leo Franklin, spiritual leader of
Temple Beth El and one of the leaders of the synagogue-center movement in

Reform Judaism. Beth El's temple center had been designed in 1903 by the well-known architect Albert Kahn. Seeking to surpass its competitor, Shaarey Zedek's new synagogue was "planned to seat 1,432 members in the main sanctuary, [and] included a large school and auditorium, numerous classrooms, a social hall, and a gymnasium." Under Rabbi Herschman, Shaarey Zedek joined the United Synagogue in 1913 as an unabashed synagogue-center.[19]

Another rabbi who crossed paths with his Reform predecessor was Samuel Margolies, the son of the Ramaz. Raised in Boston, the younger Margolies had returned to Eastern Europe for his rabbinic studies at the Telz yeshiva and then graduated from Harvard in 1902, becoming the ideal modern Orthodox rabbi. For a brief time following his college graduation, he also attended the Jewish Theological Seminary, joining the first class under Solomon Schechter (which also included Mordecai Kaplan as a postgraduate student). Ostensibly, he found Schechter's teaching too liberal and soon left. Shortly thereafter he was called to the Cleveland pulpit of Anshe Emeth, a congregation established by Polish Jews in 1857. Like his traditionalist father, Margolies became the leading rabbi of the immigrant community, and during his tenure (1904–16), Anshe Emeth rose to become the leading Orthodox congregation of Cleveland. Like his fellow modern rabbis, he became involved in the life of the greater community. In 1906, he helped organize the Union of Jewish Organizations and planned a "Jewish Institute" along the lines of Moses Gries's Council Educational Alliance. Gries, it will be recalled, was a prominent classical Reform rabbi and leading advocate of the synagogue-center; certainly he had some influence on his more conservative colleague. Margolies' plans were first realized by the creation of a modern Talmud Torah, the Cleveland Hebrew School. When he died prematurely in 1917, his congregation joined with the school to fulfill his vision for a complete Jewish center. This became the basis for the Cleveland Jewish Center, a seminal synagogue-center. Although it remained Orthodox until the 1922 arrival of Solomon Goldman (JTS, 1918), it had long been a Jewish center in the making, as envisioned by Samuel Margolies. Though not Conservative per se, Margolies was nonetheless representative of a generation of "modern-traditional" rabbis who were Zionist educators and communal workers and who saw beyond the narrow confines of the immigrant shul to an American synagogue for all.[20]

Charles Hoffman and Oheb Shalom of Newark

If Samuel Margolies stood outside the Conservative fold, a contemporary who personified Conservatism through and through was Rabbi Charles Isaiah Hoffman. Born in 1864 to a German Jewish family in Philadelphia, Hoffman first embarked on a career in the law. But there was much in his early years that foreshadowed his later calling. In 1887, while maintaining an active legal practice, Hoffman helped found a weekly newspaper, the *Jewish Exponent*, and served as

Fig. 39. Rabbi Charles Hoffman, 1900. Courtesy
of the Library of the Jewish Theological Seminary
of America.

its first editor and publisher. He was active both in Zionist activities and in efforts to help settle Jewish immigrants; all in all, he was a prototypical Jewish community activist. Yet his religious commitment overshadowed the communal. He had his early Jewish education under the tutelage of Sabato Morais (founder of the first Jewish Theological Seminary) and was classmates with Cyrus Adler—later to become the driving force behind the new seminary. As we shall see, he would later become especially close to the towering figure of Conservative Judaism, Solomon Schechter.[21]

The Hoffman family belonged to Rodeph Shalom, the oldest Ashkenazic congregation in America, and so Charles came under the influence of yet another stalwart of historical Judaism. Rabbi Marcus Jastrow was the Polish-born and German-educated scholar best known today for his dictionary of Talmudic literature. Under the rabbi's wing, Hoffman taught in Rodeph Shalom's religious school, and even served on occasion as Jastrow's English-speaking replacement in the pulpit. Soon the more Americanized element of the congregation began asking for regular sermons in the vernacular, and in 1891, Hoffman drafted the resolution calling for a new rabbi to assist the ailing Dr. Jastrow. Despite his call for "adherence to those true principles of Judaism for which it has always stood," Rodeph Shalom elected a champion of Reform Judaism to its pulpit, Henry Berkowitz. Loyal to Jastrow, Hoffman felt betrayed, and after unsuccessfully fighting to oppose the Reform tendency (the final straw was the adoption of the

Union Prayerbook), finally resigned from the congregation in October 1895. He then joined the more traditional congregation Beth Israel, known as the "Polish Synagogue," and soon became its president. Nevertheless, in the interim he had come to know Henry Berkowitz, and probably Joseph Krauskopf as well, who together were key figures in the synagogue-center movement of Reform Judaism.[22]

At the very moment Hoffman was contemplating leaving Rodeph Shalom, a savior appeared on the scene. In February 1895, Solomon Schechter arrived in Philadelphia to deliver a series of lectures under the Gratz fund. Hoffman was so impressed that he ultimately abandoned his career in law to become the great scholar's disciple. After attending the Zionist conference of 1900 and conferring with Schechter in England, he decided to enter the rabbinate at the ripe age of thirty-six. With his wife and four young children in tow, he moved to Cambridge to study under Schechter, and returned to America two years later together with his mentor. In 1904, Charles Hoffman was ordained as valedictorian of the first graduating class of "Schechter's Seminary." After serving the United Hebrew Congregation of Indianapolis (a name chosen specifically to counter the landsmanshaft principle of fragmentation, thus indicating a community synagogue), he returned to the East Coast in 1906 to assume a pulpit in Newark, New Jersey—situated, fortuitously enough, midway between his native Philadelphia and the Jewish Theological Seminary of New York. Under Rabbi Hoffman, Oheb Shalom became a model Conservative congregation, situated midway between Orthodoxy and Reform.[23]

Oheb Shalom was the third synagogue of Newark, founded in 1859 by a group of Bohemian Jews, former members of B'nai Abraham, the Polish offshoot (in 1853) of the German B'nai Jeshurun (founded 1848). All three congregations would follow the trend toward religious acculturation. Yet unlike the German Reform temple, B'nai Abraham and Oheb Shalom retained their traditionalist leanings, both later becoming founding members of the United Synagogue. In 1885, the Bohemian congregation hired Rabbi Bernard Drachman, who reported "that, in all respects except one, [the] synagogue was conducted in accordance with the regulations of the Orthodox religious code . . . at public services men and women sat together." By the turn of the century, the English-speaking second generation of Oheb Shalom achieved its majority, and began clamoring for further change. The first change was the hiring of a new rabbi in 1906. The second would be the erection of a new synagogue five years later.[24]

As always, the primary catalyst in the transformation of the American synagogue was the rise of a new generation. A new rabbi was hired precisely to cater to the youth and to ensure the future. Hoffman was probably matched with Oheb Shalom by the young Jacob Kohn, then a student at the Seminary (and also a disciple of Schechter), who had grown up in the congregation together with his younger brother, Eugene—who ended up at the Seminary as well. Their cousin and longtime member of the congregation, Sarah Kussy, would later recall that the "years (after the turn of the century) witnessed the development of a new spirit in the congregation when a number of young men and women, sons and daughters of members, inspired by religious zeal, offered their services gratuitously as teachers for the congregational school." It was just then that Rabbi Hoffman arrived on the scene and soon Oheb Shalom "became a center for Zionist activities, adult study groups, and Young Judea clubs." It almost goes without saying that Hoffman further developed the educational program of the synagogue as well.[25]

This sounds like a settlement-type Jewish center, and for good reason. Hoffman, always abreast of communal developments, was earlier inspired by the example of the Jewish sisterhoods of New York to recommend the establishment of a citywide system of religious neighborhood centers. Moreover, he was married to the former Fanny Binswanger, who, it will be recalled, had founded one of the earliest and most successful Jewish settlements in the country, the Young Women's Union of Philadelphia. Rabbi Hoffman's affinity for youth, education, and indeed, the needs of the community came directly out of his own (and his wife's) experience. The symbiosis between rabbi and community became most apparent with the founding of the *Oheb Shalom Review*. As a former newspaper man, it came naturally to him to start a synagogue newsletter. Certainly, a congregation growing in numbers and activities required some medium of communication. But Hoffman now took the idea a step further, turning the newsletter into a project of the young people in his congregation. The *Oheb Shalom Review* was edited by the rabbi's son, M. David Hoffman.

Second only to youth in importance, a new building provided another impetus for change. In fact, community synagogues were often "converted" to synagogue-centers at the point of moving into more up-to-date quarters. When Oheb Shalom's new synagogue building was constructed in 1911, certain of the youth group activities were incorporated into the congregation, and other groups were formed as well. In February 1911, M. David Hoffman offered some thoughts regarding the planned expansion of the synagogue: "With the opening of our new building a larger sphere of activity and a greater development will be afforded the congregation. . . . We should have a library and a reading room in connection with it as it is an essential part of any *Jewish centre*." The same themes were expanded upon by the young Sarah Kussy, writing in the *Oheb Shalom Fair Journal* of March, 1911:

The new synagogue will soon be completed. . . . Newark is rapidly becoming one of the large Jewish centers of America [its 1910 Jewish population of 25,000-plus would double by 1918!] . . . True, we cannot turn the house of prayer into a dance hall, but we can make of it a real Beth Hakeneseth (House of Assembly), particularly for our young people. . . . We can and should, moreover, extend the work of our school as far as possible. The large assembly hall of the new synagogue will enable us to open the doors to all the Jewish children of the neighborhood who may desire to participate. . . . Situated as we are here at the border of the densely crowded Jewish district, occupying a beautiful and spacious building, splendid opportunities are afforded us for making our synagogue the social no less than the spiritual centre of our Jewish community.[26]

The new synagogue on High Street was a synthesis of all that contemporary American Judaism had to offer. Anticipating many other such structures, it was designed by a American Jewish architect, William Lehman. At its dedication in 1911, the speakers for the occasion included Oheb Shalom's own Jacob Kohn (recently hired by Ansche Chesed of New York), as well as Solomon Schechter, Dr. Solomon Solis-Cohen of Philadelphia, and Woodrow Wilson (then governor of New Jersey). Oheb Shalom would be both fully Jewish and fully American. As the quote indicates, it also sought to attract both native Jewish residents of Newark as well as the more recently arrived immigrants. And finally, it was to be a synthesis of social and spiritual concerns, a true synagogue-center.[27]

Subsequent declarations would make the point more explicitly. Rabbi Hoffman himself said it best in "A Congregational Centre," an eloquent plea for synagogue sociability:

The synagogue is the centre of our religious activities. The worship of God is the highest expression of our service, but it by no means exhausts, it is not the only form of Jewish activity. Jewish religion is not less comprehensive and multifarious than Jewish life. It is an error to divorce our social life, our charitable and ethical activities from the religious source. In years gone by the synagogue was the centre, our faith the dynamo that supplied power to all the agencies and functions of our existence. Why not make it so again? . . . Why should we not know each other better, feel the throb of brotherhood; help and comfort each other in the hour of need, and share each other's joys and sorrows? Who is there that does not need sympathy; that does not desire appreciation; that does not long for fellowship and a responsive and an understanding heart to which he can appeal and upon which he can rely? Why not have a place where Jews shall meet together as Jews? . . . Let us bring the synagogue into the lives of our people. Let us establish an assembly, a club, a Jewish centre. Call it what you will, a congregational organization including all the men affiliated and friendly to it who will meet periodically under its aegis and influence for enjoyment, for social and for fraternal intercourse, to further all the varied interests of congregation, community and of sound Jewish development.[28]

In 1916, Oheb Shalom made a public appeal for new membership, addressing itself directly "to the Jews of Newark," issuing "the invitation to each one, old and young, man and woman, to enter into its activities, to participate in its benefits," and insisting that "every Jewish family ought, as in the past, to be identified with the Synagogue, the central power-house of Jewish life." The appeal concluded, "Make the Synagogue the Centre for all," and the following congregational offerings were listed: Services for Holidays, Memorial Services, Hebrew School, the Cemetery, Social Work (for example the ladies' auxiliary, the men's club, and young people's clubs and societies). We may infer that the initial synagogue-center experiment was not an immediate success; many Newark Jews still remained outside the synagogue. Yet the appeal to the public, congregational advertising as it were, reveals an important element of the new American synagogue: a responsiveness to the environment, as indicated by the tastes and desires of the Jewish populace. Many rabbis and other religious ideologues would denounce this as antithetical to Jewish tradition, in which authority derives from God, Torah, and *Halacha* (Jewish law). Rabbinic preference notwithstanding, however, in America the old order has been supplanted by a new authority—the will of the people. Charles Hoffman had listened to the people, especially the young people, and created a synagogue for the American future.[29]

Herbert Goldstein and the Institutional Synagogue

So far, we have reviewed rabbis who came into established congregations and attempted to turn them into synagogue-centers. We have seen a number of such experiments blossom into reality, well before the more publicized innovations of 1917: Mordecai Kaplan's Jewish Center and Herbert Goldstein's Institutional Synagogue. Though many of their colleagues succeeded in their attempts, many more (like Phineas Israeli) were intensely frustrated by their congregations and left to try their hand elsewhere. This was especially true of those young men who, subjugated to senior rabbis, languished in subordination and dreamt of breaking out on their own (such as Mordecai Kaplan). "Why not start their own synagogue?" was a thought they might understandably entertain. Certainly it occurred to Herbert Goldstein, who, like Kaplan, graduated from the Seminary and subsequently served at Kehilath Jeshurun. Like Kaplan, and like many others of his rabbinic generation, he arrived at the synagogue-center conclusion.

Herbert S. Goldstein was born on the Lower East Side in 1890. Inspired by the example of Joseph Mayor Asher, one of the first modern Orthodox rabbis in America and one of the first members of Solomon Schechter's new faculty, the young Columbia College student decided to enter the rabbinate and was admitted to the Jewish Theological Seminary in 1910. There he was elected president of the student organization, the Morais-Blumenthal literary society, and edited the *Seminary Annual*. Unlike most others at the modern rabbinical school, Goldstein remained devoutly Orthodox and resisted the liberalizing trend toward what soon would be called Conservative Judaism. In 1913, while still attending the Seminary, he received *smicha* (rabbinic ordination) from a traditionalist rabbi downtown, and shortly thereafter was elected assistant rabbi of the prestigious Orthodox congregation Kehilath Jeshurun. He graduated from the Seminary in 1914, and later that year became engaged to a daughter of Harry Fischel, the wealthy builder and Jewish philanthropist. In early 1916, while acting as English-speaking junior rabbi and principal of the Hebrew school, he was appointed director of the newly founded Central Jewish Institute. Little more than a year afterward, Goldstein resigned from both appointments to pursue a venture of his own: the formation of the Institutional Synagogue.[30]

There was much in Goldstein's educational and congregational experience to prepare him for the role of synagogue-center innovator. At the Seminary, he was exposed to the sociological teachings of Mordecai Kaplan, a religious iconoclast whom Goldstein held in low regard, but who influenced him nonetheless. Lecturing to the Morais-Blumenthal society in 1913, Professor Kaplan advised the young rabbinical students—among them the recently elected assistant rabbi of Kehilath Jeshurun—to "strive to make of the synagogue a social centre." Goldstein seemed to follow Kaplan's advice when soon after he organized the young men and women of the congregation into the popular Social Welfare Circle. As

Fig. 40. Rabbi Herbert Goldstein, upon graduation from
the Jewish Theological Seminary, 1914. *Students' Annual,
1914* (New York: Jewish Theological Seminary of America,
1914). Courtesy of the Library of the Jewish Theological
Seminary of America.

the English-speaking junior rabbi of Kehilath Jeshurun, he developed a special
rapport with the younger element of the congregation, and must have come to
see himself as the "young people's rabbi." The idea of a young people's synagogue, where as rabbi he would hold the respect of the entire congregation and
have his innovative ideas unopposed, must have held great appeal to him.[31]

Committed to the future of Orthodox Judaism in America, Goldstein took
great interest in the problem of Jewish education. While serving as principal of
the congregational Hebrew school of Kehilath Jeshurun, he was understandably
influenced by the many pedagogical innovations of the modern Talmud Torah
movement. He noted, for example, the importance of light and airy classrooms
in the educational process and worked to improve the physical condition of the
school premises. He also discerned the many practical advantages of a communal
over a congregational school, and when a new Talmud Torah was projected for
the Yorkville community he became intimately concerned with its progress. In
helping to plan the new school, Goldstein could draw upon the model of the
Uptown Talmud Torah, a pet project of his father-in-law, Harry Fischel. The
Uptown Talmud Torah, according to Goldstein, was "much more than merely a
school or religious institution. The building was also in reality a Young Men's

and Young Women's Hebrew Association, with all the many physical and social facilities to be expected in such an institution."[32]

Like its Uptown precedent, the Yorkville Talmud Torah would become something more than just a religious school by adding the social function of a center. Contrary to Goldstein, however, the model Jewish center for the Uptown Talmud Torah (UTT) was not the YMHA but the Educational Alliance and other such settlement houses. Renamed the Harlem Institute, the UTT was intended to be a more religiously Jewish version of the famous downtown settlement. Likewise, the Yorkville Talmud Torah was created in imitation of a contemporary Jewish center, the 92d Street "Y"; unlike its near neighbor, however, the YTT would be more affirmatively Jewish and staunchly Orthodox. Goldstein, wrote his biographer, "welcomed this first opportunity to demonstrate to the administrators of the "Y," right in their own shadow practically, what a positive force a community center could be in the promotion of religion." Renamed the Central Jewish Institute, the modern Orthodox "school center" would thus incorporate the recreational features of a social center within the most up-to-date school building. In a 1915 fund-raising appeal, Goldstein described the projected institution as more than an ordinary Hebrew School, "but also a Jewish Social Centre, wherein there are provided a gymnasium, room for club work, kindergarten classes, and a kosher kitchen; in short, a centre where the ideas of traditional Judaism will be fostered and encouraged in the minds of American youth."[33]

Goldstein therefore had direct experience of the merging of separate institutional functions. During his tenure at Kehilath Jeshurun, he presided over the integration of the congregational school into the new communal school. The Central Jewish Institute, whose director he became, was created as a hybrid of two institutions: the modern Talmud Torah and the Jewish center. As discussed earlier, the combination set a critical precedent for the synagogue-center. Just as the school had been merged with the settlement to form the Jewish center, the next logical step would be to add the synagogue to the school-center synthesis. Goldstein, holding joint positions as rabbi of a synagogue and director of a center, was uniquely situated to take that step. When he decided to establish a new institution, he was consciously "combining the attributes of both" the Central Jewish Institute and the traditional synagogue, a fusion reflected in the title he chose: the "Institutional Synagogue."[34]

Goldstein was appointed director of the new Central Jewish Institute in early 1916 while still officiating as rabbi of Kehilath Jeshurun. After a harried, overworked winter and spring, he finally found time to relax on a summer vacation in Long Branch, New Jersey. While daydreaming of ways to improve Jewish life back in the city—including his own, overextended Jewish life—he came up with "an idea for the future synagogue for all Jewish congregations." He would solve his own problem by creating the ideal workplace, a more efficiently organized religious institution. Upon returning home, he indicated his intentions publicly in a September 1916 article entitled "The Institutional Synagogue," in which he wrote:

I speak . . . from an uncompromisingly Orthodox point of view. . . . My plea for the future is
the Institutional Synagogue, which would embrace the Synagogue, the Talmud Torah, and
the YMHA movements. . . . The Institutional Synagogue must, first of all, be as Orthodox a
house of worship as is prescribed in Jewish codes [that is, like Kehilath Jeshurun]. It should
then be a place of study for the elders in the evenings, and for the children in the afternoons
(in large, light and well-ventilated classrooms) [that is, like the Central Jewish Institute]. It
should be a place where men and women may come after plying their daily cares and spend a
social hour in an Orthodox environment and in a truly Jewish atmosphere [that is, as the
YMHA should be].[35]

He made his intentions perfectly clear, envisioning the Institutional Synagogue
as the fusion of three separate institutions: the synagogue, the Talmud Torah,
and the YMHA/Jewish center. From his point of view, it was the logical conclusion of his own experience. In historical terms, the 1917 synagogue-center ought
to be seen as the confluence of three parallel processes: the socialization of the
Orthodox synagogue, the modernization of the Talmud Torah, and the Judaization of the center. Goldstein sought to merge three institutions whose movements were already headed in the same direction.

He justified the innovation in three ways. First, he employed the familiar argument of Jewish authenticity, claiming that "this institution would be a revival
of the historic synagogue. The synagogue of old was the center for prayer, study,
and the social life of the community. The restoration of this type of synagogue
would spell the salvation of Judaism." Second, he indicated the potential benefit
to Jewish life of an institution that served the entire family: "The father and
mother would go to the synagogue with their children; the young man and
woman would go to the building for social work; the children would go to the
Talmud Torah and thus there would be brought back to the family life that religious unity and enthusiasm which is so sorely lacking today." Indicative that
these ideas were not original with him, Goldstein launched into his main rationale with greater alacrity. The Institutional Synagogue, argued the modern Orthodox rabbi, would "serve the practical purpose of helping to solve the problem of
support of religious institutions." Instead of funding three separate institutions,
the community need only fund one. Instead of joining three separate institutions, the individual need only join one. Emulating his father-in-law, the pragmatic businessman Harry Fischel, Goldstein knew that the "bottom line" was
economic efficiency.

He was, after all, a man of his time—the era shaped by the cataclysm of the
First World War. The war had begun to affect American life and culture even before America's entry in April 1917. There arose at that time a sense of rapid
change and cultural malleability that gave new impetus to the Progressive
agenda. John Dewey, for instance, argued that the moment was pregnant with
"social possibilities." For Jews the war was a watershed event in several areas. Responding to the plight of European Jewry the American Jewish community leapt
onto the world stage and first became aware of its own robust potential, as exemplified by the 1914 formation of the Joint Distribution Committee for overseas

relief. At home, the Jewish Welfare Board was created in 1917 to provide religious and social services to Jewish servicemen. Its organization represented "a union of all the religious forces in American Jewish life," and was a significant example of the social-religious synthesis. With anti-Semitism on the rise both in Europe and in America, the Zionist movement achieved mass appeal and helped to unify American Jews, a unity realized by the founding of the American Jewish Congress in 1916–18. American Jews in general were swept up by the "wave of religious enthusiasm which spread over American communities during and immediately after the period of storm and stress." Postwar American Jewry therefore evinced a "deeper religious interest" as well as "a keener racial pride," adding up to the makings of a Jewish revival.[36]

The war also created an atmosphere of youthful rebellion and resurgence. The following account of the years 1917 and 1918 offers a vivid impression of the cultural climate:

The world was dancing in a frenzy to the discordant music of a Dance Macabre. To the tempo of cannon, to the theme of death cries, to the counterpoint of tragedy, death, sorrow, Youth and Age danced. They gyrated crazily, purposelessly. They seemed to be disjointed mannikens of a marionette show responding to the careless handling of a drunken showman. . . . The war ended. In the period of economic and social readjustment that followed, new ideals, new concepts, and a new outlook were evident among the youth of the world.[37]

This evocative portrait is quoted from a history of the founding of the Institutional Synagogue that appeared in the Twentieth Anniversary Souvenir Program of 1937. Just as the Jewish Welfare Board (JWB) had created religious centers and YMHAs in the army camps, the newly aroused generation would emerge from wartime to create analogous institutions at home during peacetime—a development fostered by the postwar JWB. As we shall soon see, the YMHA movement was instrumental in the formation of the Institutional Synagogue. It was most directly associated with the war by Isaac Siegel, cofounder with Rabbi Goldstein, when he later stated with patriotic pride (though with dubious accuracy): "The Institutional Synagogue was founded on the very day this nation entered the World War."[38]

Above all other factors, however, Goldstein was influenced by the contemporary Jewish milieu. In October 1916 (soon after the publication of his article), in private conversation with his wife and in-laws, Goldstein discussed his intention to organize a synagogue-center movement. "Herbert," his wife wrote, "has decided to launch his plans at once because the Institutional Synagogue idea is very much in the air now and Herbert thinks he ought to start it before somebody steals a march on him." Consciously competing with Mordecai Kaplan's Jewish Center movement on the West Side, he began by sending copies of his article to potential supporters in the Harlem community. He knew that to succeed, he needed a lay partner, someone of stature in the community. In November he attended the founding dinner of the Jewish Center where he attempted to convince Judge Otto Rosalsky to head his rival movement. Rosalsky demurred, but three days later Goldstein met with Congressman Isaac Siegel to broach the subject. Siegel, president of the Harlem YMHA, responded enthusiastically and became the cofounder and leading layman of the Institutional Synagogue.[39]

Though rebuffed by the Jewish philanthropic elite, Goldstein and Siegel received encouragement from I. E. Goldwasser, an official of the Council of Young Men's Hebrew and Kindred Associations. Goldwasser promised them "the cooperation of this body for the IS movement." Siegel next brought a delegation of his YMHA boys to see Rabbi Goldstein to express their interest in affiliating; shortly afterward, a group of boys from the Young People's Hebrew Orthodox League (founded at the Harry Fischel West Side Annex of the Uptown Talmud Torah in 1915) met with Goldstein for the same purpose. The league, an uptown version of the Young Israel, had distinguished itself through the formation of model synagogue services. Rabbi Goldstein, while still based in Yorkville, had been "elected Honorary President of the League in recognition of his constant encouragement of its activities." By amalgamating the YMHA and the YPHOL, therefore, the Institutional Synagogue united the efforts of a YMHA leader and a youth-oriented rabbi, and repeated the experience of other lay-rabbinic combined projects.[40]

The initial meeting of the Institutional Synagogue took place on March 6, 1917, and Goldstein later recalled, "the audience consisted of the membership of the Harlem YMHA and the Young Men's Hebrew Orthodox League. The purpose of the meeting was to amalgamate these two bodies and get them to pledge their allegiance and support to the Institutional Synagogue." That purpose was achieved by March 25 when Isaac Siegel wrote: "We have . . . amalgamated both organizations into the Institutional Synagogue." The new institution was thus a direct outgrowth of the YMHA and young people's synagogue movements. As Mordecai Kaplan later stated more bluntly, "The Institutional Synagogue was a religious 'Y.'[41]

One widely disseminated founding statement of the Institutional Synagogue emphasized its intention to reestablish the centrality of the synagogue in the Jewish community—implying, of course, that the synagogue had lost that distinction: "The Institutional Synagogue, established and incorporated in 1917, is an attempt to answer in a concrete way the problem of the function of the Synagogue in modern Jewish life." The problem of the function of the synagogue was that it seemed to have no function at all in modern society; the narrowly defined, purely religious synagogue held little if any attraction for the younger generation. The quote therefore continues: "The central idea of the Institutional Synagogue is that the Synagogue of today must become the Jewish community center which it was in former periods of Jewish history. It must be not only a house of worship, but must gather under its roof all forms of communal activities, ranging from the relief of the poor to the recreation and education of the youth." Without the added appeal of youth activities and social services, the synagogue would die. Hence the statement concludes: "The Institutional Synagogue has accordingly encouraged the organization of a Y.M.H.A."[42]

For Herbert Goldstein, moreover, the Institutional Synagogue represented the flagship of a Jewish revival movement and his own opportunity for fame and glory. He announced his intention to resign from Kehilath Jeshurun in his Passover sermon, cleverly linking his decision to the seasonal theme of rebirth and renewal (the unspoken subtext was, of course, liberation from slavery). Though the congregation reacted with shock, the announcement was greeted with excitement by the greater community. Like (Stephen S.) Wise and Magnes before him, Goldstein's willingness to abandon a prestigious position (actually two: KJ and CJI) impressed many with his idealism and individualism. Such qualities may have enabled him to strike out on his own, though the material support he enjoyed certainly played a part. The first organizational meeting was held two weeks after Goldstein's announcement and was soon followed by the purchase of the Institutional Synagogue's first building at 112 West 116th Street. The donor remained anonymous at the time, but Goldstein later admitted that it was his generous father-in-law, Harry Fischel.[43]

While the building was being remodeled as a synagogue-center, the Institutional Synagogue held its activities in the nearby YWHA on West 110th Street, a community center that included on its premises a synagogue and a swimming pool. It was incorporated on October 30, 1917, and when the first services in the new building took place a few days later, "the synagogue was packed to the doors." The new institution proved an immediate success. To accommodate the crowds that flocked to its "monster revival meetings," it began to rent public halls such as the Regent and Mount Morris theaters, where audiences of more than one thousand heard Goldstein's Billy Sunday–like sermons and mass appeals for membership. In 1918, accordingly, the Institutional Synagogue bought a larger building a few blocks away, the former Columbia Typewriter Building at 37–43 West 116th Street. The construction firm responsible for both the Central Jewish Institute and the Jewish Center was hired to renovate the building, and the architect chosen was B. Levitan. The latest structure was planned to contain the following amenities: an auditorium, classrooms, club rooms, game rooms, a library, reading room, kindergarten and nursery, gymnasium, social rooms with a radio and Victrola, a kitchen, dining room, chess room, swimming pool, steam room, showers, basketball courts, handball courts, roof garden, bowling alleys, and tennis courts. With the exception of the last three, all were eventually built.[44]

Not insignificantly, the new location was directly across the street from another synagogue, the First Hungarian Congregation Ohab Zedek. Though prestigious by virtue of its rabbi, Philip Hillel Klein, and its "world famous" chazan, Yosele Rosenblatt, Ohab Zedek was an Orthodox community synagogue of the older type. In 1908, the young Isaac Siegel had led a community protest against the elitist policies of the established synagogue. Ten years later, "barely a month after the Institutional Synagogue bought its new and huge building on 116th Street," the board of Ohab Zedek met with Siegel and Rabbi Goldstein to propose amalgamating the two institutions. Despite its former luster, the Ohab

Zedek synagogue was then in decline; whereas the star of the Institutional Synagogue was on the rise, and so the offer was turned down. The leadership clearly
understood that their institution represented an advance beyond the landsmanshaft shuls and the cantorial synagogues of the immigrant generation. Built for a
new generation of American Jews, the Institutional Synagogue was something
else again: a synagogue-center.[45]

In its first several years of existence, the Institutional Synagogue set a frantic
pace of organization and activity, including in its program: membership and
fund-raising campaigns, Friday night forums and guest lectures, a modern Hebrew School and Hebrew High School, adult education and vocational classes,
and a myriad of clubs and extracongregational societies. By 1926, the Harlem
synagogue-center had reached its apogee and began to plan its move to the West
Side. The change reflected more than a shift of population and the decline of
Jewish Harlem, however. Orthodox Judaism in America was on the decline—despite its ongoing modernization and various attempts to stem the tide (for example, the founding of Yeshiva College)—and with it, the Orthodox synagogue-
center. Rather than engendering duplication, the Institutional Synagogue
followed the general trend to settle in more fashionable areas, where many new
synagogue-centers would be established independent of its influence. The new
synagogue-centers would only rarely be modeled after the modern Orthodoxy of
Herbert Goldstein, but far more often after the Reconstructionist-Conserva-
tivism of Mordecai Kaplan. It was Kaplan, to whom we now turn, who inspired a
new movement and heralded a new era. Though Goldstein's institution appeared
simultaneously with Kaplan's Jewish Center, it ought to be seen as the culmination of a process rather than a new beginning. It was, in fact, the end result of the
half-century evolution of East European immigrant Judaism on American soil:
from landsmanshaft shul and heder, to the community synagogue and Talmud
Torah, to the youth synagogue and Jewish school-center, and finally, to the all-
inclusive modern Orthodox synagogue-center, as exemplified by the Institutional Synagogue of Herbert Goldstein.[46]

Mordecai M. Kaplan and the Jewish Center

The origination of the synagogue-center idea is most often attributed to Mordecai M. Kaplan, who is furthermore credited as the prime mover of the synagogue-
center movement. As I have argued, however, the social-religious synthesis arose
prior to and apart from Kaplan's personal involvement, which raises the question
of his rightful place in the history of the synagogue-center. Indeed, a minority of
scholars have viewed his supposed innovation with a degree of skepticism. In his
1955 study of Conservative Judaism, Marshall Sklare remarked: "Some think of
Kaplan and his group as leading a movement, but in reality their role was confined chiefly to reflecting some of the contemporary developments." Likewise,

Mel Scult has written: "Kaplan's contribution, which lies in the realm of ideology, should not be confused with the actual beginnings of synagogue-centers, which resulted from efforts by Kaplan and others."[47]

And yet, leaving ideological contributions aside for the moment, Kaplan's role in the history of the synagogue-center was significant in at least three ways beyond his involvement in "the actual beginnings of synagogue-centers." First of all, Mordecai Kaplan was teacher, mentor, and inspiration to an entire generation of American congregational rabbis. He became principal of the Teachers Institute in 1909, and one year later, professor of homiletics at the Jewish Theological Seminary. After Solomon Schechter's death in 1915, Kaplan would become a principal ideological influence in the Conservative movement. Throughout his long teaching career, he inculcated scores of future rabbis and Jewish educators with his uniquely sociological perspective. As he wrote in the opening entry of his journal in February 1913: "Religion is primarily a social phenomenon. To grasp its reality, to observe its workings, and to further its growth we must study its functioning in some social group." Hence his comment to the Morais-Blumenthal Society, suggesting that rabbis "must strive to make of the synagogue a social centre," was the logical outgrowth of his philosophy of Judaism. With admirable consistency, he would continue to recommend such innovation for many years to come. Most of his rabbinical students went on to become congregational rabbis in pulpits around the country, often creating new synagogue-centers in their adopted communities, and always remembering and giving due credit to their teacher, Mordecai Kaplan. This farflung inspiration may represent his most significant contribution to the synagogue-center movement.[48]

Second, Kaplan served as a one-man clearinghouse for nearly all the institutional trends then afloat in the American Jewish community. As a "thoroughly Americanized" rabbi he was inclined toward practical work and communal affairs, and had direct contact with several of the precedent movements described above. Though he was not instrumental in any one of them, he was involved with the YMHA, the founding of Albert Lucas's Jewish Centre and the model Talmud Torahs of the New York Kehillah, as well as in numerous examples of the emerging modern Orthodox and Conservative synagogue—all of which had their cumulative effect on his thinking. His experience spanned the entire denominational spectrum of Jewish religious life: serving as rabbi for an Orthodox congregation, teaching in the rabbinical seminary of the Conservative movement, and initiating his own "reform" movement in American Judaism. He even had some minimal contact with the proponents of classical Reform, sitting next to Emil G. Hirsch at a Chicago Rabbinical Association meeting in April 1917, and in lengthy discussions with Samuel Schulman of Temple Emanu-El in New York. His later projects would thus naturally reflect the coalescing of the various parallel trends he witnessed. Though Kaplan was not the source of the social-religious synthesis, he became its nexus, the flashpoint through which multiple tributaries flowed together to form one stream.[49]

And finally, Kaplan became the principal ideologist of the synagogue-center and deserves greater credit for championing the centrality of the synagogue at a time when its preeminence was being challenged by the Jewish school, settlement, and center. He did not invent the idea of a central Jewish institution, nor was he the first to innovate the merging of separate functions under one roof. He was not even the originator of the "synagogue as social center" concept; the earlier Reform temple center as well as the "Zionized" versions of Stephen Wise and Judah Magnes (the Free Synagogue and Magnes's Beth Am respectively) preceded his. Yet Kaplan was the first to insist that the synagogue remain the hub from which other communal functions derive. Only then might the synagogue fulfill its true purpose: the fostering of Jewish community. Herbert Goldstein gave popular expression to the notion that the Synagogue, Talmud Torah, and YMHA might be unified into one institution. Kaplan, on the other hand, did more than graft other institutions onto the synagogue; he recommended their full integration and interpenetration. He conceptualized an entirely new institutional form in which the synagogue would be transformed into a social center and the center would be imbued with a new religious emphasis. In this, Kaplan's first attempt to reconstruct Judaism, he erased the distinctions between social and religious Jewish life and blurred the lines between real and ideal. Due perhaps to the utopian reach of the vision, he never fully succeeded; yet in the attempt, he would play a major role in the emergence of the synagogue-center movement.

The most decisive influence on Mordecai Kaplan's conception of the synagogue-center may have been his negative experience at the YMHA. Just when the YMHA was about to enter its period of revival during and after the First World War, Kaplan became sorely disillusioned by the institution and lost his earlier optimism in its potential for the revitalization of Jewish life. In his private journal, he often vented his frustrations with the YMHA, as for example: "I feel so uninterested in YMHA work. . . . The whole institution is nothing but a toy to these rich men to amuse themselves with." Seated next to one of those wealthy benefactors (Felix Warburg) at a dinner for Judah Magnes's Society for the Advancement of Judaism, Kaplan reported: "He spoke for instance of what I did to improve the moral tone of young men in YMHA while I know that it amounts to practically nil." And at a meeting of YMHA directors (held a few weeks following the launching of the synagogue-center movement): "Every one of us spoke in glorious terms of YMHA work. I had the hardest time eking something out that would not amount to bald lying—for what can be said in favor of the work as it is actually carried on?"[50]

In the autumn of 1914, he described his exasperation with the YMHA religious services: "As for the services themselves they are so dull and monotonous that I can scarcely understand how they are tolerated by people who are constantly clamoring for change. It is composed of a hodgepodge of Hebrew and English, congregational responses that make one think he is in church, and renderings in traditional music with all the fancy voulades of the 'Elokenu ve-Elokei.'" Before Kaplan arrived on the scene, the YMHA "services were entirely of [the] same kind as are held in the reformed synagogues, with organ, etc." Though he derided such ineffectual imitations of Reform practice, his latest appointee as director of religious work, Aaron Robison (JTS, 1913), continued in the same vein: "Robinson [*sic*] has been at his wit's ends to get the young men of the building to attend the services. He has organized a choral union, to be led by the cantor Steinberg of Temple Beth El." Apparently, the addition of a choir was somewhat more effective, since in it there was "a preponderance of women, which means that the YMHA and religion have to introduce the feminine element to get the men to come. Maybe it is the way these matters have always had to be managed."[51]

In early 1915 Kaplan was invited to speak before "the first Sabbath afternoon services organized at the YMHA building" by the new religious director, Nathan Blechman (JTS, 1910). Apparently the attendance was not very encouraging; he complained in his journal that many young people go to the matinee on Saturday afternoon, and commented: "If some outlet for their social and intellectual desires were found that would be in keeping with the Jewish spirit, such violation of that spirit would not arise." Kaplan thus encountered one of the central challenges of his rabbinical career: how to socialize religion without degrading the synagogue to the level of a dancehall. He met with a similar problem earlier that year in Averne, New York, the preferred summer retreat of many of Kaplan's "all-rightnik" acquaintances in the bourgeois world of uptown Orthodoxy. Angered by the community's tolerance of a planned carnival to be held on Friday night and Saturday, he expressed his indignation in his guest sermon before the Averne congregation. Referring to Richard Cabot's *What Men Live By,* he declared that "the play of a people is its art and literature and social pleasures; . . . and the play [is fostered] by socializing the synagogue." He then cited the scandalous carnival "as proof of what happens when the synagogue fails to cultivate the play instinct and leaves it to be exploited by characterless men." Kaplan would learn this lesson well, both from the play-less Orthodox synagogue and the spirit-less YMHA services.[52]

In 1916 Kaplan seemed to become more positive in regard to the YMHA, as when he organized a group of religious Zionists to meet there every Saturday afternoon. Shortly thereafter a change in leadership encouraged him as well, leading him to comment: "[Judge Irving Lehman] differs from [Warburg] in a more genuine and intrinsic interest in Judaism as such, though, of course, he is far from being what may be called a Jewish Jew." His optimism was thus always tempered by sharp criticism of the YMHA and its proponents for not being Jewish enough, as at the annual convention of the YMH and Kindred Associations (held at the Central Jewish Institute): "I harped upon my old theme that the associations must be more Jewish in spirit, and that to do so they must resort to other means than holding Fri. night services or conducting Sunday School

Fig. 41. Rabbi Mordecai Kaplan as principal of the Teachers
Institute, 1915. Courtesy of the Library of the Jewish Theological Seminary of America.

classes for little children. . . . My constant hammering upon the need of having
our social institutions more Jewish may ultimately have some effect." By this period, however, Kaplan was looking beyond the YMHA and had begun formulating a new institution, the synagogue-center to be called the "Jewish Center." His
inspiration in the YMHA seems beyond doubt.[53]

For some time Kaplan had been testing his ideas in private conversation, urging acquaintances to embark upon the synagogue-center experiment. In his journal entry for April 10, 1915, he wrote:

For the last three or four years I have been urging Joseph H. Cohen to induce his friends to establish an institution that would not only provide a place of worship for the elders and a
school for the children but also an opportunity to all affiliated with it to develop their social
life Jewishly. . . . Cohen grasped my idea at once and took steps to have it realized. A little over
two years ago he called together at his house a number of people and invited me to explain to
them the kind of institution I wanted them to establish. In the meantime most of those who
were present had become pre-occupied with their own affairs, these years having been particularly strenuous, and the whole matter was left in abeyance. The various philanthropic and educational institutions in which Cohen and his friends are interested claimed all the attention
that they could devote to things Jewish, and so nothing further was heard about my scheme.[54]

The new institution would be neither a synagogue, nor a Jewish school, nor a social club like the YMHA, but rather, a combination of all three. The idea was one
of unification and simplification, meant to harmonize dissonant elements in the

cacophonic milieu of the contemporary Jewish community; as formulated by Kaplan it became the germination of the synagogue-center movement.

Yet the role played by Kaplan's close associate, Joseph H. Cohen, must not be underestimated. Cohen, a prominent businessman, served as friend, father figure, and perhaps in some sense, his alter ego. In early 1914 Kaplan had organized a private minyan/discussion group of his young disciples (later called the "Sabbath Afternoon Circle") and invited the elder Cohen to join, explaining, "Not that I expect to influence him in any way, but because he has a keen mind, and will act as a buffer to some of the wild tendencies in thought that are sure to break out from time to time." Kaplan thought so highly of Cohen that he grouped him with Judah Magnes as "the only people of all that I know who enable me to realize what a joy conversation can be,"[55] and even singled him out as "the most stimulating person in my circle of acquaintances." Cohen became Kaplan's link to the world of money and power, and paralleling Jacob Schiff's relationship to Judah Magnes, his patron and mentor. The cooperation between rabbi and businessman would be repeated time and again in the creation of synagogue-centers, all products of combined religious and secular interests.[56]

Whereas Kaplan provided the initial idea and the ideological rationale for the synagogue-center, Joseph H. Cohen was the organizer and guiding force of the project. Reminiscent of the biblical archetypes Moses and Aaron, theirs was a dual leadership, one partner in charge of practical matters, the other serving as spiritual second. Indeed, the American synagogue has historically followed the pattern in which the institution is conceived and built by a lay leadership who then hire a rabbi to serve "their" synagogue. Rather than yielding any real power to the rabbi, he is set up as a priestly figurehead, performing ceremonial and pastoral duties for the congregation.

Kaplan's similarly passive role in the creation of the Jewish Center is revealed in the words he used to introduce the new subject in his journal: "I find myself at the beginning of a new spiritual enterprise which holds out great promise. The very opening up of a new vista of possibilities is exhilarating. I refer to the new movement that has been started by some of my friends on the West Side to establish a Jewish communal centre." He would later add, "of course Cohen is the actual mover in the entire affair." At the cornerstone-laying ceremony, he reported the words of William Fishman: "The only man who had a right to lay the cornerstone was Cohen, since he was the one to whose inspiration the center owed its coming into existence." And still later, when disillusioned with the Jewish Center, Kaplan wrote: "I realize every day more clearly that the Center is nothing but a one man institution, J. H. Cohen being the man."[57]

In March 1915, at the Magnes dinner mentioned earlier, Kaplan was elated to discover that "suddenly the undertaking was revived." Meeting Cohen, William Fishman, and Abe Rothstein at the dinner, he was informed "that they had organized, and were determined to carry out the plan of having the kind of institution that I had been dreaming of." Kaplan and the group began to stay in touch regularly, discussing how Kaplan might identify with "the movement." Their initial deliberations betrayed a clash between his thinking and the outlook of the Center's founders, and foreshadowed the ideological differences that ultimately would lead to his departure. His insistence on the principle of *klal yisrael,* the indivisibility of the Jewish people, was clearly at odds with the intentions of the lay leaders to create an Orthodox, sectarian institution. Kaplan's stated ambition to "Judaize a greater fraction of the Jew's life" meant little to men who were creating an enclave of traditionalist Judaism and would thereby feel their religious obligations fulfilled. Kaplan, furthermore, was interested in undertaking a bold new venture in Jewish religious methods, whereas the lay group was notably less adventurous, fearing criticism from the greater community. Lastly, Kaplan acknowledged his debt to church experiments in social religion, which, though benign to his ecumenical mind, likely held a negative connotation of "goyish" influence to his more parochial friends.[58]

The plans for the new institution proceeded slowly. In May 1915, the same month as the cornerstone laying of "the 85th St. Yorkville Jewish Institute and Talmud Torah" (the CJI), Kaplan "met with Judge [Otto] Rosalsky and Abraham Landau to draw up the preamble to the constitution of the Jewish Communal Centre of the West Side." Judging from Kaplan's comments at the time, it appears that he viewed the West Side Centre and the East Side CJI in similar terms. He noted the opposition of Samuel Hyman who was afraid of the Centre's competition with his CJI; and at the cornerstone-laying ceremony, he remarked that it "marked the inauguration of a new method in Jewish life," a comment that could have applied to one as easily as the other. At one point he even flirted with the idea of heading both institutions simultaneously.[59]

Note also that Kaplan does not yet refer in his journal to the institution as the "Jewish Center." In fact, he persists in using the phrase in its Ahad Ha'amist sense of a central Jewish community in Palestine; not until several months later does he employ the term in its Jewish institutional sense. In October 1915, Kaplan tells us, he was invited to "Joseph H. Cohen's place of business to look over the plans for a building of the Jewish Center of the West Side." (There is some indication that he felt uncomfortable with the transposition. In the entry for June 18, 1916, he first writes "the Community Centre on the West Side," but upon second thought crosses out the word "Community" and substitutes "Jewish.") The new nomenclature may have been supplied by William Fishman and/or Otto Rosalsky, leading figures in the West Side Jewish Center movement, and both of whom, a decade before on the Lower East Side, had been officers of the Jewish Centres Association of Albert Lucas. Of course, as noted earlier, Mordecai Kaplan himself had been present at the first public meeting of the association in May of 1906.[60]

At the October 1915 meeting Cohen told Kaplan "to be prepared to take the position of [spiritual] leader as soon as the building would be completed." It was also at that time that he began a series of articles in the *Menorah Journal* on "The

Meaning of Judaism." In the fifth and concluding article, appearing in June 1916, he expounded upon "The True Functions of the Synagogue." In this, his first public statement of the synagogue-center idea, Kaplan declared:

In order that there shall be no mistake as to the spirit and motive of the social autonomy which Jews should cultivate, and that there shall not be the slightest reason to suspect it of un-Americanism, it must center about the Synagogue. America rightly resents all social autonomy that is not lifted to the plane of religion. Thus the function of the Synagogue will appear in a new light. . . . It should become a social centre where the Jews of the neighborhood may find every possible opportunity to give expression to their social and play instincts. It must become the Jew's second home. It must become his club, his theatre and his forum.[61]

One might conclude from this passage that Kaplan was less interested in the religious potential of the synagogue-center than in its social function. The Jewish community center must be configured as a synagogue, he seems to suggest, to stave off accusations of ethnic separatism. The "synagogue," functioning as a community center, would retain its name only to maintain the appearance of religiosity. Can it be that Kaplan had rejected the synagogue per se? More likely, the statement reflects his awareness that the secularist intellectuals of the *Menorah Journal* had mostly abandoned the synagogue and would need a new rationale for the continuance of what they regarded as a vestigial institution. Kaplan's pitch to this readership was that the synagogue, however defined, is the most effective guarantor of cultural pluralism. Moreover, it is the first instance of his defense of the synagogue as a viable institution, and his advocacy of the synagogue-center as the heart of the Jewish community.

At the same time, the Jewish Center movement began to pick up steam. On June 18, 1916, Kaplan wrote in his journal: "After the lapse of many months during which I had heard nothing about it, the undertaking came to life again. The organization purchased ground on West 86th St. J. H. Cohen put himself again in touch with me with a view to have me take charge of the institution when it was completed." Ironically, at this pivotal moment Kaplan ruled out his own participation in the new enterprise: "In the meantime, I have practically come to the conclusion that I could not give up either the Institute or the Seminary for the West Side Institution, particularly for the reason that I can not have it conducted the way I should like to see it conducted. Cohen has been trying hard to sway me." Apparently Cohen was persuasive, for in August Kaplan was appointed chairman of the "Plan and Scope Committee of the West Side Centre," and took part in a meeting of the "Jewish Center" organization in October; in the following month he delivered the keynote address at the founding banquet, held at the Hotel Astor.[62]

At the beginning of 1917, Kaplan reported that "the Jewish Center movement has made considerable progress the last few months." Though he alluded to the specific project on the Upper West Side of Manhattan, he may as well have been referring to the general synagogue-center movement. In September 1916, Rabbi Herbert Goldstein, then director of the Central Jewish Institute, published his article "The Institutional Synagogue." Exactly six months later, an organizational meeting was held in Harlem and Goldstein's synagogue-center was founded. Though it was related to developments in the YMHA movement and in American Orthodoxy, the effort came on the heels of the Jewish Center initiative and was clearly inspired by Kaplan's precedent-setting idea.[63]

In the meantime, planning for the West Side institution was advancing steadily. Attending a meeting of the building committee in February 1917, Kaplan commented on the "remarkable evolution" of the plans, the height of the building having increased from four to nine stories. He further noted: "It is surprising to see men whom one would judge as out and out materialists—except Cohen and Fischman—spend so much time upon an undertaking that can bring them no material advantage." We may make the opposite observation regarding a rabbi, a spiritual leader, so concerned with the physical plant of the synagogue. Kaplan answered this in May 1918, when the building of the Jewish Center, then open for services, stood only partly constructed. Lamenting the unbuilt state of floors which were to include the gymnasium, club rooms, and swimming pool, he wrote: "The entire purpose of the Center, which is that of illustrating how Judaism can be lived to some extent as a civilization instead of merely as a religion, would be frustrated if those other stories should remain unbuilt."[64]

In April 1917 America entered the World War, but still the Jewish Center project continued apace. Present at the groundbreaking on May 22, 1917, Kaplan captured the import of the moment:

This morning at 8:30 I participated in the ceremony of groundbreaking of the Jewish Center on the West Side. It was to me a thrilling experience to watch the Italian laborers . . . getting ready . . . to start building, while the passersby were hurrying to their shops and offices entirely unmindful of the spiritual significance of what we were doing. It could never have occurred to them that the ancient spirit of Israel was once again seeking a foothold. . . . The few men who have made the Jewish Centre possible and who were on the grounds were at that moment simply obeying a mysterious impulse within them which has been driving them on to make every effort to perpetuate the life of Israel. Do they themselves realize the nature and the direction of this impulse? Perhaps one or two of them. But it makes no difference. They are the tools of a will not their own and higher than their own.[65]

On August 5, he "participated in the exercises of the cornerstone laying of the Jewish Center." His remarks at the occasion, recollected in his journal, were "devoted to the further clarification of the ideal which is about to be embodied in brick and mortar." In no uncertain terms, he asserted the uniqueness and the significance of the new institution: "The Jewish Center is intended . . . to be different from any of the institutions with which we are apt to class it. We don't want the Jewish Center to be a rich man's club, with a religious chapel in one part of the building. . . . Neither do we want merely to establish a house of worship. There are plenty of synagogue[s] within easy walking distances that are more than half empty. . . . We have established a Jewish center that shall enable us to live together as Jews, because living together as Jews is an indispensable condition to Jewish Religion. Before we can have Judaism we must have Jewishness."[66]

In the course of his remarks, Kaplan singled out the Zionists as "the only Jews who realize the danger [of assimilation]. They are doing all they can to prevent the disappearance of the Jews by striving to obtain for the Jewish people a legally secure homeland." In an intriguing metaphor, Kaplan then linked his own initiative to the Zionist enterprise: "To make sure that the soldier will reach the base hospital alive you need a field hospital. Jewish centers are to Palestine what a field hospital is to the base hospital." Kaplan thereby took the earlier idea of a "Zionist synagogue" a step ahead. The earlier experiments had brought Zionism into the synagogue by redefining Jewish nationalism as a religious ideology and by reconceptualizing the synagogue as a "house of Jewish peoplehood." Kaplan went further still in drawing a direct parallel between the synagogue and Zionism, describing his project as a microcosm of the Zionist dream. The new institution would itself become a diasporic "Jewish center" to precede and help prepare for the establishment of the main center in Palestine. The object of both "centers" would remain the same: the preservation of Jewish life, and consequently, of Judaism.[67]

The connection between Judaism and Zionism became an issue of wider concern in the years following the World War, especially after the issuance of the Balfour Declaration in November 1917. Even such non-Zionists as Jacob Schiff began to publicly declare that "if Zionism is to succeed, it must adopt Judaism." Along similar lines, JTS graduate (class of 1910) Jacob S. Minkin wrote in February 1918: "Between Judaism, as a religion of the synagogue and Zionism, there has always been a marked estrangement. The latter has always been a thing apart from the synagogue, and its leaders have in the past been only too ready to accentuate the cleavage. . . . Today to place Jewish nationalism outside of Judaism, would be to strangle Zionism at its very birth. Hard as it is to conceive a Zionless Judaism, still more absurd it is to plan a Judaism-less Zion. It is in the bosom of the synagogue where Zionism was born."[68]

Rabbi Minkin's article was the second in a series of three published by the *American Hebrew* in early 1918 that collectively announced the advent of a new movement. The first had appeared in the January issue and was titled: "The Institutional Synagogue—A New Movement in American Orthodoxy That is Meeting the Problem of the Jewish Youth." Intriguingly, it was signed simply "M.K." Assuming that the author was Mordecai Kaplan, we may surmise that he sought to maintain anonymity while describing a rival institution, the synagogue-center of Herbert Goldstein. Despite his personal dislike for Goldstein, Kaplan positively profiled the new Institutional Synagogue and thus lent support to a movement in which he, after all, had a great stake. In the short piece, Kaplan relates the synagogue-center idea to the earlier experiment of the Central Jewish Institute (which, incidentally, was profiled by the *American Hebrew* in the following month). He implies that Goldstein was influenced by his brief tenure at that institution and depicts the new Institutional Synagogue as the next logical step. The innovative aspect was the centrality of the synagogue within the overall scheme;

as he continues: "The Institutional Synagogue, which [Goldstein] founded some four months ago, in the heart of Harlem, represents the co-ordination of all communal activity—social, athletic, educational—under one roof with the synagogue as the permeating influence. No boy or girl, man or woman, may become a member of the institution unless he or she first becomes a member of the Synagogue. Thus the Synagogue becomes the root of all the Jewish life of the community, sympathetic to the needs of the American youth, the guard of his Jewishness."[69]

It was, of course, an idea that Kaplan was simultaneously promoting on the West Side. About the same time, he participated in the preparation of the *Jewish Communal Register of New York City, 1917–18,* a project of the Kehillah. In his contribution, a survey of synagogue affiliation, Kaplan recited a formula that would echo throughout the subsequent history of the American synagogue. Describing the traditional role of the synagogue in Jewish life, he stated: "It was *a house of prayer,* a 'beth tephillah,' *a house of study,* a 'beth ha'midrash,' and *a meeting house,* where communal undertakings were formulated, and, where all plans for the communal good were discussed and adopted." Kaplan thereby justified the threefold functional division of the new Institutional Synagogue by linking it with the historical synagogue. Its accuracy aside, the formula "house of prayer, house of study, and house of assembly" became the unoffical motto of the synagogue-center movement. It served both to define the main areas of activity of the synagogue program and to legitimate the multifunctionality of the synagogue-center innovation.[70]

The Jewish Center opened for services in January 1918 and was dedicated on March 20. Kaplan delivered the dedicatory address and immediately thereafter published the third of the articles in the *American Hebrew,* entitled "The Jewish Center" and signed "Prof. Mordecai M. Kaplan." With eloquence and passion, Kaplan offered his statement of purpose for the new institution, providing at the same time a manifesto for the new movement. In the statement, he once again insisted upon the uniqueness and novelty of the Jewish Center experiment:

We state frankly that we are establishing the Jewish Center for the purpose of deriving from it for ourselves pleasures of a social, intellectual, and spiritual character. We are not building a settlement, nor a communal center, nor a Young Men's or Young Women's Hebrew Association; nor do we expect the Jewish Center to be an institution for the doing of so-called uplift work. This time we feel that we are as much in need of being uplifted as they for whose benefit the city is dotted with communal institutions. . . . The Jewish Center will be dominated by a purpose of far-reaching significance, if we, who are about to establish it, will do so with the deliberate and conscious aim of conducting it as an experiment to help us solve the problem of Jewish life and religion. . . . For we shall attempt to conserve and develop Jewish life by a method hitherto untried. If we succeed, our method is sure to be adopted in every part of the world, wherever the problem of conserving and developing Jewish life is the same as ours.[71]

Kaplan emphasized the self-orientation of the Jewish Center in order to differentiate it from the prevalent philanthropic institutions founded by "uptown" Jews to "uplift" those less fortunate. For the first time, a Jewish recreational and educational center would serve the sponsors themselves, for they were in need of uplift themselves. To differentiate the self-centered institution from a posh social club, Kaplan emphasized its Jewish atmosphere and religious purpose. Expanding upon the synagogue formula of "prayer, study and assembly," he offered a new metaphor to explain the functions of the synagogue-center: "The elements which are indispensable to health in human life are four in number: atmosphere, light, food and exercise. Provide Jewish life with these constituents, and you will solve the problem of Judaism." To meet all the requirements for healthy Jewish living, the synagogue-center must supply: "atmosphere," or a Jewish environment; "light," interpreted as "entertainment and joy-giving recreations"; the "food" of Jewish knowledge; and "exercise," understood as the opportunity for "practical action." In other words, the Kaplanian synagogue-center is intended to provide a spatial context for Jewishness, a recreational center, an institute of Jewish education (for all ages), and a headquarters for social and political activism. The third item corresponds directly to the familiar notion of a "house of study," but the remaining functions of Jewish atmosphere, recreation, and activism are an elaboration of the simpler "house of assembly." Kaplan's preoccupation with the social aspects of Jewish life is thus reflected in three of the four elements of his new "method." Throughout the statement, he repeats the theme of creating a proper environment for Jewish life to flourish. In his theoretical "reconstruction of Jewish life," social context is everything.[72]

The vision was utopian, however, especially when applied to the realities of the Upper West Side Jewish community. As Kaplan complained in his journal in November 1917: "It is clear to me that with the exception of three or four people, most of those affiliated with the center have gone into the undertaking blindly. Some want a synagogue primarily, others want mainly a club. The length of time it has taken to put up the building has dampened the enthusiasm even of the few. Besides, the group is of the typically successful bourgeois type." The public statements surrounding the March 1918 dedication thus may be seen as an attempt to win over the congregation by offering a "program of Jewish life [that] will be big enough and heroic enough, to thrill our souls, to captivate our imagination and to hold our allegiance . . . a program that makes for the recuperation of Israel's health of spirit." Perhaps he even sought to convince himself. For at the very same time, just prior to the dedication of the Jewish Center and the publication of his manifesto, he confided: "During the last three weeks I have been quite miserable. I am adrift again, tossed hither and thither by contrary gusts of passionate anger and disappointment. I have severed my relations with the West Side Center." After the opening of Sabbath services two months earlier, Kaplan had quickly become disillusioned by the "policy of reaction" maintained by Joseph Cohen and reflected in the Orthodox character of the synagogue service.[73]

During that period of estrangement from the Jewish Center—the first of several—Kaplan returned to his earlier plan to establish a Zionist synagogue, changing its focus to that of a "Zionist Beth-Hamidrash." He organized a group of his younger friends and thought to initiate a new institution, commenting that "they, no less than the community of the Jewish Center, are in need of a center where they could develop common social artistic and intellectual interests—a kind of club, except that with them the ultimate purpose of such intercourse would never be lost sight of, but made the basis of their principal activities." At a subsequent meeting he suggested changing the name to "Society for Jewish Culture," which later evolved to become the "Society for the Advancement of Judaism," the name of Kaplan's second synagogue-center enterprise.[74]

For the next four years, however, he would lurch back and forth between serving as the spiritual leader of the Jewish Center and severing his attachment altogether, preferring to "concentrate on studying and writing" in lieu of joining the political fray of the New York Jewish community. The final break came in early 1922, when he resigned from the Jewish Center to organize the Society for the Advancement of Judaism. Years later, Kaplan still harbored resentment toward the Center community when he wrote: "The people, however, whom I succeeded in getting to establish the first Jewish Center were unable to grasp the significance of the new experiment in Jewish living." Yet, in a sense, Kaplan himself was unable to grasp the power of the synagogue-center idea; he misunderstood its capacity to spread on its own without the philosophical comprehension of its adherents. In 1920, he wrote: "How great an amount of misdirected energy would have been saved if those who have built up synagogues had been shown that the future of many a congregation has been compromised by the failure to provide social and recreational facilities in the synagogue itself." By that time, however, the idea had begun to spread of its own accord.[75]

At the same time, Kaplan's 1917 innovation had one somewhat surprising consequence: the revivification of the Jewish (community) center movement. As we have seen, the Jewish center movement had its roots in the histories of the YMHA, the Jewish settlement, and the modern Talmud Torah. During the World War period the idea found great appeal among the army-age, American-born generation, and a national movement was formed, coordinated by the Jewish Welfare Board (succeeding the earlier CYMHKA). Kaplan's influence stemmed from both his well-publicized institution—listed in the *American Jewish Yearbook* of 1919–20 as the "Jewish Social Center"—as well as from his writings, which gave inspiration to many young social workers in search of Jewish rationale. But communal centers lacking the religious focus of the synagogue were not what he had in mind. Although in some part inspired by him, it is thus inaccurate to ascribe the secular "Jewish Center" movement to Mordecai Kaplan.[76]

He seemed to acknowledge this himself when he wrote, in his 1934 magnum opus: "Before 1918, the very term 'Jewish center' as applied to a local institution was scarcely known in the vocabulary of Jewish life. Since then, Jewish centers have been springing up in every important Jewish community. . . . In 1930, the Jewish Welfare Board included 308 constituent organizations which for the most part maintained communal centers. . . . These institutions then ministered to a membership of over 300,000. . . . All this activity was developed within little more than a decade. . . . *A phenomenon such as this calls for explanation.*" The explanation he supplied was not his own genius but an "inherent factor of conservation" in Jewish life; namely, the survivalist battle against assimilation and intermarriage. But Kaplan's Jewish Center was intended as something more than a Jewish social club where young men and women might meet. Created as a congregational entity and intended to revolve around a synagogal hub, the West Side Jewish Center was a synagogue-center and, as such, became the prototype for a new movement in American Jewish life. Like its secular counterpart, the new synagogue-center movement was also called the Jewish Center movement, causing much confusion—both for contemporaries and for the historian. The confusion will be abated somewhat as we next trace the course of a movement, from Kaplan's Jewish Center to the Brooklyn Jewish Center to the East Midwood Jewish Center to the Ocean Parkway Jewish Center and so on.[77]

Conclusion

Four individual rabbis were highlighted in this chapter: Phineas Israeli, Charles Hoffman, Herbert Goldstein, and Mordecai Kaplan. All four studied at the Jewish Theological Seminary during the years 1900–1915, and all went on to become English-speaking, youth-oriented congregational rabbis. All certainly knew one another, and more important, were part of the same American Jewish milieu. They, like their many colleagues spread across the country, grappled with similar problems of synagogue life. The solution, as Goldstein's wife put it, was "in the air": the rabbis would approach the problem scientifically, treating the synagogue as an extension of people and their wants. Or, as Kaplan put it, as a human life in need of "atmosphere, light, food and exercise." "Atmosphere," according to Kaplan, meant "Jewish spirit," and the young rabbis certainly had a well-developed religious sensibility—Solomon Schechter had seen to that. "Light" meant the "joys of Jewish life," and here the very youthfulness of both the rabbis and the rising generation of American Jews guaranteed that social and recreational pleasures would be on the program. "Food" referred to the nourishment of knowledge, and what Seminary man was not fully committed to the importance of Jewish schooling? Last, "exercise" could apply to either Jewish philanthropic or political "action." These were all the firm commitments of a new generation of rabbis—a generation that would breathe life into the American synagogue by projecting its own commitments onto the institution, making it a healthful "center" of Jewish life.

7

MOVEMENT
The Synagogue-Center Movement of the 1920s

Working with the Building Committee, the architects have co-ordinated as one. All have been imbued with responsibility placed upon them and filled with enthusiasm knowing that the results will be worthy of their untiring efforts and labor. When the final nail is driven, all are looking forward to see in the new Temple another monument to all those that have labored and made it possible, and there will be one more contribution to the Jewish community of Boston and another tangible evidence of the present renaissance of Judaism in America.

—JACOB FREDERICK KROKYN
(of Krokyn, Browne, and Rosenstein, Architects), 1923[1]

AT THE HEIGHT of the synagogue-center movement, an architect named Nathan Myers proposed a new design for Temple B'nai Jeshurun of Newark, New Jersey. Myers pointed to one feature of his design in particular, ingeniously intended to satisfy two needs of the congregation at once: "The social centre hall is provided with motion picture booth, and the picture screen is on one side of a revolving partition, the other side being provided with a small cabinet for the scrolls when the hall is used for devout services." Though the somewhat humorous scheme (were they planning on selling popcorn at services?) was never put into effect, it reveals the sympathy the Jewish architect felt for his client. It is hard to imagine a gentile architect recommending a reversible movie screen/*aron kodesh* (holy ark) to Jews wishing to build a new synagogue. Only another Jew would have had the chutzpah![2]

One wonders what the rabbi had to say. We do know, however, that hundreds of rabbis during the 1920s did sign on enthusiastically to the ambitious building projects of their congregations. It was a fortuitous convergence of interests. Just at the time that rabbis began to articulate a "theology" promoting the expansion of the synagogue, laymen across the country began to lay plans for the same. They saw their schemes in more concrete, even materialistic terms, of course, but that did not stop them from joining with their rabbis to build synagogue-centers. In fact, the confluence of rabbinic and lay interests is precisely what fueled the movement. Often alienated by their disparate worldviews, here at last was a project that could unite the two: a synagogue for the rabbis and a center for the people, all in one! Meshing the "inspiration" of the one with the "perspiration" of the other, a movement was born.

But such collaboration invites disharmony. From the start, the synagogue-center movement of the 1920s was compromised by internal conflict between laymen and rabbis, rabbis and social workers, and what might be called "synagogue people" and "center people." The nationwide drive to create synagogue-centers thus took two distinct paths. One was the "elite" ideological movement that drew upon the precedent set by Kaplan in New York City. The other was the inchoate trend of synagogue-center construction by the "folk." In the first instance, congregational rabbis and Jewish social workers provided the institutional rationale for the newly built synagogue-centers, often deriving their ideas from Mordecai Kaplan. It was on this level, too, that most debate took place. Just as rabbis were the first to openly champion the synagogue-center, they were also the first to criticize the innovation. Yet, it was not the rabbi who initiated most synagogue-center projects, but the laity. While Kaplan's name was sometimes invoked by the builders in order to legitimate their new institutions, the movement to construct synagogue-centers resulted primarily from socioeconomic factors rather than from theoretical formulations.

The ideological and socioeconomic (that is, "religious" and "social") roots of the synagogue-center are not mutually exclusive, of course, but they do reveal the differing motivations of synagogue-center creators. Rabbis, on the one hand, were swayed by the Judaizing potential of the synagogue-center. Many of these same religious ideologues later balked at what they perceived as the rampant secularization of the synagogue. Laymen, on the other hand, tended to see the synagogue-center in more pragmatic terms: as a means to "sell" the masses on synagogue membership, and even more critically, to "lure" straying youth back into the fold of the Jewish community. Despite their earnest intentions, these same balabatim never quite understood the conceptual link between the synagogue and the swimming pool they had fused together. Yet despite the absence of a common vision, rabbis and their congregants continued to build "Jewish Centers" throughout the 1920s. The extent of their cooperation reflected the extent to which their institutions synthesized the social and religious emphases.

The synagogue-center movement spread primarily through a broad-based, grassroots effort on the part of lay Jews around the country—not the rabbinic elite but the common folk, the amcha of American Judaism. Jews throughout America engaged in a flurry of synagogue-center construction in the postwar era, due, first of all, to the continued growth of the Jewish population. During the decade 1916–26, approximately three hundred thousand immigrant Jews entered the United States, bringing the total Jewish population to more than four million (an increase of 92.6 percent, as compared to increases of 40.5 percent for the preceding decade [1906–16], and 19.6 percent for the subsequent period [1926–36]). During the same period, the number of Jewish congregations nearly doubled, jumping from 1,619 to 3,118. The size of congregations also increased dramatically, from an average membership of only 221 in 1916 to more than 1,300 a decade later. Understandably, the number of new synagogue structures grew as well, more than doubling from 874 to 1,782 in 1926. Within a few short years the number would rise to more than two thousand. The new synagogues, costing an average $85,816, reflected a total expenditure of nearly $78 million. While some of this represents the acquisition of older properties, the majority of it went to finance the construction of new buildings. The characteristic institution of all this building activity was, of course, the synagogue-center.[3]

Still, some more elaborate explanation than population growth alone must be advanced as the moving force behind the synagogue building boom of the 1920s. As implied above, the more convincing argument would rely upon a complex set of socioeconomic and demographic factors. Samuel Abelow thus wrote: "The popularity of the Center was the result of a combination of circumstances. It was organized at a time when the Jews were making a great deal of money in real estate, business, in law and medicine, and the members wanted to develop an exclusive circle. The high membership fee appealed to this clientele."[4]

In May 1932, the executive director of the Jewish Welfare Board, Harry L. Glucksman, delivered a paper before the Rabbinical Assembly of the Conservative movement. It was an insightful review of a movement with which he had intimate familiarity, entitled simply "The Synagogue Center." Glucksman noted "the rapidity with which the idea seemed to spread, unstimulated by any organized propaganda," and attributed the phenomenon to the general economic prosperity following the World War, as well as to three more specific causes: (1) The postwar "resumption of peace time activity, [when] many new communal enterprises were launched, among them new congregations"; (2) "the migration of populations, within the cities, from old sections to newer areas of residence"; and (3) the "movement from congested urban neighborhoods to suburban communities which created the need for entirely new institutions." Regarding the movement itself, he continued: "In most instances where new buildings were planned, they were denominated as Synagogue Centers or Jewish Centers. It was practically a daily occurrence to read in the Jewish press of a projected Synagogue or Jewish Center structure. It would not have been an unreasonable deduction from these announcements that the Synagogue, especially the Conservative Synagogue, to some extent the Reform Temple, to a much lesser extent the Orthodox Synagogue, was reorganizing in terms of the Center concept. Millions of dollars were expended upon stone and mortar. Expectations ran high. Both Rabbis and laymen looked forward hopefully to the results."[5]

In addition to population growth, therefore, the growth of the synagogue-center movement might be attributed to the coincidence of several phenomena: Jewish social mobility, demographic shifts to new areas, postwar prosperity, and factors not mentioned before: the 1920s boom in real estate and the advent of a generation of Jewish developers, buildings, and architects. Just as traditional Jewish life had been translated into secular American terms (in education, for instance), the reverse process then came into play; the newfound creative capacity to acquire property, build apartment houses, and lay out entirely new neighborhoods, was translated by Jewish builders into the "spiritual" endeavor of erecting monuments to Judaism and Jewish life—the synagogue-center.

In earlier chapters I described prominent synagogue-centers in New York City, Chicago, Philadelphia, Boston, Cleveland, Baltimore, Newark, Detroit, Cincinnati, and other important Jewish communities. In each of these population centers, the synagogue-center phenomenon followed the path of new Jewish settlement. Chicago, with a Jewish population of nearly three hundred thousand, was the second largest community after New York. The 1920s saw the development of multiple new areas of settlement; hence the construction of new synagogue-centers, as for example the South Shore Temple, established in September 1922, "to provide a place of worship and a community social center for the rapidly growing Jewish community in the new South Shore district." Its range of social activities, including "a library and club-rooms, gymnasium, and the like," was expressly intended "to make the South Shore Temple a prime factor for Jewishness in its territory, thus adding another unit to the group of influential congregations on the South Side."[6]

The Philadelphia Jewish community was a close third behind Chicago, and it too became an important locale for the synagogue-center movement. One prominent example was the all-purpose Edward L. Rothschild Memorial Building, dedicated by Congregation Beth-El on April 10, 1927. The three-storied building contained, on the ground floor, "the chapel, where daily services are held, also classrooms and club rooms, and offices," on the second floor, "eight class rooms, spacious, airy and light, and equipped with the most modern school equipment," and on the third, "a spacious auditorium where religious services are held and School Assemblies take place as well as entertainments, lectures, dances and meetings of the congregation, Sisterhood, Men's Club, banquets, and various communal functions are held. It is equipped with stage scenery with a kitchen, dressing rooms, coat room and moving picture booth." The congregation had been founded just twenty years earlier, having "its origin in a Sunday School that was started in 1907 in a private house." In 1915, the congregation was enabled to build a synagogue and school building by the bequest of Edward L. Rothschild, a former client of lawyer-turned-rabbi Charles Hoffman. Hoffman had sent Rothschild to visit the struggling congregation in the hope that he might come to its aid—and he did. He first gave them a synagogue, and a decade later, added a center.[7]

The synagogue-center trend was just as pronounced in medium-sized communities as in Boston, Cleveland, Baltimore, and Newark (all with Jewish communities of between 50,000–90,000 during the 1920s). In Newark, for example, the three leading congregations—B'nai Jeshurun, B'nai Abraham, and Oheb Shalom—all had built impressive new synagogue-centers by 1924. In 1927, the director of the Newark YM/YWHA (Aaron G. Robison, whom we met earlier as the religious director of the New York YMHA under the tutelage of Mordecai Kaplan) wrote: "The synagogue-center movement in Newark is a very strong one and it is only a question of time before all the major congregations will use their buildings as the social centers for their respective congregations." Newark, situated midway between New York and Philadelphia, was influenced of course by both cities; but interestingly, it too became influential. In part, the intensive Jewish life of Newark had produced several rabbis who would become active in the synagogue-center movement, most notably the brothers Jacob and Eugene Kohn.[8]

Another, lesser known example is Rabbi Samuel Felix Mendelsohn, who in early 1919 was called from Newark to a new pulpit in the Albany Park section of Chicago. Upon his arrival at Temple Beth Israel, he immediately organized a young people's auxiliary known as the "Temple Center," and was soon laying plans for a building to house its activities. After an intensive fund-raising effort of two years, construction began on "a temple and community center building, and the formal laying of the cornerstone took place on October 22, 1922." Mendelsohn was a Russian immigrant who grew up in Newark. He graduated from Hebrew Union College in 1917, the same year that Temple Beth Israel was established. Of course, it was also the same year in which the Jewish Center and the Institution Synagogue were established, yet one suspects that Mendelsohn was just as influenced by the synagogue-center activity of his hometown of Newark.[9]

One other reason for the influence of Newark was the local activity of two Jewish architects, Albert Gottlieb and Nathan Myers. Gottlieb, who worked out of an office in New York, had designed the monumental structure of Temple B'nai Jeshurun, the Reform congregation of Rabbi Solomon Foster. Dedicated in 1915, the building contained a spacious sanctuary, assembly room, and numerous classrooms. In the following year, he addressed the Central Conference of American Rabbis on the subject of "Synagog and Religious School Architecture," and later published a series of articles on the same subject. Gottlieb's main competitor in Newark was Nathan Myers, who designed the synagogue-center of Temple B'nai Abraham in 1924. In addition to the amenities mentioned above, Myers's integrated "Temple and Social Centre" included a gymnasium as well.[10]

Significantly, the new generation of American-born Jews included some architects in addition to the ranks of doctors, lawyers, accountants, and teachers. The Jewish architects were a new phenomenon on the American Jewish scene and played an important role in the synagogue-center movement. Their task would be to translate synagogue-center aspirations into three-dimensional form. Within the congregation, the key players in the process of planning and construction formed a "building committee"—a new kind of synagogue *hevra,* whose "spiritual advisor" was the architect. Beyond the individual congregation, the architects played yet another role in the movement. Like the rabbis on the ideological level, they helped spread the idea on the practical level. Seeking to convince uncertain building committees to undertake ambitious projects, they referred to the impressive examples of other buildings in other cities. By thus advertising the synagogue-center idea (for their own aggrandizement, admittedly) Jewish architects joined rabbis as harbingers of the movement.

To view the processes of influence and imitation in the synagogue-center movement more closely, we turn now to two case studies of particular communities. One, the Jewish community of Brookyn, New York, became ground zero for the movement in the wake of Mordecai Kaplan's uptown experiment. A key figure in the course of influence from Manhattan to Brooklyn was Rabbi Israel Levinthal, but as we shall discover, laymen played an even more significant role. The second case study is of Boston, more typical of other communities around the country. There, only the most affluent congregations succeeded in erecting synagogue-center structures, but the relationships between them—with each other, with other communities—betrays the workings of a grassroots movement. Our first stop, however, is the colorful borough of Brooklyn—home of the hot dog, Coney Island, Ralph Kramden, Jackie Robinson, a fantastic number of Jews, and, it might be said, the synagogue-center.

The Brooklyn Jewish Center Movement

In 1936, Rabbi Israel H. Levinthal uttered a statement that has been quoted many times since: "If the Synagogue as a *Beth Hatefilah* has lost its hold upon the masses, some institution would have to be created that could and would attract the people so that the group consciousness of the Jew might be maintained. The name center seems to work this magic with thousands who would not be attracted to the place if we simply called it Synagogue or Temple." A pioneer of the synagogue-center movement and the congregational rabbi "whose life intertwined thoroughly with that of the [Brooklyn Jewish] center," Israel Levinthal was well situated to comment on the effectiveness of the novel Jewish institution. His oft-quoted statement testifies to both an important impetus for the creation of the synagogue-center, the attempt of the synagogue to reclaim the disaffected and unaffiliated, as well as to its extraordinary popularity. Most revealing of all, however, is Levinthal's reference to the "magic" of the name. The institution succeeded, he implied, because it was something more than a synagogue; it was, at the same time, a "center."[11]

In his 1937 history of the Brooklyn Jewish community, Samuel Abelow included a chapter entitled "The Center Movement," surveying several prominent synagogue-centers of the 1920s: the Brooklyn Jewish Center (23 on map opposite), the East Midwood Jewish Center (26), The Ocean Parkway Center (25), and the Flatbush Jewish Center (24), and Congregation Shaare Torah; but these were only a few of the many synagogue-centers that covered the borough during the 1920s and after. The Jewish Center movement succeeded so phenomenally in

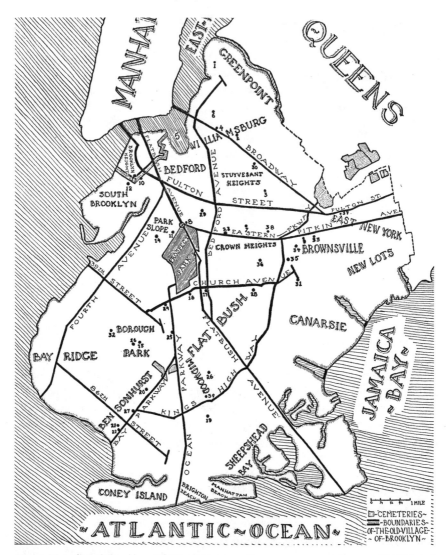

Fig. 42. Map of Jewish Brooklyn. Of 36 institutions noted, over 20 are synagogue-centers. *The Universal Jewish Encyclopedia* (New York: Funk & Wagnalls, 1939–43).

Brooklyn for a combination of two reasons. One was the explosive growth of its Jewish community during the interwar period. By 1923, Brooklyn was the New York City borough with the largest Jewish population, with 740,000 Jews compared to Manhattan's 706,000. By World War II, the fourth-largest city in America was home to nearly one million Jews, constituting the "largest Jewish community of any city in the history of the world." Second was the fragmented character of Brooklyn, made up of a myriad of distinct neighborhoods. As Israel Levinthal wrote in 1940: "The story of Brooklyn Jewry is made complex by the fact that communities developed in more than twenty-five villages and districts, independently and often simultaneously." Each newly developed area of Jewish settlement would need a focus of Jewish communal life, and the synagogue-center, for reasons we shall consider, recommended itself time and again.[12]

The first of them, the Brooklyn Jewish Center, has been called "the model Jewish Center of American Jewish life" and "the most well known prototype of the synagogue-center." The Brooklyn Jewish Center certainly led the way for the other congregations mentioned, though it was not the first such institution in Brooklyn. Fully two years prior to its organization at the start of 1919, a congregation calling itself the Jewish Communal Center of Flatbush was established "for the purpose of erecting a suitable communal center . . . [that] will have school rooms, a library, auditorium, a gymnasium and a synagogue." The Brooklyn Jewish Center would be more ambitious in terms of size and cost, but not in the originality of its program. In fact, the premier synagogue-center of Brooklyn was directly influenced by several precedent movements and institutions; it was anything but prototypical.[13]

The first source of influence was the Jewish Center of the West Side. In an early history of the Brooklyn Jewish Center, Joseph Goldberg notes the appearance in 1918 of "a new movement, the Jewish Center . . . launched by Professor Mordecai M. Kaplan," and further recalls the more direct link between the two Centers: "The President of [Kaplan's] Center was the late Joseph H. Cohen. His brother, Louis Cohen, also deceased, was then a recent arrival in the newly developed Jewish community of Eastern Parkway. He, together with Moses Ginsberg and Samuel Rottenberg, sponsored the organization of the Brooklyn Jewish Center." Louis Cohen, the principal founder of the Brooklyn Jewish Center, was directly exposed to the synagogue-center idea when he accompanied his brother Joseph H. Cohen, William Fischman, and Mordecai Kaplan on a vacation retreat (in Tannersville, New York) during the summer of 1917—at the height of preparatory activities for the Jewish Center. Though Louis Cohen struck Kaplan as "a much more matter-of-fact person than his brother," apparently uninterested in religion, he must have been impressed with the enthusiasm and vision of the founding group of the Jewish Center. He called the first organizational meeting for the new Brooklyn institution in his own home on December 29, 1918, at the end of a year that saw the dedication of the Jewish Center on the upper West Side. That model institution had been designed by Jewish architect Louis Allen Abramson, and not surprisingly, the same man was chosen to design the Brooklyn project as well. The new "Brooklyn Jewish Center" was to be, quite plainly, a Jewish Center for Brooklyn.[14]

Yet the Jewish Center was not the only model for the Brooklyn Jewish Center. The "Eastern Parkway Jewish community," also known as Crown Heights, was contiguous with the older and larger community of Brownsville. Many of the founders of the Brooklyn Jewish Center had come from that nearby ghetto, often called the "Jerusalem of America," and the memory of its array of Jewish institutions would also influence the creation of the new synagogue-center. The Brooklyn Jewish Center may be seen, in fact, as a merger of the three most prominent institutions of the Brownsville Jewish community: (1) the leading Jewish community center, the Hebrew Educational Society (see fig. 18); (2) the leading communal Hebrew school, the Stone Avenue Talmud Torah (see fig. 21); and (3) the leading community synagogue, Congregation Ohav Sholom. The three had served their functions separately in the old neighborhood; in the new district they would, in effect, be combined into one.[15]

A more direct connection between Brownsville and the Brooklyn Jewish Center was provided by Rabbi Israel Herbert Levinthal (JTS, 1910), whose second pulpit was the modern orthodox Temple Petach Tikvah in Brownsville, serving there from 1915 to 1919. As noted earlier, Petach Tikvah had been founded in 1914 as a young men's synagogue, a tenuous experiment in modernism reflected by its "Zionist" name; as such, it was a transitional institution between the community synagogue and the synagogue-center. Its founders "consisted mainly of real estate builders and operators who came originally from 'Ohev Sholem' Synagogue," the leading community synagogue of Brownsville. As they moved westward, settling a new area on the border of Brownsville and Crown Heights, they established a new synagogue.[16]

Like its indeterminate location, the congregation too was ambivalent, split between traditionalists and progressives. William Roth, president of the congregation, was of the former group. According to Samuel Rottenberg, one of the founders of the Brooklyn Jewish Center and a former member of Petach Tikvah, because Roth "wanted to develop the congregation into a close corporation and did not want to encourage any interest in Zionism and charitable work, a group rebelled and seceded from the organization." It was that very group that organized the Brooklyn Jewish Center, soon luring away the rabbi of Petach Tikvah as well: "When some of the members of Petach Tikvah, together with some of the neighborhood of Brooklyn Avenue and Eastern Parkway, organized the Brooklyn Jewish Center, they extended a call to Rabbi Levinthal to become their spiritual leader. He unhesitatingly accepted the call."[17]

In October 1919, therefore, at the age of thirty-one, Levinthal began his long and illustrious career as rabbi of the Brooklyn Jewish Center; rarely noted is that he brought his Brownsville experience with him. At Petach Tikvah, Levinthal had introduced Friday evening services whose main feature was his English sermon. In one such address, entitled "Local Patriotism," delivered on March 10, 1916, he extolled the virtues of Brownsville and its Jewish institutions, and concluded: "All these facts have made of Brownsville a truly Jewish centre—a centre characteristic of all that is best in Jewish life. . . . And I feel that [this Temple being the centre] of inspiration of all that is best in Jewish life and in this community, must spread among its adherents first of all an appreciation, a love and a pride for the community of which it is a part"[18] (brackets in original).

While still at Petach Tikvah, Levinthal had begun to advance the concept of the synagogue-center. As early as February 4, 1916, he described "the Function of the Synagogue" as the sum of three functions: prayer, study, and meeting. In December 1917, the editor of the temple bulletin, *Petach Tikvah News,* wrote: "Our Rabbi has often pointed out to us the various names by which the Synagogue was known to the Jew of old. It was the Beth Hatfilah, the House of Prayer; it was the Beth Hamidrash, the House of Study, and it was also the Beth Hakeneses, the House of Assembly or Meeting House for the Jew." As proof of the return to the former synagogue ideal, the editor cited the recent organization of a Men's Club, which amply demonstrated the desirability of re-creating "the Synagogue as a Social Centre."[19]

The men's club would become a universal feature of the Conservative synagogue-center (in much the same way that the sisterhood had been popularized a generation earlier by the Reform movement). Temple Ansche Chesed of Harlem, for example, instituted a men's club in early 1918. The "new feature of congregational life" was again legitimated in social terms, and as a response to urban anomie: "The feeling of the organizers of the men's club was that a congregation like the Temple Ansche Chesed could be made the rallying point for all of the Jewish forces of Harlem, which, because of the peculiar condition of aloofness characteristic of life in New York City, are out of contact. Too many New Yorkers boast that they don't know their next door neighbor. The neighborliness and local pride of the small town is lacking here."[20]

Soon after Levinthal's departure to the Brooklyn Jewish Center, the new editors of the *Petach Tikvah News* announced plans for a "Synagogue Centre" to be constructed next door to the 1914 temple building. Five years later, they regretted having built too small a synagogue, one that lacked "a Jewish Centre for educational and social purposes." Their statement neatly captures the forward-looking and constructive spirit of the synagogue-center.

a building cannot be a structure for a day or a year. It must be planned with vision. It must be a legacy from one generation to its successors. Not only our requirements must be considered, but the next generation's must be adequately met. We owe it to our successors as a sacred duty. . . . We need to build and build we will; but shall it be only for to-day or also for to-morrow? Let us be builders with vision. Let us be builders for our children. Let us give the next generation a structure that will be an inspiration for Jewish constructive activity and a monument to its builders.[21]

The monumental structures created by the synagogue-center movement cost vast sums of money and saddled their builders with enormous debt. In later years, after populations moved and the buildings were left behind (unforeseeable events in the 1920s), they came to be lamented as white elephants, and the urge to have built them was derided as an "edifice complex." The stated intention to create "a monument to its builders" supports this notion (to be further explored below); on the whole, however, as the quote also attests, synagogue-center builders were motivated by far nobler sentiments overall.

Similar sentiments must have been echoed at the cornerstone-laying ceremony of the new Brooklyn Jewish Center building in June 1920. Reminiscent of the patriotic Institutional Synagogue, "An American flag used by the Jewish soldiers on

Fig. 43. Cornerstone-laying ceremony of the Brooklyn Jewish Center, June 13, 1920; *l.* to *r.:* Rabbis Israel Levinthal, Simon Finkelstein, and Bernard Levinthal (in top hats). *Jubilee Book of the Brooklyn Jewish Center* (April 1946). Courtesy of the Library of the Jewish Theological Seminary of America.

the battlefields of France during the World War and a Jewish flag given by David Reiner were displayed on poles erected for the occasion." And like the traditional Star of David marking the Jewish flag, the keynote theme of the occasion was the continuity represented by the new Brooklyn Jewish Center: "The event was an important one in the annals of the Center. About three thousand people were present. The honor of laying the corner stone was conferred upon Rabbi B. L. Levinthal, his son, Rabbi I. H. Levinthal, and Rabbi Simon Finkelstein [of Ohav Sholom of Brownsville]. . . . Rev. Josef Rosenblatt, the well-known cantor, sang Hebrew melodies."[22]

The presence of two prominent Orthodox rabbis—Levinthal, "chief rabbi of Philadelphia," and Finkelstein, "Dean of the Brooklyn Orthodox Rabbinate"— as well as the famous *hazan* Yosele Rosenblatt assured the crowd that this would be a tradition-bound Jewish institution. The sight of Israel Levinthal and his father standing side by side on the podium was a vivid demonstration of the passing of the torch from one generation to the next. Like other contemporary "Conservative" synagogues such as Temple Petach Tikvah, the Brooklyn Jewish Center of 1920 saw itself as an Orthodox synagogue, remaining traditional while appealing to the American-born generation. Though the Jewish Center of Manhattan and the Jewish Center of Brooklyn are thought of today as Orthodox and Conservative respectively, at their inception they both fell somewhere in between.[23]

Perhaps the best indicator of the Brooklyn Jewish Center's religious conservatism (small c) was its solution to the problem of seating. Rather than settling upon one extreme or the other, the Brooklyn Jewish Center adopted the compromise solution of allowing congregants an alternative: mixed seating in the center rows, and separate seating on the sides. Despite its affiliation with the Conservative movement, therefore, the Brooklyn Jewish Center still leaned to the religious right. Historian Deborah Dash Moore notes that even after "the more Orthodox leadership of the center resigned . . . many continued to describe the center's Judaism as Orthodox." Furthermore, Moore writes: "The contractors were efficient and did not work on the Sabbath or any Jewish holidays, thus upholding the religious commitments of the leadership. The latter noted with satisfaction that such adherence to Jewish law did not cost the center any extra money." The combination of Jewish traditionalism and economic efficiency recalls the building policies of Harry Fischel from an earlier chapter; likewise, much of the Brooklyn Jewish Center program would bear a remarkable similarity to earlier institutional expressions we have described.[24]

Moore also draws a familiar analogy between community, home, and synagogue: "Crown Heights was their American home, and at its heart would stand their Jewish home, the Brooklyn Jewish Center." The idea of the synagogue qua Jewish home is one we encountered as early as the synagogue-center experiment of Henry Berkowitz in Kansas City; and the notion of the Jewish center defining its concentric community has also been dealt with at length. But the intertwining of all three is novel. By overlaying the themes of community, home, and synagogue, Moore struck upon the essence of the synagogue-center: "at home" in their new Jewish neighborhoods, American Jews reconfigured the synagogue as the "home" of the Jewish community, and subsumed the functions of an entire Jewish community within the synagogue. The new synagogue type came to replace both the Jewish home and the Jewish community, each having lost its former role as an instrument of Jewish continuity. The intensive Jewish home life of the immigrant generation was fast disappearing by the 1920s, as were the organic Jewish communities of areas of first and second settlement. By addressing the two deficiencies at once, the synagogue-center became the characteristic Jewish institution of both the second generation and of areas of third settlement.[25]

Thus, at the same time that the synagogue-center combined features of the traditional synagogue (the Brooklyn Jewish Center sponsored a daily minyan and a *hevra kadisha*) with the amenities of a modern synagogue (a Hebrew school, a sisterhood, a youth group, Friday evening lectures and musical services, a forum lecture series on Monday nights, and a synagogue bulletin), it also incorporated various aspects of the Jewish home and of the Jewish community. Institutionalizing the idea of a proper Jewish household, the Brooklyn Jewish Center included a library, a dining room, and a kosher kitchen. In this regard, Moore cites Rabbi Levinthal's Friday evening programming as a home-inspired innovation:

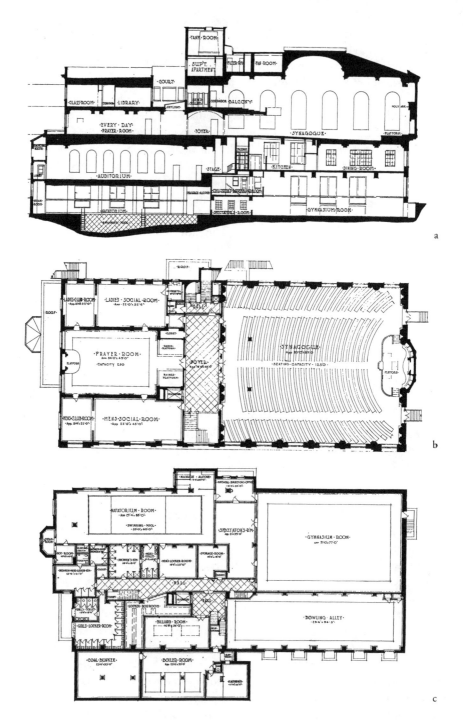

Fig. 44. Brooklyn Jewish Center, Eastern Parkway, Brooklyn, built 1920. (a) Longitudinal section. (b) Second-floor plan, showing synagogue, prayer room, and social rooms. (c) Basement plan, showing "natatorium" (swimming pool), gymnasium, and bowling alley. Courtesy of the Library of the Jewish Theological Seminary of America.

Not wanting to supplant the traditional Friday evening service held before the meal at sun-down, Levinthal justified his efforts to supplement this service by speaking of the transfer of the "singing of the *Zmiroth* from the supper table to the Synagogue or Public Forum." In fact, the late Friday night lecture and musical service, as it was called from years at the Brooklyn Jewish Center, did represent the shift to a public place of the previously private, familial cele-bration of the Sabbath. The *oneg shabbat* that had traditionally occurred in the home now ac-quired a new locale and form.[26]

Perhaps the clearest expression of the synagogue-center as communal home was in the architecture. As in his earlier design for the Jewish Center, architect Louis Allen Abramson did not conceive the Brooklyn Jewish Center as a recog-nizable "church" edifice, but as a functional institution. The institution it most resembled was the characteristic "house" of the second-generation Jewish family: the apartment house. Just as the "tenement" synagogue had typified the ghetto and had blended in with its urban environment, the synagogue of the postwar Jewish neighborhood would again be a residential analogue. The synagogue was thus construed as a home by the Reform temple, the immigrant shul, *and* the synagogue-center.[27]

There is a beautiful parallel here. The Jewish community center, it will be re-called, was analogized with the commercial department store. Both were service institutions offering many "wares" under one roof, and in many cases, they were built by the same German-Jewish *balabatim*. Where earlier Jewish entrepreneurs such as Abraham and Straus had pioneered the department store, Jewish builders such as Harry Fischel were later instrumental in the development of the apart-ment house. And what is an apartment building but a service (for example, elevator- and doorman-service) institution offering many "homes" under one roof? In both cases, the secular building experience was translated into Jewish in-stitutional terms. The same men who lined avenues such as Eastern Parkway with rows of luxurious apartment houses had built luxurious synagogue-centers to match.[28]

Housed in its compartmentalized structure, the synagogue-center became a Jewish community in microcosm, welcoming on its premises: Hadassah meet-ings, Federation fund-raising, college extension classes, etc. The new BJC even came to be seen as the new communal center of Brooklyn Jewry, representing the borough as a whole. In April 1921, the porch of the unfinished building was used as the reviewing platform for a Zionist youth parade down Eastern Parkway, honoring the presence of Chaim Weizmann, Menachem Ussishkin, and Shmarya Levin. The event "was the first time that [Brooklyn] was selected as a place for a citywide function." Thus it was that the ambition of the community synagogue to be a "stadt shul," a central institution embodying and representing the entire Jewish community, was realized by the synagogue-center, in both form and content.[29]

As a reconstructed community synagogue, the Brooklyn Jewish Center adopted the most characteristic feature of its predecessor, the star *hazan*. "With all the worship services in place, the leaders began to search for a cantor, eventually choosing Samuel Kantor of Boston over Samuel Rothstein." Years later, in 1943, the future opera star Richard Tucker was engaged as well (staying three years before moving on to the metropolitan Opera). At the same time, the Brooklyn Jewish Center was a young people's synagogue, like its predecessor Young Israel, emphasizing the more pleasurable aspects of life. The oft-stated intention to "show the world that one might be a Jew and enjoy life at the same time" was realized through Saturday night dinners and dances, as well as by the social and recreational facilities of the Center: its swimming pool and gymnasium. Such amusements should not be underestimated in importance; the popularity and success of the synagogue-center rested largely on its attraction to the young. Older members of the community fully approved, for they understood that social activities bringing young men and women into contact might help stem the tide of intermarriage. Besides, they liked the steam bath (yet another carryover from European Jewish culture).[30]

Like earlier youth synagogues, the Brooklyn Jewish Center was infused with the Zionist spirit. From the cornerstone-laying ceremony to the Friday night services, all Brooklyn Jewish Center events were concluded with the singing of both the "Star Spangled Banner" and "Hatikvah." Zionist leaders such as Shmarya Levin were frequent lecturers, and Rabbi Levinthal, who often sermonized on the theme, was an active Zionist. According to Joseph Goldberg, "the Eastern Parkway Zionist District became synonymous with" the Brooklyn Jewish Center. But above all, the Center Hebrew school and the later Center Academy day school (from 1927) were twin founts of cultural Zionism, heirs to the Hebraism of the modern Talmud Torah movement.[31]

In essence, the Brooklyn Jewish Center, like the Institutional Synagogue and the Jewish Center before it, was the culmination and consolidation of the many religious and social trends of contemporary Jewish life. Harry Seinfel, chairman of the Dedication Committee and first vice president of the BJC (and who was earlier associated with the Stone Avenue Talmud Torah, Congregation Ohav Sholom, and Temple Petach Tikvah) summed it up well when he wrote, in December 1920: "Our aim: To unite the fathers and mothers of Israel with their children—to provide a common meeting place under Jewish auspices—for all the members and their families—to give the best in spiritual guidance—to provide a Jewish education for all of the family—to establish a place for recreation and play—to encourage thought—to help the members in the art of self-expression—to bring forth the best in each of us. In all, to reinterpret Jewish life so that it may continue to be a living force."[32]

The new synagogue-center was judged a great success by all concerned, an assessment based on the growth of its membership and the popularity of its programs. An even better indication of its success lies in the phenomenal pace of imitation in the years following the 1920 dedication. To some degree, the imitators were Conservative rabbis, several of whom were present at that auspicious occasion: Elias Solomon (then president of the United Synagogue as well as associate rabbi of Kehilath Jeshurun), Julius Greenstone (of Gratz College), Jacob Kohn (of Ansche Chesed), Israel Goldfarb (of Beth Israel Anshe Emeth), and Alexander Basel (of Mount Sinai). If the synagogue-center idea had not impressed the young rabbis of the Conservative movement by that time, then surely the inspiring unveiling of the monumental edifice on Eastern Parkway would. Of the congregational leaders mentioned, Solomon, Kohn, and Basel would build their own synagogue-centers in the years ahead.[33]

More directly related to the Brooklyn Jewish Center precedent was the series of synagogue-centers founded throughout Brooklyn during the 1920s. As Rabbi Levinthal wrote in 1940: "The Center's diversified program has set the pattern for the synagogue centers which have been erected in a number of Brooklyn districts since; several of the Reform congregations have likewise followed the example of the Jewish Center in erecting costly physical plants." Contemporary with the Brooklyn Jewish Center, the Jewish Center of Kings Highway dedicated its two buildings in 1920. Its first rabbi was Joseph Lookstein, who soon moved uptown to begin his lengthy association with Kehilath Jeshurun of Yorkville. He was succeeded by Rabbi Abraham M. Heller, who served for two years and then switched to the Flatbush Jewish Center, where his half-century career matched both Lookstein's at Kehilath Jeshurun and Levinthal's at the Brooklyn Jewish Center. Organized in October 1921, the Flatbush Jewish Center was "the first of a number of synagogue centers formed in the region south of Prospect Park." In the next year, the West Flatbush Center was founded, and the East Midwood Jewish Center and the Ocean Parkway Jewish Center followed in 1924. At last count, there were some thirty-three congregations in Brooklyn named "Jewish Center."[34]

As greater numbers of synagogue-centers were established, they became less ambitious in scope. The first had been called simply the Jewish Center, without geographic designation; the second, the *Brooklyn* Jewish Center, made reference to an entire borough; the third, the *Flatbush* Jewish Center, encompassed an expansive neighborhood (larger in area and population than many cities); and the fourth, the *West Flatbush* Center, a section of that larger region; it later became the *Ocean Parkway* Jewish Center, thus reducing the scope of the Center to a single thoroughfare—eventually the most common designator. Can it be mere coincidence that this brings us back to the "Street Shul" usage of the shtetl and immigrant ghetto?

Certainly, the location of nearly all synagogue-centers on wide boulevards was no coincidence. In Manhattan, both the Institutional Synagogue and the Jewish Center were situated on main avenues, West 116th Street and West 86th Street respectively, the latter address being particularly fashionable. The siting of the BJC on Eastern Parkway was even a grander statement. Eastern Parkway had been designed in the 1870s by Frederick Law Olmsted, the great landscape architect responsible for Boston's Emerald Necklace, Manhattan's Central Park, and his masterpiece, Brooklyn's Prospect Park. Eastern Parkway was billed as the nation's first parkway, a blissful combination of city and country. What better location for the nation's model synagogue-center? The idea of siting on a major thoroughfare certainly resonated with the later builders of synagogue-centers, for they all followed suit, similarly seeking to make their presence known.

Like the Brooklyn Jewish Center, most Brooklyn synagogue-centers were counted as the pioneering institutions of new Jewish neighborhoods, initiated by individual Jews without the aid of rabbis. Aside from the direct influence of the BJC, therefore, the very act of settling a new area gave rise to the synagogue-center concept. The first Jews in such a new neighborhood soon felt the need for either a religious congregation (as in the case of the Ocean Parkway Jewish Center) or a Hebrew school for their children (as in the case of the East Midwood Jewish Center). But since the neighborhood had no other Jewish institutions as yet, the first to be created would naturally tend to fulfill all the needs of a Jewish community. Like the earlier immigrant builders of community synagogues, urban pioneers of the second generation hoped to attract more Jews to the area. So, like their predecessors, they built the most modern Jewish institution they knew of. In the earlier period, that had been the "up-to-date" community synagogue; in the new era it was the synagogue-center, as exemplified by the Brooklyn Jewish Center.

The Ocean Parkway Jewish Center originated as the first community synagogue of Kensington, a new area of Jewish settlement in Brooklyn located between Flatbush and Borough Park. The First Congregation of Kensington was founded in June 1907, and its first synagogue built four years later. Following the establishment of the Brooklyn Jewish Center and the Flatbush Jewish Center, the congregation began to redefine itself as a synagogue-center. In October 1922, an adjoining building was acquired for use "as a schoolhouse and by the various clubs of the congregation." Two years later the group amalgamated with the West Flatbush Center, and altered its building on E. 2d St. "to provide a meeting place for the steadily growing auxiliary organizations. With three buildings at the disposal of the members, the religious, social and educational needs of the community could not be satisfied. . . . The congregation decided, therefore, to build the Ocean Parkway Jewish Center, a modern building with all facilities to satisfy the needs of the community." The cornerstone laying took place on April 19, 1925, and the dedication in the fall of 1926. Its cost was a mere $450,000.[35]

The East Midwood Jewish Center was organized by a former member of Temple Petach Tikvah, Dr. Jacob R. Schwartz, D.D.S., who "was very much concerned over the fact that his two boys had no Hebrew school in the immediate vicinity of his home . . . [and] interested one or two men in a movement for the organization of a school." On November 18, 1924, the first annual meeting was held at "the Jewish Communal Center of Flatbush, whose officers had generously offered the facilities of their building to the new organization." The Jewish Communal Center, located on Avenue I in West Midwood, served as the launching pad for the establishment of what was to be "the first synagogue in

East Midwood." Under the headline, "Midwood Hebrew Congregation Building Center and Synagogue," the *Brooklyn Daily Eagle* of August 20, 1925, published a rendering of the proposed structure. The architect, interestingly enough, combined the apartment-house layout of the Brooklyn Jewish Center with the temple facade of the West End Synagogue so widely copied by earlier community synagogues. At the June 1926 cornerstone laying, the invocation was delivered by Rabbi A. M. Heller of the Flatbush Jewish Center; and at the meeting of November 1927, new officers were installed by Samuel Rottenberg, president of the Brooklyn Jewish Center. The monumental structure on Ocean Avenue was finally completed in 1929 under its new rabbi, Harry Halpern. As described in the local press, the new $1,000,000 center was to include "a synagogue, auditorium, kitchens, restaurant, classrooms, gymnasium and swimming pool"—exactly the same as the Brooklyn Jewish Center.[36]

Of course, not all Brooklyn Jewish Center–influenced synagogues in Brooklyn were created anew and called "Jewish Centers." Temple Petach Tikvah added a center to its synagogue in 1922. Congregation Shaari Zedek, formerly of Williamsburg, moved to Crown Heights and built its synagogue-center in 1924, a half-million-dollar building containing "a synagogue, a Sunday school, a dance hall, a gymnasium, and special rooms for the meetings of the board of directors and other attractive features." Congregation Sons of Israel, founded in 1896 in Bath Beach, began its drive for a new building as early as 1916, completing construction in 1919. Only after the Brooklyn Jewish Center, however, did its rabbi launch "a movement for an educational center that would house the Talmud Torah and related activities. . . . During 1926–29, the educational building was erected. . . . The new building provided ample facilities for the expanding work of the community. . . . The bazaars, the festivals, entertainments and dinners are also held in the building."[37]

As Rabbi Levinthal indicated, the Brooklyn Jewish Center inspired imitation among Reform temples in Brooklyn as well. Congregation Beth Sholom–Peoples Temple, for example, built its new synagogue-center in 1922. Since most Reform congregations had been established earlier, most of their synagogue-center construction took the form of an additional structure. Temple Beth Emeth of Flatbush built a new community house in 1922 to adjoin its 1914 temple on Church Avenue. In 1924, Congregation Beth Elohim, known as the "Garfield Place Temple," built a new community house across the street from its 1910 temple building. Temple Beth El of Manhattan Beach, "the first religious organization in that section," was organized in 1919 and its first building dedicated in 1924. In 1929, its men's club resolved to build a club- and schoolhouse adjoining the temple.

The Reform temple that followed the precedent of the Brooklyn Jewish Center most closely was descended from the oldest congregation in Brooklyn, Beth Elohim, founded at the midpoint of the nineteenth century. In 1869, a group of reform-minded members seceded to found Temple Israel, whose rabbi would later be the young Judah Magnes. When Beth Elohim built its first synagogue building on Keap Street (in Williamsburg) in 1876, it joined the Reform movement also and became known as Temple Beth Elohim. It remained at that location for nearly half a century until, in 1921, the two congregations decided to come back together. The new Union Temple then relocated to a prime address at the western end of Eastern Parkway, in conscious competition with the popular Brooklyn Jewish Center further up the avenue. The socially conscious Reform congregation would rise above its predecessor, however, moving ever further away from Brownsville to the border of fashionable Park Slope. The newest synagogue-center was to be built on the tree-lined circle called Grand Army Plaza, Brooklyn's version of the Champs-Élysées, there to join the grand Neoclassical structures of the Soldiers' and Sailors Memorial Arch (modeled on the Arc de Triomphe), the Public Library, and just up the parkway, the monumental Brooklyn museum. Rabbi Simon R. Cohen wrote in the spring of 1924: "the Jewish Centre here on Eastern Parkway has a very fine building. . . . Our Congregation 'Union Temple' is now having plans completed for the finest Temple and Community House in the Country." The public announcement went even further, projecting the new synagogue-center to be "one of the greatest and most beautiful temples in the world."[38]

The architect chosen was Arnold Brunner, who earlier had designed synagogue structures for Temple Beth El (1891), Shaaray Tefila (1894), and Shearith Israel (1897), as well as numerous other Jewish centers—including the Educational Alliance building of 1890 and the YMHA of 1900. For Union Temple, Brunner designed two complementary structures: a Neoclassical temple, and a ten-story community center building immediately adjoining. The temple was planned to seat two thousand, and was to be fronted by "four huge marble columns," a grand facade to visually balance the library across the street. The center, completed in 1926, bore striking similarity to the multistory Jewish Center on the Upper West Side. Since the temple was never built (due to the stock market crash of 1929; note which building took precedence), the community center alone would serve as "a modern synagogue," characterized by "a swimming pool, a gymnasium, club rooms for all kinds of activities, a Men's Club, a Sisterhood, a Hebrew school, and a beautiful synagogue [with frescoed ceiling] that seats about 1100 people."[39]

Created in the mold of the Brooklyn Jewish Center, Union Temple thus became an integrated, all-in-one synagogue-center complex, as glowingly described in the *American Hebrew:*

Union Temple, long one of the strongest spiritual factors in the borough, exercises through its new center an immense influence communally, socially and culturally. The new temple consists of two buildings, one of the temple proper for religious services, and adjoining it a 10-story temple house to be used as a social, educational and recreational center for the members. . . . The Temple house has every facility for community purposes. It contains, under one roof, a religious school, a club for Temple members, a community center, a theatre with a stage as modern as any on Broadway, a gymnasium, pool-room and swimming-pool, hand-ball courts and all the

Fig. 45. Union Temple, Eastern Parkway, Brooklyn. Architect's drawing (center built 1926). *American Jewish Year Book*, vol. 28 (1926–27).

other appurtenances for up-to-date physical culture as well as religious and social development. . . . The new home of the Union Temple marks the last word in the modern policy of combining all forms of social activity with religious worship.[40]

The Brooklyn Jewish Center was the major influence in the spread of a Jewish Center movement during the 1920s, extending beyond New York: "In 1926, as a direct inspiration by the Brooklyn Jewish Center, the West Philadelphia Jewish Center was established" under Rabbi C. David Matt. Even further afield, Levinthal was later instrumental in "the organization and the construction of The Jeshurun Synagogue in Jerusalem, the first and only Synagogue Center in Israel." Even so, to gauge the true significance of the Brooklyn Jewish Center, we need only ask, What if it had never been? What if Israel Levinthal had followed his parents' advice, and not gone into the rabbinate? For that matter, what if Herbert Goldstein had stayed in a law school, or what if Mordecai Kaplan had opted to go into business? Would there have been a synagogue-center movement to speak of? Of course there would. Just as Levinthal, Goldstein, and Kaplan were inextricably bound to their rabbinic identities, the masses of second-generation American Jews were pulled toward the synagogue-center solution.[41]

"A Synagogue-Center Movement Grows in Brookline"[42]

The case of Boston provides an excellent example of the synagogue-center movement as it unfolded locally, on the individual urban scene. During the 1920s, four major synagogue-center projects were undertaken, thus identifying—and at the same time helping to determine—the four leading congregations of the Boston Jewish community: Mishkan Tefila, Kehillath Israel, Ohabei Shalom, and Temple Israel. The first two were Conservative congregations, the latter two Reform. The first was located in the then thriving middle-class community of Roxbury/Dorchester, and the rest in the somewhat more upscale Brookline. All four undertook their synagogue-center projects with some awareness of the others' plans, and were clearly motivated by their mutual competition. They also had cognizance of synagogue-center progress in other cities, revealed by the fact that the architectural material of Albert Gottlieb and Nathan Myers—as well as much other enlightening information—found its way into the archives of Temple Israel.

The congregation that laid claim to being the leading synagogue-center of Boston was Temple Mishkan Tefila, the self-described "oldest Conservative congregation in New England." Mishkan Tefila was in fact deemed a "Conservative" congregation as early as 1892. As described earlier, however, JTS graduate Herman H. Rubenovitz was called to Mishkan Tefila in 1910 and only then did the transition to Conservativism begin in earnest. Later that same year, the congregation celebrated its golden jubilee (two years too late) whereupon Rabbi Rubenovitz proclaimed that "after an existence of fifty years, Cong. Mishkan Tefila this day unfurls the banner of Conservative Judaism."[43]

Jewish Advocate editor and YMHA director Jacob de Haas was also present at the occasion, and contributed an editorial in which he described "the synagogue as the natural center of Jewish life":

The celebration was the occasion for serious appeals for conservative Judaism, and if we mistake not the immediate future of Boston is bound up in a conservative advance. . . . But conservatism is itself but a phase if the synagogue is not made the center of the social life and other activities. The synagogue was not intended to be an austere meeting place for prayer. It was in olden times a good deal of a discussion hall, a place for study and debate, and there is no reason why the adjuncts of the synagogues should not be used for purposes other than class rooms for Sabbath schools. Nor does there seem to be apparent reason why the administrators of a congregation should regard the holdings of social reunions as other than part of their general duties. . . . There is no reason why a first-class program could not be evolved which would bring every generation of a congregation's members within the walls of its fane frequently. And if this were accomplished in what is called the secular side, it would not require the effort it does today to get people to attend regular religious services.[44]

The synagogue-center impulse was thus present at that early date, as reflected by the editorial declaration of de Haas. In all likelihood, the younger men and women of the congregation stood in full agreement. Their rabbi, on the other hand, would not take up such ideas for another decade. In 1910 he was more concerned with becoming a part of the emerging national movement for Conservative Judaism. Three years later, in the spring of 1913, Rubenovitz accompanied "a Mishkan Tefila delegation headed by Mr. Joseph Sonnabend, our president at that time," to the founding convention of the United Synagogue. As discussed in the previous chapter, however, the United Synagogue at that time was hardly a bastion of non-Orthodox Conservatism. In an attempt to stake out a definitive Conservative position, Rubenovitz together with his liberal cohorts Israel Friedlaender, Max Margolis, Julius Greenstone, Jacob Kohn, and Mordecai Kaplan issued a group statement in June 1919 that stated, in part: "In view of the upheaval in the world at large [World War I], and in view of the changes which will necessarily take place in the spiritual life of Jewry, as a result of the restoration of Palestine to the Jewish people [the Balfour Declaration], we maintain that the time has come for us to state frankly and emphatically what we believe in, and what we regard as authoritative in Jewish practice, and to develop the religious implications of the Zionist movement. . . . It is our duty to point the way to a Judaism that shall be both historic and progressive." Further emphasizing the Zionist element of Conservatism, Rubenovitz claimed that "Temple Mishkan Tefila was a Zionist pulpit," and later added: "it became one of my chief aims to make of Temple Mishkan Tefila a center of Zionist propoganda [sic] and activity."[45]

The 1919 missive turned out to be the founding statement of the "Society of the Jewish Renascence," eventually to develop into the Reconstructionist movement of Mordecai Kaplan. Rubenovitz thus became Kaplan's disciple and followed closely the events at the Jewish Center of the West Side. In a letter dated February 3, 1921, Jacob Kohn wrote to Rubenovitz to inform him of, among other things, Kaplan's continued efforts "in magnifying the Social Center idea of the Synagogue." In Kaplan's footsteps, he would turn his own congregation into a youth-oriented, multifaceted synagogue-center. Besides various Zionist, cultural, and educational groups, Mishkan Tefila also sponsored an active men's club, which in February 1921 began an in-house publication entitled "The Jewish Center, a Magazine of Progressive Judaism" and ran under the slogan "Liberalism, Zionism and Social Service."[46]

The campaign to build a new "Jewish Center" for the rapidly growing Roxbury-Dorchester Jewish community was launched at Mishkan Tefila's anniversary banquet on December 18, 1918. The "fine site at the corner of Seaver Street and Elm Hill Avenue, facing Franklin Park, was purchased" in 1919, and the architectural firm chosen was Krokyn, Browne, and Rosenstein. Sometime in 1920–22, just as the nationwide synagogue-center movement was under way, the architects joined the building committee on an inspection tour of potential models for the new project. As committee chairman Morris Bronstein recalled:

When I called for volunteers to go with the architects and myself to inspect various temples for the purpose of incorporating new ideas such as architectural designs, elevations, inside decorations, etc., the entire Building Committee was willing to go at their own expense and time, and we visited nearly every modern temple in New York City, Brooklyn and New Jersey. From there we gained wonderful ideas of designs in architecture which have been of help to us in our plans.[47]

Jacob Krokyn, a local Jewish architect who had grown up in the North End ghetto and was educated at Harvard, was inspired by the project to wax somewhat poetic on the significance of the new synagogue. In a letter to the editor signed "J. Frederick Krokyn," he elaborated on the theme of an American Jewish renaissance: "The new building represents an event in the progress of the faith and is evidence of the Jewish renaissance here. Its location, in the heart of the largest Jewish population in New England, is unsurpassed in beauty and accessibility and lends itself perfectly for the purpose. The building will be an expression of modern American architecture, a striking symbol to the world of our harmony with American culture and traditions. . . . The architects are thus planning a building to express the ideals and aspirations of a great Jewish community."[48]

Prior to the ceremony of the ground-breaking in the fall of 1922, press releases were sent to all the Boston papers to announce the "New $500,000 Temple and Jewish Community Center." The articles included a beautiful rendering of the proposed structure, and described its architectural style as the "American Renaissance." What better form of construction for a synagogue imbued with the Reconstructionist principles of the "Jewish Renascence"?

Present at the ground-breaking was Alexander Brin, the new editor of the *Jewish Advocate*. In March 1923, Brin ran a special issue that announced in bold type, "Temple Mishkan Tefila Launches Victory Drive to Complete New Edifice." He personally advocated the "realization of the Model Temple Mishkan Tefila" and appealed to the public in this editorial: "The new Temple Mishkan Tefila is not a luxury; it is a necessity. It is impossible to develop Jewish life if our buildings handicap rather than encourage us. A weakened spiritual condition makes it easier for the anti-Semites to attack us. This community could do more work—NECESSARY WORK—if we had proper facilities. Ours is a job of education. That is why we need modern temples and centres."[49]

The editor provocatively suggested antisemitism as a motive for the construction of the synagogue-center. The issue also included articles by members of the congregation, such as: "Mishkan Tefila's Success is Accounted For—[A. A. Bloome] Points Out Why This 'Young Men's Congregation' Prospers Spiritually and Materially," in which the author noted "the fact that the majority of our members are under thirty-five years of age." There was also a major piece by Rabbi Rubenovitz proclaiming "The Synagogue as a Community Center," and further suggesting the inclusion of "meeting rooms, assembly halls, reading rooms, a well equipped gymnasium, a swimming pool and athletic field." The final construction did not include the proposed athletic facilities, for the same year and just one block away on Seaver Street, the Boston YMHA Gymnasium Building was constructed with those very amenities. A popular Jewish center known as Hecht House was located within short walking distance as well. It ought to be noted, however, that Rubenovitz served as director of religious education for the YMHA; and the architect for the new YMHA building was (who else?) Jacob Krokyn. The YMHA and its neighboring synagogue-center were not overlapping and competing institutions, therefore, but complementary and complete.

Sans swimming pool but synagogue-centered nonetheless, the monumental Temple Mishkan Tefila was dedicated on September 13, 1925, having cost approximately $750,000. A schoolhouse building was added to the rear of the main structure in 1929, at a further cost of $300,000, bringing the total outlay to more than one million dollars. Rabbi Rubenovitz later recalled the significance of the new complex: "It can be said without exaggeration that the dedication of our temple on Seaver Street marked the beginning of a new epoch in the evolution of Jewish life in New England. Here was finally realized the old idea of a *Stadt Shul,* a great central synagogue which could serve as a place of assembly for the entire community whenever some special occasion demanded it. And many such occasions did arise." The description of Mishkan Tefila as a "stadt shul" was common through the 1950s. Indeed, throughout the interwar heyday of the second-generation Jewish community, Mishkan Tefila was the dominant institutional presence in Roxbury-Dorchester—due in no small part to the imposing synagogue-center edifice of 1925.[50]

Kehillath Israel, or "K.I." as it came to be known, was established in 1915 as the original congregation of Brookline. KI provides an example of many trends we have seen before. The congregation was created as a private minyan of thirty-six members but soon "began to realize that in order to fulfill its purpose, it would have to accommodate the social and educational demands of the Jewish neighborhood also." Land was purchased in May 1921, and the cornerstone for a new synagogue was laid in October 1923. Originally defined as "a modern orthodox congregation," KI adopted mixed seating only after the dedication of its new building in January 1925. As late as 1942, Kehillath Israel could still claim: "Some people call us Progressive orthodox; others call us Right Wing Conservative. We should like to rise above appellations and confine ourselves within no party lines but to be humble and worthy servants of *Klal Yisroel.*"[51]

In August 1925, the noted scholar Louis M. Epstein (JTS, 1913) was called to the Brookline pulpit from the Crawford Street Shul of Roxbury. Many of the members of KI during its early years had also moved from Roxbury where they had been members of either the Crawford Street or the Blue Hill Avenue Shuls. In a very real sense, KI was the descendant of the two older congregations. Epstein had first arrived in Boston in 1918 to become rabbi of Beth Hamidrash Hagadol on Crawford Street, the "Litvishe" (Lithuanian, as was Epstein) shul of Roxbury. Under Rabbi Epstein, the congregation thrived, soon developing into both a congregational and a communal center. By 1924, he could boast: "We have thirteen hundred souls permanently organized into our congregational system and we serve on the average—some more, some less—approximately ten thousand Jewish souls in our community." In that year, the congregation had the architectural firm of Krokyn, Browne, and Rosenstein draw up plans for a new community building to be added to the original structure—complete with banquet hall, classrooms, club rooms, and gymnasium. Jacob Krokyn had earlier designed the 1906 building of Adath Jeshurun on Blue Hill Avenue (Phineas Israeli's congregation), and was also responsible for the 1917 synagogue of Beth Hamidrash Hagadol. Like its contemporary congregation on Blue Hill Avenue, the Crawford Street Shul never succeeded in creating a synagogue-center on Crawford Street. However, both its rabbi and Jewish architect would later realize the vision elsewhere, albeit with different congregations.[52]

Rabbi Epstein moved to Kehillath Israel in 1925, the same year in which that congregation dedicated its new synagogue. In its new building and under its new rabbi, KI continued to grow: in 1929 it added a new school building and social hall, and in 1947 a new community house and auditorium building (whose architect was Jacob Krokyn) was added next door. At its central location on Harvard Street—which thereafter became a main Jewish shopping street—KI became the most active congregation in Brookline and a leading synagogue-center of the Boston Jewish community. KI described its activities in 1934:

As an institution, Kehillath Israel is the religious center for nearly a thousand families that comprise the membership in the Congregation, the Brotherhood and the Sisterhood. To them there is a ceaseless flow of religious inspiration, education and activity out of their sanctuary on Harvard Street by means of the daily, Sabbath and Holy Day services, the daily Hebrew School, the lectures and courses and classes, the Brotherhood's and Sisterhood's rich activities and interesting meetings. But it is not only an institution for members; it is a community institution in the full sense of the word. Kehillath Israel does not distinguish between member and non-member when it is a question of rendering service. . . . Whether it is of any material benefit to the institution or not, it is always a source of pride to us to see our synagogue thronged day after day with hundreds and thousands of men and women and children; every one finding some spiritual service there.[53]

At the same time that KI was being built on Harvard Street, a third major synagogue-center was under construction not far away on Beacon Street, the main avenue of Brookline. Ohabei Shalom, the first congregation of Boston, was founded in the old South End in 1842. It had built a small synagogue in 1851, moved into a neighboring church building in 1863, and purchased yet another church in a more fashionable area in 1887. The congregation remained in the South End until the end of World War I, by which time most of its membership had left that district, many moving to Brookline. In 1921, therefore, land was purchased along the main artery of Brookline for a new congregational home.

At its new site on Beacon Street, Temple Ohabei Shalom would be geographically located between Kehillath Israel on Harvard Street and Temple Israel on Commonwealth Avenue, its two historic offshoots. Religiously as well, Ohabei Shalom was midway between them; while KI was moderate Orthodox and Temple Israel was classical Reform, Ohabei Shalom wavered between moderate Reform and classical Conservatism. More to the point, it directly competed with the other two congregations for prestige and influence: as opposed to Temple Israel, it saw itself as the rightful "leading congregation" of Boston; and as opposed to Kehillath Israel, it aspired to be the "central synagogue" of Brookline. Ohabei Shalom therefore hired the architect of the 1906 Temple Israel, and planned a magnificent new temple to overshadow both its competitors.

In 1920 a new rabbi, Samuel J. Abrams, arrived, and a new fraternity was formed, the Temple Ohabei Shalom Brotherhood. In April 1922 the congregation held a banquet to raise funds for their building project. The rabbi, followed by the president of the brotherhood, offered stirring messages for the occasion. Rabbi Abrams spoke of "a possession forever": "What is this New Temple Ohabei Shalom? Let me tell you at least what we shall strive to make it—a monument of the standing of the Jews of this metropolis of the 20th century! More than that; it is to be a witness to the fact that though we have risen in wealth and power, and though we yield to none of our fellow-citizens in love of country, we have not forgotten the rock whence we were hewn. In its artistic completeness, is it to be an offering recording for years, or—may God grant—for centuries to come, at once the prosperity and the gratitude which are ours in being privileged to be counted among those who served this holy cause."[54]

President F. Wingersky added the following, once again alluding to anti-semitism as a motivating factor: "Our Brotherhood must continue to play its important part in the building of the New Temple. Majestically our new edifice will stand, a monument for all time, and a sacred memory to the men and women whose time and money made the project possible. The erection of this Temple is a public answer to the arguments that the Jew is a rank materialist, a Godless people."[55] The architect made his statement in stone and brick. Clarence Blackall had designed the first "skyscraper" in Boston as well as many of the leading the-aters of the city. His design for the new Ohabei Shalom would be Boston's version of the Hagia Sophia, the great monument of ancient Byzantium. The Byzantine revival had, in fact, become the reigning style of synagogue architecture in America, adapted for contemporary synagogue-centers in San Francisco, Chicago, Cleveland, Newark, New York, Providence, and now, Boston (see figs. 47c–d). The style was thought to refer to recent excavations of Byzantine synagogues in Palestine, and bore allusions of an oriental Mediterranean civilization; one not far removed from Judaism. The eminent urban historian Lewis Mumford contributed to the trend in a 1925 article for the *Menorah Journal* entitled "Towards a Modern Synagog Architecture." Mumford advocated the use of the Byzantine style so as to "recognize the reintegration of the Jewish culture and Jewish civilization." The central dome would serve to unify the spiritual, cultural, communal, and social functions of the modern synagogue. Even Lewis Mumford, it seems, was a staunch defender of the synagogue-center idea.[56]

The rabbi, president, and architect of Ohabei Shalom could not have agreed more, together foreseeing the planned edifice as a monument to the arrival of the Jews in Brookline and the presence of Judaism in Boston. In 1925, the same year as the dedications of Kehillath Israel and Mishkan Tefila, Ohabei Shalom dedicated its new "Temple Center" school and administration building; its "cultural purposes" would be served by an auditorium, a supper and play room—to be used as a gymnasium or recreation room—dressing rooms, class and meeting rooms, music rooms, a museum, library and reading room. Three years later, in 1928, the adjacent temple edifice was dedicated, minus the minaret but impressive nonetheless.[57]

Not to be outdone by its fellow Boston congregations, Temple Israel began planning for its new synagogue-center complex in 1923. In 1917 the congregational historian had written, "Adath Israel is now unquestionably the strongest individual Jewish institution, the most influential Congregation in New England." But that image would soon be threatened, as Mishkan Tefila, Kehillath Israel, and Ohabei Shalom all announced plans for institutional expansion during the next few years. The alert became alarm after Temple Israel's president, Felix Vorenberg, attended the UAHC convention of January 1923. There he listened to the keynote speech of Louis Marshall, and also heard tell of the conspicuous construction of Reform synagogue-centers around the country. In no uncertain terms, Marshall had declared: "Let us . . . direct our thoughts to a revival, not a temporary, but a continuous one, in our religious lives. Let the call go forth: 'Back to the Synagogue!' . . . The Synagogue should not be visited solely on holiday occasions, or merely by the women or the aged of our Congregations. Parents and children should gather there habitually. It should again become the centre of our life and of our activities, as it was of yore. As I have had occasion to say quite frequently of late, it should be a house of prayer, a house of assembly, and a house of learning."[58]

Following his return to Boston, Vorenberg wrote the following open letter to his congregation:

"Back to the Synagog" was the strong note sounded by many speakers at the recent Convention of the Union of American Hebrew Congregations held in New York in January, and "Back to the Synagog" means to start with our children and our young people. . . . It is difficult to understand why, here in this progressive Community, we should be so far behind the Jews of other cities. In Baltimore a new school and Community House has been built recently at a cost of over $300,000. In Detroit a new Temple and a Community House, including a religious school, have been erected at an expense of nearly $1,000,000. In Cleveland a New Temple and Community House have been built, costing over $1,000,000. In almost every other city of any size the Jews have begun to realize that our children must be made to understand what we are and what we stand for. . . . Your Board has considered this matter very seriously and is now ready to recommend a Sunday School Building and a Community House to be built at once. . . . Last Fall 600 attended Yom Kippur services at Whitney Hall in addition to the 1200 who participated in the services at the Temple. Does not all this evidence inspire you to immediate action? A Community House will fill just this need, and more than that, it will be in keeping with our ambition to make this Congregation the strongest in New England. . . . The time has come to purchase a suitable piece of land large enough to build a religious school and Community House for the present, as well as a new Temple, when the time comes, which may be sooner than we think. . . . May God grant that each of us will take to heart the responsibilities which are ours as members of the leading congregation of Boston, leading not merely in members but in strength and influence.[59]

In April 1924, land was purchased on the Riverway, along the border between Brookline and Boston proper; and the process of planning the new Temple complex began. Rabbi Harry Levi immediately became involved by writing to his Reform colleagues around the country to seek their advice and learn from their experience in erecting synagogue-centers. Rabbi Maurice Harris of Temple Israel in

New York City wrote back to Rabbi Levi and suggested: "It would be worth your while to run over to New York to visit three or four Centers, of which ours would be one, and another the remarkable Brooklyn Jewish Center." Similarly, Rabbi Samuel Hirshberg of Temple Emanuel in Milwaukee wrote: "Mr. A. B. Beal of Ohabei Shalom was recently here and I secured for him blueprints. . . . I would suggest that it would repay you and any committee . . . to come here and see personally the building, as also Franklin's in Detroit and Silver's in Cleveland."[60]

Finally, the rabbi of Union Temple in Brooklyn, Simon Cohen, wrote to Rabbi Levi:

My dear Harry, I have your letter of Friday touching the matter of a Centre connected with the Synagogue. The Jewish Centre here on Eastern Parkway has a very fine building, but it is a De Luxe Y.M.H.A. and my impression is that now the members themselves feel that in spite of all their efforts the club features of the Centre are failures. I have not discussed the matter with Rabbi I. H. Levinthal, but if you write him informing him that I referred you to him I am sure he will give you the information that you want. It might be wise also to confer with those institutions which have Community Houses or centres attached to the Synagogues to find just what is permanently needed and also the kind of activities best suited for the clientele you desire to cater to. Our Congregation "Union Temple" is now having plans completed for the finest Temple and Community House in the Country.[61]

Levi also received letters from Rabbis Abba Hillel Silver and Louis Wolsey, and in addition to the congregations mentioned, was sent photographs and brochures depicting synagogue-centers in Baltimore (Eutaw Place Temple), Chicago (both K.A.M. [Kehilath Anshe Mayriv] and the Sinai Social Center), and Newark (B'nai Jeshurun and B'nai Abraham). Thus the synagogue-center movement was spread throughout the land.

As noted before, the rabbis were joined by architects in spreading the idea. As soon as the word got out that the wealthy Temple Israel was planning a new building, architects began to write in to solicit the commission. One of the first was Albert Gottlieb, who explained: "In conversation yesterday with Rabbi Solomon Foster of Temple B'nai Jeshurun in Newark, N.J. which I designed for his congregation, he told me that your Temple in Boston is contemplating the erection of a new one and suggested that I write you to tell you about my work in Newark thinking that perhaps I might be given the opportunity to design your Temple also provided an architect has not already been selected." Other architects who wrote included Nathan Myers, Jacob Krokyn, Tachau and Vought (rejected as not being Boston architects), and S. S. Eisenberg who wrote: "you may have met me frequently at the affairs of the New Century Club. . . . I might add, in closing, that my office has designed and supervised the construction of most of the Temples and Talmud Torahs in greater Boston within the past ten years."[62]

The firm of Krokyn, Browne, and Rosenstein was particularly eager to win the commission and wrote repeatedly. In a letter dated May 23, 1924, Arthur Rosenstein wrote to A. C. Ratchesky, the chairman of the Land and Buildings Committee: "Some time ago Mr. Felix Vorenberg had advised us that he had forwarded to you data that we had sent him in relation to the professional activities of this office. With this and our general reputation in the community, we felt that we would be given serious consideration when choice of architects came up. . . . The enclosed photographs of the Temple Mishkan Tefila, the Boston Young Men's Hebrew Assoc. Gymnasium Building, . . . indicate the character of the work we do." Though the building committee of Temple Israel chose not to hire the leading Jewish architects of Boston, it was well aware of their various synagogue-center designs.[63]

After choosing the architectural firm of McLaughlin and Burr—interestingly, the designers of the nearby Harvard Medical School—the congregational leadership remained involved in the design process. In August 1924, Felix Vorenberg wrote to A. C. Ratchesky to inform him that "Rabbi Levi wrote me, from Kennebunkport, that he hoped we would visit other cities for the purpose of studying similar structures, before we proceed." At the same time, they were careful to retain the interest and the input of the entire congregation. At the annual meeting of December 1924, plans of the proposed buildings were submitted to the congregation for their approval. In early 1926, when construction was ready to proceed, the trustees presented "to the Congregation a résumé of just what has been done to date with regard to the new buildings. In doing this the Trustees emphasize that this is a Congregational enterprise and that each and every step that has been taken from the beginning to the present has been taken by the Congregation itself and not by the Trustees or by any committee. At every stage of progress the matter has been put before the members at a meeting and the vote of the Congregation taken."[64]

In February 1926, the new design was publicized in the local press. Architects McLaughlin and Burr described their project as follows:

The Congregation Adath Israel will begin early in March the erection of the first building of a religious center to be built on the new location on the Riverway. . . . This is one of the most sightly locations in Boston for an imposing religious group having an unobstructed view from practically all directions.

Much time, thought and deep research has been given to this problem by the architects and the drawings have been studied and re-studied to the end that this group of buildings when completed will be best adapted to every need of a great religion and the most beautiful architectural expression in the Country. The final design and the model presented by the architects, McLaughlin & Burr with Chas. H. Coolidge and C. Howard Walker as advisory architects show a beautiful structure of classic design facing on the Riverway, with the great Temple as the central dominating building flanked on either side by the less important entrances of the Social and Administrative units.

The architecture of the group is to be pure classic in conception and built of white limestone. The main entrance to the Temple is dignified by a lofty 6 column Corinthian portico richly decorated and surmounted by a Pediment. Behind this and covering the auditorium of the Temple is the roof of the dome which rises 125 feet from the ground. . . .

The religious activities of the Congregation are divided into four phases: Spiritual, Social, Educational, and Administrative. Each of these phases is adequately expressed in the plan.

The east wing contains the executive quarters and offices for the Rabbi and Assistant Rabbi with ample provision for accommodating all the religious club life of the Congregation.

At the rear of the group and fronting on Plymouth Street is the Educational building of the

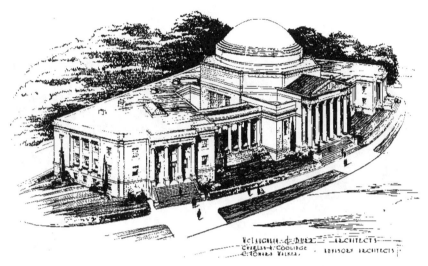

Fig. 46. Temple Israel, Boston. Architects' drawing. Courtesy of Temple Israel.

group. Here are rooms where approximately 1000 pupils will be given religious instruction. . . .

The west wing of the group along Longwood Avenue contains provision for social functions. In this wing is located the assembly hall to accommodate 1200 with adequate stage facilities for the proper presentation of social and religious drama.[65]

The west wing, called the "Meeting House," and the connected school building were dedicated in 1928, and have served the congregation ever since. The remainder of the monumental project was never completed due to the stock market crash of 1929 and the ensuing Great Depression. But the synagogue-center movement of Boston, as in the rest of the country, had left its mark.

Conclusion

The synagogue-center movement was most concretely expressed by the building boom of the 1920s, but its communal and even theological implications reverberate in American Jewish life to this day. Generated both by the socioeconomic success of second-generation American Jews and by the simultaneous religious revival of American Judaism, the synagogue-center idea had emerged in city after city. It became a local movement within each city as congregations competed for predominance, and a national movement as rabbis, lay leaders, and architects spread the word. The universal action that followed was to build. Indeed, it is the pervasive quality of the building phenomenon that is so striking. One can travel to just about any large city in the United States today, and locate the former Jewish neighborhood(s) of the interwar years. There one will find one or more remnants of the golden age of synagogue-center construction, once proud monuments now

Fig. 47a. Cleveland Jewish Center. Collection of Peter Schweitzer.

either abandoned or converted to new uses. Most often they have been turned into black churches, as with the recent conversion of Mishkan Tefila of Boston; yet some remain in Jewish hands, as in the case of the Brooklyn Jewish Center, now a Lubavitcher yeshiva. There are still others, such as the Jewish Center of the West Side, which remain in use by the original owners and continue to serve as active synagogue-centers. Whatever their current status, however, they remain as stark architectural testaments to a world gone by.

They also serve as vivid reminders of a movement that harks back to the intensive Jewish communal activity of turn-of-the-century America. Though the synagogue-center was a unified institution—bringing its religious, educational, and social functions together under one roof—it had emerged from diverse religious,

Fig. 47b. Temple de Hirsch, Seattle. *American Jewish Year Book*, vol. 28 (1926–27).

Fig. 47c. Temple Emanu-el, San Francisco. *American Jewish Year Book,* vol. 28 (1926–27).

Fig. 47d. Isaiah Temple, Chicago. *American Jewish Year Book,* vol. 28 (1926–27).

educational, and social trends. When interpreted properly, the historical legacy of the synagogue-center is the memory of the classical Reform "open temple," the Orthodox community synagogue, the Jewish educational settlement, the modern Talmud Torah, and the ideally synthetic Jewish Center—all uniquely American Jewish institutions, now all but lost to history. The phenomenal rise of the synagogue-center movement following World War I might lead one to see it only in terms of its immediate context. But the energy underlying the movement was just as surely drawn from the preceding period in which religious institutions vied with educational centers, educational institutions competed with social centers, and all jostled together within a fractious yet lively community. The organizational and communal cacophony of the first two decades of the twentieth century was then quieted by the dramatic resolution of the 1920s: the synagogue-center movement. But we ought not let the calm after the storm blind us to the reality of a fascinating era in American Jewish history.

The synagogue-center movement held profound implications for the future of American Jewish life as well. By unifying the diverse elements of the immigrant-era Jewish community, the synagogue-center movement was a principal factor in the creation of a unified American Jewish culture. As the central Jewish institution of the second-generation neighborhood (the public school was the central American institution), the synagogue-center set the religious and communal tone for Jewish community building in succeeding generations as well. As the first and most successful experiment in social-religious consolidation, it provided a model for the contemporary American Jewish syntheses of the suburban synagogue, Jewish community center, and communal federation. Perhaps most important, the synagogue-center established the predominance of the congregational synagogue in American Jewish life. Because the "Jewish center" idea was most often adopted by a congregation, and realized in the form of a synagogue (hence, "synagogue-center"), the synagogue rather than the settlement or school remained the central institution of the Jewish community. Because the original concept was to combine the separate functions on an equal basis, the congregational synagogue-center may be said to be a compromised institution, and the movement might be judged a failure. However, whereas the ideal version never quite succeeded as such, the idealization had produced a new kind of Jewish institution—short of the ideal, but unique and original nonetheless. That the contemporary American synagogue contains educational and social functions as a matter of course—in sharp contrast to synagogues elsewhere in the world—testifies to the success of the synagogue-center movement. And the fact that American Jewish life continues to be energized by the dynamic interrelationship between ethnic culture and religious commitment is testament to the essential truth of the synagogue-center idea: contrary to modernity, Jews and Judaism are one.

EPILOGUE

Relations between the synagogue and the Jewish center are in many instances neither close nor cordial; certainly not, if the participation of rabbis in the center program is an adequate test. . . . The lack of cooperation between the center and the synagogue is conditioned by a number of factors—institutional, personal, attitudes toward formal religion, and differing conceptions of Jewish life. . . . It is quite simple to assign "religion" to the synagogue, and cultural, recreational and social activities to the center.   —OSCAR JANOWSKY, 1948[1]

As IN THE HISTORY of the synagogue-center, a tension between the ideal and the real can be discerned throughout this book. Seduced by the noble dream of the era's rabbis, educators, and other communal workers to create a perfectly synthetic Jewish institution, the historian may be tempted to describe the real institution in idealized terms. One way to do this would be to cut off the story in its prime, to end the account at the highpoint of the saga, thereby implying that the synagogue-center lived on forever in its robust state of maturity. But this is not the case. Rather than succeeding in its attempt to heal the basic schism of American Jewish life, that is, to bridge the gap between the social and religious tendencies of Jewish identity, the synagogue-center movement actually ended up institutionalizing the divide. A brief account of this reversal of fortune must be added as an epilogue to an otherwise heroic tale. For in the end, the story of the failure of the synagogue-center holds as much relevance for contemporary American Jewish life as does the story of its success.

The Elite Movement: Debates over the Synagogue-Center

Even as the synagogue-center movement united American Jews on the local level, the ideological movement was split apart by opposing boosters of the synagogue and the center. Because the synagogue-center was a centrist phenomenon, it came under criticism from both the left and the right, that is, from both the social and religious ends of the continuum. Perhaps the sharpest attacks came from rabbis across the denominational spectrum who were less enthused than their sociologically attuned colleagues to the social potential of the house of God.

Defenders of the traditional synagogue, they offered consistent critique concerning the apparent secularization of what was an essentially religious institution. As early as 1915, anticipating the objections of later years, Solomon Schechter issued a warning in what turned out to be his last public address (at the commencement exercises of the Seminary held on June 6, 1915):

> the great danger of our age is the tendency towards secularizing life and thought in all its aspects, even those aspects which originated in the Sanctuary. . . . The Sacred Writ, it is maintained, is to be studied as a mere ancient classic, not as a Torah of *Chesed*. . . . Jewish endeavor in the line of Jewish settlements and kindred social work is to be conducted on non-religious lines. . . . The synagogue itself, affectionately called by our ancestors *Makom Kadosh,* a Sacred Place, is to be largely stripped of its sacred features. It is to make room for the Institutional Synagogue in which the worship of God by reason of its organization must become in the end subordinated to the material service of man and his amusements.[2]

The debate between pro- and anti-synagogue-center rabbis did not emerge into the open until a decade later. One of the first to object was the right-of-center Rabbi Joel Blau, who contributed an article to the annual publication of the Brooklyn Jewish Center of 1925, in which he wrote: "The Center Movement has decidedly had its birth in what I called above, 'the whistling of God's word through the keyhole.' The argument had been that since the young . . . want athletics, swimming pools, dances, lectures on not too difficult subjects, we will give it to them, and incidentally we will lure them to a little bit of a religious service with a little bit of a sermon, preferably on the topics of the day; so that little by little they might become used to going to the Synagogue and imbibing what is called Jewishness." According to several sources, it was Blau who first employed the phrase "shul with a pool" to describe the synagogue-center in a derogatory way, as an epithet.[3]

The debate was taken up by the New York Board of Jewish Ministers, which held a symposium in 1926 entitled "Problems of the Jewish Ministry," later published under that title in book form. On the subject "The Synagogue Center," Rabbi Samuel M. Cohen noted that while "members and leaders of Centers, as a rule, express satisfaction with the development of their institutions . . . deep down in their hearts there are many misgivings." Cohen had extensive experience with synagogue-center development. While serving as the first executive director of the United Synagogue of America, he "personally helped establish more than 150 congregations on behalf of the United Synagogue, promoting the concept of the synagogue-center" all the while. He cited the following problems: "In many Centers, there seems to be no integration of the various activities and departments in the Center. The Hebrew School, for instance, will be supervised by a principal who is a secular, cultural Hebraist. The gymnasium will be in charge of a retired pugilist. The director of clubs, a social worker, and the director of the whole institution, a suave business executive. The Rabbi is in charge of the Synagogue, teaches several classes and occasionally helps secure speakers for the Forum. He does not seem to exercise much influence on the institution as a whole."[4]

Two of the best-known critics were, interestingly enough, also leading Zion-ists—recalling our earlier discussion (Chapter 1) of Reform Zionists who op-posed the synagogue-center concept. They were Reform rabbi Abba Hillel Silver and Conservative rabbi Israel Goldstein, both of whom presided over the con-struction of center facilities by their congregations only to later disavow the con-cept entirely. In 1926, after four years of the synagogue-center program of the "Temple" (Tifereth Israel) in Cleveland, Abba Hillel Silver delivered an address to the Thirteenth Annual Recreational Congress in which he stated: "I am not at all convinced, as some others are, that the church ought to try to bring under its roof all the recreational enterprises of a community. I am not that ambitious for organized religion. I rather think that in some instances such an all-comprehensive and embracing policy is distinctly harmful; for very often the still, small voice of the church—its spiritual message—is drowned in the din of the multifarious ac-tivities which go on under its roof. Very often, the church, in attempting to sanc-tify secular activities, finds itself profaned and secularized, and that is a distinct social loss." Three years later, in 1929, Rabbi Silver recommended the abandon-ment of the synagogue-center program. In a report to his congregation, later reprinted in the *American Hebrew,* he explained: "The crowding of many secular activities into the life of a congregation frequently causes men to lose sight of the real purposes of a religious institution. . . . The Synagogue ought to concentrate upon those basic community needs which, from its inception, have been its par-ticular province—religious inspiration and religious education."[5]

Israel Goldstein was similarly disappointed with the progress of his congrega-tion in New York, B'nai Jeshurun. In a paper delivered before the Rabbinical As-sembly in 1928, Goldstein "declared himself an "agnostic" on this subject" of the synagogue-center, and added in the following year: "No doubt there is much still to be said in its favor, but it is true, as has been repeatedly stated by its critics, that whereas the hope of the Synagogue Center was to Synagogize the tone of the secular activities of the family, the effect has been the secularization of the place of the Synagogue. Card parties and fat reducing exercises under Synagogue aus-pices have not made people more Synagogue-minded or even more Jewish con-scious; witness the attempt to introduce the Jewish note into the secular activities of the Synagogue Center, regarded as an intrusion by the lay powers and inter-dicted as a menace to the popularity of the institution. . . . If the Synagogue Cen-ter has had the effect of erasing the distinction between the sacred and the secu-lar, it has been at the expense of the sacred. The Synagogue as a week-end institution may have seemed aloof and ineffective. As a week-day institution, functioning through the Center, it has become banal, and even vulgar."[6]

Nevertheless, as Leon Spitz noted, "Synagogue Centers continued to flourish" despite the criticism of their rabbis, no matter how influential. The point was that rabbis were occupationally and temperamentally committed to the religious side of the equation. They rarely comprehended the synagogue-center concept from a balanced perspective, in which the social and religious elements might be equally weighted and thus fully integrated. When they said "synagogue-center," they meant a synagogue with an appended center, rather than the synthetic institution originally intended. Mordecai Kaplan himself lamented the failure of the rabbis to "get it" when he wrote, in 1932: "Opportunity has brought to the Rabbi the institution of the Jewish Center. If he had only known how to utilize it, he could have made of it the means to a Jewish spiritual and cultural renaissance. But lacking the training in the human sciences, he regards it merely as a means of inveigling the young people to the Synagogue." When *Judaism as a Civilization* was published two years later, Kaplan was still trying to convey the message to his hardheaded colleagues.[7]

In that same year, Horace Stern wrote in the *American Jewish Yearbook:* "We all know that the synagogue of today is vastly shrunken in its activities as compared with periods previous to the present. The synagogue was formerly the centre of all Jewish life. Abrahams says that the medieval Jew not only prayed in the synagogue, he lived in it. It was the common meeting place and in it the communal life expressed itself.... It is true that some synagogues have so-called 'centres' or community houses attached to them, where there are gymnasiums and even swimming pools, and assembly halls where brotherhoods and sisterhoods and Sunday School alumni have dinners and receptions and dramatic and vaudeville performances and lectures. These kinds of entertainment are not to be condemned nor criticized, but on the other hand their religious and ethical value should not be exaggerated in the minds of those who sponsor and those who enjoy them." Even as late as 1934, the synagogue-center idea had still not taken hold.[8]

The Synagogue-Center Split

Ultimately, it was neither the expensive building projects nor the single-minded rabbis that doomed the synagogue-center movement to failure. Just as rabbis had criticized the idea from the religious standpoint, another group of Jewish professionals represented the opposing viewpoint. They did more than criticize, however, they created an alternative movement: the so-called Jewish (Community) Center movement, as institutionalized by the Jewish Welfare Board, led by Jewish social workers, and promulgated through the pages of the *Jewish Center,* a periodical that began publication in October 1922. Prior to 1920, the name "Jewish Center" had referred to the pioneer synagogue-center of Mordecai Kaplan; as when Isaac Berkson noted "a new and very interesting institution, "The Jewish Centre" [on W. 86th St.]," in his chapter on "The CJI—A *Jewish Community Center.*" In the early 1920s, however, while congregational "Jewish Centers" proliferated in Brooklyn and elsewhere, a separate movement co-opted the name and redefined it to include any institution—settlement, YMHA, school center, *or* synagogue— that fostered Jewish communal life.[9]

When Jewish Center workers invoked the name of their movement, they intended a generic Jewish institution whose religious component was negligible. It might have a synagogue, it might not; certainly the synagogue need not be the central element. A synagogue-center was simply one type of Jewish Center; without its synagogue, it would be another type, just as acceptable. The Jewish Center movement thus advocated a multipurpose Jewish institution that could exist outside of, and even without the synagogue. The implication was that Jewish religious life was obsolete, in line to be replaced by the cultural and ethnic Jewishness of the secular center. The patron saint of the Jewish Center movement, remarkably enough, was Mordecai Kaplan. But Kaplan never intended the demolition of the synagogue, only its reconstruction.

In the March 1928 issue of the *Jewish Center,* YMHA director Aaron Robison reviewed the earlier publication of *Problems of the Jewish Ministry,* and wrote: "Of particular interest to Jewish Center workers is the symposium on "The Synagogue Center." . . . There seems to exist a state of bewilderment as to the advisability of the Synagogue Center and, if it is to continue, much doubt as to what it ought to be. . . . In many places, one is struck by the fact that the Synagogue Center has the same goal and purpose as our Jewish Community Centers."[10]

The confusion he spoke of was due to the phenomenon of two opposing groups—rabbis and social workers—laying claim to the same institutional type. That is to say, the religious and the social spheres of Jewish community were fighting for predominance. Both wanted to be at the "center" of Jewish life. If the rabbis had their way, the center would be the Synagogue; if the social workers prevailed, the center would be . . . the Center! In between them stood a range of synagogue-center institutions, pulled to and fro like so much ideological taffy. The social-religious rivalry plagued individual synagogue-centers as well. In 1932, looking back at a decade of synagogue-center activity, the executive director of the Jewish Welfare Board observed: "Sometimes, because of lack of self-assurance in problems of Center management, and other times because of the feeling that the Center represents mundane influences that had no essential relationship to the Synagogue, the Rabbi often remained aloof from Center activities. A sharp distinction was drawn between the sphere of the spiritual and the realm of the secular, a division that was inconsistent with the program unity implied in the concept of the Center. Indeed, it is an unreal and forced distinction."[11]

The debate raged on throughout the 1920s (most prominently in the pages of the *Jewish Center*) without resolution. Both congregational synagogue-centers and Jewish community centers continued to be constructed, often competing for the same constituencies and funding. In some cases, the tendency toward synthesis prevailed, as in the case of the YMHA Temple of Aurora, Illinois (1927); and in the 1930s at Congregation Hebrew Educational Alliance of Denver (1932), and the JCC of Norristown, Pennsylavania, which was the merger of Congregation Tiferes Israel and the local YMHA (1936). And during the same era, back at the YMHA of New York, the "Religious Council" was instituted in

1927 as "a membership group that was to be the nucleus for a permanent con-gregation." The "Young People's Synagog" opened in the fall of 1931.[12]

Nevertheless, the synagogue-center split became the principal legacy of the 1920s, as it grew into an institutional rivalry through the 1930s, and then spurred the development of separate movements during the 1940s. The timing was pro-pitious; the move to suburbia was on and the new communities seemed to hold great promise for both the synagogue and center. Most often, the first Jewish in-stitution to be founded in suburbia was either a school for the children or a social group for the adults. In either case, for reasons most famously elucidated by Will Herberg, the incipient institution came to be defined in religious terms and soon evolved into a full-service "temple." The most important of its services inevitably became the Hebrew school, so that in suburbia, the formerly communal func-tion of Jewish education became solely the province of the congregation. The Jewish "denomination" most often chosen was the one thought to appeal to the broadest clientele: centrist Conservativism. As had occurred earlier in the cen-tury, the creation of a synagogue-center preceded its affiliation with the Conserv-ative movement.[13]

The synagogal synagogue-center was therefore reinvigorated as a Conservative institution at a time when the ideas of Mordecai Kaplan were finally gaining cur-rency in the movement. By 1940 his followers had attained a majority of sorts, and in that year the presidency of the Jewish Theological Seminary passed from the anti-Kaplan Cyrus Adler to Louis Finkelstein, heralding a new era in Conser-vative Judaism. In 1941, the *Synagogue Center* periodical was established by the United Synagogue, and five years later, two articles by Conservative rabbis de-scribed the synagogue-center movement as coextensive with their own: Leon Spitz's "The Synagogue Center Marches On—The History of the Synagogue Center Movement in the United States," and Jacob Agus's "On the Furtherance of the Synagogue-Center Movement," in 1946 and 1947 respectively. The notion of a Conservative monopoly on the synagogue-center dates back to the 1940s, no further.[14]

About the same time, the Jewish (Community) Center movement began to reconsider its mission. If Jewish suburbanites were opting to build synagogues rather than centers, than something must be amiss. The Jewish Center move-ment's soul-searching culminated with the 1948 publication of *The JWB Survey,* by Oscar Janowsky. Harking back to Louis Marshall's pronouncement of four decades before, Janowsky's major theme was the need for the "Judaization" of the center. Apparently, the educational emphasis associated with the Benderly boys and the early days of the Jewish center movement had been lost as the social and recreational functions took precedence in practice, and the function of Jewish education was taken over by the synagogue. Still a sectarian agency, however, the center required a Jewish rationale. This was found in the emergent ideology of "civil Judaism"—the secular Jewish faith characteristic of the UJA (United Jewish Appeal) fund-raising campaign, federations, and the Jewish Community Center.

As ethnic Jewish identification grew in acceptability, the JCC became the preferred institution of Jewish suburbia and experienced a mini-boom of its own.[15]

The tension between the religious synagogue and the social center thus persisted throughout the post–World War II period, as reflected by the pattern of
Jewish institutions built in suburbia. Unlike the earlier building booms of the
turn of the century and the 1920s, the boom of the 1950s–1970s is well documented. Because the only institutions built along the "suburban frontier" were
synagogues and JCCs (no settlement houses or Talmud Torahs to confuse the
picture), the building activity seemed that much more concentrated. Our study
of the earlier building boom may now yield some insight into the synagogue and
center efflorescence of the post–World War II era. If the original synagogue-
center had been, in Deborah Dash Moore's phrase, a "metaphor for community,"
how much more urgent would the need be in the cultural wasteland of Jewish
suburbia? In turn, this observation helps to explain the failure of the synagogue-
center during the 1920s. Second-generation Jews living in urban Jewish neighborhoods had no use for communal metaphors; they had the real thing. At the
time, however, they could not see the familial, tight-knit community for what it
was. Only by comparison with the atomized environment of suburbia would
they wax nostalgic, and once again, reconstruct the fondly remembered Jewish
institution of the old neighborhood: the synagogue-center.[16]

Simultaneously, they re-created the split between synagogue and center. There
exists an extensive literature documenting the ongoing ideological debates during those years, most notably two symposia "on the relationship between the
Synagogue and the Center" in the pages of *Conservative Judaism*. By the 1960s,
however, the original synagogue-center idea had long since faded away in the
public mind. Third-generation American Jews knew what a synagogue was of
course, and they knew well the JCC, but the two combined? Only in the late
1960s and 1970s would the religious-social synthesis again be attempted in American Jewish life—by the fabled Havurah movement. The subject of the Havurah—an informal and intimate, nonhierarchal and participatory synagogue-
community—and its analogous relationship to the synagogue-center must be left
to another time.[17]

Conclusion

Thus the synagogue-center ideal—that is, an integration of the religious and social functions of Jewish life—never came to fruition. For this reason, the term
"Jewish Center"—representing the aspiration to perfect synthesis, that is, the
ideal synagogue-center—was replaced by "Jewish *Community* Center." Both the
synagogue-center and Jewish Center movements, insofar as they promoted an
idealized institution, must therefore be judged failures; due, in no small part, to
their split into two separate groups. Just as institutions competed to detrimental

effect on the local level, resources on a national level were squandered by the existence of dual movements.

Despite its failure to achieve a perfect synthesis between synagogue and center, the synagogue-center movement left both institutions permanently changed. The synagogue was "socialized," now including a school, library, assembly hall, kitchen, and other institutional trappings as a matter of course. Whatever its congregational name, the American synagogue of today customarily perceives itself as a "Jewish center." As Marshall Sklare has pointed out, one need only compare the contemporary synagogue to its counterpart in Israel to see the innovation of the American version. Likewise, the synagogue-center movement left its impress upon the Jewish center: while the synagogue socialized, the center Judaized. The cultural pluralist aspect of the synagogue-center, its role as a guarantor of Jewish identity, became the Jewish center's raison d'être and the rationalization for its separate existence. To this day, the Center movement has maintained an independence from the synagogue movements, perpetuating itself through a national organization (the JCC Association, formerly JWB), ideological elaboration, professionalization of its staff and systems, and by the ever-growing number of Jewish community centers constructed during the past half-century. The JCC, it is fair to say, has become the "secular synagogue" of contemporary American Jewry. And the split remains.

As I have described in great detail, the synagogue-center had numerous historical sources: the institutional church, Reform temple, YMHA, Jewish settlement, Talmud Torah, Orthodox synagogue, Mordecai Kaplan, and the second-generation Jewish neighborhood—each and every one a discrete origin of the synagogue-center innovation. I have implied throughout that the synagogue-center would have emerged from any one of these movements alone. To what do we attribute this phenomenon? Quite simply, to the one theme that underlies all of these movements and much else in American Jewish life: the tension between the social and religious elements of Jewishness, between Jews and Judaism. The synagogue-center was the American Jewish institution whose founders self-consciously attempted to synthesize the two sides of the Jewish dichotomy and thus cannot be understood without this basic conception. The primary paradigm for the study of the American Jewish experience has been, and assuredly will continue to be, the balance between American integration and Jewish survival, the creative tension between "America" and "Jewish." But the principal underlying theme of this study has been the dialectic between the religious "synagogue" and the social "center." In the final analysis, it must be seen as yet another essential paradigm for the understanding of American Jewish life.

NOTES

INTRODUCTION

1. Salo Baron, *A Social and Religious History of the Jews* (Philadelphia: The Jewish Publication Society of America, 1952) 1:3–4. See also Heinrich Graetz, "The Construction of Jewish History" (1846); and Yehezkel Kaufmann, *Gola-ve-Nekhar* "Diaspora and alien lands" (Palestine, 1929–30); both excerpts found in English translation in Michael Meyer, ed., *Ideas of Jewish History* (New York: Behrman House, 1974), 224–28, 277.

2. In the existing literature, the phrase "synagogue-center" will be seen often as two separate words. I have chosen the hyphenated version in order to emphasize the synthetic nature of the institution. For chapter-length treatments of the subject, see Samuel Abelow, "The Center Movement," chap. 3 in *History of Brooklyn Jewry* (New York: Scheba, 1937); Leon Spitz, "The Synagogue Center Marches On—The History of the Synagogue Center Movement in the United States," in the *Brooklyn Jewish Center Jubilee Book* (April 1946); Jeffrey Gurock, "Harlem Jewry and the Emergence of the American Synagogue," chap. 5 in *When Harlem Was Jewish, 1870–1930* (New York: Columbia University Press, 1979); Deborah Dash Moore, "From Chevra to Center," chap. 5 in *At Home in America: Second Generation New York Jews* (New York: Columbia University Press, 1981); and Jenna Weissman Joselit, "'Bigger and Better' Orthodox Synagogues," chap. 2 in *New York's Jewish Jews: The Orthodox Community in the Interwar Years* (Bloomington: Indiana University Press, 1990). Note that all these studies are relegated to New York City. The exception, as well as the most incisive discussion, is Marshall Sklare, "Social Activities and Jewish Education in the Conservative Synagogue," chap. 5 in *Conservative Judaism: An American Religious Movement* (Lanham, Md.: University Press of America, 1955; 2d ed., 1985; orig. publ. Glencoe, Ill.: Free Press, 1955).

3. Quote from Marshall Sklare, *America's Jews* (New York: Random Press, 1971), 127. For a more in-depth study by the same author, see his *Conservative Judaism.*

4. Abraham G. Duker, "Structure of the Jewish Community," in *The American Jew: A Composite Portrait,* ed. Oscar I. Janowsky (New York: Harper & Bros., 1942), 148–49: "It is the common meeting place of the orthodox, reform, conservative, as well as those Jews who have no connection with synagogue or temple. Through the center, the work of the local organizations is co-ordinated, and its membership becomes well-nigh synonymous with conscious adherence to the Jewish community." Deborah Dash Moore, *At Home in America: Second Generation New York Jews* (New York: Columbia University Press, 1981), 70–71: "Each [Jewish communal] organization staked a claim to supremacy by supporting a visible building as a physical symbol of its collective presence in the world of the neighborhood." Article III of the *Statement of Principles on Jewish Center Purposes* (adopted by Annual Meeting of JWB [Jewish Welfare Board] National Council, Chicago, May 9, 1948): "The functions of the Jewish Center include: A Service as an agency of Jewish identification . . ." [Reprinted in *A Documentary*

Story of a Century of the Jewish Community Center, 1854–1954, ed. Philip Goodman (New York: Jewish Community Center Centennial Committee, 1954), 64.]

5. On the notion of "a good Jew," see Marshall Sklare's discussion of "The Image of the Good Jew in Lakeville," in *Jewish Identity on the Suburban Frontier* (Chicago: University of Chicago Press, 1967, 1979), 321–32. Also, by the same author, *America's Jews* (New York: Random House, 1971), 122.

6. Aaron I. Abell, *The Urban Impact on American Protestantism, 1865–1900* (Cambridge: Harvard University Press, 1943). Charles H. Lippy, "Social Christianity," in *Encyclopedia of the American Religious Experience,* ed. Charles H. Lippy and Peter W. Williams (New York: Scribner, 1988), 2:917–31.

7. *The Jews of the United States,* ed. Priscilla Fishman (Jerusalem: Keter, 1973), 135–36. See also Sidney Goldstein, *The Synagogue and Social Welfare* (New York: Stephen Wise Free Synagogue, 1955): "The synagogue center probably arose out of two trends. One was that of the institutional church. . . . The synagogue center movement [also] owes its existence in large part to a growing interest in social life, and to an effort on its part to retrieve its prestige as a communal center" (44).

8. Aaron I. Abell, *The Urban Impact on American Protestantism, 1865–1900* (Cambridge: Harvard University Press, 1943), 137. On the influence of the institutional church, Louis Kraft wrote in 1944: "Many of our best group work agencies had a church origin. Rabbi Philip Goodman, director of educational activities of the National Jewish Welfare Board, believes that the spread of the Synagogue Center in America was largely influenced by the work of [the Reverend] Jenkins Lloyd Jones in Chicago." See also Mordecai Kaplan, *Judaism as a Civilization: Toward a Reconstruction of American-Jewish Life* (New York: T. Yoseloff, 1957; repr., New York: Schocken Books, 1967), 52.

9. *Congregation Beth Emeth Year Book, 1914–1922* (Albany, N.Y.: 1922), 16.

10. Lee I. Levine, "The Second Temple Synagogue: The Formative Years," in *The Synagogue in Late Antiquity,* ed. Lee I. Levine (Philadelphia: American Schools of Oriental Research, 1987), 15.

11. An example of two together can be found in *Pesikta de-Rav Kahana* 121a: "He said to them: Go and pass before their Houses of Study and Houses of Prayer." Common enough, this type of listing only supports the argument that they were distinct institutions. *Hammer on the Rock: A Midrashic Reader,* ed. Nahum Glatzer (New York: Schocken Books, 1962), 33.

12. Mel Scult, *Judaism Faces the Twentieth Century: A Biography of Mordecai M. Kaplan* (Detroit: Wayne State University Press, 1993).

13. Paula Hyman, "From City to Suburb: Temple Mishkan Tefila of Boston," in *The American Synagogue: A Sanctuary Transformed,* ed. Jack Wertheimer (Cambridge: Cambridge University Press, 1987), 185. See also Marshall Sklare, *Conservative Judaism.* While acknowledging the existence of Reform and Orthodox synagogue-centers, Sklare subsumes his examination of the synagogue-center within an analysis of the Conservative synagogue, thereby obscuring the pervasive quality of the synagogue-center phenomenon. Rather than being the sole province of one Jewish denomination, the synagogue-center was the ubiquitous product of a historical period affecting every sector of American Judaism.

14. In addition to Hyman, "From City to Suburb," see Gurock, "Harlem Jewry," Moore, "From Chevra to Center," and Joselit, "Bigger and Better."

1. TEMPLE

1. Israel Mattuck, "America Revisited: Leader of Progressive Judaism in England Discusses Developments in Liberal Movement in America and the Jew's Place in American Life," *Ameri-*

can Hebrew 121:24 (Oct. 28, 1927), 863. The Lithuanian-born Mattuck (1883–1954) was raised in Worcester, Massachusetts, attended Harvard College, and received ordination from Hebrew Union College in 1910. Leaving for England the following year, he cofounded—with Claude Montefiore and Lily Montagu—the movement for "Liberal Judaism." In 1926, the same group created the World Union for Progressive Judaism. Michael Meyer, *Response to Modernity* (New York: Oxford University Press, 1988), 220–21, 335–40.

2. Mattuck, "America Revisited."

3. The Pittsburgh Platform of 1885; see Meyer, *Response to Modernity,* 388. Note the distinction between "religion" and "religious community." It is subtle yet significant, as it points to a later corruption of our understanding of classical Reform Judaism. A more accurate definition of classical Reform would acknowledge the continuum between moderate and radical extremes that was embodied and to some degree resolved by the classical synthesis.

4. Mordecai M. Kaplan, *The Greater Judaism in the Making: A Study of the Modern Evolution of Judaism* (New York: Reconstructionist Press, 1960), 311.

5. Although founded as an Orthodox institution, Mordecai Kaplan's Jewish Center served as the prototype for the Conservative synagogue in America; see Marshall Sklare, *Conservative Judaism: An American Religious Movement* (Lanham, Md.: University Press of America, 1985; orig. pub. Glencoe, Ill.: Free Press, 1955); and for further discussion, Chapter 6 below.

6. Michael Meyer is the latest and most authoritative historian to describe the period following 1885 as "classical" Reform; *Response to Modernity*, 265. The observation that classical Reform is a synthesis of Wise and Einhorn has its origin in Kaufmann Kohler's 1895 comment that "in the new ritual [the Union Prayer Book] Einhorn and Wise dwell together," quoted in Moshe Davis, "Jewish Religious Life and Institutions in America," *The Jews*, ed. Louis Finkelstein (Philadelphia: JPS, 1960), 528. Meyer does not repeat the truism but implies as much by the juxtaposition of his chapters 6 (on Wise and Einhorn) and 7 (on "classical" Reform Judaism). Mattuck, "America Revisited," 863. On the development of the synagogue, see Abraham Karp, "Overview: The Synagogue in America—A Historical Typology," in *The American Synagogue: A Sanctuary Transformed*, ed. Jack Wertheimer (Cambridge: Cambridge University Press, 1987). There is as yet no equivalent typological treatment of the American rabbinate.

7. On the earlier period of American Reform, see Leon Jick, *The Americanization of the Synagogue, 1820–1870* (Hanover, University Press of New England, 1976). Jonathan Sarna has described the post-1870 period as a "religious revival" for American Judaism and more recently, as the "American Jewish Awakening." Sarna, *JPS: The Americanization of Jewish Culture, 1888–1988* (Philadelphia: JPS, 1989); and "The Late 19th-Century American Jewish Awakening," in *Religious Diversity and American Religious History*, ed. Walter H. Conser, Jr., and Sumner B. Twiss (Athens, Ga.: University of Georgia Press, 1997), 1–25.

8. Michael Meyer, "A Centennial History," part 1 of *HUC-JIR At One Hundred Years*, ed. Samuel Karff (Hebrew Union Press, 1976). For more on the new roles of the American rabbi, see Marc Lee Raphael, *Profiles in American Judaism: The Reform, Conservative, Orthodox, and Reconstructionist Traditions in Historical Perspective* (San Francisco: Harper & Row, 1984), 38.

9. The literature on the reforming of the American synagogue is extensive. For a general narrative, see Jick, *Americanization of the Synagogue*; and on a specific aspect, Jonathan Sarna, "The Debate over Mixed Seating in the American Synagogue," in *The American Synagogue: A Sanctuary Transformed*, ed. Jack Wertheimer (Cambridge: Cambridge University Press, 1987). On the question of architectural style, see Rachel Wischnitzer, *Synagogue Architecture in the United States* (Philadelphia: JPS, 1955); and regarding the term "temple," Wischnitzer, *Synagogue Architecture,* 48; and Meyer, *Response to Modernity*, 42.

10. American Jewish Archives, MS Coll. 56, 2/4.

11. *American Israelite,* 34:22 (Nov. 25, 1887), 5; 34:28 (Jan. 6, 1888), 3.

12. *American Hebrew* 37:1 (Nov. 9, 1888), 2, under the title, "Congregational Work" (em-

phases added). The editorial is in praise of the solution of Henry Berkowitz (see note 21). As Simon Rawidowicz first suggested, such portents of doom may serve as Jewish "early warning systems," averting the very evil of which they forewarn. See Jonathan Sarna, "Jewish Identity in the Changing World of American Religion," in *Jewish Identity in America*, ed. David M. Gordis and Yoav Ben-Horin (Los Angeles: University of Judaism, 1991).

13. Aaron Hahn, "The Relation of the Rabbi to the Congregation," *CCAR Yearbook* (1890), 1:71.

14. *The Changing World of Reform Judaism: The Pittsburgh Platform in Retrospect*, ed. Walter Jacob (Pittsburgh: Rodef Shalom Congregation, 1985), 92. On the calling of the conference, see Meyer, *Response to Modernity*, 265–68.

15. Jacob, *Changing World*, 94–95.

16. David Einhorn Hirsch, *Rabbi Emil G. Hirsch, The Reform Advocate* (Northbrook, Ill.: Whitehall, 1968).

17. *The Reform Advocate* 1:1 (Feb. 20, 1891), 6. Ibid., 1:2, 1.

18. "The Social Features of Congregational Life," *Reform Advocate* 3:2 (Feb. 27, 1892), 66 (emphasis added). On Social Christianity, see Aaron I. Abell, *The Urban Impact on American Protestantism, 1865–1900* (Cambridge, Mass.: Harvard University Press, 1943).

19. Kerry Olitzky, in "Sunday-Sabbath Movement," *American Jewish Archives* 34:1 (April 1982), 75–88; Sidney Regner, "The Rise and Decline of the Sunday Service," *Journal of Reform Judaism* (Fall 1980), 30–37. See relevant comments by Kaufmann Kohler in *Changing World*, 96–95, and as quoted in Moshe Davis, "Jewish Religious Life and Institutions in America," in *The Jews: Their History, Culture, and Religion*, ed. Louis Finkelstein (Philadelphia: JPS, 3d ed., 1960), 519. Also see Joseph Krauskopf's recommendation in the *CCAR Yearbook* (1904), 14: 25–27. The quotation is by Julius Rosenthal, *Reform Advocate* (Jan. 14, 1898).

20. Joseph Silverman, "The Paramount Duty of Temple Emanuel," in *Emanu-El Pulpit* 11:2 (1908), 8.

21. Hirsch, in *Reform Jewish Advocate*, May 8, 1891, "Sinai Congregation's Radicalism," 197 [7]. Berkowitz, in part 2 of "Judaism and the New Education," reprinted in *Jewish Messenger* 64:1 (July 6, 1888), 4.

22. Myer Stern, *The Rise and Progress of Reform Judaism: Embracing a History Made from the Official Records of Temple Emanu-El of New York* (New York: Myer Stern, 1895), 73. Quoted in W. Gunther Plaut, *The Growth of Reform Judaism*, vol. 2 in his *The Rise of Reform Judaism*, 2 vol. (New York: World Union for Progressive Judaism, 1963–65), 342.

23. Quoted from "Ten Years of Fruitful Work for Humanity," *Cleveland Leader*, Nov. 16, 1902; AJArchives, MS. Coll. 53, Box 4/2. Similarly, Henry Berkowitz's biographer described him as "modern and at the same time reverent toward tradition; American, and also Jewish to the core." Max Berkowitz, *The Beloved Rabbi: An Account of the Life and Works of Henry Berkowitz, D.D.* (New York: Macmillan, 1932), 449.

24. Leonard J. Mervis, "The Social Justice Movement and the American Reform Rabbi," *AJA* 7 (1955), 171–230; Jerrold Goldstein, "Reform Rabbis and the Progressive Movement" (M.A. thesis, University of Minnesota, 1967); Egal Feldman, "The Social Gospel and the Jews," *American Jewish Historical Quarterly* 58 (March 1969), 308–22.

25. Michael Meyer, "A Centennial History," in *Hebrew Union College-Jewish Institute of Religion at One Hundred Years*, ed. Samuel Karff (Cincinnati: Hebrew Union College Press, 1976), 21–23.

26. Ibid., 28–29.

27. Significantly, "Atzilei Bene Israel" was Wise's term for both the student literary society and a title to confer upon ordination. See *American Israelite* 34:31 (Jan. 27, 1988), 6; Meyer, "A Centennial History," 29, 37. *CCAR Yearbook* (1902), 12:138. As the solution to synagogue

inattendance on Saturday, Wise favored the introduction of Friday night services over the more radical innovation of Sunday services.

28. Joseph Krauskopf (1858–1923) was born in Ostrowo, Prussia, and came to the United States in 1872 at the age of fourteen. Three years later he enrolled in the first class of the Hebrew Union College. After ordination in 1883, he served as rabbi for B'nai Jehudah Congregation in Kansas City, until 1887 when he was called to Philadelphia to succeed S. Hirsch at Keneseth Israel. Henry Berkowitz (1857–1924) was born and educated in Pittsburgh; in 1883, was graduated from Hebrew Union College; served Temple Shaare Shamayim in Mobile, Alabama from 1883 to 1888; succeeded Krauskopf at Temple B'nai Jehudah of Kansas City in 1888; and in 1892 was called to succeed Marcus Jastrow at Rodeph Shalom of Philadelphia, thus joining Krauskopf in that city. With David Philipson and Israel Aaron, they were members of an elite group, the first graduating class of Hebrew Union College. They did not, of course, make a radical break from Wise, but merely shifted their emphasis. The Wiseian conception persisted, as when Krauskopf promised "to make this place a house of God, and you must come hither with no other purpose but to seek here the word of God." Inaugural Address (Oct. 22, 1887) delivered to Temple Keneseth Israel, Philadelphia: "The Minister and the Congregation," printed in *American Israelite* 34:21 (Nov. 18, 1887).

29. *American Israelite* 32:11 (Sept. 11, 1885), "The Acceptance of the Key," 4.

30. Bernhard Felsenthal, in *Sermons by American Rabbis* (Chicago: Central Conference Publication Committee, 1896). "K.A.M. Dedication," *Reform Advocate* 1:18 (June 19, 1891), 3 (295).

31. On Wise's advocacy of the Friday night service (Kaufmann Kohler as well), see Moshe Davis, "Jewish Religious Life," 519. On literary societies, see Morris Gutstein, "Cultural and Literary Freedom: The Story of the Jewish Literary Societies in the Nineteenth Century," in *Profiles of Freedom: Essays in American Jewish History* (New York: Bloch, 1967).

32. Stanley Nadel, "Jewish Race and German Soul in Nineteenth-Century America," *American Jewish History* 77:1 (Sept. 1987), 8. Meyer, *Response to Modernity,* 266.

33. Quoted in Jonathan Sarna, *JPS.* Sarna is right in emphasizing that "Keneseth Israel originally hired Krauskopf to win back some of the young, native-born Jews who had deserted the congregation. . . . Being young himself—just twenty-nine—the new rabbi quickly created a rapport with young Jews, for he shared many of their concerns."

34. American Jewish Archives, Chicago Sinai collection (MS. Coll. 56), 2/6, 3/1.

35. *American Israelite* 32:20 (Nov. 13, 1885), 8.

36. Irving Katz, "A Chronology of the History of Temple Beth El," in *The Beth El Story* (Detroit: Wayne State University Press, 1955), 90–91. *American Israelite* 32:31 (Jan. 29, 1886), 3.

37. Sarna, *JPS.*

38. Henry Berkowitz, "The Jewish Chautauqua Society: An Account of its Origin and Activities," Appendix A in Max Berkowitz, *Beloved Rabbi,* 130–33.

39. *CCAR Yearbook* (1895), Report of Committee on "Jewish Summer School & Assembly," 4:43–52.

40. Correspondence of September 27, 1881, Henry Berkowitz to Max Heller, American Jewish Archives, MS. Coll. 33, Box 1/ 7.

41. Ibid., Jan. 6, 1884.

42. Ibid., Oct. 4, 1887.

43. The phrase "New Education" predates the movement of Progressive Education associated with John Dewey, and refers to the naturalist, holistic educational theories of Jean Jacques Rousseau (1712–78), Johann Heinrich Pestalozzi (1746–1827), Friedrich Froebel (1782–1852), and others. See Adrian M. Dupuis and Robert C. Craig, *American Education: Its Origins and Issues* (Milwaukee, Wis.: Bruce, 1963), chap. 10, "The New Education," 239–67. *American Israelite* 34:53 (June 29, 1888).

44. The Jewish *hevra* predated and developed in parallel to the parish confraternity, an established institution in American Christianity. For example, see the discussion of the immigrant "verein" in Jay P. Dolan, *The Immigrant Church: New York's Irish and German Catholics, 1815–1865* (Baltimore: Johns Hopkins University Press, 1975), 80–81. *American Israelite* 35:18 (Nov. 2, 1888), 3.

45. *American Israelite* 35:18 (Nov. 2, 1888).

46. *American Israelite* 35:20 (Nov. 16, 1888), 7. *American Israelite* 35:22 (Nov. 30, 1888), 9.

47. *American Israelite* 35:22 (Nov. 30, 1888), 9.

48. *American Hebrew* 37:1 (Nov. 9, 1888), 2. Frank Adler, *Roots in a Moving Stream: The Centennial History of Congregation B'nai Jehudah of Kansas City, 1870–1970* (Kansas City, Mo.: Congregation B'nai Jehudah, 1972), 83, 85.

49. *American Israelite* 35:24 (Dec. 14, 1888), 3. Adler, *Roots in a Moving Stream,* 85–86.

50. American Jewish Archives, Histories File. Kansas City, Mo., Congregation B'nai Jehudah. Announcement of Congregational Activities for 1891–92.

51. Adler, *Roots in a Moving Stream,* 96.

52. "The Jewish Ministers' Semi-Annual Conference," *American Hebrew* 37:5 (Dec. 7, 1888), 89 [5].

53. The intriguing question of the relationship between the rabbi and his female congregants will be taken up in a later chapter. For a more women-centered treatment of the sisterhood, see Karla Goldman, "Beyond the Gallery: American Jewish Women in the 1890s," chap. 5 in "Beyond The Gallery: The Place of Women in the Development of American Judaism" (Harvard University, Ph.D. diss., 1993). Goldman lists two major factors leading to the creation of the sisterhood: the influence of Christian women's activism and the growing need for social service in the Jewish immigrant ghetto. Goldman also notes "the influence of male rabbis upon the organization of these women's groups" (225). Relevant to our earlier discussion, Jenna Weissman Joselit adds: "In much the same way that the modern American Jewish woman had made of her home a miniature temple, she was now to make of her temple a miniature home." Joselit, "The Special Sphere of the Middle-Class American Jewish Woman: The Synagogue Sisterhood, 1890–1940," in *The American Synagogue,* ed. Jack Wertheimer (New York: Cambridge University Press, 1987), 211–12.

54. *Reform Advocate* 1:1 (Feb. 20, 1891), 1.

55. Selig Adler and Thomas Connolly, *From Ararat to Suburbia* (Philadelphia, JPS, 1960), 209.

56. Berkowitz, *Beloved Rabbi,* 30. Henry S. Morais, *The Jews of Philadelphia* (Philadelphia: Levy-type, 1894), 83, 168.

57. *American Israelite* 34:45 (May 4, 1888), 4. Berkowitz, *Beloved Rabbi,* 43. Harry Mayer, *History of Cong. Bnai Jehudah—1800–1950* (1953), American Jewish Archives, Histories File under "Kansas City, Mo.," 31–32. Morais, *Jews of Philadelphia,* 81. Malcolm Stern, "Philadelphia's Reform Rabbis," 192. Joseph Leiser, *American Judaism: The Religion and Religious Institutions of the Jewish People in the United States: A Historical Survey* (New York: Bloch, 1925), 235–36.

58. *Congregation Rodeph Shalom—Annual* 7 (1899), 8–9. William Rosenau, "Henry Berkowitz," *American Jewish Yearbook* (1924–25), 26:448–58. Henry Berkowitz, *Intimate Glimpses of the Rabbi's Career* (Cincinnati: Hebrew Union College Press, 1921).

59. *American Israelite* 34:40 (March 30, 1888), 6.

60. Hyman L. Meites, ed., *History of the Jews of Chicago* (Chicago: Jewish Historical Society of Illinois, 1924; facsimile reprint, 1990), 518. See dedication addresses in the *Reform Advocate* 10:21 (Jan. 11, 1896). Charles E. Gregersen, *Dankmar Adler: His Theatres and Auditorium* (Athens: Swallow Press/Ohio University Press, 1990) includes discussion of Adler's synagogue

buildings. Also see Emil G. Hirsch's remarkable eulogy for Adler in the *Reform Advocate* (April 28, 1900), 304–8. Lauren Weingarden Rader, *Faith and Form: Synagogue Architecture in Illinois* (Chicago: Spertus College of Judaica Press, 1976), 48.

61. Lloyd P. Gartner, *History of the Jews of Cleveland* (Cleveland, Ohio: Western Reserve Historical Society, 1978), 157.

62. "A New Jewish Temple" (1893), AJArchives, MS. Coll. 53, 4/1–2. Wischnitzer, *Synagogue Architecture,* 104; photograph on 107.

63. "To Be Open To All—The Advantages Offered by The New Temple Society." (Nov. 1894), AJArchives, MS. Coll. 53, Box 4.

64. *The Temple, 50th Anniversary,* AJA, MS. Coll. 53, 2/8.

65. Meyer, *Response to Modernity,* 304. AJArchives, MS. Coll. 53, 4/2.

66. Sidney Regner, "The History of the Conference," in *Retrospect and Prospect: Essays in Commemoration of the Seventy-Fifth Anniversary of the Founding of The Central Conference of American Rabbis, 1889–1964,* ed. Bertram Korn (New York: Central Conference of American Rabbis, 1965), 1–19.

67. *CCAR Yearbook* (1898–99), 9:64–72; and reprinted in the *Reform Advocate* 15:22 (July 16, 1898), 1. It was this paper in which Rosenau advised the establishment of People's Synagogues.

68. *CCAR Yearbook* (1899), 8:147–60, 163.

69. Ibid., 165.

70. While Ahad Ha'am leaned toward a cultural approach and Dubnow to the political, both conceptions were "social" in their stress on Jewish peoplehood. For their relationship, see Robert M. Seltzer, "Ahad Ha'am and Dubnow: Friends and Adversaries," in *At the Crossroads: Essays on Ahad Ha'am,* ed. Jacques Kornberg (Albany: State University of New York Press, 1983), 60–72. Mordecai Kaplan attributed his own shift of emphasis from Jewish religion to Jewish peoplehood to the influence of Ahad Ha'am. See Meir Ben Horin, "Ahad Ha'am in Kaplan," in *The American Judaism of Mordecai M. Kaplan,* ed. Emanuel S. Goldsmith, Mel Scult, and Robert M. Seltzer (New York: New York University Press, 1990), 221–33.

71. Israel Abrahams, *Jewish Life in the Middle Ages* (New York: Atheneum, 1969), 1–2, 7.

72. Ibid., 15. This last observation is discussed in greater depth by Samuel Heilman, *Synagogue Life: A Study in Symbolic Interaction* (Chicago: University of Chicago Press, 1976), 33–35, 129–49.

73. On the public reception of Abrahams's work, see Sarna, *JPS,* 60. Jacob Rader Marcus, for example, read *Jewish Life in the Middle Ages* before beginning his studies at HUC; personal conversation with the author, August 1991. *CCAR Yearbook* (1902), 12:207. Abrahams is mentioned as well in the CCAR proceedings of 1898 (8:40), 1901 (11:79), and 1904 (14:117). Sometime later, Reform rabbi Joseph Leiser would refer to Abrahams in the same vein: "A synagog exclusively devoted to prayer is as unJewish as one exclusively given over to extra congregational activities. Israel Abraham's Jewish Life in the Middle Ages describes the range of activities encompassed by the synagogs during that period and these correspond to the clubs and classes now in vogue." Leiser, *American Judaism* (1925), 234 n.48. Also see Sidney Goldstein, *The Synagogue and Social Welfare* (New York: Bloch, 1955), 40.

74. *CCAR Yearbook* (July 1901), 11:145–49.

75. *CCAR Yearbook* (1902), 12:204, 209.

76. *CCAR Yearbook* (1902), 208, 12:210–12.

77. Ibid., 209, 213, 217.

78. Letter of Dec. 14, 1902, AJArchives, MS. Coll. 53, 1/4.

79. "Rabbi Gries and the Open Temple," *Jewish American* 5:13 (Detroit, Mich.: January 9, 1903), 1.

80. "Rabbi Gries and the Open Temple." Also printed in the *Reform Advocate* 24:20 (Jan. 17, 1903), 482–86.

81. "The Open Temple and Rabbi Gries," "Dr. Gries Defense of the Open Temple," [probably from the *Jewish American* of the week following the article of January 9, 1903], AJArchives, MS. Coll. 53.

82. Max Heller, "The Institutional Synagog Again," AJArchives, MS. Coll. 53.

83. *CCAR Yearbook* (1905), 15:22.

84. *Report of Committee on Social Religious Union, CCAR Yearbook* (1905), 15:156–57.

85. *CCAR Yearbook* (1906), 16:147.

86. Ibid., 149.

87. Ibid., 148.

88. *CCAR Yearbook* (1907), 17:144. Marshall Sklare, *Jewish Identity on the Suburban Frontier* (Chicago: University of Chicago Press, 1967; 2d ed., 1979), 57–59.

89. *CCAR Yearbook* (1909), 19:129, 132.

90. *CCAR Yearbook* (1908), 18:123.

91. Ibid., 127.

92. *CCAR Yearbook* (1916), 26:247.

93. Ibid., 249.

2. YMHA

1. *American Israelite* (March 15, 1878); repr. in *A Documentary Story of a Century of the Jewish Community Center,* ed. Philip Goodman (New York: Jewish Community Center Centennial Committee, 1953), 22.

2. The standard history of the YMHA is Benjamin Rabinowitz, "The Young Men's Hebrew Associations" (cited hereafter as "YMHA") *Publications of the American Jewish Historical Society* (PAJHS) 37 (1947): 222–323.

3. Sydney E. Ahlstrom notes the still earlier origins of the YMCA in Germany. *A Religious History of the American People* (New Haven: Yale University Press, 1972), 742. Winthrop S. Hudson, *Religion in America: An Historical Account of the Development of American Religious Life,* 2d ed. (New York: Scribner, 1973), 229.

4. Clifford Putney, "From Character Building to Personal Growth: Changing YMCA Attitudes Toward Fitness, Religion, and Social Reform in the Twentieth Century" (unpublished paper, 1988), 5–6. F. Michael Perko, "Religious Education," in *Encyclopedia of the American Religious Experience,* ed. Charles H. Lippy and Peter W. Williams (New York: Scribner, 1988), 3:1606.

5. Hudson, *Religion in America,* 180, 229. Ahlstrom, *Religious History of the American People,* 742–43. Putney, "From Character Building," 6.

6. Leonard Sweet, "Nineteenth-Century Evangelicalism," and F. Michael Perko, "Religious Education," in *Encyclopedia of the American Religious Experience,* ed. Charles H. Lippy and Peter W. Williams (New York: Scribner, 1988), 877 and 1606. Putney, "From Character Building," 8. Aaron I. Abell, *The Urban Impact on American Protestantism, 1865–1900* (Cambridge, Mass.: Harvard University Press, 1943), 205. Dwight Moody quoted in Hudson, *Religion in America,* 233.

7. For example, Herbert Goldstein, "From the Synagogue Back to the Synagogue," *Jewish Center* 2:3 (June 1924), 29: "We began by imitating the YMCAs of our neighbors, substituting an "h" for the "c", of course." Charles Nemser, "The Jewish Center in the Life of American Jewry," *Jewish Center* 3:3 (Sept. 1925), 4–5: "Founded in 1874, the YMHA, in the first stage of

its development until the year 1890, was a more or less vicarious insitution, a substitute for Jewish young men for its counterpart, the YMCA. It was, therefore, entirely imitative."

8. Horace Kallen, "The Dynamics of the Jewish Center," in *Judaism at Bay* (New York: Bloch, 1932), 223.

9. Benjamin Rabinowitz, "YMHA," 223. For an example of the German-Jewish connection, see Selig Adler and Thomas E. Connolly, *From Ararat to Suburbia: The History of the Jewish Community of Buffalo* (Philadelphia: JPS, 1960), 75.

10. Naomi W. Cohen, *Encounter with Emancipation: The German Jews in the United States, 1830–1914* (Philadelphia: JPS, 1984), 53. Rabinowitz, "YMHA," 231–32.

11. *Jewish Messenger* 64:20 (Nov. 16, 1888).

12. *Jewish Messenger* 90:21 (Nov. 22, 1901), 10. Barbara Solomon, *Pioneers in Service: The History of the Associated Jewish Philanthropies of Boston* (Boston, 1956), 9. *A Documentary Story of a Century of the Jewish Community Center, 1854–1954,* ed. Philip Goodman (New York: Jewish Community Center Centennial Committee, 1953), 17.

13. *Minutes* (1910), meetings of Feb. 13, March 20, and June 22. Archives of the 92d Street "Y" (NY YMHA).

14. Bertram W. Korn, *American Jewry and the Civil War* (Philadelphia: JPS, 1951), 4.

15. William R. Langerfeld, *The Young Men's Hebrew Association of Philadelphia, A Fifty-Year Chronicle* (Published by the YM/YWHA of Philadelphia, 1928), 6–7. On Jewish orphanages more generally, see Reena Sigman Friedman, *These Are Our Children: Jewish Orphanages in the United States, 1880–1925* (Hanover: University Press of New England, 1994).

16. Lloyd P. Gartner, *History of the Jews of Cleveland* (Cleveland, Ohio: Western Reserve Historical Society, 1978), 24.

17. Cohen, *Encounter with Emancipation,* 54.

18. Rabinowitz, "YMHA," 222 and 225.

19. Rabinowitz, "YMHA," 225, 227. *American Israelite* 2:20 (Nov. 23, 1855), 166.

20. *Jewish Times* (Dec. 10, 1869); reprinted in *A Documentary Story,* 13; and in Rabinowitz, "YMHA," 227.

21. *Sinai* 1:2–3 (March-April 1856); reprinted in *A Documentary Story,* 9–10. Rabinowitz, "YMHA," 224.

22. *The Occident* 16:9 (Dec. 1858); reprinted in *A Documentary Story,* 12.

23. Rabinowitz, "YMHA," 230–32. Fred Rosenbaum, *Architects of Reform: Congregational and Community Leadersip Emanu-El of San Francisco, 1849–1980* (Berkeley, Calif.: Judah H. Magnes Memorial Museum, 1980), 72.

24. [The Rev. Dr.] Nathan Stern, "Historical Review of Congregation Shaaray Tefila," *West End Synagogue–Ninetieth Anniversary Celebration* (Feb. 14–17, 1935).

25. Jeffrey S. Gurock, *When Harlem Was Jewish, 1870–1930* (New York: Columbia University Press, 1979), 11–12. Rabinowitz, "YMHA," 223.

26. Rabinowitz, "YMHA," 229–30. Philipson quoted in Isaac M. Fein, *The Making of an American Jewish Community: The History of Baltimore Jewry from 1773 to 1920* (Philadelphia: JPS, 1971), 132.

27. Rabinowitz, "YMHA," 230.

28. *A Documentary Story,* 20.

29. Rabinowitz, "YMHA," 244. *A Documentary Story,* 22.

30. *Boston Hebrew Observer* 1:3 (January 19, 1883).

31. *Cleveland Hebrew Observer* 1:1 (July 5, 1889), and 1:2 (July 12, 1889).

32. Quoted in Rabinowitz, "YMHA," 264.

33. Ibid., 256. See Jonathan D. Sarna, *JPS: The Americanization of Jewish Culture, 1888–1988* (Philadelphia: JPS, 1989), 300 n. 9.

34. *American Hebrew* 29:3 (Nov. 26, 1886), 41.

35. Ibid.

36. Philip Cowen, *Memories of an American Jew* (New York: International Press, 1932), 400–401.

37. Sarna, *JPS,* 15; also see his "The Late 19th-Century American Jewish Awakening," *Religious Diversity and American Religious History,* ed. Walter H. Conser, Jr., and Sumner B. Twiss (Athens, Ga.: University of Georgia Press, 1997), 1–25. Moshe Davis, *The Emergence of Conservative Judaism: The Historical School in 19th Century America* (Philadelphia: JPS, 1973). Note that Davis's title obscures the fact that the "Conservative" appellation did not come into popular use until the twentieth century, only then referring to the centrist movement between Reform and Orthodoxy; its nineteenth century precursor was not a denominational movement per se, but the response of some rabbis and laymen to the perceived excesses of Reform Judaism.

38. *American Israelite* (Nov. 6, 1868); in Rabinowitz, "YMHA," 227–28.

39. *Jewish Times* (Dec. 24, 1869); quoted in Rabinowitz, "YMHA," 229.

40. Rabinowitz, "YMHA," 260, 267.

41. On the *American Hebrew,* see Cowen, *Memories of An American Jew* 40–111. *A Documentary Story,* 26. Rabinowitz, "YMHA," 256, 271.

42. Langerfeld, YMHA of Philadelphia, 9–10. Moshe Davis, *Emergence of Conservative Judaism,* 355. Wise first proposed a unified ritual in 1847 and published "Minhag America" ten years later. Nathan Glazer, *American Judaism* (Chicago: University of Chicago Press, 1957; 2d ed. rev., 1972), 36–38. Michael Meyer, *Response to Modernity* (New York: Oxford University Press, 1988), 254–55.

43. *Jewish Messenger* 38 (November–December 1875); quoted by Davis, *Emergence of Conservative Judaism,* 162–63.

44. Rabinowitz, "YMHA," 230–31.

45. *Monthly Bulletin* 3:7 (Oct. 1902), 2. Archives of the 92nd St. "Y" (NY YMHA).

46. *Boston Hebrew Observer* 1:3 (Jan.19, 1883).

47. Rabinowitz, "YMHA," 289. It may be argued alternatively that the downtown Y was a "mission" intended to maintain separation between the Jewish classes. But if this were the case, why call it and structure it as a YMHA? Instead, it is far more likely that the enthusiasts of the uptown Y were merely attempting to spread the "movement" to areas of greater Jewish concentration. Hence, the argument is made for "unification."

48. *A Documentary Story,* 31.

49. Rabinowitz, "YMHA," 267–69.

50. *American Hebrew* 31:3 (May 27, 1887), 42.

51. *Jewish Messenger* (October 16, 1874), 5; in *A Documentary Story,* 15.

52. Cyrus Adler, *I Have Considered the Days* (Philadelphia: JPS, 1941), 20–21; in *A Documentary Story,* 18.

53. Rabinowitz, "YMHA," 272. The YMHA solution is analogous to so-called Kosher style. See Joseph L. Blau, *Judaism in America* (Chicago: University of Chicago Press, 1976), 134–35; for a more scientific discussion of folk religion, Charles S. Liebman, *The Ambivalent American Jew: Politics, Religion, and Family in American Jewish Life* (Philadelphia: JPS, 1973).

54. Rabinowitz, "YMHA," 237, 257. Cowen, *Memories of an American Jew,* 50. The title page of de Sola Mendes's article is reprinted in *A Documentary History,* 28.

55. Rabinowitz, "YMHA," 235–36. *A Documentary Story,* 24. The phrase "post-biblical history" possibly refers to the title of the 1866 textbook written by the rabbi Morris Raphall of Congregation B'nai Jeshurun.

56. Rabinowitz, "YMHA," 264.

57. Ibid., 266–68. See also *American Hebrew* 37:3 (Nov. 23, 1888), 2: "Abuse Not Criti-

cism," referring to an attack by the *Jewish Messenger* on the YMHA and the involvement of rabbis. *A Documentary Story,* 34–35.

58. Rabinowitz, "YMHA," 237.

59. Sarna, *JPS,* 15.

60. *A Documentary Story,* 25.

61. Jack Nadel, "Our Seventy-Five Years: A Brief History of the YM & YWHA During Three-Quarters of a Century of Service to the Community," in *Building Character For 75 Years* (New York: Published on the Occasion of the 75th Anniversary of the Young Men's & Young Women's Hebrew Association, 1949), 13–14.

62. Religious Department History, YMHA Archives, New York City.

63. YMHA Archives.

64. *The Bulletin* 3:6 (Sept. 1902), 1.

65. *The Bulletin* 3:3 (June 1902), 3–4.

66. *The Bulletin* 3:5 (Aug. 1902), 1.

67. *The Bulletin* 3:8 (Nov. 1902), 3.

68. Rabinowitz, "YMHA," 305. I. E. Goldwasser, "The Work of Young Men's Hebrew and Kindred Associations in New York City," *Jewish Communal Register* (New York: The Kehillah, 1917), 482.

69. *The Bulletin* 3:1 (April 1902), 1; 3:8 (Nov. 1902), 1.

70. *The Bulletin* 3:8 (Nov. 1902), 1, 3.

71. "In the Beginning," in *Gala Benefit* journal, 1988, YMHA Archives, New York City.

72. *Boston Advocate* 1:26 (Oct. 27, 1905). *The Bulletin* 3:9 (December 1902), 5.

73. *The Bulletin* 4:10 (Jan. 1903), 1.

74. *The Bulletin* 3:1 (April 1902), 2.

75. *Hebrew Standard* 45:35 (April 8, 1904), 4. See issue 45:39 (May 6, 1904) for a photograph of the occasion.

76. *Gala Benefit* journal, 1988.

77. Philip Cowen, *Memories of an American Jew,* 409–10.

78. Ibid., 410.

79. *The Bulletin* 3:4 (July 1902), 2.

80. Religious Department *Minutes* (Sept. 25, 1910), YMHA Archives, New York City.

81. *YWHA History,* YMHA Archives, New York City.

82. *The Bulletin* 4:11 (Feb. 1903), 6–7.

83. *Jewish Advocate* 16:2 (March 15, 1912), 1.

84. Kaplan journal, 67 (August 23, 1914). Ibid.

85. *Boston Advocate* 1:25 (Oct. 20, 1905), 2.

86. *Jewish Advocate* (Sept. 22, 1911), 6. *Oheb Shalom Fair Journal* (March 1911). [Ratner Center Archives, Cong. Oheb Shalom (Newark), 3/1.] Both Israeli and Hoffman are discussed in greater detail in Chapter 6.

87. "Rudolph Isaac Coffee (1878–)—rabbi and social worker," *Universal Jewish Encyclopedia,* 10 vols. (New York: Universal Jewish Encyclopedia, 1939–43).

88. Religious Department History, YMHA Archives, New York City.

89. Kaplan journal, 104 (October 20, 1914).

90. Mel Scult, "Mordecai M. Kaplan: His Life," in *Dynamic Judaism: The Essential Writings of Mordecai M. Kaplan,* ed. and with introds. by Emanuel S. Goldsmith and Mel Scult (New York: Schocken Books, Reconstructionist Press, 1985), 8.

91. Kaplan journal, 104 (October 20, 1914).

92. Ibid., 105.

93. Ibid.

94. YMHA Archives, New York City.

95. Mordecai M. Kaplan to Felix Warburg, Nov. 1, 1913; quoted by Moshe Davis, "Jewish Religious Life and Institutions in America (A Historical Study)," in *The Jews: Their History, Culture, and Religion,* ed. Louis Finkelstein (Philadelphia: JPS, 1960), 1:545.

96. Rabbi Aaron G. Robison, "Religious Work of the Y.M.H.A.," *Publications of the Council of Y.M.H. and Kindred Associations,* ser. 1915, Document no. 7, p. 6.

97. As reflected by their articles in the movement journal: R. Aaron Robison, "The Program of the Newark YM and YWHA," *Jewish Center* 2:2 (March 1924); and "The Status of Jewish Activities in Jewish Centers," *Jewish Center* 3:3 (Sept. 1925). R. Lee Levinger, "The Jewish Center and the Synagogue," *Jewish Center* 1:3 (May 1923); and "The Jewish Center in the Universities," *Jewish Center* 4:1 (March 1926).

98. Rabinowitz, "YMHA," 306–7. CYMKHA existed independently for only eight years, merging with the Jewish Welfare Board in 1921.

99. I. E. Goldwasser, "Work of Young Men's Hebrew Associations."

100. Rabinowitz, "YMHA," Alexander Shecket Korros and Jonathan D. Sarna, *American Synagogue History: A Bibliography and State-of-the-Field Survey* (New York: Markus Wiener Publishing, 1988). Ratner Center, Jewish Theological Seminary.

101. Religious Department History, YMHA Archives, New York City.

102. Fein, *Making of an American Jewish Community,* 219.

103. *Fourth Annual Report of the United Synagogue of America* (New York: United Synagogue of America, 1917), 19–20.

104. Mordecai M. Kaplan, *Judaism as a Civilization: Toward a Reconstruction of American Jewish Life* (New York: T. Yoseloff, 1957; repr., New York: Schocken Books, 1967), 52–53.

105. Max I. Dimont, *The Jews in America: The Roots, History, and Destiny of American Jews* (New York: Simon & Schuster, 1978), 178–79.

3. SETTLEMENT

1. Abraham Heller as quoted in the *Jubilee Book of the Brooklyn Center* (April 1946), 82.

2. Leon Harris, *Merchant Princes: An Intimate History of Jewish Families Who Built Great Department Stores* (New York: Harper & Row, 1977). Other department store magnates who supported Jewish settlement activity include Edgar Kaufmann of Pittsburgh's Irene Kaufmann Settlement and Louis Bamberger of Newark, who "contributed generously toward the building funds of virtually every Jewish Community Center erected in New Jersey in the 1920s." Bernard Postal and Lionel Koppman, *American Jewish Landmarks,* rev. ed. (New York: Fleet Press, 1977) 1:217.

3. Richard Hofstadter, *The Age of Reform: From Bryan to F.D.R.* (New York: Vintage Books, 1955); Allen F. Davis, *Spearheads for Reform: The Social Settlements and the Progressive Movement, 1890–1914* (New York: Oxford University Press, 1967); Robert M. Crunden, *Ministers of Reform: The Progressives' Achievement in American Civilization, 1889–1920* (Urbana: University of Illinois Press, 1982). Deborah Dash Moore, "A New American Judaism," in *Like All the Nations?—The Life and Legacy of Judah L. Magnes,* ed. William M. Brinner and Moses Rischin (Albany: State University of New York Press, 1987), 41–55; Evyatar Friesel, "The Age of Optimism in American Judaism, 1900–1920," in *A Bicentennial Festschrift for Jacob Rader Marcus,* ed. Bertram Korn (New York: Ktav Publishing, 1976); 131–55.

4. Rivka Shpak Lissak, *Pluralism & Progressives: Hull House and the New Immigrants, 1890–1919* (Chicago: University of Chicago Press, 1989). John Higham, *Strangers in the Land: Patterns of American Nativism, 1860–1925* (New Brunswick: Rutgers University Press, 1955), 121,

236. Horace M. Kallen, *Culture and Democracy in the United States* (New York: 1924); Milton R. Konvitz, "Horace Meyer Kallen (1882–1974): Philosopher of the Hebraic-American Idea," *American Jewish Yearbook* (1974–75), 75:55–80.

5. Quoted in Friesel, "Age of Optimism," 131.

6. Judah Magnes, February 1909; quoted in Moses Rischin, *The Promised City: New York's Jews, 1870–1914* (Cambridge: Harvard University Press, 1962, 1977), 243. Also see Israel Friedlaender, "The Present Crisis in American Jewry (A Plea for Reconciliation)," in *Past and Present: Selected Essays* (New York: Burning Bush, 1961). For a concise and balanced historical treatment of the opposition of the two groups, see Henry Feingold, *Zion in America* (New York: Twayne, 1974), chap. 10, "The Old and the New Immigrant: Conflict and Philanthropy"; more specifically, Zosa Sjakowski, "The Attitude of American Jews to East European Jewish Immigration (1881–1893)," *PAJHS* 40:3 (March 1951). Rischin, *Promised City,* esp. chap. 6, "Germans versus Russians," and chap. 12, "Dawn of a New Era." Compare Selma Berrol's "update" of Rischin in *American Jewish History* 73:2 (Dec. 1983), 142–56; and Rischin's response to Berrol in *American Jewish History* 73:2 (Dec. 1983), 193–98. Isaac B. Berkson, *Theories of Americanization: A Critical Study, with Special Reference to the Jewish Group* (New York: Teachers College, 1920), 37; Oscar Handlin, *Adventure in Freedom: Three Hundred Years of Jewish Life in America* (New York: McGraw-Hill, 1954), 158; Irving Howe, *World of Our Fathers* (New York: Harcourt Brace Jovanovich, 1976), 230–35.

7. Seraphine Pisco, "Denver's Settlement Work," quoted by William Toll, *Women, Men, and Ethnicity: Essays on the Structure and Thought of American Jewry* (Lanham, Md.: University Press of America, 1991), 77–78.

8. Hutchins Hapgood, *Spirit of the Ghetto* (1902), ed. Moses Rischin (Cambridge: The Belknap Press of Harvard University Press, 1967), 35–36.

9. John Daniels quoted in Charles S. Bernheimer, "Jewish Americanization Agencies," *AJYB* (American Jewish Year Book) 23 (1921–22), 87.

10. Rabinowitz, "The Young Men's Hebrew Associations) (hereafter cited as "YMHA") *Publications of the American Jewish Historical Society (PAJHS)* 37 (1947): 222–323, 287–88, 298. Hyman B. Grinstein, "In the Course of the Nineteenth Century," chap. 2 in *A History of Jewish Education in the United States,* ed. Judah Pilch (New York: American Association for Jewish Education, 1969), 37. Jonathan D. Sarna, "The Impact of Nineteenth-Century Christian Missions on American Jews," in *Jewish Apostasy in the Modern World,* ed. Todd M. Endelman (New York: Holmes & Meier, 1987), 242. Alvin I. Schiff, *The Jewish Day School in America* (New York: Jewish Education Committee, 1966), 23. Lawrence A. Cremin, *American Education: The Metropolitan Experience, 1876–1980* (New York: Harper & Row, 1988), 141–42.

11. Philip Cowen, *Memories of an American Jew* (New York: International Press, 1932), 92–93.

12. *Fifty Years of Social Service: The History of the United Hebrew Charities of The City of New York* (New York: Jewish Social Service Association, 1926), 8. Boris David Bogen, *Jewish Philanthropy: An Exposition of Principles and Methods of Jewish Social Service in the United States* (New York: Macmillan, 1917), 160. The history of the Jewish orphanage has been most recently documented by Reena Sigman Friedman, *These Are Our Children: Jewish Orphanages in the United States, 1880–1925* (Hanover: University Press of New England, 1994). Her valuable chapter 6, on the religious life of the orphanage, portrays in greater detail many of the same issues covered here; see esp. p. 93 of that work.

13. Nurith Zmora, "A Rediscovery of the Asylum: The Hebrew Orphan Asylum Through the Lives of Its First Fifty Orphans," *American Jewish History* 77:3 (March 1988), 461.

14. Interestingly, Abraham Hoffman had earlier served as rabbi of the Baltimore Hebrew Congregation but left the pulpit because "his controversial reforms threatened to divide the

congregation." Apparently, the orphans would give Hoffman no such trouble in his efforts to "reform" them. Zmora, "Rediscovery of the Asylum," Barbara Solomon, *Pioneers in Service: The History of the Associated Jewish Philanthropies of Boston* (Boston, 1956), 16–17. Solomon Schindler, *Israelites in Boston* (Boston, 1889). Jacob Neusner, "The Impact of Immigration and Philanthropy Upon the Boston Jewish Community (1880–1914)," *PAJHS* 46:2 (Dec. 1956), 84.

15. Gary Edward Polster, *Inside Looking Out: The Cleveland Jewish Orphan Asylum, 1868–1924* (Kent: Kent State University Press, 1990), 32. See especially chap. 4, "Reforming the Orthodox: Religious Indoctrination."

16. Lawrence A. Cremin, *The Transformation of the School: Progressivism in American Education, 1876–1957* (New York: Knopf, 1969), chap. 2, "Education and Industry," 23ff. *Fifty Years of Service,* 9–17. Annual Report of the Board of Relief of the United Hebrew Charities, 1875–99 (AJHS, MS. Nat. J29—Jewish Social Service Association). Rischin, *Promised City,* 100–101. Barbara Solomon, *Pioneers in Service,* 23. Rabinowitz, "YMHA," 288.

17. Cowen, *Memories of an American Jew,* 103–4.

18. Rabinowitz, "YMHA," 290–92. Solomon, *Pioneers in Service,* 24.

19. *6th Annual Report of the Board of Relief of the United Hebrew Charities* (1880), 30.

20. *20th Annual Report of the United Hebrew Charities of the City of New York,* October 1894 (New York: Press of Philip Cowen, 1895), 28.

21. Albert Ehrenfried, *A Chronicle of Boston Jewry: From the Colonial Settlement to 1900* (Boston: privately published, 1963), 563. Rabinowitz, "YMHA," 289–90. *American Hebrew* 21:11 (Jan. 23, 1885), 161.

22. On the origins of the general settlement movement, see Henry Steele Commager's 1960 foreword to Jane Addams's *Twenty Years at Hull-House* (New York: Penguin Books, 1981), ix. Allen F. Davis, *Spearheads for Reform: The Social Settlements and the Progressive Movement, 1890–1914* (New York: Oxford University Press, 1967), 8–11. On the Jewish settlement movement, see Linda Gordon Kuzmack, *Woman's Cause: The Jewish Woman's Movement in England and the United States, 1881–1933* (Columbus: Ohio State University Press, 1990), 104.

23. Lillian D. Wald, *The House on Henry Street* (New York: Henry Holt, 1915).

24. William Toll, "A Quiet Revolution: Jewish Women's Clubs and the Widening Female Sphere, 1870–1920," *AJA* (American Jewish Archives) 41:1 (Spring–Summer, 1989). Edwin Wolf II, "The German-Jewish Influence in Philadelphia's Jewish Charities," in *Jewish Life in Philadelphia, 1830–1940,* ed. Murray Friedman (Philadelphia: ISHI Publications, 1983), 133. Evelyn Bodek, "'Making Do': Jewish Women and Philanthropy," in *Jewish Life in Philadelphia,* ed. Friedman, 157: "In its activities the Young Women's Union, founded four years before the first settlement house in the United States, was taking on the trappings of a settlement house. Philip Rosen adds that the activities of the YWU—its kindergarten, nursery, and day care center—"were models for similar Gentile and secular philanthropy on behalf of children"; "German Jews vs. Russian Jews in Philadelphia Philanthropy," in *Jewish Life in Philadelphia,* ed. Friedman, 200.

25. Marvin Lowenthal, *Henrietta Szold: Life and Letters* (New York: Viking Press, 1942), 39. Ida Selavan calls the innovation "the first evening school for immigrants in the U.S."; and Isaac M. Fein adds: "Perhaps the most important cultural institution in East Baltimore was the so-called Russian night school. It was one of those undertakings in which Germans and Russians met and worked hand in hand . . . a pioneering effort in night-school education"; *The Making of an American Jewish Community: The History of Baltimore Jewry from 1773 to 1920* (Philadelphia: JPS, 1971), 173–74. Also see Benjamin H. Hartogensis, "The Russian Night School of Baltimore," *PAJHS* 31 (1928), 225–28. Solomon, *Pioneers in Service,* 22–25. Fein, *Making of an American Jewish Community,* 218.

26. Hannah B. Einstein, "Sisterhoods of Personal Service," *Jewish Encyclopedia* (New York:

Funk and Wagnalls, 1905), 11:398. For another view of the role of synagogue sisterhoods, see Karla Goldman, "Beyond the Gallery: The Place of Women in the Development of American Judaism" (Ph.D. diss., Harvard University, 1993), especially chap. 5.

27. *Fifty Years of Service,* 51.

28. Rabinowitz, "YMHA," 294–95. Selig Adler and Thomas F. Connolly, *From Ararat to Suburbia: The History of the Jewish Community of Buffalo* (Philadelphia: Jewish Publication Society, 1960), 209–10.

29. Joseph Jacobs, "Jewish Clergy and Jewish Clergy—I," *Jewish Charity* 3:2 (Nov. 1903), 29–30.

30. Samuel Schulman, "Jewish Charity and Jewish Clergy—II," *Jewish Charity* 3:3 (Dec. 1903), 63.

31. Rabinowitz, "YMHA," 295. Ida Libert Uchill, *Pioneers, Peddlers, and Tsadikim* (Denver: Sage Books, 1957), 190. Ida Selavan, "From Settlement to Center," 3. Rabinowitz, "YMHA," 294, 296. William Toll, "Maternal Surveillance and the Jewish Settlement Idea in the American West," chap. 7 in *Women, Men, and Ethnicity: Essays on the Structure and Thought of American Jewry* (Lanham, Md.: University Press of America, 1991).

32. Rabinowitz, "YMHA," 292. Solomon, *Pioneers in Service,* 26–27.

33. "Blaustein, David," *Jewish Encyclopedia,* vol. 3 (1903), and *Encyclopedia Judaica.* Also, Miriam Blaustein, ed., *Memoirs of David Blaustein* (New York: McBride, Nast, 1913). Solomon, *Pioneers in Service,* 20. On the origin of the Zionist flag see "Miscellany—The First Zionist Flag," *Jewish Social Studies* 6:1 (Jan. 1944), 55–57. Mark Raider, "Pioneers and Pacesetters: Boston Jews and American Zionism," in *The Jews of Boston: Essays on the Occasion of the Centenary (1895–1995) of the Combined Jewish Philanthropies of Greater Boston,* ed. Jonathan Sarna and Ellen Smith (Boston: Combined Jewish Philanthropies, 1995), 244–45.

34. Lissak, *Pluralism and Progressives,* 85. Maxwell Whiteman, "Zionism Comes To Philadelphia," *Early History of Zionism in America,* ed. Isidore S. Meyer (New York: American Jewish Historical Society, 1958), 200.

35. Rabinowitz, "YMHA," 272–73, 290–91.

36. Ibid., 292. Mitchell E. Panzer, "Gratz College—A Community's Involvement in Jewish Education," in *Gratz College Anniversary Volume* (Philadelphia: Gratz College, 1971), 1–19.

37. Adam Bellow, *The Educational Alliance: A Centennial Celebration* (New York: Educational Alliance, 1990). Howe, *World Of Our Fathers,* 230. Bogen, *Jewish Philanthropy,* 227.

38. Selma C. Berrol, "Julia Richman and the German Jewish Establishment: Passion, Arrogance, and the Americanization of the Ostjuden," *AJA* 38:2 (Nov. 1986), 152.

39. Ibid., 76–77. Quoted in Bogen, *Jewish Philanthropy,* 228; also see Myron Berman, "The Attitude of American Jewry Toward East European Jewish Immigration, 1881–1914" (Ph.D. diss., Columbia University, 1963), 401.

40. Hapgood, *Spirit of the Ghetto,* 34–36.

41. Abraham H. Fromenson, "East Side Preventive Work," National Conference of Jewish Charities, *Proceedings* (1904), reprinted in *Trends and Issues in Jewish Social Welfare in the United States, 1899–1958,* ed. Robert Morris and Michael Freund (Philadelphia: JPS, 1966), 118–23.

42. Edward A. Steiner, *On the Trail of the Immigrant* (New York: Fleming H. Revell, 1906), 163–64. Cowen, *Memories of an American Jew,* 91. Bogen, *Jewish Philanthropy,* 231–32.

43. J. K. Paulding, "Educational Influences—New York," in *The Russian Jew in the United States,* ed. Charles Bernheimer (Philadelphia: John C. Winston, 1905), 192–93.

44. Quoted in *The Old East Side: An Anthology,* ed. Milton Hindus (Philadelphia: JPS, 1971), 118.

45. Bogen, *Jewish Philanthropy,* 231. Blaustein, *Memoirs,* 28–29, 106.

46. In response to conference paper by Louis Marshall, *Proceedings of the Fifth National Conference of Jewish Charities* (1908), 123. Berkson, *Theories of Americanization,* 58.

47. Blaustein, in supplement to the *Nineteenth Annual Report, 1911,* Educational Alliance (New York, 1912).

48. Bogen, *Jewish Philanthropy,* 233–34.

49. Blaustein, *Memoirs,* 36–37.

50. Chapter 472, New York State Laws of 1899; quoted in "The Religious Department—The People's Synagogue," Jacob Grossman Collection, Ratner Center Archives.

51. On the significance of Zvi Hirsh Masliansky, see Jeffrey Gurock, "Resisters and Accomodators: Varieties of Orthodox Rabbis in America, 1886–1983," in *The American Rabbinate,* ed. Jacob Rader Marcus and Abraham Peck (Hoboken, N.J.: Ktav Publishing House, 1985), 35. See also *Masliansky's Memoirs: Forty Years of Life and Struggle* (New York: Turberg, 1924) (in Yiddish). Quoted in Samuel P. Rudens, "A Half Century of Community Service—The Story of the New York Educational Alliance," *American Jewish Year Book* 46 (1944–45), 81–82. Letter to Louis Marshall, Dec. 12, 1901; quoted in Berrol, "Julia Richman," 154–55. Berman, *The Attitude of American Immigration Towards East European Jewish Immigration, 1881–1914,* 468. *Nineteenth Annual Report—1911—The Educational Alliance* (New York: Isaac Goldmann, 1912), 28. "The Religious Dept.—The People's Synagogue," Jacob Grossman Collection, Ratner Center Archives, Jewish Theological Seminary, 2–3.

52. Educational Alliance Committee on Moral Culture Report, 1899. Eighth Annual Report, The Educational Alliance, Nov. 25, 1900.

53. Blaustein, *Memoirs,* 38–39. Proceedings of the Fifth National Conference of Jewish Charities (1908), 124–25. Also see Blaustein, *Memoirs,* 219, for alternate version.

54. For disparaging comments, see Howe, *World of Our Fathers,* 232: "The [Educational] Alliance tried almost everything. A People's Synagogue with sedate services in Hebrew and German was set up in 1900, never very successful." See also Henry Feingold, *Zion in America* (New York: Twayne, 1974), 134. *Nineteenth Annual Report—1911—The Educational Alliance* (New York, 1912), 28–29. In his eulogy of Blaustein, Louis Marshall pointed to the "mushroom synagogues" as the principal reason for Blaustein's making "effort after effort to establish a model synagogue." Blaustein, *Memoirs,* 267.

55. Lloyd P. Gartner, *History of the Jews of Cleveland* (Cleveland, Ohio: Western Reserve Historical Society and The Jewish Theological Seminary of America, 1978), 222–25.

56. Samuel Joseph, *History of the Baron de Hirsch Fund: The Americanization of the Jewish Immigrant* (Philadelphia: Published for the Baron de Hirsch Fund by JPS, 1935), 266–67. Alter F. Landesman, *Brownsville: The Birth, Development and Passing of a Jewish Community in New York* (New York: Bloch, 1969), 176, 170.

57. Judith E. Endelman, *The Jewish Community of Indianapolis: 1849 to the Present* (Bloomington: Indiana University Press, 1984), 71–72, 91–93.

58. Rabinowitz, "YMHA," 292; Meites, *History of the Jews of Chicago,* 558. Regarding Baltimore, see Fein, *World of Our Fathers,* 218: "In 1909 these two pioneer organizations in Jewish settlement work [the Maccabeans and the Daughters of Israel] united and formed the Jewish Educational Alliance."

59. Rabinowitz, "YMHA," 296–97.

60. Ibid., 301–2.

61. Arthur A. Goren, ed., *Dissenter in Zion: From the Writings of Judah L. Magnes* (Cambridge: Harvard University Press, 1982), 100.

62. Rabinowitz, "YMHA," 302.

63. Morris M. Feuerlicht, "A Hoosier Rabbinate," in *Lives and Voices,* ed. Stanley F. Chyet (Philadelphia: JPS, 1972), 170–71.

64. Adler and Connolly, *Ararat to Suburbia*, 262.

65. Steven Hertzberg, *Strangers Within the Gate City: The Jews of Atlanta, 1845–1915* (Philadelphia: JPS, 1978), 136.

66. Fein, *Making of an American Jewish Community*, 218–19.

67. Harry Barnard, *The Forging of an American Jew: The Life and Times of Judge Julian W. Mack* (New York: Herzl, 1974), 52. Philip Bregstone, quoted in Morris A. Gutstein, *A Priceless Heritage: The Epic Growth of Nineteenth Century Chicago Jewry* (New York: Bloch, 1953), 357. Gutstein, 358. Also see Lissak, *Pluralism and Progressives*, 82–83.

68. Lissak, *Pluralism and Progressives*, 85.

69. Quoted in Lissak, *Plurals and Progressives*, 85–86. See also Mrs. Benjamin Davis quoted in Anita Libman Lebeson, "Recall to Life . . . ," in *The Sentinel's History of Chicago Jewry* (Chicago: Sentinel Publishing, 1961), 10–11.

70. Bogen, *Jewish Philanthropy*, 238–40.

71. The phrase "cultural Zionism" is, of course, identified with Ahad Ha'am and European Zionism; but as interpreted by Israel Friedlaender and others, it became the keynote of American Zionism as well. See Ben Halpern, "The Americanization of Zionism, 1880–1930," in *Solidarity and Kinship: Essays on American Zionism,* ed. Nathan Kaganoff (Waltham, Mass.: American Jewish Historical Society, 1970). Lissak, *Pluralism and Progressives*, 85.

72. Mrs. Benjamin Davis, "Religious Activity—Chicago," in *The Russian Jew in the United States,* ed. Charles Bernheimer (Philadelphia: John C. Winston, 1905), 180–82.

73. Blaustein, *Memoirs*, 32, 87, 277–78.

74. Bogen, *Jewish Philanthropy*, 240–41.

75. Maxwell Whiteman, "Zionism Comes to Philadelphia," in *Early History of Zionism in America,* ed. Isidore Meyer (New York: American Jewish Historical Society, 1958), 200.

76. Ruth L. Deech, "Jacob de Haas: A Biography," in *Herzl Year Book* (1971), 7:331ff. Solomon, *Pioneers in Service*, 53. Allon Gal, *Brandeis of Boston* (Cambridge: Harvard University Press, 1982), 103–4. Jacob de Haas, "Jacob de Haas Points to the History-Making Endeavors of the Jewish Advocate—No New England Jewry Until Paper Began to Function—Attributes Homogeneity to Its Influence," *Silver Jubilee Edition of the Jewish Advocate* 49:1 (March 17, 1927), 8, 132.

77. *Boston Advocate* 6:17 (Jan. 1908), 1. Ibid., 7:4 (April 3, 1908). Ibid., 8:5 (Oct. 9, 1908), 1.

78. Ibid., 8:6 (Oct. 16, 1908).

79. *Jewish Advocate* 15:20 (Jan. 19, 1912), 1. Ibid. (Oct. 4, 1917), 7. Rabinowitz, "YMHA," 308.

80. Rabinowitz, "YMHA," 300.

81. Blaustein, in eulogy of Isidor Straus, *Memoirs*, 235.

82. Bogen, *Born a Jew,* in collab. with Alfred Segal (New York, Macmillan, 1930), 80. Ronald Sobel, "A History of New York's Temple Emanu-El: The Second Half Century (Ph.D. diss., New York University, 1980), 217.

83. Stephen S. Wise, *Challenging Years: The Autobiography of Stephen Wise* (New York: Putnam, 1949), 102.

84. *Boston Advocate* 7:5 (April 10, 1908), 8; also see follow-up editorial in 7:10 (May 15, 1908), 8.

85. Louis Marshall, "The Need of a Distinctly Jewish Tendency in the Conduct of Jewish Educational Institutions," *Proceedings,* Fifth Biennial Session, The National Conference of Jewish Charities in the United States, held in the city of Richmond, Va., May 4–6, 1908 (Baltimore: Press of Kohn & Pollack, 1909), 112–22.

86. Ibid., 126.

87. Blaustein, *Memoirs*, 210.

88. "Necrology—David Blaustein (1866–1912)," *PAJHS* 22 (1914), 210. Blaustein, *Memoirs*, 212.

89. Presciently, David Blaustein predicted the westward move of American Jewish life: "As soon as it will be found out that there is a religious and social life for the Jews also in the interior of the country and even in the far West, they will gradually spread and establish Jewish communities." Blaustein, *Memoirs*, 259–60.

90. Rabinowitz, "YMHA," 293. *Jewish Advocate*, "Building Like YMHA Indispensable at Camp Devens—Truly American and Jewish," by Coleman Silbert, Jan. 10, 1918.

91. Alexander Dushkin, *Jewish Education in New York City* (New York: Bureau of Jewish Education, 1918), 366. Dushkin was the first of the "Benderly boys"—and probably the first American Jew—to write his dissertation on the subject of American Jewish life. On the "Benderly boys" see Chapter 4; Arthur Goren, *New York Jews and the Quest for Community: The Kehillah Experiment, 1908–1922* (New York: Columbia University Press, 1970) 118–20, 281 n. 29; and Meir Ben-Horin, "From the Turn of the Century to the Late Thirties," in *A History of Jewish Education in the United States*, ed. Judah Pilch (New York: American Association for Jewish Education, 1969), 75. Alexander Dushkin, *Living Bridges: Memoirs of an Educator* (Jerusalem: Keter, 1975), 19.

4. SCHOOL

1. Samson Benderly, "Jewish Education in America," lecture of January 12, 1908; reprinted in *Jewish Education* 20:3 (Summer 1949), 86.

2. Ibid., 85–86.

3. On Benderly, see Nathan H. Winter, *Jewish Education in a Pluralist Society: Samson Benderly and Jewish Education in the United States* (New York: New York University Press, 1966). For more on the "Benderly boys," see Alexander Dushkin, *Living Bridges: Memoirs of an Educator* (Jerusalem: Keter, 1975), and David Kaufman, "Jewish Education as a Civilization: A History of the Teachers Institute," in *Tradition Renewed: A History of the Jewish Theological Seminary of America*, ed. Jack Wertheimer (New York: Jewish Theological Seminary, 1997).

4. Mark Twain's comment was made at the Educational Alliance in 1906, when the two made a joint appearance. Adam Bellow, *The Educational Alliance: A Centennial Celebration* (New York: Educational Alliance, 1990), 50–51. On Dewey's influence, see Isaac Berkson, "John Dewey's Ideas and their Implications for Hebrew Education in America," in *Shviley Hahinuch* (1927); "John Dewey and the Community Centered School," *Jewish Education* (Spring 1950), 3–5; Samuel Blumenfeld, "John Dewey and Jewish Education," in *Judaism and the Jewish School: Selected Essays on the Direction and Purpose of Jewish Education*, ed. Judah Pilch and Meir Ben-Horin (New York: Bloch, 1966), 145–55; Ronald Kronish, "John Dewey's Influence on Jewish Education in America: The Gap Between Theory and Practice," *Studies in Jewish Education*, ed. Barry Chazan (Jerusalem: Magnes, 1983), 1:168–91.

5. Alexander Dushkin's 1917 Ph.D. dissertation was published in the following year as *Jewish Education in New York City* (New York: Bureau of Jewish Education, 1918), 366. On the "Benderly Boys," see note 91 to Chapter 3; *Jewish Education* 20:3 (Summer 1949), special issue dedicated to Samson Benderly; Kaufman, "Jewish Education as a Civilization." Of John Dewey's writings, see esp. *The School and Society* (1900; rev. ed., 1915); *Democracy and Education* (1916); "The School as Social Center," *National Educational Association (NEA) Journal of Proceedings* (1902), 381; an earlier statement of the same was James K. Paulding, "Public School as a Center of Community Life," *Educational Review* 15 (Feb. 1898): 147–54. Dushkin may also have been influenced by the writings of Edward J. Ward, esp. "The Schoolhouse as the Community

Center," *NEA Journal of Proceedings* 50 (1912), 438; Ward was the leader of the school center movement in Rochester (1907–11). See also Robert A. Woods, *The Neighborhood in Nation-Building* (New York: Houghton Mifflin 1923), 265–84. Edward W. Stevens Jr., "Social Centers, Politics, and Social Efficiency in the Progressive Era," *History of Education Quarterly* (Spring 1972).

6. Allen F. Davis, *Spearheads for Reform: The Social Settlements and the Progressive Movement, 1890–1914* (New York: Oxford University Press, 1967), 77. Paulding, "Public Schools"; Dewey, "School as Social Center," 381. For other aspects of Deweyan influence, see Kronish, "John Dewey's Influence."

7. Originally intended as the introduction to an abridgement of Graetz's *History,* Dubnow's essay "What is Jewish History? An Attempt at a Philosophical Analysis," was first published in Russian in 1893, and "later translated into German by Israel Friedlaender, and then into English by Henrietta Szold [for the Jewish Publication Society]. It was the first work by Dubnow to be acclaimed abroad." Koppel S. Pinson, "Simon Dubnow: Historian and Political Philosopher," in *Nationalism and History: Essays on Old and New Judaism (by Simon Dubnow),* ed. Koppel S. Pinson (Philadelphia: JPS and Meridien Books, 1961), 16. Lionel Kochan, *The Jew and His History* (New York: Schocken Books, 1977), 93–94.

8. Ahad Ha'am, "The Jewish State and the Jewish Problem" (1897) reprinted in *The Zionist Idea: A Historical Analysis and Reader,* ed. Arthur Hertzberg (New York: Atheneum, 1979), 267. Samson Benderly, "Jewish Education in America" (1908), and "The School Man's Viewpoint" (1927), reprinted in *Jewish Education* 20:3 (Summer 1949), 81, 91.

9. Ahad Ha'am, letter to J. L. Magnes (September 18, 1910), 261 in *The Zionist Idea,* ed. Hertzberg. The Magnes quote is from a letter read on the occasion of the death of David Blaustein; quoted by Deborah Dash Moore, "A New American Judaism," in *Like All The Nations?—The Life and Legacy of Judah L. Magnes,* ed. William M. Brinner and Moses Rischin (Albany: State University of New York Press, 1987), 44–45. On the Kehillah experiment, see Arthur A. Goren, *New York Jews and the Quest for Community: The Kehillah Experiment, 1908–1922* (New York: Columbia University Press, 1970).

10. Charles S. Bernheimer, ed. *The Russian Jew in the United States* (Philadelphia: John C. Winston, 1905), 214. Also see Morris A. Gutstein, *A Priceless Heritage: The Epic Growth of Nineteenth Century Chicago Jewry* (New York: Bloch, 1953), 244. Lloyd P. Gartner, *History of the Jews of Cleveland* (Cleveland: Western Reserve Historical Society, 1978), 201. Bernard Drachman, *The Unfailing Light* (New York: The Rabbinical Council of America, 1948), 211. Jeffrey S. Gurock, *When Harlem Was Jewish, 1870–1930* (New York: Columbia University Press, 1979), 98–99. Issac M. Fein, *The Making of an American Jewish Community: The History of Baltimore Jewry from 1773 to 1920* (Philadelphia: JPS, 1971), 187. Joseph Shalom Shubow, "The Historic Aspect of New England Jewry," *Jewish Advocate* (silver jubilee ed.), March 17, 1927, 190. Robert A. Woods, ed., *Americans in Process: A Settlement by Residents and Associates of the South End House* (Boston: Houghton Mifflin, 1902).

11. *Hebrew Standard* 47:19 (August 18, 1905), 7. Boris David Bogen, *Jewish Philanthropy: An Exposition of Principles and Methods of Jewish Social Service in the United States* (New York: Macmillan, 1917), 222. William Toll, *Women, Men, and Ethnicity: Essays on the Structure and Thought of American Jewry* (Lanham, Md.: University Press of America, 1991), 76–77.

12. Bogen, *Jewish Philanthropy,* 222.

13. Selig Adler and Thomas F. Connolly, *From Ararat to Suburbia: The History of the Jewish Community of Buffalo* (Philadelphia: Jewish Publication Society, 1960), 240. Louis Levin, "Suggestions for Jewish Settlement Work," cited in Bogen, 221. On Levin, see Fein, *Making of an American Jewish Community,* 173.

14. Bogen, *Jewish Philanthropy,* 221–22. Albert Isaac Gordon, *Jews in Transition* (Minneapolis: University of Minnesota Press, 1949), 41.

15. Compare Samson Benderly's description of the Talmud Torah curriculum quoted in Winter, *Jewish Education in a Pluralist Society*, 10–11. Arthur Goren, *New York Jews*, 90–91. Goren, *New York Jews*, emphasizes the philanthropic aspect of the Talmud Torah, describing the institution as a sort of Jewish settlement. Winter, *Jewish Education in a Pluralist Society*, 10. Hyman B. Grinstein, "In the Course of the Nineteenth Century," chap. 2 in *A History of Jewish Education in the United States*, ed. Judah Pilch (New York: American Association for Jewish Education, 1969), 49.

16. New York—1st Talmud Torah, 1881 or 1883; Chicago—1878, 1880, and 1883; Cleveland—1883; Boston—1883. Barnett Brickner, "The History of Jewish Education in Cincinnati," *Jewish Education* 8:3 (Oct.–Dec. 1936), 120.

17. Gutstein, *A Priceless Heritage*, 241. Adler and Connolly, *From Ararat to Suburbia*, 240–41. Emanuel Gamoran, *Changing Conceptions in Jewish Education*, Book One: *Jewish Education in Russia and Poland* (New York: Macmillan, 1925), 197–200; Zevi Scharfstein, "Fifty Years of Jewish Education in America" (in Hebrew), *Sefer haYovel . . .* , ed. Scharfstein (New York: 1944), 157; Leo Honor, "Jewish Elementary Education in the U.S. (1901–1950)," *PAJHS* 42:1 (Sept. 1952), 10.

18. Jonathan Sarna, trans. and ed., *People Walk On Their Heads: Moses Weinberger's Jews and Judaism in New York* (New York: Holmes & Meier, 1981), 5. Dushkin, *Jewish Education*, 33, 37, 69.

19. Jenna Weissman Joselit, *New York's Jewish Jews: The Orthodox Community in the Interwar Years* (Bloomington: Indiana University Press, 1990), 125. Sarna, ed. *People Walk On Their Heads*, 51, 53. Dushkin, *Jewish Education*, 70.

20. Goren, *New York Jews*, 90–91.

21. Meir Ben-Horin, "From the Turn of the Century to the Late Thirties," chap. 4 in *A History of Jewish Education in America*, ed. Judah Pilch (New York: American Association for Jewish Education, 1969), 57; hereafter cited as Ben-Horin. Also see the constitution of the Machzike Talmud Torah extracted in Dushkin, *Jewish Education*, appendix E, 47ff.

22. See Deborah Dash Moore's chapter on the public school in *At Home in America: Second-Generation New York Jews* (New York: Columbia University Press, 1981), and Joselit, *New York's Jewish Jews*, 124. *Jewish Advocate* 15:8 (October 27, 1911), 1. Israel Konovitz, ed., *A Brief Survey of Thirty-one Conferences Held by Talmud Torah Principals in New York City* (New York: Bureau of Jewish Education, 1912), 3.

23. Dushkin, *Jewish Education*, 68. Robert A. Woods and Albert J. Kennedy, *The Settlement Horizon* (New York: Russell Sage Foundation, 1922), 292–93, 462.

24. Woods and Kennedy, *Settlement Horizon*, 210, 215.

25. Henry Berkowitz, "The Junior Congregation," in the *Jewish Comment* of Baltimore (issue of Aug. 10, 1917), quoted in Max Berkowitz, *The Beloved Rabbi: An Account of the Life and Works of Henry Berkowitz, D.D.* (New York: Macmillan, 1932), 72. Also in the American Jewish Archives, Henry Berkowitz file.

26. Samuel Abelow, *History of Brooklyn Jewry* (New York: Scheba Publishing Co., 1937). Note: the phrase "Biblical instruction" may have been intended simply as a translation of "Talmud Torah." Dushkin, *Jewish Education*, 69.

27. According to historian Jeffrey Gurock, Lucas's primary concern was to counter the missionary efforts of settlement workers such as Jacob Riis. Gurock, *American Jewish Orthodoxy in Historical Perspective* (Hoboken, N.J.: Ktav Publishing House, 1996), chaps. 5, 7, and 8.

28. "Pike Street Religious Classes," *Hebrew Standard* 44:13 (March 27, 1903), 4. Albert Lucas, "Religion in Education" (Paper read before the third convention of the Union of Orthodox Jewish Congregations, June 21, 1903), *Hebrew Standard* 14:26 (June 26, 1903), 3; 44:36 (September 4, 1903); 44:42 (October 16, 1903), 5; 47:53 (May 19, 1905), 3.

29. *Hebrew Standard* 47:14 (July 14, 1905), 8. "Worthy of Emulation," *Hebrew Standard* 48:8 (December 15, 1905), 8.

30. *Hebrew Standard* 48:17 (May 11, 1906), 20; 49:9 (September 28, 1906), 4.

31. *Hebrew Standard* 49:12 (October 19, 1906), 4; 54:2 (January 22, 1909), 5.

32. Ehud Luz, *Parallels Meet: Religion and Nationalism in the Early Zionist Movement, 1882–1904* (Philadelphia: JPS, 1988), 127–33.

33. Ibid., 131. Scharfstein, "Fifty Years of Jewish Education in America," 156. Elazar Goelman, "Some Aspects of the Development of Ivrit Be-Ivrit in America," in *Gratz College Anniversary Volume,* ed. Isidore D. Passow and Samuel T. Lachs (Philadelphia: Gratz College, 1971), 73–82.

34. Ben-Horin, 63. For a more complete description (and a photograph of an early class), see Dushkin, *Jewish Education,* 81–83. Goelman, "Some Aspects," 74–75.

35. Honor, "Jewish Elementary Education," 10. Goelman, "Some Aspects," 76.

36. "Izhac Epstein (1862–1943)," in *Encyclopedia Judaica* (Jerusalem: Keter, 1972), 6:826–27. Fein, *Making of an American Jewish Community,* 188–90. Julius H. Greenstone, *Statistical Data for Jewish Religious Schools of Baltimore and Pittsburgh for 1908–1909* (Philadelphia: Gratz College, 1909). Honor, "Jewish Elementary Education," 11–12. Ben-Horin, 66. Goren, *New York Jews,* 96ff.

37. Louis Hurwich, "Jewish Education in Boston (1843–1955)," *Jewish Education* 26 (Spring 1956), 23. Goelman, "Some Aspects," 76–78. See Honor, "Jewish Elementary Education," 11–14, for Philadelphia, Detroit, Chicago, Minneapolis, and Pittsburgh. Zevi Scharfstein called Friedland "the reviver of Jewish education in America" (in Ben-Horin, 64), inviting comparison to Benderly; cf. Mordecai M. Kaplan Journal, volume I (Rare Books Room of the Jewish Theological Seminary, New York), 118–21 (Oct. 28, 1914), 153 (March 23, 1915); hereafter cited as Kaplan Journal. Ben–Horin, 65.

38. Ben-Horin, 66. *Jewish Advocate* 14:26 (Sept. 1, 1911), 8.

39. Israel Goldstein, *A Century of Judaism in New York: B'nai Jeshurun 1825–1925: New York's Oldest Ashkenazic Congregation* (New York: Congregation B'nai Jeshurun, 1930), 223–24. Malachowsky (1860–1943) quoted in Ben-Horin, 64. Gurock describes "Zvi Malacovsky" as one of the key modernizers of the Talmud Torah. Gurock, *When Harlem Was Jewish,* 100–1. Harry Fischel's biographer reports that he had organized a religious school for girls at Machzike Talmud Torah over a decade earlier; Herbert Goldstein, ed. *Forty Years of Struggle for a Principle: The Biography of Harry Fischel* (New York: Bloch, 1928), 38–39. Joseph Bluestone remained active in the Machzike Talmud Torah for more than fifty years and was instrumental in the pre-Kehillah movement to organize the Talmud Torahs of New York City. His collected papers are housed in the American Jewish Historical Society, and were summarized by Hyman Grinstein in "Memoirs and Scrapbooks of Dr. Bluestone," *PAJHS* 35 (1939), 61. Edward Orentlicher, *The Talmud Torah in America—Its Structure, Philosophy, and Decline (1860–1960)* (Dropsie College, 1962), quoted in Ben-Horin, 66.

40. Gordon, *Jews in Transition,* 25, 41, 178–82. Kaplan Journal (February 7, 1917), 273–74.

41. Grinstein, "Memoirs and Scrapbooks of Dr. Bluestone," 62. Also see Gurock, *Harlem,* 103.

42. Grinstein, Ibid., 61. For more on the Teachers Institute, see David Kaufman, "Judaism as a Civilization: A History of the Teachers Institute of the Jewish Theological Seminary of America," in *Tradition Renewed,* ed. Wertheimer. For a reprint of the Kaplan-Cronson Report, see *American Hebrew* 86:18 (March 4, 1910), 458–59.

43. See Goren's chap. 5 "Education as a Communal Responsibility," in *New York Jews.* Cf. Uriah Zevi Engelman, "Community Responsibility for Jewish Education," *A History of Jewish Education in the United States,* ed. Judah Pilch (1969).

44. Goren, *New York Jews,* 115–16; Dushkin, *Jewish Education,* 105–6.

45. Dushkin, *Jewish Education,* 112–13.

46. Alter F. Landesman, *Brownsville: The Birth, Development and Passing of a Jewish Community in New York* (New York: Bloch, 1969), 228. Abelow, *History of Brooklyn Jewry,* 112.

47. Abelow, *History of Brooklyn Jewry,* 114. Landesman, *Brownsville,* 228.

48. Landesman, *Brownsville,* 231. Abelow, *History of Brooklyn Jewry,* 231.

49. The following is based largely upon Jeffrey Gurock's capsule history of the Uptown Talmud Torah in *When Harlem Was Jewish,* 98–110.

50. *Hebrew Standard* 48:7 (March 2, 1906), 9; 49:18 (November 30, 1906), 5.

51. *Hebrew Standard* 54:8 (March 5, 1909), 4. Later that month, a photograph appeared of the newly dedicated "Harlem Hebrew Institute" at 132–142 East 111th Street. *Hebrew Standard* 54:11 (March 26, 1909).

52. Gurock, *Harlem,* 101–5.

53. Rabbi Herbert S. Goldstein, ed., *Forty Years of Struggle for a Principle.* Fischel's building projects included the Beth Israel Hospital, Grand (Yiddish) Theatre, Jewish Orphan Asylum, Uptown Talmud Torah and West Side Annex, Home of the Daughters of Jacob, Central Jewish Institute, Hebrew Sheltering and Immigrant Aid Society, and the Yeshivah College. On a humorous note, Fischel included a personal Sukkah in his new Park Avenue apartment house of 1925. A fourteen-story building, halachic requirements demanded a twelve-flight skylight above the second-floor Sukkah. Goldstein, *Forty Years of Struggle for a Principle,* 370.

54. Ibid., 94. Gurock, *Harlem,* 108.

55. *Hebrew Standard* editorial quoted in Goldstein, *Forty Years of Struggle for a Principle,* 114. Ibid. 97–104. Gurock, *Harlem,* 105–6.

56. Gurock, *Harlem,* 122.

57. Ibid., 126. Regarding Kehilath Jeshurun, "leading" refers not only to its social prestige and economic status, but also to its religious authority derived from its rabbi, the renowned Ramaz. For an excellent study of the history of the congregation, see Joselit, *New York's Jewish Jews.* Ben-Horin, 94.

58. Joseph Epstein, "The Early History of the Central Jewish Institute—The Emergence of a Jewish Community School Center" (M.A. thesis, Bernard Revel Graduate School, 1978). Also see Kaplan Journal, 175 (May 20, 1915) and 225 (June 20, 1916).

59. Aaron I. Reichel, *The Maverick Rabbi* (Norfolk, Va.: Donning, 1984), 59–68. Kaplan journal, 98 (Oct. 4, 1914): "[Goldstein] has no ideas and no originality. . . . Plagiarizing others' thoughts and presenting them as his own is an ordinary procedure with him."

60. "Teachers Inspect Jewish Institute," *New York Tribune,* July 3, 1916; quoted by Reichel, *Maverick Rabbi,* 68.

61. Ibid., 66.

62. Kaplan Journal, 175 (May 20, 1915); 225 (June 20, 1916).

63. Ibid., 252–53 (Sept. 30, 1916).

64. Joselit, *New York's Jewish Jews,* 129–33.

65. *The Jewish Teacher* (December 1917).

66. Reprinted in Isaac B. Berkson, *Theories of Americanization: A Critical Study with Special Reference to the Jewish Group* (New York: Teachers College, 1920), 189.

67. Dushkin, *Jewish Education,* 368–71.

68. Berkson, *Theories of Americanization,* 190.

69. Ibid., 191–92.

70. Dushkin, *Jewish Education,* 368.

71. Drachman, *Unfailing Light,* 210–12.

72. *Hebrew Standard* 47:19 (August 18, 1905), 7.

73. Abelow, *History of Brooklyn Jewry*, 115–16.

74. *American Hebrew* 102:9 (Jan. 4, 1918), 283: Item—"New Rabbi for Brooklyn Cong." Also see Kaplan Journal, 95 Oct. 4, 1914, for quote on the transitory state of the Talmud Torah and the inevitability of a "religious school system to be established by congregations."

75. Philip Cowen, *Memories of an American Jew* (New York: International Press, 1932) 105–6. Abelow, *History of Brooklyn Jewry*, 103.

76. Abelow, *History of Brooklyn Jewry*, 114.

77. Other New York City hybrid congregations included Beth Hamedrosh Hachodesh Talmud Torah (1900), Ohel Torah Talmud Torah (1901), Uptown Talmud Torah Association (1902), Tiphereth Israel Talmud Torah (1906), Tiphereth Zion Talmud Torah (1907), Talmud Torah Tiphereth Jerusalem (1908), Talmud Torah Israel Salanter (1909), Machzike Talmud Torah (1910), Chevrah Talmud Torah Anshei Ma'arovi (1911), Talmud Torah Beth Machseh L'Yesomim Anshei Zitomir (1912), Talmudical Institute of Harlem (1912), Talmud Torah Rabbi Chaim Berlin of Harlem (1912), Atereth Israel Talmud Torah (1912), Mishkan Israel of Jamaica Talmud Torah (1914), Torath Moses Talmud Torah (1914), Zion Congregation Talmud Torah of Manhattan (1914), Talmud Torah Tiphereth Israel (1915), Hunt's Point Talmud Torah (1916), Talmud Torah B'nai Israel (1916), and Talmud Torah Anshei Poland (1917). In the New York region one could find the Agudath Achim and Hebrew Institute in Orange, New Jersey (1904), Tannersville Talmud Torah in upstate New York (1910), the Hebrew Free School of White Plains, New York (1917), and the Keneseth Israel Hebrew Free School Congregation of Bayonne, New Jersey. These and many more are all cited as congregations in the listings of local Jewish organizations found in the *American Jewish Yearbook* for the years 5671 (1910–11), 5675 (1914–15), 5680 (1919–20).

78. Ben-Horin, 65.

5. SHUL

1. Quote from *The Autobiography of Lincoln Steffens*, as cited in Arthur Hertzberg, *The Jews in America—Four Centuries of an Uneasy Encounter: A History* (New York: Simon and Schuster, 1989), 197; *What Did They Think of the Jews?* ed. Allan Gould (Northvale, N.J.: Jason Aronson, 1991), 294; Gerald Sorin, *A Time for Building: The Third Migration, 1880–1920*, vol. 3 in *The Jewish People in America*, ed. Henry Feingold (Baltimore: Johns Hopkins University Press, 1992).

2. *Boston Advocate* 8:17 (Jan. 1, 1909), 5; 8:18 (Jan. 8, 1909), 5. On Philip Davis, see his memoir, *And Crown Thy Good* (New York: Philosophical Library, 1952).

3. *Boston Advocate* 8:18 (Jan. 8, 1909), 8.

4. Jeffrey S. Gurock, "Harlem Jewry and the Emergence of the American Synagogue," chap. 5 in *When Harlem Was Jewish, 1870–1930* (New York: Columbia University Press, 1979), 114–36. Deborah Dash Moore, *At Home in America: Second-Generation New York Jews* (New York: Columbia University Press, 1981). On the issue of decorum, see Jenna Weissman Joselit, "Of Manners, Morals, and Orthodox Judaism: Decorum Within the Orthodox Synagogue," in *RAMAZ: School, Community, Scholarship and Orthodoxy*, ed. Jeffrey Gurock (Hoboken, N.J.: Ktav, 1989).

5. I am generalizing about the many cities that received large-scale Jewish immigration; e.g., New York, Chicago, Philadelphia, Boston, Baltimore, Cleveland, Newark, and so forth. An example of a pioneering Russishe shul was in Philadelphia (B'nai Abraham) in 1883; a similar Litvishe shul was in Boston (Shomre Shabbes) in 1875. See Robert Tabak, "Orthodox Judaism in Transition," in *Jewish Life in Philadelphia, 1830–1940*, ed. Murray Friedman (Philadelphia:

ISHI Publications, 1983), 50–51. David Kaufman, "Temples in the American Athens: A History of the Synagogues of Boston," in *The Jews of Boston: Essays on the Occasion of the Centenary (1895–1995) of the Combined Jewish Philanthropies of Greater Boston,* ed. Jonathan Sarna and Ellen Smith (Boston: Combined Jewish Philanthropies, 1995), 178–79.

6. "Anshe" (literally, men of) often forms the first part of the congregational title, such as Anshe Vilna, Anshe Lubawitz, and so forth. "Hevra" (literally, society) is usually associated with the various auxiliary societies of the traditional kehillah community. *Hevrot* often met together for daily prayer in addition to their stated purpose. In the New World, *hevrot* were either attached to the synagogue-community, or themselves constituted small shuls. Like "anshe," "hevra" was often used to designate a congregation; for example, Hevra Tehillim. "Shtibl" (literally, small room) is self-explanatory in its generic sense; its Hasidic connotations are discussed below. The phrase "Beth Hamedrash Hagodol" appeared in the following cities among others: New York, 1859; Chicago, 1867; Denver, 1897; Roxbury (Boston), 1913. Often, the name signified the "Litvishe" (Lithuanian/Mitnagdic) orientation of the shul. The phrase "community synagogue" was chosen over the alternative "central synagogue," which was preempted by the prominent Reform temple of that name in New York City. Reflecting the transitional nature of the institution, neither the sociological nor the historical literature contains a better alternative: E.g., Sklare employs such unwieldy phrases as "large Orthodox synagogue" and "second settlement synagogue," while Gurock offers the equally awkward "proto-American[ized] synagogue." See Marshall Sklare, *Conservative Judaism: An American Religious Movement* (New York: Free Press, 1955), chap. 2, "Orthodoxy in Transition," 47–60. Gurock, *Harlem,* chap. 5, "Harlem Jewry and the Emergence of the American Synagogue." Jenna Weissman Joselit, *New York's Jewish Jews: The Orthodox Community in the Interwar Years* (Bloomington: Indiana University Press, 1990), chap. 2, "Bigger and Better" "Orthodox Synagogues."

7. Joselit, *New York's Jewish Jews,* 28. Abraham Karp, "An East European Congregation on American Soil: Beth Israel, Rochester, New York, 1874–1886," in *A Bicentennial Festschrift for Jacob Rader Marcus,* ed. Bertram W. Korn (New York: Ktav, 1976), 90.

8. J. D. Eisenstein, "The History of the First Russian-American Jewish Congregation. The Beth Hamedrosh Hagodol," *PAJHS* 9 (1901), 63–64.

9. Ibid., 69.

10. Karp, "East European Congregation," 264. It should be pointed out that many and perhaps most immigrants from Eastern Europe (especially from White Russia and the Ukraine) were influenced by Hasidic custom; hence, congregations named either "Anshe Russia" or "Anshe Sfard" tended to be Hasidic in their liturgical style, that is, employing "*Minhag Sfard.*"

11. Quoted in Moore, *At Home in America,* 124. See Charles Liebman, "Orthodoxy in American Jewish Life," *AJYB* 66 (1965), 21–92. Moore, *At Home in America,* 124.

12. Charles Bernheimer, ed., *The Russian Jew in the United States: Studies of Social Conditions in New York, Philadelphia, and Chicago, with a Description of Rural Settlements* (Philadelphia: John C. Winston, 1905), 162. Michael R. Weisser, *A Brotherhood of Memory: Jewish Landsmanshaftn in the New World* (New York: Basic Books, 1985), 81, 14. Moore, *At Home in America,* 126–27.

13. Nathan Kaganoff, "The Jewish Landsmanshaftn in New York City Before World War I," *American Jewish History* 76:1 (September 1986), 58. Nathan Glazer, *American Judaism* (Chicago: University of Chicago Press, 1957; 2d ed., 1972), 67: "Just how many of the immigrants adhered to one point of view and how many to the other is hard to say. It is perhaps most accurate to conceive of them as forming a continuum, with the religious Jews at one end, the most radical at the other, and many in the middle who were both religious and radical in varying degrees."

14. For example, Samuel C. Heilman, *Synagogue Life: A Study in Symbolic Interaction* (Chicago: University of Chicago Press, 1976). Also see Jack Kugelmass, *The Miracle of Intervale Avenue: The Story of a Jewish Congregation in the South Bronx* (New York: Columbia University Press, 1996).

15. Quote is from Moore, *At Home in America,* 124.

16. Bernheimer, ed., *Russian Jew,* 249–50.

17. Louis Wirth, *The Ghetto* (Chicago: University of Chicago Press, 1928), 184. Glazer, *American Judaism,* 62. Gerard R. Wolfe, *The Synagogues of New York's Lower East Side* (New York: Washington Mews Books, 1978), 33–34.

18. Irving Howe, *World of Our Fathers* (New York: Harcourt Brace Jovanovich, 1976), 183.

19. See Daniel Soyer, *Jewish Immigration Associations and American Identity in New York, 1880–1939* (Cambridge: Harvard University Press, 1997).

20. Moses Weinberger, *Jews and Judaism in New York* (1887; in Hebrew); trans. and ed. Jonathan D. Sarna under the title *People Walk On Their Heads* (New York: Holmes and Meier, 1981), 41. Wirth, *The Ghetto,* 184.

21. Moses Rischin, *The Promised City: New York's Jews, 1870–1914* (Cambridge, Mass.: Harvard University Press, 1962; 2d ed. 1977), 104–5. Howe, *World of Our Fathers,* 191. Goren quoted by Slobin, *Chosen Voices: The Study of the American Cantorate* (Urbana: University of Illinois Press, 1989), 52.

22. Louis Lipsky in Bernheimer, ed., *Russian Jews,* 149.

23. Jonathan D. Sarna, "From Immigrants to Ethnics: Toward a New Theory of 'Ethnicization,'" *Ethnicity* 5 (1978). Joselit, "Of Manners, Morals." Mark Slobin, *Chosen Voices: The Story of the American Cantorate* (Urbana: University of Illinois Press, 1989).

24. Eisenstein, "History," 63–74. See also Jeffrey Gurock's "A Stage in the Emergence of the Americanized Synagogue . . . ", 265–83 in *American Jewish Orthodoxy in Historical Perspective* (Hoboken, N.J.: Ktav, 1996), which is essentially a case study of Beth Hamedrosh Hagodol, utilizing the recently discovered minutes of the congregation. Wolfe, *Synagogues,* 25.

25. Eisenstein, "History," 71.

26. *Boston Hebrew Observer* 12:6 (Boston: August 21, 1885).

27. Eisenstein, "History," 74.

28. Jeffrey S. Gurock, "The Orthodox Synagogue," in *American Jewish Orthodoxy,* 78. Sarna, introduction to Weinberger, *Jews and Judaism,* 12–13.

29. Slobin, *Chosen Voices,* 51–60. Weinberger, *Jews and Judaism,* 42, 41. Eisenstein, "History," 73.

30. Abraham Karp, "New York Chooses a Chief Rabbi," *PAJHS* 44:3 (March 1955), 129–87. Wolfe, *Synagogues,* 53.

31. Wolfe, *Synagogues.* Gurock, *American Jewish Orthodoxy,* 78: "As soon as finances permitted, congregations looked to move from storefront *shtibls* to renovated former churches, newly built synagogues edifices or to buildings previously occupied by German congregations." His examples: Beth Hamedrash Hagodol (church), Khal Adas Jeshurun (new edifice on Eldridge Street), Ohab Zedek (moved into former Anshe Chesed on Norfolk).

32. Sarna, "From Immigrants to Ethnics," 12.

33. Julius H. Greenstone, "Religious Activity. Philadelphia," in Bernheimer, ed., *Russian Jew,* 162–63.

34. See Rachel Wischnitzer, *Synagogue Architecture in the United States* (Philadelphia: JPS, 1955), 25–28. Wolfe, *Synagogues,* 66.

35. Wolfe, *Synagogues,* 80. Also see my discussion of church buildings converted to synagogues in "Temples in the American Athens" in *The Jews of Boston,* 172–80.

36. Wolfe, *Synagogues,* 43–44.

37. Ibid., 41, 43.

38. Weinberger, *Jews and Judaism,* 41, 44.

39. Mrs. Benjamin Davis (Jeanette Isaacs) in Bernheimer, ed., 175. Minutes, Eldridge Street Synagogue, 3:53. *Reform Advocate* (May 5, 1900), 336.

40. Moshe Davis, *The Emergence of Conservative Judaism: The Historical School in 19th-Century America* (Philadelphia: JPA, 1965). Wischnitzer, *Synagogue Architecture.*

41. Quoted in the Report of the President, *Annual No. VII—Cong. Rodeph Shalom* (Philadelphia, 1899), 27–28.

42. *Hebrew Standard* 38:22 (June 3, 1898), 6: "Temples and Synagogues."

43. During the period from July 1903 to October 1909, the *Hebrew Standard* ran some thirty-two depictions of synagogue buildings. Of these, seven were European, eleven were established American congregations, and the remainder were new synagogues. For every older synagogue, therefore, the paper printed a new one constructed by an immigrant congregation. Bernard Drachman, *The Unfailing Light: Memoirs of an American Rabbi* (New York: Rabbinical Council of America, 1948), 208–10. Wischnitzer, *Synagogue Architecture,* 82, suggests that Zichron Ephraim's picturesque design was influenced by Rodeph Shalom in Philadelphia.

44. *Hebrew Standard* 44:13 (March 27, 1903), 8.

45. The "Chicago school" of American Jewish sociology is best represented by Louis Wirth, *The Ghetto* (Chicago: University of Chicago Press, 1928), and Marshall Sklare, *Conservative Judaism: An American Religious Movement* (Glencoe, Ill.: Free Press, 1955). On those "Americanized immigrants" who had immigrated at an early age and were neither first- nor second-generation per se, see W. Lloyd Warner and Leo Srole, *The Social Systems of American Ethnic Groups* (New Haven: Yale University Press, 1945), 31, and Gurock, "Time, Place and Movement in Immigrant Jewish Historiography," in *Scholars and Scholarship: The Interaction Between Judaism and Other Cultures,* ed. Leo Landman (New York: Yeshiva University Press, 1990). For the definitive study of "the second ghetto," see Jeffrey Gurock, *When Harlem Was Jewish.* In his study of Harlem, Gurock stresses that many so-called areas of second settlement were simultaneously areas of first settlement for many immigrants, thus complicating the Chicago scheme adopted by Sklare. Table VI, "Jewish and General Immigration into the United States from 1899 to 1914," in *The Jew in the Modern World, A Documentary History,* ed. Paul R. Mendes-Flohr and Jehuda Reinharz (New York: Oxford University Press, 1980), 530.

46. Egon Mayer, *From Suburb to Shtetl: The Jews of Boro Park* (Philadelphia: Temple University Press, 1979), 27. Reprinted in the *Boston Advocate* 7:10 (May 15, 1908), 4. *Boston Advocate* 7:1 (March 13, 1908), 8.

47. Alter F. Landesman, *Brownsville: The Birth, Development, and Passing of a Jewish Community in New York* (New York: Bloch, 1969), 73.

48. Rabbi Louis M. Epstein, "The Crawford Street Synagogue," *Tenth Anniversary Souvenir Book—Crawford Street Synagogue* (Boston: Congregation Beth Hamidrash Hagadol, 1923).

49. Wischnitzer, *Synagogue Architecture,* 120–21. Interesting to note, Brunner was Jewish while Pelham was not. Shaaray Tefila had chosen Brunner as the architect responsible for the renowned Temple Beth El on Fifth Avenue, completed three years before, and because Brunner was a great-grandson of the founder of the synagogue. Simon Cohen, *Shaaray Tefila: A History of its Hundred Years, 1845–1945* (New York: Greenberg, 1945), 14–15, 36.

50. Wolfe, *Synagogues,* 90.

51. *Hebrew Standard* 47:20 (September 1, 1905), 3.

52. Karp, "East European Community," 274.

53. *Hebrew Standard* 47:57 (June 16, 1905), 4.

54. S. N. Behrman, *The Worcester Account* (New York: Random House, 1954), 106; Norma

Feingold, *Shaarai Torah: Life Cycle of a Synagogue* (Worcester, Mass.: Worcester Historical Museum, 1991), 24.

55. Like Arnold Brunner, Lewis Weissbein was a member of the German Jewish community. See Albert Ehrenfried, *A Chronicle of Boston Jewry: From the Colonial Settlement to 1900* (Boston: privately published, 1963), 696. Isaac M. Fein, *Boston—Where It All Began: An Historical Perspective of the Boston Jewish Community* (Boston Jewish Bicentennial Committee, 1976), 52. Kaufman, "Temples in the American Athens."

56. Kaplan Journal (Rare Books Room, Jewish Theological Seminary of America, New York), 110 (October 28, 1914).

57. Joselit, *New York's Jewish Jews,* 29.

58. Ibid., 41. Kaplan Journal, 109 (October 21, 1914).

59. The term "German Orthodox" is borrowed from Marsha Rozenblit, "Choosing a Synagogue: The Social Composition of Two German Congregations in 19th-Century Baltimore," 327–62, in *The American Synagogue: A Sanctuary Transformed,* ed. Jack Wertheimer (Cambridge, U.K.: Cambridge University Press, 1987). "Orthodox" alone is problematic as applied to nineteenth-century American Judaism, as is the term "Conservative." There did not yet exist the ideological and institutional divisions between Orthodoxy and Conservatism, and neither of the twentieth-century terms accurately applies to the earlier religious mode. Some commonly employed terms are "Counter-Reform," "Historical School," and "traditional," but none is fully satisfactory. Also see Wertheimer, "The Conservative Synagogue," 111–49 in *The American Synagogue.*

60. Mendes, "A Young People's Synagogue," *American Hebrew* 65 (October 20, 1899); cited by Davis, *Emergence of Conservative Judaism,* 264. Jeffrey Gurock, "A Generation Unaccounted For," *American Jewish History* 77:2 (December 1987), 251.

61. Jeffrey Gurock, "Jewish Endeavor Society," in *Jewish American Voluntary Organizations,* ed. Michael N. Dobkowski (Westport, Conn.: Greenwood, 1986), 228–231. For some contemporary sources, see Bernheimer, ed., *Russian Jew,* 153 (on New York), 169–71 (Philadelphia); also, 176–77: Mrs. Benjamin Davis (Chicago) laments that "the young people are gradually drifting away from religious influences" and recommends that "a young people's synagogue should be established on the West Side with attractive services and a sermon on Sabbath afternoons." Sydney E. Ahlstrom, *A Religious History of the American People* (New Haven: Yale University Press, 1989), 858.

62. Gurock, "Jewish Endeavor Society."

63. Jeffrey Gurock, "Consensus Building and Conflict Over Creating the Young People's Synagogue of the Lower East Side," chap. 13 in *American Jewish Orthodoxy,* 285–98. The phrases are Bernard Drachman's, as quoted by Gurock. Kaplan Journal, vol. 15 (Sept. 17, 1950), also quoted by Gurock, "Consensus Building."

64. *Hebrew Standard* 44:51 (Dec. 18, 1903), 8. Merely three examples of the scores of "anshei" congregations (that is, landsmanshaftn) founded on the Lower East Side and in other immigrant districts. *The Jewish Communal Register of New York City, 1917–18* (New York: Kehillah, 1918), "List of Congregations," 145–285.

65. *Hebrew Standard* 45:4 (Jan. 22, 1904), 4. Ronald Sobel, "The Emanu-El Brotherhood," in "A History of New York's Temple Emanu-El" (Ph.D. diss., New York University, 1980), 216–21, Myron Berman, "A New Spirit on the East Side: The Early History of the Emanu-El Brotherhood, 1903–1920," *AJHQ* (September 1964).

66. *Hebrew Standard* 45:6 (Feb. 5, 1904), 4. Jeffrey Gurock, "Consensus Building."

67. Jeffrey S. Gurock, "Jewish Endeavor Society," in *Jewish American Voluntary Organizations,* ed. Michael Dobkowski (Westport, Conn.: Greenwood Press, 1986), 231. *Hebrew Standard* 45:37 (April 22, 1904), 4; emphases mine.

68. *Hebrew Standard* 44:2 (Jan. 9, 1903), 4; 45:4 (Jan. 22, 1904), 4.

69. Henry Pereira Mendes (1852–1937) was a founder and first president of the Union of Orthodox Congregations (1898–1914) and interim president of the Jewish Theological Seminary (1897–1902), and had also attended the second and third Zionist Congresses (1898 and 1899). His interest both in the modernization of Orthodox Judaism and the rebirth of Jewish nationhood placed him on the cutting edge of the Jewish revival of the 1890s. See Davis, *Emergence of Conservative Judaism,* 351.

70. *Boston Advocate* 3:18 (Sept. 14, 1906), 3.

71. *Jewish Advocate* (October 6, 1911), 5. *American Jewish Yearbook* 5671 (Philadelphia: JPS, 1910), 258. Gorovitz went on to become the rabbi of the United Orthodox Congregations of Cambridge and Somerville, and later, of various congregations in Roxbury. His 1952 obituary described him as "the Dean of the Orthodox Rabbinate in Greater Boston." R. Aaron Gorovitz, Papers, American Jewish Historical Society. "Rabbi Gorovitz Again Honored," newspaper clipping in R. Aaron Gorovitz papers, AJHS. *American Jewish Yearbook* 5680 (1919–20), 390, 394.

72. Sarah Schmidt, "Horace M. Kallen and the "Progressive" Reform of American Zionism," *Midstream* 22:10 (Dec. 1976), 15. "Religion and Daily Life," *Boston Advocate* 8:15 (Dec. 18, 1908), 6.

73. Ida Libert Uchill, *Pioneers, Peddlers, and Tsadikim* (Denver: Sage Books, 1957), 215.

74. Maxwell Whiteman, "Zionism Comes to Philadelphia," in *Early History of Zionism in America,* ed. Isidore Meyer (New York: American Jewish Historical Society, 1958), 191–218; Tabak, "Orthodox Judaism in Transition."

75. Other likely "Zionist synagogues" include Sons of Zion, Holyoke, Massachusetts (1903); Ohave Zion, Dayton, Ohio (1907); Ohave Israel, Brownsville, Pennsylvania (1907); Tikvath Zion Cong., New York (1912); Ahavath Zion (Zionist) Congregation, Cleveland, Ohio (1913); Love of Israel, Dunmore, Pennsylvania (1913); Brith Israel, Buffalo, New York (1914?); Ohavei Zion (1914) and Ahavath Zion (1915), Lexington, Kentucky; Chevrah Zionei Galicia Anshei S'phard, New York (1915); Congregation Ahavath Zion, Marinette, Wisconsin (1916); and B'nai Zion Society of Savannah, Georgia (1917). *American Jewish Yearbook* 5675 (1914–15), 5680 (1919–20), 389.

76. Arthur Goren, ed., *Dissenter in Zion: From the Writings of Judah L. Magnes* (Cambridge: Harvard University Press, 1982), 88, 93, 125. Kaplan Journal, 286 (April 12, 1917). On the Zionism of Magnes, Kaplan, and Friedlaender, see Deborah Dash Moore, "A New American Judaism, in *Like All the Nations—The Life and Legacy of Judah L. Magnes,* ed. William Brinner and Moses Rischin (Albany: State University of New York Press, 1987), 41–55.

77. The following sources have been consulted: Hyman Goldstein, "History of the Young Israel Movement," *Jewish Forum* (Dec. 1926); David Warsaw, "A History of the Young Israel Movement, 1912–1937" (Master's thesis, Bernard Revel Graduate School, Yeshiva University, 1974); Shulamith Berger, "The Early History of the Young Israel Movement" (seminar paper, YIVO Institute, Fall 1982), courtesy of the author.

78. Jeffrey Gurock, "Orthodox Synagogue," in Wertheimer, *The American Synagogue,* 56. Goldstein, 529. Warsaw, "History," 9; *Free Synagogue—Annual Reports* (New York, 1914), 28.

79. Warsaw, "History," 10. Compare Landesman, *Brownsville,* 217–18. Berger suggests that the word "young" was inspired by the Young Turks, whose revolution of 1908 Magnes had applauded; "Early History," 3. Norman De Mattos Bentwich, *For Zion's Sake: A Biography of Judah L. Magnes, first chancellor and first president of the Hebrew University of Jerusalem* (Philadelphia: JPA, 1954), 62. The English phrase "Young Israel" appears as early as 1856 in a German editorial on the YMHA; *Sinai* 1:2–3 (March–April 1856). In 1871, it was the name of a new journal for young people in New York; Judah Pilch, ed., *A History of Jewish Education in the*

United States (New York: American Association for Jewish Education, 1969), 50. About the turn of the century, Marcus Jastrow wrote: "The difference between orthodoxy and reform is unimportant in the face of the indifference of our young people to both. Young Israel is suffering"; quoted in Moshe Davis, *Emergence of Conservative Judaism*, 401. See, for example, Abraham Karp, "Overview: The Synagogue in America," in Wertheimer, *The American Synagogue*, 29–31.

80. Warsaw, "History," 10.

81. *American Hebrew* (January 10, 1913), 303; *Hebrew Standard* (January 12, 1913), 9. Quoted in Berger, "Early History," 1.

82. Berger, "Early History," 6, 10.

83. *Jewish Advocate* 16:10 (May 10, 1912), 1.

84. Warsaw, "History," 12–13.

85. Warsaw, "History," 15.

86. *Hebrew Standard* (September 29, 1916); quoted in Berger, "Early History," 12–13.

87. Warsaw, 18. Gurock, *American Jewish Orthodoxy*, 88.

88. *Hebrew Standard* (Jan. 18, 1918), 9; quoted by Gurock, ibid.

89. *American Hebrew* 102:18 (March 8, 1918), 501. Landesman, *Brownsville*, 191, 219.

90. Landesman, *Brownsville*, 218.

91. Cf. Gurock, *American Jewish Orthodoxy*, 395 n. 78. Also see Berger, "Early History," 6–9.

92. Marshall Sklare, *Conservative Judaism*. The title of this chapter is a nod to Sklare's chap. 2, "Orthodoxy in Transition."

6. RABBI

1. Mordecai M. Kaplan Journal (Rare Books Room, Jewish Theological Seminary, New York), 159 (April 10, 1915) (hereafter Kaplan Journal).

2. Mel Scult, *Judaism Faces the Twentieth Century: A Biography of Mordecai M. Kaplan* (Detroit: Wayne State University Press, 1993). Jeffrey Gurock and Jacob J. Schachter, *A Modern Heretic and a Traditional Community: Mordecai M. Kaplan, Orthodoxy, and American Judaism* (New York: Columbia University Press, 1997).

3. On the history of the Jewish Theological Seminary, see *Tradition Renewed: A History of the Jewish Theological Seminary of America*, ed. Jack Wertheimer (New York: Jewish Theological Seminary, 1997). For the Reform precedent, see my Chapter 1.

4. Biographical information on Phineas Israeli is scarce. For the *Slutsker Rav* incident, see Scult, *Judaism Faces the Twentieth Century*, 72–75. Jeffrey Gurock, *American Jewish Orthodoxy in Historical Response* (Hoboken, N.J.: Ktav, 1996). For more in-depth treatments of Roxbury and the Blue Hill Avenue Shul, see Gerald Gamm, "In Search of Suburbs: Boston's Jewish Districts, 1843–1994," and David Kaufman, "Temples in the American Athens: A History of the Synagogues of Boston," in *The Jews of Boston: Essays on the Occasion of the Centenary (1895–1995) of the Combined Jewish Philanthropies of Greater Boston*, ed. Jonathan D. Sarna and Ellen Smith (Boston: Combined Jewish Philanthropies, 1995).

5. Jeffrey Gurock, *American Jewish Orthodoxy*, 19–23; and Jenna Weissman Joselit, *New York's Jewish Jews: The Orthodox Community in the Interwar Years* (Bloomington: Indiana University Press, 1990), 61–63. For the apocryphal story of Ramaz's return home, see S. N. Behrman, *The Worcester Account*, 138.

6. *Boston Advocate* 6:18 (Jan. 10, 1908), 2. *Our Golden Jubilee—Temple Mishkan Tefila, 1860–1910* (Boston, 1910), 34. See also *Temple Mishkan Tefila: A History, 1858–1958* (Newton,

Mass., 1958), 14; and *Jewish Advocate* 13:17 (Dec. 30, 1910), 1. Reminded by Israeli's address of his symposium of the year before, editor Jacob de Haas took the occasion to write a lengthy editorial in favor of "the synagogue as the natural center of Jewish life," continuing, "there is no reason why a first-class program could not be evolved which would bring every generation of a congregation's members within the walls of its fane frequently. And if this were accomplished in what is called the secular side, it would not require the effort it does today to get people to attend regular religious services."

7. *Jewish Advocate* 14:18 (July 7, 1911), 1. The accusation was later leveled that the invitation "was partly created in order to destroy the Kehillah." *Jewish Advocate* 15:1 (Sept. 8, 1911), 1.

8. *Jewish Advocate* (Nov. 17, 1911), 8; 15:17 (Dec. 29, 1911), 2.

9. Kaplan Journal, 126 (Dec. 29, 1914).

10. Ibid., 127.

11. Ibid., 128, 143.

12. Ibid., 262 (Feb. 2, 1917). It was the same speech he had given a few months earlier at the banquet for the establishment of a "Jewish Center." Ibid., 263. *American Hebrew* 102:11 (Jan. 18, 1918), 326. *Jewish Advocate* 29:5 (Oct. 3, 1918), 1.

13. *JTS Student's Annual,* vol. 2 (New York: Jewish Theological Seminary of America, May 1915); "Alumni Notes" lists eighty-four JTS graduates up to 1915.

14. *Jewish Advocate* (May 28, 1909), 1. Rabbi Herman H. Rubenovitz and Mignon L. Rubenovitz, *The Waking Heart* (Cambridge, Mass.: Nathaniel Dame, 1967), 34.

15. Pamela Nadell, "A Union of Conservative Congregations: The United Synagogue of America," in her *Conservative Judaism in America: A Biographical Dictionary and Sourcebook* (Westport, Conn.: Greenwood, 1988), 326. Also see Abraham Karp, *A History of the United Synagogue of America, 1913–1963* (New York, 1964) and Herbert Rosenblum, "The Founding of the United Synagogue of America, 1913" (Ph.D. diss., Brandeis University, 1970).

16. Nadell, *Conservative Judaism in America,* 156.

17. On Kaplan's tenure at Kehilath Jeshurun, see Scult, *Judaism Faces the Twentieth Century,* 65–76, 87–98; and regarding Solomon's graduation, 60.

18. Entry for "Congregation Baith Israel Anshei Emes (Kane Street Synagogue)" in Kerry Olitzky, *The American Synagogue: A Historical Dictionary and Sourcebook* (Westport, Conn.: Greenwood, 1996), 226–27. Entry for "Herman Abramowitz" in Nadell, *Conservative Judaism in America,* 26. For more on Israel Goldfarb and the Kane Street Synagogue, see its archives, on file at the Ratner Center of JTS.

19. Eli Grad and Bette Roth, *Cong. Shaarey Zedek, 1861–1981* (Southfield, Mich.: 1982), 40, 45.

20. Lloyd Gartner, *History of the Jews of Cleveland* (Cleveland, Ohio: Western Reserve Historical Society, 1978), 172, 178, 204, 279. For some comments regarding Margolies by Mordecai Kaplan, see his Journal, vol. 1:298 (July 27, 1917). On Goldman, see Jacob Weinstein, *Solomon Goldman: A Rabbi's Rabbi* (New York: Ktav, 1973), 12–17.

21. M. David Hoffman, "Charles Isaiah Hoffman: One Hundredth Anniversary (1864–1964)," *American Jewish Historical Quarterly* 55:2 (Dec. 1965), 212–34. Also see entry for Charles Isaiah Hoffman (1864–1945) in Nadell, *Conservative Judaism in America,* 142–43.

22. Edward Davis, *The History of Rodeph Shalom Congregation [of] Philadelphia, 1802–1926* (Philadelphia: Edward Stern, 1927), 103–8. On Berkowitz and Krauskopf, see Chapter 1.

23. M. David Hoffman, "Charles Isaiah Hoffman: One Hundredth Anniversary (1864–1964), *AJHQ* 55:2 (Dec. 1965), 212–34. For some sense of his relationship to Schechter, see Charles I. Hoffman, "Memories of Solomon Schechter," chap. 5 in *The Jewish Theological Seminary of America: Semi-Centennial Volume,* ed. Cyrus Adler (New York: The Jewish Theological Seminary of America, 1939).

24. Bernard Drachman, *The Unfailing Light: Memoirs of an American Rabbi* (New York: Rabbinical Council of America, 1948), 169.

25. Sarah Kussy quotes from the *75th Anniversary Journal* (Newark, N.J.: Oheb Shalom, 1935), 19.

26. *75th Anniversary Journal,* 19. *Oheb Shalom Review* 1:3 (February 1911), 2. *Oheb Shalom Fair Journal* (March 1911). Ratner Center Archives, Congregation Oheb Shalom Collection, Box 3.

27. Hoffman, "Charles Isaiah Hoffman," 226.

28. Charles Hoffman, "A Congregational Centre," *Oheb Shalom Review* 1:7 (June 1911), 1.

29. Oheb Shalom Yearly Schedule, "Announcements for the Coming Year/ Arrangements for 5676 (1916)." Ratner Center Archives, Cong. Oheb Shalom Collection, Box 2:11.

30. Aaron I. Reichel, *The Maverick Rabbi: Rabbi Herbert S. Goldstein and the Institutional Synagogue—"A New Organizational Form"* (Norfolk, Va.: Donning, 1984). Reichel, Goldstein's grandson, lauds his forebear as "the first Orthodox rabbi of American birth to receive a traditional ordination in America," that is, the first fully "Americanized" Orthodox rabbi. Scult claims that Goldstein was influenced by Mordecai Kaplan to enter the rabbinate, whom he heard speak at Joseph Mayor Asher's funeral. Emanuel S. Goldsmith, Mel Scult, and Robert M. Seltzer eds., *The American Judaism of Mordecai Kaplan* (New York: New York University Press, 1990), 89 n. 9. For more on Asher, see Israel Goldstein, *A Century of Judaism in New York: B'nai Jeshurun, 1825–1925* (New York: Cong. B'nai Jeshurun, 1930), 223–26. Other examples of the first generation of English-speaking traditionalist rabbis include Bernard Drachman, Henry Pereira Mendes, and Henry Schneeberger. Drachman and Schneeberger were American-born; Mendes, like Asher, was British. Jeffrey Gurock, "Resistors and Accommodators: Varieties of Orthodox Rabbis in America, 1886–1983," in *The American Rabbinate*, ed. Jacob Rader Marcus and Abraham Peck (Hoboken, N.J.: Ktav, 1985).

31. Kaplan Journal, 31 (Dec. 15, 1913). Reichel, *Maverick Rabbi,* 60–62.

32. Herbert Goldstein, *Forty Years of Struggle for a Principle: The Biography of Harry Fischel* (New York: Bloch, 1928), 121.

33. Reichel, *Maverick Rabbi,* 65. The projected site of the new institution was next door to Kehilath Jeshurun on East 85th Street, a short walk from the 92nd Street "Y."

34. Ibid., 72.

35. Ibid., 108. *Hebrew Standard* (Sept. 15, 1916), 1; and later reprinted in the *Jewish Social Service Quarterly* 11:4 (June 1926). Quoted extensively in Reichel, *Maverick Rabbi,* 92–94.

36. Quote from David M. Kennedy, *Over Here: The First World War and American Society* (New York: Oxford University Press, 1980), 50. Israel Goldstein, *Century of Judaism in New York,* 247, 250.

37. Reichel, *Maverick Rabbi,* 107.

38. "The Institutional" (synagogue bulletin of the Institutional Synagogue) 17:32 (April 13, 1934), 2.

39. Reichel, *Maverick Rabbi,* 109.

40. Ibid., 112–13. Parenthetically, Goldwasser was the grandfather of Ruth Messinger, a candidate for mayor of New York City in 1997.

41. Ibid., 96, 115. *American Jewish Chronicle* (April 3, 1917); quoted by Reichel, *Maverick Rabbi,* 119.

42. *Jewish Communal Register* (New York Kehillah, 1918), 208–9.

43. Herbert Goldstein, *Forty Years of Struggle for a Principle,* 144.

44. Reichel, *Maverick Rabbi,* 127, 170–71.

45. Jeffrey Gurock, *When Harlem Was Jewish, 1870–1930* (New York: Columbia University Press, 1979), 92–93, 130–31. Reichel, *Maverick Rabbi,* 324.

46. Reichel, *Maverick Rabbi,* chaps. 17–33.

47. Marshall Sklare, *Conservative Judaism: An American Religious Movement* (Lanham, Md.: University Press of America, 1985), 305 n. 9. Goldsmith, Scult, and Seltzer, eds. *American Judaism of Mordecai M. Kaplan,* 53–93. Also see Scult's "The Quest for Community: The Jewish Center," chap. 6 in his *Judaism Faces the Twentieth Century.*

48. Kaplan Journal, 3 (Feb. 24, 1913); 31 (Dec. 15, 1913). Mel Scult makes the same point regarding the logic of Kaplan's position in *Judaism Faces the Twentieth Century,* 155.

49. Kaplan Journal, 291, 347.

50. Ibid., 131 (Dec. 29, 1914); 156 (April 3, 1915); 171 (April 23, 1915).

51. Ibid., 103 (Oct. 20, 1914); 107 (Oc. 21, 1914).

52. Ibid., 132–33 (Feb. 8, 1915); 59–70 (Aug. 23, 1914).

53. Ibid. (Jan. 1916); 227 (June 29, 1916); 255 (Jan. 6, 1917).

54. Ibid., 159 (April 10, 1915).

55. Ibid., 230 (June 30, 1916).

56. Ibid., 32 (Jan. 1914); 245 (Aug. 24, 1916).

57. Ibid., 158–62 (April 10, 1915); 204 (Oct. 21, 1915); 302 (Aug. 29, 1917); 336 (Jan. 27, 1918).

58. Ibid., 159–62 (April 10, 1915). For a more complete telling of Kaplan's differences with the board of directors, see Mel Scult, *Judaism Faces the Twentieth Century,* 157–63, 193–98.

59. Ibid., 176 (May 18, 1915); 175 (May 20, 1915); 253 (Sept. 30, 1916).

60. Ibid., 137 (Feb. 20, 1915); 204 (Oct. 21, 1915). *Hebrew Standard* 48:17 (May 11, 1906), 20; 49:9 (Sept. 28, 1906), 4.

61. Mordecai M. Kaplan, "The Future of Judaism," *Menorah Journal* (June 1916), 160–72.

62. Kaplan Journal, 223–24 (June 18, 1916); 245–46 (Aug. 24, 1916); 253 (Jan. 1, 1917); 262 (Feb. 2, 1917).

63. Ibid., 253 (Jan. 1, 1917). Herbert Goldstein, "The Institutional Synagogue," *Hebrew Standard* (Sept. 15, 1916), 1. For another view on this matter, see Mel Scult, *Judaism Faces the Twentieth Century,* 200–201.

64. Kaplan Journal, 280 (Feb. 22, 1917); 352 (May 7, 1918).

65. Ibid., 294–95 (May 22, 1917).

66. Ibid., 300–301 (Aug. 29, 1917).

67. Ibid.

68. Jacob Schiff, "Need of a Jewish Revival," *American Hebrew* 102:9 (Jan. 4, 1918), 262. Compare Cyrus Adler, *Jacob H. Schiff: His Life and Letters* (New York: Doubleday, Doran and Company, 1928), 2:307–20. Rabbi Jacob S. Minkin, "The Synagogue—A New Interpretation of an Old Theme," *American Hebrew* 102:14–15 (Feb. 8–15, 1918).

69. "The Institutional Synagogue—A New Movement in American Orthodoxy That is Meeting the Problem of the Jewish Youth," *American Hebrew* 102:11 (Jan. 18, 1918), 322. "The Central Jewish Institute," *American Hebrew* 102:16 (Feb. 22, 1918), 433–34.

70. M. M. Kaplan, "Affiliation with the Synagogue," in *The Jewish Communal Register of New York City, 1917–1918* (New York: Kehillah, 1918), 118; emphasis added.

71. Mordecai M. Kaplan, "The Jewish Center," *American Hebrew* 102:20 (March 22, 1918), 529–31.

72. Ibid. It was not until 1920 that Kaplan highlighted the term "reconstruction" in his famous article "A Program for the Reconstruction of Judaism." *Menorah Journal* 6:4 (Aug. 1920), 181–96. Its application here to the synagogue-center is nonetheless significant. Compare the comment by Mel Scult regarding the term "civilization"; *American Judaism of Mordecai M. Kaplan,* 88 n. 1.

73. Kaplan Journal, 331 (Nov. 11, 1917). Compare Mel Scult's description of Kaplan's relationship to his wealthy congregants; *American Judaism of Mordecai M. Kaplan,* 67, 69, 82. Kaplan, "The Jewish Center," 531. KJ 337 (March 2, 1918).

74. Kaplan Journal, 345 (April 5, 1918).

75. Kaplan Journal, 331 (Nov. 11, 1917). Kaplan, "The Way I Have Come" in *Mordecai M. Kaplan: An Evaluation,* ed. Ira Eisenstein and Eugene Kohn (New York: Jewish Reconstructionist Foundation, 1952), 312. Kaplan, "A Program for the Reconstruction of Judaism (The Need of Fostering Jewish Communal Life)," *Menorah Journal* 6:4 (Aug. 1920), 192.

76. *AJYB* (5680), 470.

77. Mordecai M. Kaplan, *Judaism as a Civilization: Toward a Reconstruction of American Jewish Life* (New York: Macmillan, 1934), 51–52; emphasis added.

7. MOVEMENT

1. J. Frederick Krokyn, "Mishkan Tefila," *The Jewish Advocate* 41:2 (March 12, 1923).

2. "A Brochure of Architectural Work from the Office of the Architect—Nathan Myers—Newark, N.J." Archives of Temple Israel, Boston, Massachusetts.

3. Paul R. Mendes-Flohr and Jehuda Reinharz, eds. *The Jew in the Modern World: A Documentary History* (New York: Oxford University Press, 1980), 374, 530. Jacob Marcus, *To Count a People: American Jewish Population Data* (Lanham, Md.: University Press of America, 1990), 241. *Census of Religious Bodies—1936—Jewish Congregations* (U.S. Dept. of Commerce, Bureau of the Census, 1940), Table 2.

4. Samuel Abelow, *History of Brooklyn Jewry* (New York: Scheba, 1937), 78.

5. *Proceedings of the Rabbinical Assembly* 4:3 (May 1932), 270–71.

6. Hyman L. Meites, *History of the Jews of Chicago* (Chicago: Chicago Historical Society, 1924; facsimile reprint, 1990), 543.

7. "Are You Well Centered? (A Roster of New Communal Institutions)," *American Hebrew* 121 (May 20, 1927), 52ff. M. David Hoffman, "Charles Isaiah Hoffman: One Hundredth Anniversary (1864–1964)," *AJHQ* 55:2 (December) 1965, 228.

8. Aaron G. Robison, "The 'Y' as the Jewish Community Center," *Jewish Center* 5:2 (June 1927), 26.

9. Meites, *Jews of Chicago,* 497–98.

10. *CCAR Yearbook* (Wildwood, N.J., 1916), 26:247–55. *American Hebrew* (April 14, 1916; April 11, 1919). *Union Bulletin of American Hebrew Congregations* (Oct. 1922; May–June 1923).

11. Levinthal's statement was first cited by Marshall Sklare, *Conservative Judaism: An American Religious Movement* (Lanham, Md.: University Press of America, 1985; orig. pub., 1955), 136. Deborah Dash Moore, "A Synagogue Center Grows in Brooklyn," in *The American Synagogue: A Sanctuary Transformed,* ed. Jack Wertheimer (Cambridge: Cambridge University Press, 1987), 297–89.

12. Abelow, *History of Brooklyn Jewry.* Ron Miller, Rita Seiden Miller, and Stephen Karp, "The Fourth Largest City in America—Sociological History of Brooklyn," in *Brooklyn USA: The Fourth Largest City in America,* ed. Rita Seides Miller (Brooklyn: Brooklyn College Press, 1979), 3–44. Bernard Postal and Lionel Koppman, *American Jewish Landmarks* (New York: Fleet Corporation, 1954, rev. ed. 1977), 1:485. Entry for "Brooklyn," *Universal Jewish Encyclopedia* (New York: Universal Jewish Encyclopedia, 1939–43), 2:550. In 1937, the *American Jewish Yearbook* estimated the Jewish population of Brooklyn at 947,765, some 37 percent of the total population of the borough.

13. Stephen S. Wise, *Jubilee Book of the Brooklyn Jewish Center* (April 1946), 69. Marc Lee Raphael, *Profiles in American Judaism: The Reform, Conservative, Orthodox, and Reconstructionist Traditions in Historical Perspective* (San Francisco: Harper & Row, 1984), 108. The best source on the development of the Brooklyn Jewish Center is Deborah Dash Moore's article, "A

Synagogue Center Grows in Brooklyn," in *The American Synagogue*, ed. Jack Wertheimer 297–326. *American Hebrew* 102:11 (Jan. 18, 1918), 330.

14. Joseph Goldberg, "Twenty-Five Years of Brooklyn Jewish Center History," *Jubilee Book of the Brooklyn Jewish Center* (April 1946), 7. Mordecai M. Kaplan Journal (Rare Books Room, Jewish Theological Seminary, New York), 305 (Aug. 29, 1917) (hereafter Kaplan Journal). Abelow, *History of Brooklyn Jewry*, 73.

15. Goldberg, "Twenty-Five Years," 7. The 1925 *Jewish Communal Survey of Greater New York* also identifies Eastern Parkway as its own district, containing a Jewish population of 47,570, comprising 48.8 percent of the total population of that area. At the same time, next-door Brownsville was 95 percent Jewish with 169,906 population (New York: Bureau of Jewish Social Research, 1928). This reflects the classic distinction between areas of second and third settlement; compare Sklare, *Conservative Judaism*.

16. *Petach Tikvah Temple News* 18:5 (May 1955).

17. Abelow, *History of Brooklyn Jewry*, 79–80.

18. Ratner Center Archives (JTS), Israel Levinthal papers, sermons and addresses, "Local Patriotism," March 10, 1916.

19. *Petach Tikvah News* 3:2 (Dec. 1917), editorials, p. 1: "The Synagogue As A Social Centre."

20. *American Hebrew* 102:15 (Feb. 15, 1918), 430.

21. Ibid., Passover issue of April 1920, p. 2.

22. Abelow, *History of Brooklyn Jewry*, 75.

23. Goldberg, "Twenty-five Years," 10.

24. Jonathan Sarna calls this "compromise seating." On the seating controversy in the Conservative movement, see his "The Debate over Mixed Seating in the American Synagogue," in *The American Synagogue*, Wertheimer, 379ff. Moore, "A Synagogue Center," 300.

25. The "second generation" explanation is identified with Deborah Dash Moore; compare her *At Home in America: Second-Generation New York Jews* (New York: Columbia University Press, 1981); the "area of third settlement" theory with Marshall Sklare. In the case of the synthetic synagogue-center, neither is sufficient without the other.

26. Moore, "A Synagogue Center," 312.

27. Deborah Dash Moore describes the rise of Jewish apartment house living in *At Home in America*, chap. 2, "Jewish Geography," 19–58.

28. In fact, the other building type recalled by the design was the private (or university) club. From the perspective of architectural history, this is the more proper design source to cite, and there is certainly a parallel to be drawn. Moore notes the analogy in *At Home in America*, 136, and points out its limitations. I have tried to elicit a more layered (multistoried?) metaphor.

29. Moore, "A Synagogue Center," 303. Goldberg, "Twenty-Five Years," 11.

30. Moore, "A Synagogue Center," 303. Abelow, *History of Brooklyn Jewry*, 73.

31. Quoted by Moore, *At Home in America*, 142. Moore, "A Synagogue Center," 317.

32. Ibid., Abelow, *History of Brooklyn Jewry*, 75–76.

33. Ibid., 77–78.

34. Article on "Brooklyn," *Universal Jewish Encyclopedia* (New York: Universal Jewish Encyclopedia, 1939–43), 2:550–51.

35. Abelow, *History of Brooklyn Jewry*, 92.

36. Ibid., 87–88. Brooklyn *Daily Eagle* (April 7, 1929).

37. Abelow, *History of Brooklyn Jewry*, 56–57.

38. Like the Brooklyn Jewish Center in Crown Heights, the Keap Street Temple is today located in a Hasidic neighborhood and has been converted to use as a yeshiva. See Deborah Dash Moore, "A Synagogue Center Grows in Brooklyn," for more on this irony of Jewish his-

tory. Letter to Rabbi Harry Levi, May 19, 1924. Temple Israel Archives, Boston, Mass. "Plans for One of World's Finest Synagogues, To Be Built on Eastern Parkway, Disclosed At Testimonial Dinner to Philip A. Lustig," *Brooklyn Daily Eagle*, April 4, 1924.

39. Abelow, *History of Brooklyn Jewry*, 22. Oscar Israelowitz, *Synagogues of New York City* (New York: Dover, 1982), 24, 34, pl. 54.

40. "Are You Well Centered?" 53.

41. Leon Spitz, "The Synagogue Center Marches On: The History of the Synagogue Center Movement in the United States," *Brooklyn Jewish Center Jubilee Book* (April 1946), 59.

42. Another version of this section, with illustrations, appears in my article "Temples in the American Athens: A History of the Synagogues of Boston," in *The Jews of Boston*, ed. Jonathan D. Sarna and Ellen Smith (Boston: Combined Jewish Philanthropies, 1995), 190–97. There, architectural developments are highlighted, whereas here the context is the synagogue-center movement.

43. Herman N. Rubenovitz, *The Waking Heart* (Cambridge, Mass. Nathaniel Dame, 1967). *Jewish Advocate* 13:17 (December 30, 1910), 1.

44. *Jewish Advocate* 13:17 (Dec. 30, 1910), 8; editorial, "The Synagogue."

45. Herman Rubenovitz, "My Rabbinate at Temple Mishkan Tefila: A History from 1910 to 1946," in *Temple Mishkan Tefila: A History, 1858–1958* (Newton, Mass.: Temple Mishkan Tefila, 1958), 20–22. *Waking Heart*, 57–58, 69, 105.

46. *Waking Heart*, 60, 146.

47. Rubenovitz, "My Rabbinate," 24. Morris Bronstein quoted in the *Jewish Advocate* (March 12, 1923).

48. Letter of February 27, 1923; reprinted in the *Jewish Advocate* (March 12, 1923).

49. *Jewish Advocate* (March 12, 1923).

50. Rubenovitz, "My Rabbinate," 24. Paula Hyman, "From City to Suburb: Temple Mishkan Tefila of Boston, "in *The American Synagogue*, ed. Wertheimer, 187.

51. D. Margolis, "Purposes of Kehillath Israel," typescript document, K.I. archives.

52. *Congregation Kehillath Israel—Jubilee Banquet* (Brookine, Mass., Dec. 20, 1942). *Tenth Anniversary Souvenir Book—Crawford Street Synagogue* (Boston: Beth Hamidrash Hagadol, 1924), 12.

53. Kehillath Israel—An Institution and an Ideal," temple publication on the tenth anniversary of the synagogue building, 1934.

54. *Brotherhood T.O.S. Banquet and Hall Program*, April 4, 1922.

55. Ibid.

56. Rachel Wischnitzer, *Synagogue Architecture in the United States* (Philadelphia: JPS, 1955), 106–17. Lewis Mumford, "Towards a Modern Synagog Architecture," *Menorah Journal* 11:3 (June 1925), 225ff. Mumford, it is rarely noted, was half-Jewish.

57. "The Temple Center and The Temple," undated brochure (c. 1925), Temple Ohabei Shalom archives.

58. Stella D. Obst, *The Story of Adath Israel* (Boston, Mass., 1917), 27. Louis Marshall, in an address delivered at the opening of the UAHC convention, New York, Jan. 23, 1923. Charles Reznikoff, ed., *Louis Marshall: Champion of Liberty* (Philadelphia: JPS, 1957), 820.

59. "Extracts from the message of President Felix Vorenberg given at the 69th Annual Meeting of Congregation Adath Israel," April 8, 1923. Temple Israel archives.

60. Letter of May 5, 1924; Temple Israel archives.

61. Letter of May 19, 1924; Temple Israel archives.

62. Letters of May 12, 1924, and May 29, 1924; Temple Israel archives.

63. Ibid.

64. "History of Our New Buildings." Temple Israel archives.

65. Press release describing "Temple Israel," Jan. 31, 1926. Temple Israel archives.

EPILOGUE

1. Oscar Janowsky, *The JWB Survey* (New York: Dial, 1948), 317–18.

2. Solomon Schechter, *Seminary Addresses and Other Papers* (Burning Bush Press, 1959), 251–52.

3. Blau, "The Prospect of the Center Movement," *Jewish Center Annual* (Brooklyn Jewish Center, 1925); quoted by Leon Spitz, "The Synagogue Center Marches On: The History of the Synagogue Center Movement in the United States," *Brooklyn Jewish Center Jubilee Book* (April 1946), 61. Among others, the phrase is attributed to Blau by Abraham J. Feldman, "The Changing Functions of the Synagogue and the Rabbi," in *Understanding American Judaism Toward the Description of a Modern Religion,* ed. Jacob Neusner (New York: Ktav, 1975), 1:106.

4. *Problems of the Jewish Ministry* (New York Board of Jewish Ministers, Jan. 1927), 110. Pamela S. Nadell, *Conservative Judaism in America: A Biographical Dictionary and Sourcebook* (New York: Greenwood, 1988), 61. Marc Lee Raphael, *Profiles in American Judaism: The Reform, Conservative, Orthodox, and Reconstructionist Traditions in Historical Perspective* (San Francisco: Harper & Row, 1984), 110, 118.

5. Quoted in Harry Glucksman, "Tendencies in the Jewish Center Movement" (1923), reprinted in *Trends and Issues in Jewish Social Welfare in the United States, 1889–1958,* ed. Robert Morris (Philadelphia: JPS, 1966), 272; cf. Spitz, "Synagogue Center Marches On," 62, and Marc Lee Raphael, *Abba Hillel Silver: A Profile in American Judaism* (New York: Holmes and Meier, 1989), 52–53. Abba Hillel Silver, "Leisure and the Church," *Jewish Center* 4:4 (Dec. 1926), 3.

6. Quoted in full from Glucksman, "Synagogue Center," 271–72; also cited in Spitz, "Synagogue Center Marches On, 61–62; and more recently, by Jack Wertheimer, "The Conservative Synagogue," in *The American Synagogue: A Sanctuary Transformed* (Cambridge: Cambridge University Press, 1987), 122.

7. Spitz, "Synagogue Center Marches On," 62. Kaplan, "Need Rabbi and Social Worker Clash?" *Opinion*, March 28, 1932; quoted in Glucksman, "Synagogue Center," 272.

8. Horace Stern, "The Synagogue and Jewish Communal Activities," *AJYB* 35 (1933–34), 161.

9. Isaac Berkson, *Theories of Americanization: A Critical Study, with Special Reference to the Jewish Group* (New York: Teachers College and Columbia University, 1920; reprinted by Arno Press, 1969); emphasis added.

10. Aaron Robison, "New York Judaism," *Jewish Center* 6:1 (March 1928), 21.

11. Harry Glucksman, "The Synagogue Center," *Proceedings of the Rabbinic Assembly* (May 1932), 276.

12. See esp. Max Kadushin, "The Function of Synagogue and Center," *Jewish Center* 1:4 (Sept. 1923), 6–11; Charles Nemser, "The Jewish Center in the Life of American Jewry," *Jewish Center* 3:3 (Sept. 1925), 4–8; Aaron Robison, "The Status of Jewish Activities in Jewish Centers," *Jewish Center* 3:3 (Sept. 1925), 41–42; Mordecai Soltes, "A Program of Jewish Activities for Jewish Community Centers" (including discussion with Alter Landesman), *Jewish Center* 3:3 (Sept. 1925), 42–50; Max Kadushin, "The Place of the Jewish Center in American Jewish Life," 11–26 (including discussion with Ezekiel London and Charles Nemser), *Jewish Center* 4:2 (June 1926). Alexandra Shecket Korros and Jonathan D. Sarna, *American Synagogue History: A Bibliography and State-of-the-Field Survey* (New York: Markus Wiener, 1988). Ida Libert Uchill, *Pioneers, Peddlers, and Tsadikim* (Denver: Sage Books, 1957). Ratner Center, Jewish Theological Seminary, New York. *Religious Department History,* 2–3, YMHA Archives, New York.

13. Albert Gordon, *Jews in Suburbia* (Boston: Beacon Press, 1959). Marshall Sklare, *Jewish Identity on the Suburban Frontier: A Study of Group Survival in the Open Society* (New York: Basic Books, 1967). Will Herberg, *Protestant—Catholic—Jew: An Essay in American Religious Sociology* (Garden City, N.Y.: Doubleday, 1955).

14. Spitz, in the *Brooklyn Jewish Center Jubilee Book* (April 1946); and Agus, in the *Rabbinical Assembly Proceedings* 10 (1947).

15. Jonathan Woocher, *Sacred Survival: The Civil Religion of American Jews* (Bloomington: Indiana University Press, 1986).

16. See esp. Lance Sussman, "The Suburbanization of American Judaism as Reflected in Synagogue Building and Architecture, 1945–1975," *American Jewish History* 75:1 (Sept. 1985), 31–47.

17. *Conservative Judaism* 2:3 (April 1946); 16:2–3 (Winter–Spring 1962). On the Havurah, see Riv-Ellen Prell, *Prayer & Community: The Havurah in American Judaism* (Detroit: Wayne State University Press, 1989).

INDEX

Boldface type indicates figures.
For individual institutions, see under location.
For small cities, see under state.

Temple, 36, 47, **273**; Jewish Training School, 100; Kehillath Anshe Maarav (KAM), 36, 59, 269; Knights of Zion, 102; Maxwell Street Settlement, 118; school center, 139; Self-Educational Club, 118; Sinai Congregation, 13, 16, **17**, 24, 32, 35; Talmud Torah, 135; Temple Beth Israel, 246; YMHA, 76

Chicago Hebrew Institute, 89, 118–21, 145

Christianity, influence of American, 3, 4, 5, 8, 12, 13, 16–17, 38, 44, 49, 213, 234; "Billy Sunday" revivalism, 211, 227; Chautauqua retreats, 5, 25; Christian Endeavor, 5, 193; Institutional Church, 4–5, 17, 40, 44, 49, 165, 173, 284n7, 284n8; reaction to proselytizing, 94, 95, 122, 142; Social Gospel, 16; Young Men's Christian Association (YMCA), 3, 5, 44, 52–55, 290n7

Cleveland, 34, 35, 45, 268; Anshe Emeth, 216; B'nai Jeshurun (Scovill Avenue Temple), 60; Cleveland Jewish Center, 216, **272**; Council Educational Alliance, 113, 216; Hebrew Free School, 133; Hebrew Literary Association, 56; *Hebrew Observer*, 60; orphanage, 95; Talmud Torah, 136; Tifereth Israel (the Temple), 37, 44, 277

Coblenz, Rabbi Adolph, 84, 85

Coffee, Rabbi Rudolph, 71, 72, **74**, 75, 83, 194–95, **208**

Cohen, Joseph H., 205, 232, 233, 234, 235, 239, 249

Cohen, Rabbi Samuel, 215, 276

Cohen, Rabbi Simon, 260, 269

Community, American Jewish, 3, 8, 15, 23, 26–27, 30, 57, 253, 274; internal relations, 63–66, 92, 99–100, 109, 113, 117–18, 183; national, 62–63

Connecticut: New Haven, 34, 35; Stamford, 160

Conservative Judaism: 19th Century ("early Conservative"), 14, 61, 67, 69, 183, 262, 292n37, 309n59; 20th Century, 11, 69, 80, 82–83, 192, 229, 252, 262, 280; Rabbinic Assembly (RA), 244, 277; *Synagogue Center* (periodical), 280; United Synagogue, 20, 88, 199, 213, 214, 216, 257, 262–63, 276. *See also* Jewish Theological Seminary

Council of Young Men's Hebrew and Kindred Associations (CYMHKA), 51, 63, 85,

86, 127, 226, 231. *See also* Jewish Welfare Board

Cowen, Philip, 67, 75, 94, 96, 160

Cultural pluralism, 44, 49, 92, 93, 105, 158, 235. *See also* Americanization, movement for

Davis, Mrs. Benjamin (Jeanette Isaacs), 120, 173, 182

Davis, Philip, 133, 165

De Haas, Jacob, 121–23, 124, 165–66, 262

Delaware: Wilmington, 83

Denver, 34, 35, 93; Beth Hamedrosh Hagodol, 161, 214; Cong. Hebrew Educational Alliance, 279; Council for Jewish Women, 101; Denver Hebrew School, 161; Dorshe Zion Society, 198; West Denver Hebrew School and Synagogue, 162

Department store, 89, 90, 107, 119, 127, 255, 294n2

De Sola Mendes, Rabbi Frederick, 64, 67, 68, 70–71, 97

Detroit, 32, 35, 44, 268; Beth El, 24, 32, 47; Hannah Schloss Memorial and Jewish Institute, 114, 116; Hebrew schools, 145; *Jewish American*, 45; Shaaray Zedek, 215–16

Dewey, John, 41, 130, 138, 148, 163, 224

Downtown Talmud Torah. *See under* Lower East Side

Drachman, Rabbi Bernard, 143, 159, 184, 194, 218

Dubnow, Simon, 41, 132

Dushkin, Alexander, 127, 131, 138, 156, 158, 159

Educational Alliance (former Hebrew Institute), 76, 89, **90**, 92, 93, 103–10, **105**, 113, 116, 124, 142, 143, 147, 202, 203; People's Synagogue, 110–12, 126, 194–95

Eisenstein, Judah David, 169, 170

Enelow, Rabbi Hyman G., 19, 35

Epstein, Izhac, 144–45

Epstein, Rabbi Louis, 83, 186, 265–66

Ethical Culture, 14, 183. *See also* Adler, Felix

Feuerlicht, Rabbi Morris, 116

Finkelstein, Rabbi Louis, 280

Finkelstein, Rabbi Simon, 252, **252**

House, 101; Hebrew Free School, 133; Hebrew Orphan Asylum, 95, 195; Hebrew Technical Institute, 96, 97; Rodeph Shalom, 32; Shaaray Tefila, 32, 58, 70, 186; Shearith Israel, 77; Talmud Torah Chevra Kadisha, 161; Temple Emanu-El, 19, 20, 32, 58, 61, 99–100, 124, 142, 183, 195, 200; Tiphereth Achim Talmud Torah, 162; Zichron Ephraim, 133, 159, 184–85. *See also* Bronx; Brooklyn; Lower East Side; Harlem

New York State: Albany, 23, 114; Buffalo, 32, 35, 58, 100, 117, 215; Elmira, 161; Kingston, 47, 83; Rochester, 65

North Carolina: Asheville, 162

Ohio: Cincinnati, 35, 57, 136; Columbus, 114, 115; Toledo, 115; Youngstown, 161. *See also* Cleveland

Olmstead, Frederick Law, 257–58

Omaha (Nebraska), 40

Orphanage, Jewish, 56, 94–96; Hebrew Orphan Asylum (New York), 83, 94

Orthodox Judaism, 137, 142, 168, 175, 228, 252; Association of American Orthodox Congregations, 177; modernization of, 80, 110–12, 174, 175–76, 195, 200, 265; Union of Orthodox Jewish Congregations (UOJC), 142, 193; Young People's Hebrew Orthodox League, 226. *See also* Young Israel

Palestine. *See* Israel

Passover. *See under* Jewish holidays

Paulding, James K., 106, 138

Pelham, George, 186, 187

Pennsylvania: Altoona, 83, 161; Norristown, 87, 279; Pittsburgh, 35, 83, 101, 114, 162; Reading, 162; Williamsport, 208. *See also* Philadelphia

People's Synagogue. *See under* Educational Alliance; Settlement movement, Jewish; Synagogue

People's Synagogue Association, 195

Philadelphia, 24, 25, 32–33, 35, 36, 67, 245; Adath Jeshurun, 215; Gratz College, 103; Hebrew Education Society, 96; Keneseth Israel, 15, 24, 36, 37; Edward Rothschild Memorial, 245; Hebrew schools, 145;

Jewish Foster Home, 56, 95; Mikveh Israel, 63, 103; Rodeph Shalom, 25, 33, 47, 140, 183–84, 217–18; Talmud Torah congregations, 162; Touro Hall, 103, 116; West Philadelphia Jewish Center, 261; Young Men's Hebrew Literary Association, 54, 56, 57; Young Women's Union, 99, 296n24; Zion Institute, 103, 121

Philanthropy, 8, 29, 32, 49, 92, 93–94, 238; Baron de Hirsch fund, 89, 113; federations, 95; National Conference of Jewish Charities, 125

Philipson, Rabbi David, 59, 68

Portland (Oregon), 34, 101, 134

Progressivism, 8, 65, 91–92, 224; progressive education, 129–31

Providence (Rhode Island), 47, 107, 126

Public school, 20, 138, 162; school center movement, 131, 132, 138–40

Rabbis: assistant rabbis, 36, 192, 209, 214, 217, 222; "chief rabbis," 177, 208–9, 210; and Christian clergy, 16; and the community, 26, 30, 88, 216, 217; English-speaking, 12, 36, 192, 208, 210, 212, 217, 222; and industrial schools, 97; and laity, 9, 23–24, 46–47, 205, 226, 233, 242–43; modern Orthodox, 184, 189, 194, 196, 197, 216, 221–22, 313n30; New York Board of Jewish Ministers, 31, 61, 64, 195, 276; and orphanages, 95–96; and philanthropy, 101, 124; *Problems of the Jewish Ministry* (1927), 276, 279; seminary training, 12, 21, 86, 124, 207, 212; sermons, 18–19, 20, 26–27, 61, 210, 227, 231, 250; and synagogues, 11–12, 35; and women, 94, 100–101, 219; and the YMHA, 57–61, 64–65, 68, 69, 71, 82–86; and Zionism, 44, 49, 120, 196, 197, 199, 210, 217, 218, 277. *See also* CCAR; individual rabbis by name

Rabinowitz, Benjamin, 56, 62, 115, 116

Radin, Rabbi Adolph, 110–12

Reconstructionist Judaism, 7, 88, 206, 240, 263

Recreational facilities, 135, 149; bowling alley, 54, **254**; gymnasium, 39, 44, 48, 54, 67, 72, 81–82, 85, 103, 104, 110, 116, 119, 120, 121, 151, 153, 158, 203, 216, 223, 227, 236,

UNIVERSITY PRESS OF NEW ENGLAND publishes books under its own imprint and is the publisher for Brandeis University Press, Dartmouth College, Middlebury College Press, University of New Hampshire, Tufts University, and Wesleyan University Press.

Library of Congress Cataloging-in-Publication Data
Kaufman, David, 1959–
    Shul with a pool : the "synagogue-center" in American Jewish
history / David Kaufman.
        p.   cm. — (Brandeis series in American Jewish history,
culture, and life)
    Includes bibliographical references and index.
    ISBN 0-87451-876-8 (cl : alk. paper). — ISBN 0-87451-893-8
(pbk : alk. paper).
        1. Synagogues—United States—History.   2. Jewish community
centers—United States—History.   3. Judaism—United States—
History.   4. Jews—United States——Politics and government.
I. Title.   II. Series.
BM205.K39   1998
296.6'5'0973—dc21   98–4180